Adversarial Reasoning

Computational Approaches to Reading the Opponent's Mind

CHAPMAN & HALL/CRC
COMPUTER and INFORMATION SCIENCE SERIES

Series Editor: Sartaj Sahni

PUBLISHED TITLES

HANDBOOK OF SCHEDULING: ALGORITHMS, MODELS, AND PERFORMANCE ANALYSIS
Joseph Y.-T. Leung

THE PRACTICAL HANDBOOK OF INTERNET COMPUTING
Munindar P. Singh

HANDBOOK OF DATA STRUCTURES AND APPLICATIONS
Dinesh P. Mehta and Sartaj Sahni

DISTRIBUTED SENSOR NETWORKS
S. Sitharama Iyengar and Richard R. Brooks

SPECULATIVE EXECUTION IN HIGH PERFORMANCE COMPUTER ARCHITECTURES
David Kaeli and Pen-Chung Yew

SCALABLE AND SECURE INTERNET SERVICES AND ARCHITECTURE
Cheng-Zhong Xu

HANDBOOK OF BIOINSPIRED ALGORITHMS AND APPLICATIONS
Stephan Olariu and Albert Y. Zomaya

HANDBOOK OF ALGORITHMS FOR WIRELESS NETWORKING AND MOBILE COMPUTING
Azzedine Boukerche

HANDBOOK OF COMPUTATIONAL MOLECULAR BIOLOGY
Srinivas Aluru

FUNDEMENTALS OF NATURAL COMPUTING: BASIC CONCEPTS, ALGORITHMS, AND APPLICATIONS
Leandro Nunes de Castro

ADVERSARIAL REASONING: COMPUTATIONAL APPROACHES TO READING THE OPPONENT'S MIND
Alexander Kott and William M. McEneaney

Adversarial Reasoning

Computational Approaches to Reading the Opponent's Mind

Edited by

Alexander Kott
William M. McEneaney

Chapman & Hall/CRC
Taylor & Francis Group
Boca Raton   London   New York

Chapman & Hall/CRC is an imprint of the
Taylor & Francis Group, an informa business

Chapman & Hall/CRC
Taylor & Francis Group
6000 Broken Sound Parkway NW, Suite 300
Boca Raton, FL 33487-2742

© 2007 by Taylor & Francis Group, LLC
Chapman & Hall/CRC is an imprint of Taylor & Francis Group, an Informa business

No claim to original U.S. Government works
Printed in the United States of America on acid-free paper
10 9 8 7 6 5 4 3 2 1

International Standard Book Number-10: 1-58488-588-2 (Hardcover)
International Standard Book Number-13: 978-1-58488-588-7 (Hardcover)

Library of Congress Cataloging-in-Publication Data

Kott, Alexander W.
   Adversarial reasoning : computational approaches to reading the opponent's mind / Alexander Kott and William M. McEneaney.
      p. cm.
   Includes bibliographical references and index.
   ISBN 1-58488-588-2 (9781584885887 : alk. paper)
   1. Psychology, Military. 2. Enemies (Persons)--Psychology. 3. Opponents--Psychology. 4. Intention. 5. Game theory. I. McEneaney, William M. II. Title.

U22.3.K56 2006
355.4'8--dc22
                                          2006003725

Visit the Taylor & Francis Web site at
http://www.taylorandfrancis.com

and the CRC Press Web site at
http://www.crcpress.com

About the Authors

Sven A. Brueckner
Co-author of Chapter 1.3

Dr. Sven Brueckner received his Diploma (1997) and Dr.rer.nat (2001) degrees in Computer Science at Humboldt University, Berlin. He is a senior systems engineer in the Emerging Markets Group of New Vectors LLC in Ann Arbor, Michigan, where he manages and leads projects in multi-agent systems and swarm intelligence applied to domains as diverse as combat simulation, industrial process design, and logistics analysis. Prior to his employment with New Vectors LLC and its predecessor, the Altarum Institute, he was a research scientist at DaimlerChrysler AG, Research and Technology, in Berlin. He has authored or co-authored more than 30 technical articles and reports and is the named inventor on five patents pending.

Gregory Calbert
Author of Chapter 3.4

Dr. Gregory Calbert completed a doctorate in Game Theory and Behavioral Ecology at the University of Adelaide in 1998. That same year, he joined the Australian Defence Science and Technology Organisation (DSTO) as a research scientist. His work at DSTO focuses on modeling and simulation research covering such topics as wargame representations, command-control, and alliance modeling. His main research interest is in the application and development of machine learning methods to agent-based wargaming.

Jacob Crossman
Co-author of Chapter 1.2

Jacob Crossman is a research engineer at Soar Technology. He researches, designs, and develops agent technology, agents, and agent-based simulations. Crossman's recent projects include leading a team to design and build a system to abduce adversarial intent in urban environments; designing a next generation, high-level language for engineering cognitive agents; developing heuristic formalisms for user-level behavior specification and diagrammatic behavior specification; architecting an agent-based simulation system for modeling country leadership; and intra-country diplomacy for intelligence analysis. His research focuses on advanced design and programming methodologies and technologies, user-programmable agent systems, knowledge systems, and reusable software and knowledge. Crossman earned a B.S. (1998) and M.S. (2000) degrees in Computer Science at the University of Michigan (Dearborn).

Christopher Elsaesser
Co-author of Chapter 2.1

Dr. Christopher Elsaesser is a principal engineer at the MITRE Corporation in McLean, Virginia, where he has been applying plan recognition to counter-terrorism indications and warnings problems. His prior research includes work in counter-deception, adversarial planning, computer intrusion forensics, and robotics. Dr. Elsaesser received an M.S. in Mathematics and an M.S. in Industrial and Systems Engineering from Ohio University and his Ph.D. in Engineering and Public Policy from Carnegie Mellon University.

Christopher Geib
Author of Chapter 1.4

Dr. Christopher Geib is a research fellow in the School of Informatics at the University of Edinburgh in Scotland. He is the principal author of the Probabilistic Hostile Agent Task Tracker (PHATT) software and theory. Dr. Geib's research interests also include artificial intelligence (AI) planning methods and the handling of uncertainty in AI planning methods. His Ph.D. thesis work concerned the use of hierarchical incremental planning for uncertain domains. Since then, Dr. Geib has worked on a number of issues involving action under uncertainty. He has also explored the issues presented by uncertain domains using decision theoretic methods to extend hierarchical planning and general AI methods of abstraction. Dr. Geib earned his Ph.D. from the University of Pennsylvania in 1995, held a post-doctoral fellowship at the University of British Columbia until 1997, and was a principal research scientist at Honeywell Labs from 1997 until 2006 when he joined the faculty at Edinburgh.

João Pedro Hespanha
Author of Chapter 2.3

Dr. João Hespanha received a Ph.D. degree in Electrical Engineering and Applied Science from Yale University in 1998. He is currently on the faculty of the Department of Electrical and Computer Engineering at the University of California, Santa Barbara. Dr. Hespanha is the associate director for the Center for Control, Dynamical Systems, and Computation. His research interests include hybrid and switched systems, distributed control over communication networks, the use of vision in feedback control, stochastic modeling in biology, and game theory. He is the author of over 100 technical papers and the principal investigator and co-principal investigator in several federally funded projects. Dr. Hespanha is the recipient of Yale's Henry Prentiss Becton Graduate Prize for exceptional achievement in research in Engineering and Applied Science, a National Science Foundation CAREER Award, the 2005 Automatica Theory/Methodology best paper prize, and the best paper award at the Second International Conference on Intelligent Sensing and Information Processing. Since 2003, he has been an associate editor of the *IEEE Transactions on Automatic Control*.

Pu Huang
Co-author of Chapter 3.5

Dr. Pu Huang is a research staff member at the IBM Thomas J. Watson Research Center in Yorktown Heights, New York. His current research interests include stochastic optimization, machine learning, and games and their applications to business. His research has led to several sense-and-respond systems that intelligently monitor business situations and execute/recommend corrective actions. Dr. Huang received the Ph.D. degree from Carnegie Mellon University.

Randolph M. Jones
Co-author of Chapter 1.2

Dr. Randolph Jones is a senior scientist at Soar Technology and scientific lead for intelligent systems projects. He has over 20 years of experience researching agent architectures, machine and human learning, graphical user interfaces, cognitive modeling, and related areas. Dr. Jones has held academic positions at Colby College, the University of Michigan, the University of Pittsburgh, and Carnegie Mellon University. His current research focuses on architectures for knowledge-intensive intelligent agents, computational models of human learning and problem solving, executable psychological models, computer games, automated intelligent actors, and improved usability and visualization in information systems. He received a B.S. degree (1984) in Mathematics and Computer Science at UCLA and his M.S. (1987) and Ph.D. (1989) degrees from the Department of Information and Computer Science at the University of California, Irvine.

Alexander Kott
Co-editor

Dr. Alexander Kott earned his Ph.D. from the University of Pittsburgh, where his research focused on applications of artificial intelligence for innovative engineering design. Later he directed research and development organizations at technology companies including the Carnegie Group, Honeywell, and BBN. Dr. Kott's affiliation with the Defense Advanced Research Project Agency (DARPA) included serving as the chief architect of DARPA's Joint Forces Air Component Commander (JFACC) program and managing the Advanced ISR Management Program, as well as the Mixed Initiative Control of Automa-Teams Program. He initiated the Real-Time Adversarial Intelligence and Decision-Making (RAID) program and also manages the DARPA program called Multicell and Dismounted Command and Control. Dr. Kott's research interests include dynamic planning in resource-, time- and space-constrained problems; in dynamically changing, uncertain, and adversarial environments; and dynamic, unstable, and "pathological" phenomena in distributed decision-making systems. He has published over 60 technical papers and served as the editor and co-author of several books.

William M. McEneaney
Co-editor and Co-author of Chapter 2.4

Dr. William McEneaney received his B.S. and M.S. in Mathematics from Rensselaer Polytechnic Institute, Troy, New York, in 1982 and 1983, respectively. He worked at PAR Technology and Jet Propulsion Laboratory, developing theory and algorithms for estimation and guidance applications. Dr. McEneaney attended Brown University from 1989 through 1993, obtaining his M.S. and Ph.D. in Applied Mathematics. His thesis research, conducted under advisor Dr. W. H. Fleming, was on nonlinear risk-sensitive stochastic control. Dr. McEneaney has since held positions at Carnegie Mellon University and North Carolina State University prior to his current appointment at the University of California, San Diego. He is a full professor at UCSD with an interdisciplinary position across mechanical and aerospace engineering and mathematics. His recent interests have been in risk-sensitive and robust control and estimation, max-plus algebraic methods for Hamilton–Jacobi–Bellman partial differential equations, and partially–observed stochastic games.

Dana Nau
Co-author of Chapter 3.1

Dr. Dana Nau is a University of Maryland professor in the Department of Computer Science and Institute for Systems Research, and director of the University's Laboratory for Computational Cultural Dynamics. He received his Ph.D. from Duke University in 1979. He has received an NSF Graduate Fellowship, NSF Presidential Young Investigator Award, Outstanding Faculty Award, and several "best paper" awards. He is a Fellow of the American Association for Artificial Intelligence (AAAI). Dr. Nau's research interests include AI planning and searching, game theory, and computer-integrated design and manufacturing. He has more than 250 publications, including *Automated Planning: Theory and Practice,* a textbook on automated planning. He co-authored the version of Bridge Baron that won the 1997 world championship of computer bridge. His SHOP2 program won one of the top four prizes in the 2002 International Planning Competition and has been used in hundreds of research projects worldwide.

Paul E. Nielsen
Co-author of Chapter 1.2

Dr. Paul Nielsen has experience in academic, industrial, and research environments, including artificial intelligence, cognitive modeling, intelligent control, intelligent agents, qualitative physics, and machine learning. Dr. Nielsen was a vice president and co-founder of Soar Technology, which was spun off from the University of Michigan to expand work he had been involved with while on the faculty there. Prior to joining the University of Michigan, he was a staff member of the GE Corporate Research and Development Center. Dr. Nielsen has over 40 publications in the areas of intelligent simulation, intelligent control, knowledge fusion, and qualitative physics. He has served on program and paper review committees and scientific panels. Dr. Nielsen received his Ph.D. in Computer Science from the University of Illinois (1987).

Austin Parker
Co-author of Chapter 3.1

Austin Parker is a graduate student at the University of Maryland. He studied mathematics and philosophy at Haverford College, where his thesis work on the Hilbert Conjecture earned him honors. As an undergraduate student, he participated in RoboCup 2000 and has contributed to the understanding of the physical structure of DNA. He is currently working on the partial-information game, Kriegspiel, and is the author of a high-performance computer program to play the entire game. As a member of the University of Maryland's Laboratory for Computational Cultural Dynamics, his other interests include probabilistic databases, game theory, adversarial reasoning, planning, machine learning, and the general subject of computer science, from system administration to complexity theory.

H. Van Dyke Parunak
Co-author of Chapter 1.3

Dr. H. Van Dyke Parunak holds a B.A. in Physics from Princeton University (1969), an M.S. in Computer and Communications Sciences from the University of Michigan (1982), and a Ph.D. in Near Eastern Languages and Civilizations from Harvard University (1978). He is Chief Scientist at New Vectors LLC in Ann Arbor, Michigan, and a corporate analyst in its Emerging Markets Group. He has previously worked at Comshare, the University of Michigan, and Harvard University. He is the author or co-author of more than 75 technical articles and reports and holds four patents and nine patents pending in the area of agent technology. His research focuses on applications of agent-based and complex systems to distributed decentralized information processing. Dr. Parunak is a member of the American Association for Artificial Intelligence and the Association for Computing Machinery, and serves on numerous editorial and conference boards.

Eugene Santos Jr.
Co-author of Chapter 1.1

Dr. Eugene Santos is a professor of engineering at the Thayer School of Engineering at Dartmouth and the director of the Distributed Information and Intelligence Analysis Group (DI2AG). Dr. Santos received his B.S. (1985) in Mathematics and Computer Science and his M.S. (1986) in Mathematics (specializing in numerical analysis) from Youngstown State University, Ohio. He received both his Sc.M. (1988) and Ph.D. (1992) degrees in Computer Science from Brown University. Dr. Santos specializes in modern statistical and probabilistic methods with applications to intelligent systems, uncertain reasoning, and decision science. He has chaired or served on numerous major conferences and professional society meetings and has over 100 refereed technical publications. He is currently an associate editor for the *IEEE Transactions on Systems, Man, and Cybernetics* and the *International Journal of Image and Graphics*.

Rajdeep Singh
Co-author of Chapter 2.4

Rajdeep Singh received his Bachelor of Engineering with honors in Aeronautical Engineering from Punjab Engineering College, Chandigarh, India (1999). He briefly worked for the Defense Research Development Organization in India before joining the Department of Mechanical and Aerospace Engineering at the University of California, San Diego, as a Ph.D. student in 2001. He finished his Ph.D. in March 2006 and is currently working part-time as a Senior Technology Consultant/Research Engineer with Orincon/Lockheed Martin, San Diego. His current research focus is on partially observed games and applications to UAV task allocation, non-linear control, modeling and simulation, algorithm development, filtering and estimation.

Jason L. Speyer
Co-author of Chapter 3.2

Dr. Jason L. Speyer received his B.S. in Aeronautics and Astronautics from the Massachusetts Institute of Technology in 1960 and his Ph.D. in Applied Mathematics from Harvard University in 1968. His industrial experience includes research at Boeing, Raytheon, and the Charles Stark Draper Laboratory. He was the Harry H. Power Professor in Engineering Mechanics at the University of Texas. He is currently a professor and past chairman in the Mechanical, Aerospace, and Nuclear Engineering Department (now the Mechanical and Aerospace Engineering Department) at the University of California, Los Angeles. Dr. Speyer has twice been an elected member of the Board of Governors of the IEEE Control Systems Society and Chairman of the Technical Committee on Aerospace Controls. He served as an associate editor for a number of journals including the *Journal of Optimization Theory and Applications*, 1981 to the present. From 1987 to 1991 and from 1997 to 2001, he served as a member of the USAF Scientific Advisory Board.

Frank J. Stech
Co-author of Chapter 2.1

Dr. Frank Stech is a principal engineer at the MITRE Corporation in McLean, Virginia, where he supports national intelligence agencies and combatant commands with deception support and counter-deception analysis. Dr. Stech received his B.A. from Dartmouth College in Psychology and Economics and his M.A. and Ph.D. in Psychology from the University of California, Santa Barbara. Dr. Stech has taught or lectured at the Joint Military Intelligence College, CIA University, the Naval Postgraduate School, Carnegie Mellon University, University of California, and Chaminade College, Honolulu. A retired army colonel, he served as both a deception planner in psychological and special operations and a deception analyst in military intelligence. As a cognitive-social psychologist, he has studied the effects of deception on intelligence analysis for over 30 years.

Boris Stilman
Co-author of Chapter 3.3

Dr. Boris Stilman received M.S. in Mathematics from Moscow State University in 1972 and a Ph.D. in Computer Science and a Ph.D. in Electrical Engineering from the National Research Institute for Electrical Engineering, Moscow, in 1984. From 1972 through 1988, Dr. Stilman was involved in the research project PIONEER in Moscow led by a former World Chess Champion, Dr. Mikhail Botvinnik. The goal of the project was to discover and formalize an approach utilized by chess experts in solving chess problems almost without a search. In 1991, while at McGill University, Montreal, employing results of the PIONEER project, Dr. Stilman originated linguistic geometry (LG), a theory for solving abstract board games. Since 1991, he has been developing the theory and applications of LG at the University of Colorado at Denver as professor of Computer Science and, simultaneously, since 1999, at STILMAN Advanced Strategies as chairman and CEO. He has published several books and contributed to books as well as over 180 research papers.

V. S. Subrahmanian
Co-author of Chapter 3.1

Dr. V. S. Subrahmanian is a professor in the Department of Computer Science, Institute for Advanced Computer Studies and Institute for Systems Research at the University of Maryland, College Park. He is Director of the Institute for Advanced Computer Studies (UMIACS). He received the NSF National Young Investigator Award in 1993 and the Distinguished Young Scientist Award from the Maryland Science Center/Maryland Academy of Science in 1997. His primary area of research is in databases and artificial intelligence. His work in AI spans rule-based expert systems and logic programs, non-monotonic reasoning, probabilistic reasoning, temporal reasoning, hybrid reasoning, and software agents. His work in databases focuses on heterogeneous database integration and interoperability, logic databases, probabilistic databases, and multimedia databases. He has also worked extensively on multimedia systems.

Ashitosh Swarup
Co-author of Chapter 3.2

Dr. Ashitosh Swarup received his B.E. in Electronics Engineering from the University of Bombay in 1997 and his M.S. and Ph.D. in Electrical Engineering from the University of California, Los Angeles, in 2000 and 2004, respectively. Dr. Ashitosh has worked as a Systems Engineer at BAE Systems and is currently a Senior Engineer at SySense in Burbank, California.

Katia Sycara
Co-author of Chapter 3.5

Dr. Katia Sycara is a professor in the School of Computer Science at Carnegie Mellon University and holds the Sixth Century Chair (part-time) in Computing Science at the University of Aberdeen. She is also the Director of the Laboratory for Agents Technology and Semantic Web Technologies at Carnegie Mellon. She holds a B.S. in Applied Mathematics from Brown University, an M.S. in Electrical Engineering from the University of Wisconsin, and a Ph.D. in Computer Science from the Georgia Institute of Technology. Dr. Sycara is a Fellow of the American Association for Artificial Intelligence (AAAI), a Fellow of the Institute of Electronic and Electrical Engineers (IEEE) and the recipient of the ACM/SIGART Autonomous Agents Research Award. She has given numerous invited talks and has authored or co-authored more than 300 technical papers dealing with multiagent systems, multiagent learning, web services, the semantic web, human-agent interaction, negotiation, case-based reasoning, and the application of these techniques to various domains. Dr. Sycara's group has developed the widely used RETSINA multiagent infrastructure, a toolkit that enables the development of heterogeneous software agents that can dynamically coordinate in open-information environments.

Paul Thompson
Author of Chapter 2.2

Dr. Paul Thompson received his Ph.D. from the University of California, Berkeley, in 1986. He is currently a research professor in Dartmouth College's Computer Science Department. His graduate research was on probabilistic information retrieval. From 1986 through 1988, he was an assistant professor at Drexel University's College of Information Studies. Subsequently, from 1988 to 1993, he was a member of PRC's Artificial Intelligence Development group, where he conducted research in natural language understanding and information retrieval. From 1993 until 2001, he worked for West Publishing Company, later West Group, where his research involved natural language understanding, information retrieval, and machine learning/text categorization. Since joining Dartmouth College's Institute for Security Technology Studies in 2001, he has continued his earlier research and is also working in the areas of semantic attacks, robust parsing, and adversarial reasoning.

Oleg Umanskiy
Co-author of Chapter 3.3

Oleg Umanskiy received an M.S. in Computer Science and Engineering from the University of Colorado at Denver in 2001. Currently, he is a Ph.D. student in Computer Science at UCD under Dr. Boris Stilman's supervision. While doing research and developing applications of linguistic geometry, he was a recipient of a number of top student awards at UCD and has published 13 research papers. In 1996 through 1998, Umanskiy worked at Maxtor and from 1998 to 2000, he ran the software development division for another company, STS, before committing to STILMAN Advanced Strategies full-time in 2000, where he currently is the chief software architect. Umanskiy has been the lead developer of a number of systems for government agencies and defense contractors.

Vladimir Yakhnis
Co-author of Chapter 3.3

Dr. Vladimir Yakhnis received an M.S. in Mathematics from Moscow State University in 1975 and a Ph.D. in Mathematics/Computer Science from Cornell University in 1990. His mentor was Dr. Anil Nerode. Dr. Yakhnis co-developed a new algorithm for generating finite memory winning strategies for a large class of infinite games. Since 1991, he has worked as a research scientist at IBM, Sandia National Laboratories, and at the Rockwell Science Center. Since 2002, he has been the chief scientist at STILMAN Advanced Strategies. His work is focused on representing applied problems, including military, with formal game-board models. Dr. Yakhnis contributed to foundations and applications of linguistic geometry, gaming algorithms, formal methods for object-oriented software development, program correctness, and validation of software requirements. He has published 42 research papers.

Qunhua Zhao
Co-author of Chapter 1.1

Dr. Qunhua Zhao received his B.S. (1990) in Botany from Nanjing University and his Ph.D. (2001) in Plant Science from the University of Connecticut. He received his Sc.M (2003) in Computer Science from the University of Connecticut. Dr. Zhao is currently working as a Research Associate at the Thayer School of Engineering at Dartmouth College. His research interests include knowledge engineering, user modeling, intelligent information retrieval, automatic document summarization, and biosystem modeling.

Introduction

As implied by the subtitle of this volume, adversarial reasoning is largely about understanding the minds and actions of one's opponents. It is relevant to a broad range of practical problems where the actors are actively and consciously contesting at least some of each others' objectives and actions. Obvious and very important examples of such problems are found in military practice: Planning and intelligence, command and control, and simulation and training. The burgeoning field of military robotics deals with related problems as well. Of growing importance and urgency are adversarial reasoning challenges in the areas of domestic security and terrorism prevention. The rising tide of transnational criminals and cybercrime calls for greater sophistication in tools and techniques for law enforcement and commercial security professionals. With less dramatic outcomes but with great commercial importance, battles of opposing minds unfold in the enormous industry of recreational games. Adversarial reasoning is highly relevant to the world of business transactions, including corporate takeovers, computer trading of investment instruments, and automated negotiation of sales.

To make the term *adversarial reasoning* more concrete, let us consider one of the aforementioned domains — military operations. Historically, this is where adversarial reasoning is applied most extensively and explicitly. In military command and control, a fundamental need exists to understand the intents, plans, and actions of the adversary. To address this need, a number of researchers (including several of this book's authors) are developing computational means to reason about and to predict an opponent's future actions.

What is particularly striking and daunting about such problems is their multidimensional, diverse, and heterogeneous nature. Attempts to decompose a military problem, to decouple its interleaved aspects, are often counterproductive and misleading. To address the problem at a level where a solution is relevant to real-world applications, researchers and practitioners learn to respect the intricate interdependencies of its multiple aspects. A meaningful approach must consider the opponent's perception of one's strengths, weaknesses and intents; the opponent's intelligent plans to achieve his objectives by effective use of his strengths and opportunities; and the opponent's tactics, doctrine, training, morale, cultural, and other biases and preferences. One must also account for the impact of physical factors such as terrain, environment (including noncombatant population), weather, time and space available, the influence of personnel losses, consumption of ammunition and other supplies, logistics, communications, and other critical elements of a military operation.

All this information must be woven into the complex interplay and mutual dependency of both one's own and the opponent's actions, reactions, and counteractions that unfold during the execution of the operation. Adversarial reasoning is the process of making inferences over the totality of such heterogeneous factors. This begins to explain why the problems of adversarial reasoning exhibit great complexity and why they call for the convergence of techniques from multiple fields.

Changing Times and Needs

Problems of such a complex and theoretically "untidy" nature do not always endear themselves to either researchers or technology practitioners. Yet a growing interest exists in adversarial reasoning. We see several reasons for such growth and, by extension, the need for a book on computational approaches to adversarial reasoning.

- First, the post-9/11 security posture of the United States fuels investments and growing interest in innovative computational techniques suitable for practical applications in military intelligence, military robotics, counterterrorism, law enforcement, and information security.

- Second, recent years have seen a dramatic rise in computational capabilities applicable to adversarial reasoning, making them for the first time relevant to problems of a practical scale and complexity.

- Third, an emerging confluence of diverse fields is applicable to adversarial reasoning (artificial intelligence planning, game theory, cognitive modeling, control theory, machine learning), and few books strive to bridge theory and applications in this area as this one attempts to do.

To give an example that illustrates the first of the above points, the Defense Advanced Research Projects Agency (DARPA), the central research and development agency of the United States Department of Defense, recently initiated a major program in adversarial reasoning. Several chapters of this book refer to that program. The program is one of several major initiatives that reflect interest in adversarial reasoning.

Let us elaborate on the second of the above arguments. The 1950s and 1960s saw critical developments in the understanding of game theory, a key element of adversarial reasoning. Game problems are much more complex than those for systems without antagonistic inputs. Game-theoretic formulations of practical problems, with the attendant level of detail and scale, result in complexity levels that until recently could not be satisfactorily handled. In this book, we describe a number of computational techniques that offer the promise of robustness and scalability appropriate for practical applications.

Further, diversion and deception have often been critical factors in the outcomes of adversarial conflicts. Reasoning about diversion and deception has not been a major focus of work in either game theory or other disciplines. Thus, since the 1960s and the development of the Kalman filter, researchers and practitioners have had excellent (and continually improving) tools for handling *random* noise in observation processes and system dynamics. However, these tools are utterly inadequate for determining an opponent's hidden actions and plans. They are particularly inadequate in the presence of intentionally false data generated by an opponent. In this book, we offer a venue for discussing recent computational approaches to these critical aspects of adversarial reasoning.

Finally, we address the third argument. We are not aware of a publication that covers the topic from the integrated perspective we have tried to pursue in this book. For example, although voluminous literature exists on game theory, the overwhelming majority of that literature is dedicated to applications in economics and management; it does not consider issues of active deception (critical in military and antiterrorism problems, among others); and rarely covers the important related work in fields like artificial intelligence planning or stochastic control theory. As another example, a tremendous amount of literature also exists on stochastic control and estimation. However, the applications tend toward aircraft, spacecraft, and ground vehicle control, queuing networks, job shops, and finance applications. This literature views all unknown inputs as stochastic in nature and so does not deal well with those applications where the most important unknown inputs are often adversarial in nature.

Overall, the confluence of new theoretical developments in game theory, control theory, artificial intelligence, and machine learning allows significant advances in adversarial reasoning. A need exists for decision aids in this area on today's military battlefield, both conventional and unconventional. A need for algorithms exists that enable coordinated decision making for the emerging application of autonomous vehicles operating in hostile environments. A need exists for mechanisms to defend against the growing number of cyberattacks. All these have created a pull for further development in the area of adversarial reasoning. We hope this book provides an introductory review of the current thinking and opportunities in this area for researchers and practitioners who solve these diverse problems.

Interdisciplinary Perspective

Clearly, the potential scope of a book on adversarial reasoning can be immense. To focus our effort, we have attempted to concentrate on computational solutions to determining (or anticipating) the state, intent, and actions of one's adversary in an environment where one strives to effectively counter the adversary's actions. Within this still very broad subject, we have selected such subtopics as belief and intent recognition, opponent strategy prediction, plan recognition, deception discovery, deception planning, and strategy generation. Even with such restrictions, the subject necessarily encompasses (and interrelates) multiple fields of study.

One of the disciplines that contributes to adversarial reasoning is readily recognized: Game theory is a mature field that is traditionally focused on the rigorous study of problems in which two or more actors strive to achieve their respective goals while interacting in a certain domain. Problems in game theory are notoriously difficult, particularly from a computational standpoint, even when addressing highly simplified problems that are far removed from the real world. Even the clearly defined and fully observable game of chess has only recently been successfully addressed with computational tools, if one measures success as outperforming unassisted humans.

Yet many of the problems that concern us today, and which are discussed in this book, are far less tidy and well-defined than chess. For instance, the set of possible inputs can be very large and ill-defined, the dynamics might not be completely known, and the dynamics can contain random elements. Further, in contrast to chess, one seldom knows the true state of the system. In fact, the players typically have only imperfect observations of some portion of the domain in which the game is being played. Thus, a tremendous gap exists between problems that can be rigorously solved and the real-world problems that confront us.

To fill this immense gap, many tools outside of the traditional realm of game theory must be brought to bear. As this volume demonstrates, practical adversarial reasoning calls for a broad range of disciplines, including but not limited to stochastic processes, artificial intelligence planning, cognitive modeling, robotics and agent theory, robust control theory, and machine learning. In fact, a key objective of this book is to demonstrate the important and close relations between ideas coming from such diverse areas. As a result, this volume combines contributions from disciplines that are rarely seen under the same cover.

Besides stressing the relevance of multiple academic disciplines, our desire was also to make this volume of interest to applied communities. From the perspective of developers, engineers, policy makers, and practitioners, the applications of the techniques described in this book cover a broad range of practical problems: Military planning and command, military and foreign intelligence, antiterrorism and domestic security, law enforcement, financial fraud detection, information security, recreational strategy games, simulation and training systems, and applied robotics.

Indeed, even though new theoretical contributions constitute the core of each chapter of this book, most chapters also include discussions and recommendations regarding at least one application or a prototype actually developed or potentially enabled by the class of techniques described in the chapter. For example, Chapter 3.3 and Chapter 3.4 focus on applications in military operations planning and command, whereas Chapter 1.1, Chapter 1.3, Chapter 2.1, and Chapter 2.4 discuss applications in intelligence gathering. Chapter 3.1 describes systems designed for playing entertainment games, and a number of other chapters use wargaming as their applied subject, also of relevance to strategy games in the entertainment industry. Applications and prototypes relevant to network security, Internet fraud detection, and e-commerce are addressed in Chapter 1.4, Chapter 2.2, and Chapter 3.5.

The Road Map of the Book

To help our readers navigate the structure of this book, let us explain the motivation for the three parts of this volume. Faced with an intelligent adversary, a decision maker — whether human or computational — often must begin by using the available information to identify the intent, the nature, and the probable plans of the adversary. Hence, the first part of our volume, *Intent and Plan Recognition*. However, a capable adversary is likely to conceal his plans and to introduce crucial deceptions. Therefore, the second part of our volume, *Deception Discovery*, focuses on the detection of concealments and deceptions. Having made progress in identifying the adversary's intent, and guarding himself against possible deceptions, the decision maker must formulate his own plan of actions that takes into account potential counteractions of the adversary — and this is the theme of our third part, *Strategy Formulation*.

Although the chapters of this book were written by a large group of authors with diverse interests and backgrounds, we strived to assure strong connectivity and logical flow between the chapters. Let us review briefly the significance of, and relations between, the topics in the chapters to follow.

In Chapter 1.1, we begin with the concept of inferring the intent of our adversary from the actions that we observe. In this chapter, the authors introduce Bayesian networks as a tool for intent inferencing. This topic is further elaborated in Chapter 1.2, where a beliefs, desires, and intentions (BDI) model is described in detail, and experimental results in a military wargaming simulation are used to verify the approach. Having estimated the opponent's intent, one wishes to anticipate the opponent's future actions, and to this end, Chapter 1.3 describes an agent-based approach to make inferences about an opponent and to predict its future behavior using BDI as a key input. Virtual agents are used to map out potential futures and to take into account both the agents' external environment and their internal emotional influences.

Going beyond the inference of an opponent's intent is the additional question of plan recognition addressed in Chapter 1.4. This concept differs from intent recognition in that one is looking not only for the goals, but also for the steps that the opponent may be following to achieve his goal. Probabilistic techniques are developed for plan recognition under partial observations as well as under full information. Unlike previous chapters that use military intelligence as their example application domain, here we explore practical applications in network security. This chapter concludes by introducing us to the significance of our next major topic — deception.

With that introduction, Chapter 2.1 begins the detailed analysis of topics related to deception by discussing historical cases of deceptions, the psychological underpinnings of deception, and what is needed for a successful deception. Two approaches for detecting a deception — the method of competing hypotheses and an extension to it — are presented and illustrated within the framework of historical military examples. However, other domains exist, such as information security on the Internet, where deceptions can have a very different nature, being extremely frequent, numerous, and unfolding within very short periods of time. Therefore, Chapter 2.2 introduces another class of deceptions — the semantic attack, also known as a cognitive attack. Methods and classes of semantic attacks are considered. Concepts, such as linguistic countermeasures and information trajectories, are presented. In this context, the author demonstrates how a process query system can act as a countermeasure.

Having outlined qualitatively the key concepts and challenges related to deception, we begin a more quantitative, mathematical journey into deception and methods for counterdeception. Chapter 2.3 uses the theory of static, partially observed games to analyze the utility of deception. Nash equilibria are used and conditions under which deception could be fruitful are obtained. Considerations of the cost of deception vs. the potential gains are weighed. Given that deception can be useful, as indicated in Chapter 2.3, the question then becomes how to deal with it. In Chapter 2.4, the authors use the theory of dynamic, stochastic, partially observed games to develop techniques for minimizing the effects of deception by one's adversary. A small game where an attacker uses deception to hide his true intentions is used as a basis for a discussion of the application of these methods.

This latter chapter makes a critical point: Even the best understanding of the opponent's intentions and deceptions is useless unless one can find ways to act on this understanding. Thus, Chapter 3.1 focuses on how to find effective strategies for acting in adversarial, imperfect-information environments. The authors discuss how to extend game-tree search to work in imperfect information games and consider methods for reducing the search-space. Games such as Kriegspiel chess and Texas hold 'em are used to illuminate the issues. Comparisons are also made under the condition of fixed computation time.

However, methods for handling deception, such as those in Chapter 2.4 and Chapter 3.1, are inherently computationally expensive. If the system were not too nonlinear, one could then use methods specific to linear systems to avoid these computational problems. In Chapter 3.2, the authors use the theory of linear, stochastic dynamic, partially observed games to determine optimal actions. A blocking filter is developed for processing the observational data. Methods unique to linear systems lead to elegant results.

Returning to the highly nonlinear systems found in most real-world problems, we look for other ways to handle computational complexity. Even in full-information games, game-tree searches can be prohibitively costly for realistic-scale games. To overcome this challenge, Chapter 3.3 uses the theory of dynamic games and introduces linguistic geometry, a theory of abstract board games, for large-scale problems, such as complex military operations. This approach permits the solving of large problems in real-time by constructing strategies rather than searching for them.

Yet another approach to handling this search-size issue is learning. In Chapter 3.4, we explore how one can use reinforcement learning within a stochastic dynamic games context, with appropriate extensions to handle adversarial components. A complex game from a military domain is used as a means for exploring issues one must handle in applying such techniques. Continuing the reinforcement learning theme, Chapter 3.5 extends this concept to games with multiple interacting and learning agents. One question that faces developers considering this approach is whether the algorithm will converge. The authors obtain some convergence results, verify convergence in an example game, and offer suggestions for practical applications of such results.

Answering the How-To Questions

As we have said, the authors would like this book to be of value to practitioners. Ideally, it should help answer specific questions on how to build specific capabilities in applications that require elements of adversarial reasoning. The following table shows where in this book one can find answers to specific "how-to" questions.

Where to Find 'How-to' Answers

How To...	Chapters												
	1.1	1.2	1.3	1.4	2.1	2.2	2.3	2.4	3.1	3.2	3.3	3.4	3.5
Estimate an opponent's goals	✓	✓										✓	
Estimate an opponent's emotional state		✓	✓										
Learn opponent's preferences and patterns				✓									
Infer an opponent's plans	✓			✓							✓		
Anticipate an opponent's actions and moves			✓	✓					✓	✓	✓	✓	✓
Detect a possible deception						✓	✓	✓	✓				
Detect concealed assets or decoys									✓	✓			
Understand the mechanism of deception						✓		✓					
Assess the likelihood of deception						✓		✓	✓				
Minimize the impact of deception							✓		✓	✓			
Devise a deception						✓		✓					
Strategize against a deception							✓	✓	✓		✓		
Devise specific actions and moves											✓		✓
Devise a mix of assets and deployment											✓	✓	
Formulate an effective course of action									✓		✓	✓	✓

Contents

1.1

Adversarial Models for Opponent Intent Inferencing

Eugene Santos Jr. and Qunhua Zhao

CONTENTS

Taking into account the characteristics and behaviors of one's adversary is essential for success in any competitive activity, such as in sports, business, or warfare. Obviously, if one's enemies are well understood, their actions can then be better anticipated and countered. To do so, the key is to capture the adversary's intentions. An intuitive approach that immediately comes to mind is to think what you would do if you were "in your opponent's shoes." However, "thinking as your enemy" is difficult because your perception of the world is quite likely to be very different from your opponents'. To address this problem and correctly infer adversary intent, the model of the adversary should capture critical aspects such as their history of movements and responses in different situations, their policies (e.g., military doctrines), capabilities, infrastructure, and human factors (e.g., social, political, cultural, and economic*). In this chapter, we focus primarily on adversary modeling (and, in particular,

---

* We only briefly touch upon human factors in this chapter. Chapter 1.2 provides a more detailed discussion of such factors.

adversary intent inferencing) for military planning and operations, but note that the concepts can be readily applied across a broad range of domains.

To successfully model the adversary, not only the opponent's capabilities but also the intent should be considered. The adversary's intent is composed of the adversary's desired end-states, reasons for pursuing such end-states, methods to achieve the goals, and the levels of commitment to achieving the goals. In this chapter, we present a comprehensive adversarial modeling approach that accounts for opponent intent inferencing in a dynamic and interactive environment. The model has been applied to military wargaming, resulting in an action-reaction-counteraction simulation environment where actions are initiative events (i.e., the offense from one side), reactions are the responses from the other side, and counteractions are the first side's responses to the reactions. In such a simulation environment, the sequence of action-reaction-counteraction is continued until the critical event is completed or the commander determines to use another *course of action* (COA) to accomplish the mission [20]. Thus, the model helped break the barrier of prescripted adversaries in wargaming, i.e., those that act in a predetermined fashion. Furthermore, we demonstrated that models of adversaries can be readily constructed and modified in real-time during a simulation to reflect the dynamic battlefield.

We begin with a discussion of intent inferencing and adversary intent inferencing, concentrating on providing a brief overview of concepts and definitions. We then present some background on representing and reasoning over noisy, incomplete, and uncertain information that is at the heart of modeling intent prediction, explanation, and understanding. Next, we describe our adversary intent inferencing framework, the semantics for building adversary models, and the inferencing process. With the framework in place, we describe its application to conflict analysis and wargaming. In particular, we provide details on some of the testbeds used in our experiments for inferring adversary intent. Finally, we present our thoughts and conclusions.

1.1.1   Intent Inferencing

In Bratman's belief-desire-intention (BDI) model [5,6], the *intentions* are viewed as partial plans committed by an intelligent entity to achieve certain goals (*desires*) based on the perception or knowledge of the world (*beliefs*). The *intentions* in the BDI model are also understood as a subset of desires upon which an entity chooses to act. In Geddes' view [11], intent inferencing involves deducing an entity's goals (desired end-states) based on observations of its actions. Such deduction typically involves the construction of one or more behavioral models that are optimized to represent the entity's behavior patterns. After data and knowledge representing observations of an entity, its actions, and its environment (collectively called *observables*) are

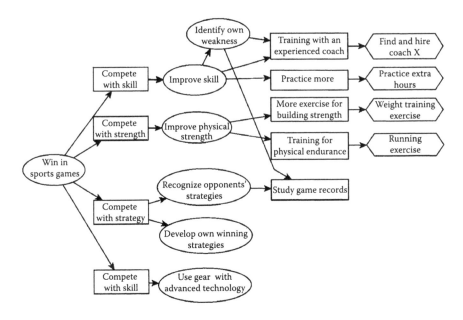

FIGURE 1.1.1
An example PGG for winning strategies in sports games.

gathered, these models attempt to match the observables against behavior patterns and derive *inferred intent* from those patterns [1,29].

Various methodologies have been developed for building computational models for intent inferencing. A plan-goal-graph (PGG) is a network of plans and goals where each high-level goal is decomposed into a set of plans for achieving it, and the plans are decomposed into subgoals that, in turn, are decomposed into lower-level plans [12]. Thus, the hierarchical structure of PGG is composed of alternating plans and goals. Intent inferencing is thus the process of searching for a path in the PGG from an observed action to a plan or goal. Figure 1.1.1 shows a PGG of an athlete's effort to win in sports games where ovals are goals and subgoals, rectangles are plans, and diamonds are the actions. As shown in the figure, the observation of a "running exercise" (action) can be traced back to the plan for training to improve physical endurance and further linked to the goal of improving physical condition, and so on.

In another approach, the operator function model (OFM), an expert system uses a heterarchic-hierarchic network of finite-state automata for intent interfering. In the network, nodes represent an entity's activities and arcs represent conditions that initiate/terminate certain activities [7,9,27]. From the topmost level to the lower-most levels, high-level activities (major operation functions) are hierarchically decomposed into subactivities, then tasks, and finally, actions. Each node has inputs and outputs: Inputs to a node are outputs from higher-level nodes or exogenous events, in the case of the top network level (heterarchic level) [27]. For inferencing, hierarchical structures of goal-plan-task-action are derived from the OFM, and the inferencing process maps an observed operator action onto model-derived tasks that, in turn, support model-derived plans. As operator actions are performed, the system tries to connect each action to one or more appropriate activity trees [9,27]. A third approach is generalized plan recognition [8,17,22], which tries to recognize the entity's plan for carrying out the task based on observations, an exhaustive set of discrete actions (a plan library), and constraints. Generally when an action from a user is observed, the system tries to search and match the observation against the plan library and then choose the preferred plan or extend the currently identified plan according to given knowledge regarding typical user plans. Lastly, the Soar model [13] is based on operators (plans) and states (beliefs). Operators are selected based on preconditions (pattern matching) and executed based on the current state. Selecting high-level operators leads to certain related subgoals. In Soar, a selected operator constrains the option of new operators that the software agent intends to consider, which constrains the search space of the problem. This methodology is compatible with Bratman's insights in the BDI model [13].

Although intent inferencing has been applied to different fields, the usual goal is to infer the user's intention from monitoring the individual's interactions with the system and then anticipate the user's future actions to provide proactive support to them. An example is the application of a user model for predicting the intelligence analyst's intent during information retrieval and assisting him/her to achieve better results [32]. This intent inferencing model consists of three formative components: The first, *interests and foci*, captures the user's key interest in the process of retrieving the information. The second, *actions and preferences*, describes the activities that can be used to carry out the user's goals with an emphasis on how the user tends to carry them out. The third, *knowledge and reasoning*, provides insight into the deeper motivations behind the goals upon which the user is focused and illuminates connections among the goals. Assume that an intelligence analyst is seeking information on weapons of mass destruction (WMD) in a certain geographic region and that they issue a query about "facilities for WMDs in…". After receiving the query, the intent inferencing model tries to recall prior information about the user's searching behavior and discovers three items: (1) The user has been focusing in the biological warfare domain (which has been identified in the interests set); (2) that biological weapons are a type of WMD (from the knowledge of reasoning component); and (3) this analyst tends to quickly narrow down his query so as to search for detailed information (searching style, found in the actions and preferences component). The system then modifies the user query to reflect the analyst's interests and searching style and subsequently presents information, appropriately ranked, concerning biological weapon facilities. The analyst goes through the returned documents and indicates which are relevant. This relevancy information is then fed back into the system for the user intent inferencing model to update itself [32,33]. Besides the intelligence domain, this user modeling approach has also been applied to the medical domain [4,23,31]. Many other applications of intent inferencing exist, including recommender systems [16,36], tutoring systems [3,9], and team intent identification [10].

We are interested in inferring the intent of a special entity, the adversary. As we shall see, many of the same underlying principles for intent inferencing hold for adversary intent inferencing, where observed adversarial actions are used to deduce the goals or plans that those actions try to achieve or carry out. Adversary intent inferencing starts by collecting information (observables) regarding the adversary from different sources, such as sensors and intelligence sources. The next step is to infer adversary intentions and goals with regards to given adversary perceptions and beliefs. Finally, the inferencing process can predict the adversary's COA. However, note that the adversary intent inferencing model should be constructed by taking into account the adversary's perception of the world, how they view the situation, what they believe about themselves and their opponents, what their desired end-states are, and what they can and intend to accomplish.

In this chapter, the discussion on adversarial modeling focuses primarily on intent inferencing. Alternative approaches exist not based on intent that have been applied to other domains and applications. For example, game-tree search approaches have been successful in games such as chess and cards. More discussion on these other approaches can be found in Chapter 3.1, Chapter 3.2, and Chapter 3.5.

1.1.2 Representing and Reasoning under Uncertainty

Capturing the uncertainties inherent in the adversarial model as well as those found in the observables is important. A wide variety of approaches to modeling uncertainty exist including fuzzy logic, possibility theory, Dempster-Shafer, and qualitative reasoning (see [19] for a brief survey of models for uncertainty). We focus here on probabilistic models, specifically discrete models. For probabilistic reasoning, random variables (abbreviated *r.v.s.*) are used to represent discrete events or objects in the world. By making assignments to these *r.v.*s, the current state of the world can be modeled probabilistically. The reasoning process involves computing joint probabilities of the given *r.v.s.*

Bayesian networks (BNs) [25] are directed acyclic graphs in which the conditional dependency (such as a causal relationship) is represented through arcs between the *r.v.s.* When all parents of a given *r.v. A* are instantiated, that *r.v.* is said to be conditionally independent of the remaining *r.v.*s that are not descendants of *A* given its parents.* This approach provides a structural and

---

* For more details on this, see *d*-separation in [25].

visual (graphical) organization of information and direct relationships among *r.v.s.*

While BNs have been successfully used to prototype intelligent systems, including a tool for adversarial intent inferencing [29] and a causal analysis tool for military planning and wargaming [21,26], limitations exist for constructing such networks due to BN requirements such as completeness of conditional probability tables. In this chapter, we recommend another uncertainty model called *Bayesian knowledge bases* (BKBs) [34].

BKBs are a generalization of BNs. BKBs have been extensively studied both theoretically [35] and empirically for use in knowledge engineering [28] in a wide variety of domains such as space shuttle engine diagnosis, medical information processing, and data mining [2]. BKBs provide a highly flexible and intuitive representation following a basic "if-then" structure in conjunction with probability theory. Furthermore, BKBs were designed with typical domain incompleteness in mind to retain semantic consistency as well as soundness of inference in the absence of complete knowledge. Conversely, BNs typically assume a complete probability distribution is available from the start. BKBs have also been shown to capture knowledge at a finer level of detail as well as knowledge that would be cyclical (hence, disallowed) in BNs.

BKBs can also be depicted as directed graphs consisting of two types of nodes — *instantiation nodes* (I-nodes) and *support nodes* (S-nodes). In Figure 1.1.2, the I-nodes are labeled nodes that represent unique specific assignments to individual *r.v.s.* The I-nodes are related via edges to the S-nodes, which are depicted as dark nodes. Each *conditional probability rule* (CPR) is represented by an S-node where the parents of the S-node are the antecedents of the CPR and the child of the S-node denotes the

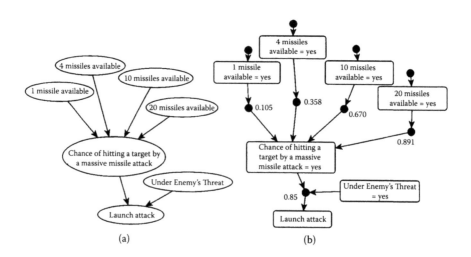

FIGURE 1.1.2
An example of probability networks for decision making process in (a) BN and (b) BKB.

consequence. Inferencing over BKBs can be conducted similarly to "if-then" rule chaining. As such, sets of CPRs collectively form inferences where the probability of the collection is a product of the probabilities associated with the CPRs.

As described in [35], probabilistic models exhibiting significant local structure are common. In such models, explicit representation of that structure — as done in BKBs — is advantageous as the resulting representation is much more compact than the full table representation of the *conditional probability tables* (CPT) in a BN. For example, as shown in Figure 1.1.2, the decision of whether to launch a missile attack against an enemy target is dependent upon two conditions: The chance of being able to hit and destroy/damage the target and whether a threat exists from that target. The chance of hitting the enemy target depends on the number of missiles that can be launched at the same time in the attack (consider the enemy having the ability to defend against those missiles). In this example, each random variable has only two states (*yes* or *no*). The structures of BNs and BKBs are very similar, except that BKBs have additional S-nodes (dark circles). However, in BNs, the CPT for the random variable "Chance of hitting the target by a massive missile attack" has 2^5 entries. The size of the representation of the conditional probabilities in terms of rules in the BKB is only 4.

Given the rule-based nature of BKBs, introducing new rules and modifying or removing existing rules is also relatively easy. This attribute allows the development of automatic algorithms for generating BKB fragments, i.e., small sets of CPRs, in real-time or stored in a BKB fragments library for use as needed. As we shall see, BKB fragments are successfully instantiated and used within our adversary intent inferencing framework for wargaming and mission planning and analysis.

1.1.3   Adversary Intent Inferencing Model (AII)

The *adversary intent inferencing* (AII) model strives to represent the perceptions of the adversary. It explicitly defines what the adversary believes about themselves, such as their capabilities and doctrines, and what the adversary believes about their opponents (see detailed discussion below). This is one major difference between the AII model and other approaches, such as the Soar system. Also, unlike the Soar and BDI models where the committed plans or chosen operators constrain the search space, the AII model's reasoning space is defined by the current state of the world as seen through the eyes of the adversary. In addition to inferring the possible goals, intentions, and actions, the AII model also emphasizes the explanation of inferred results by relating them to the adversary's beliefs. In general, intent inferencing should be able to provide three kinds of hypotheses: (1) Descriptive intent inference provides insight into the motivations behind actions that have just occurred; (2) predictive intent inference can anticipate future actions given the individual's inferred goals; and (3) diagnostic intent inference detects deviations between predicted and observed actions to reveal possible errors [1]. Instead of just focusing on prediction, the AII model provides all three types of intent inferencing.

1.1.3.1 Architecture of AII Model

In the AII model, we decompose the adversary intent inferencing architecture into the what/how/why components to provide a natural and intuitive organization of the adversarial decision-making process. The three core components are as follows:

Goals/Foci (what): A prioritized, weighted short- and long-term goals list representing adversary objectives or foci, which evolves over time.

Rationale network (why): A probabilistic network representing the influences of the adversary's beliefs, both about themselves and about their opponents, on their goals and on high-level actions associated with those goals.

Action network (how): A probabilistic network representing the detailed relationships between adversary goals and possible actions to realize those goals.

Due to the uncertainty involved in adversary course of action prediction, we use BNs [25] or BKBs [34,35] as the knowledge representation for the rationale and action networks.* The *r.v.*s involved in the probabilistic networks are classified into four classes:

Axioms (X) represent the beliefs of the adversary about themselves. This can be an adversary's beliefs about their own true capabilities or even a fanatic belief of invulnerability. Axioms typically serve as inputs or explanations to the other *r.v.*s, such as adversary goals.

Beliefs (B) represent the beliefs regarding their opponent. For example, an adversary might believe that their opponent will conduct air strikes before moving ground troops but will not conduct carpet-bombing given their opponent's current political situation. Beliefs are further decomposed into tactical and strategic beliefs as we will describe in more detail later. (Note that for this chapter, we use *Red* to refer to the adversary and *Blue* for the friendly side as our models are used by the "friendly" side.)

---

* We initially employed BNs, but have moved to BKBs, as we mentioned earlier.

Goals (G) are the adversary's desired end-states. They are either short-term or long-term and are stored in a weighted, prioritized list. The goals can be further partitioned into two types: Abstract and concrete. Abstract goals are those that cannot be executed directly — for example, the abstract goal of damaging world opinion concerning Blue. Concrete goals could be something like destroying a Blue force checkpoint.

Actions (A) can be carried out to achieve adversarial goals. Actions typically can be observed by friendly forces — for example, launching a surface-to-air missile against Blue aircrafts.

These four *r.v.* types occur within the two networks. The rationale network contains all the Belief, Axiom, and Goal variables, as well as any Action variables that have Goals as inputs. This network is used to infer the adversary's short-term and long-term goals. Once the goals are determined, the action network is used to reason out what the most likely enemy actions will be. The action network contains the entire set of Action variables and any concrete Goal variables. These Action variables serve as the "connective" interface between the rationale and action networks. Figure 1.1.3 shows an example of a rationale network and an action network.

1.1.3.2 Model Construction

As described above, the AII model contains three major components. Besides the goal list, two probabilistic networks are also used: The action network and the rationale network. These two networks represent the knowledge of the adversarial decision-making process. Generally, the process of establishing any probabilistic network consists of three steps: (1) Identify the important random variables; (2) build the causal relationships among random variables and their assignments, which then gives a graphical structure; and (3) set the probability distribution values.

We begin by examining the high-level variables belonging to Beliefs. In the AII model, Belief variables are independent and serve as inputs to Axioms, Goals, or Actions. Belief variables can be categorized into two basic types: Strategic Beliefs and tactical Beliefs. Strategic Beliefs include philosophy, strategic goals, and general characteristics or behaviors of Blue forces from the adversary's point of view. Tactical Beliefs represent actionable Blue events such as the physical repositioning of assets, specific kinetic attacks, and so on. While constructing a dependency structure among the Belief variables (especially, tactical beliefs) that represent sequences or hierarchies of Blue actions seems reasonable, this practice increases the complexity of the networks. The complexity is easily mitigated by the fact that when the Blue actions are known with certainty, the belief variables can be set as evidence, which has the effect of rendering the Beliefs independent [29,30].

The rest of the semantic structure is intuitive and is as follows: Axioms have strategic Beliefs as inputs and serve as inputs to Goals and other

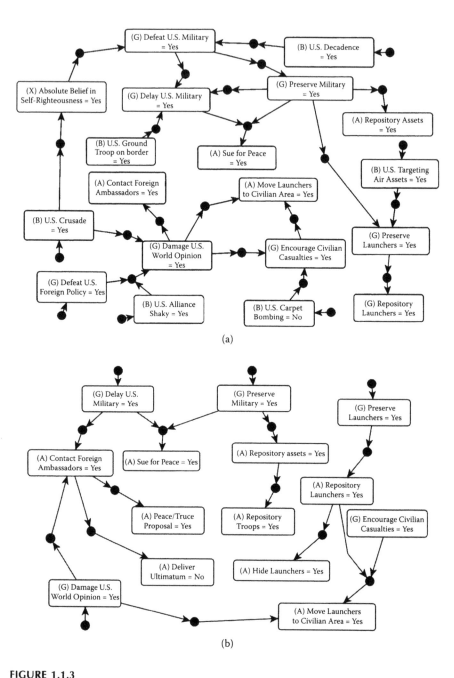

FIGURE 1.1.3

(a) Rationale network and (b) action network. The random variables are labeled according to their categories, with X for Axioms, B for Beliefs, G for Goals, and A for Action.

Axioms. Goals have Axioms and Beliefs as inputs and serve as inputs to Actions or other Goals. Actions have Goals and tactical Beliefs as inputs and can only be inputs to other Actions. Basically, the structure follows an intuitive hierarchical pre- and post-condition organization. Hence, a natural dominance relationship exists between related variable types, for example, Axioms that are descendants of other Axioms. This dominance reflects the fact that one variable can be "more general," "more abstract," "aggregate," "precondition," and so on, with respect to a descendant variable.

To maintain the appropriate division of variables among the rationale and action networks, Goal variables are partitioned into abstract Goals and concrete Goals. Abstract Goals are Goals composed of additional Goal variables. Concrete Goals are Goals that are immediately actionable. As such, abstract Goals can only appear in the rationale network and are critical to providing the proper explanations for adversary rationale. Concrete Goals must appear in both networks and serve as the causal "glue" between networks.

Finally, two basic rules maintain the semantic integrity of the AII: (1) All Axioms, Beliefs, Goals, and Actions occur in at least one of the adversary rationale or action networks; and (2) given a concrete Goal G, if A is an Action node with input G, then G, A, and the inputs of A must occur in both networks with the same connection structure. The second rule makes sure that the propagation of reasoning between the two networks occurs properly. Such propagation actually happens in both directions, rationale to action to rationale, which reflects the predictive and explanatory process in the AII.

As we can see, the construction of the AII model is a process of identifying potential adversarial goals based on what the enemy believes about the Blue forces and the Red themselves, then generating possible actions that can be carried out to achieve these goals based on their capabilities and history movements. Human factors can be modeled by or show their impacts through the Axiom or Belief variables in the model as we shall see later.

1.1.3.3 Reasoning over the Model

Reasoning over the AII model is an iterative process that allows the adversary model to adapt to changes over time (Figure 1.1.4). It includes several steps: Take inputs (observables, currently inferred adversary goals, intelligence, and user feedback) as evidence and infer the new goals; use the new information as evidence to reason about the potential adversarial actions and present them to the user; update the model according to the environmental inputs, reasoning results, and user feedback; and get ready for the next cycle. More specifically, the intent inferencing and prediction process functions as follows:

(1) Observables regarding the adversary are set as evidence in both rationale and action networks. Feedback from the analyst (if any) is set as evidence.

(2) Current short- and long-term enemy foci from foci lists are also set as evidence in both networks.

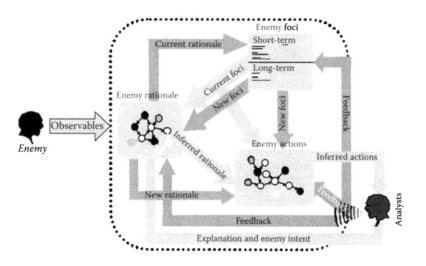

FIGURE 1.1.4
AII process (from [29]).

(3) The rationale network infers new goals that are set as evidence for the action network.

(4) The action network is now used to predict adversarial actions.

(5) The analyst is presented with the inferred goals, predicted actions, and the explanation behind such predictions.

(6) The analyst provides feedback in terms of corrected goals and actions, if desired.

(7) The goals list is updated based on newly inferred goals and current strength of existing goals. If goals exceed a given threshold value, they are added to the list. If goals fall below a set threshold, they are removed. If goals in the short-term list persist beyond a given time threshold, they become long-term goals.

(8) Networks are updated based on analyst feedback (if any) and go to Step 1.

The inference process on both the rationale and action networks is based on Belief updating for probabilistic networks. In essence, given a target variable R and evidence set E, belief updating computes $P(R/E)$.

1.1.3.4   AII and Wargaming

Our AII model has been integrated into military wargaming environments to assist in simulating intelligent forces. This practice helps to reduce the overall level of human expert involvement while effectively assisting in the rapid construction and execution of the simulations and "what-if" analysis in the after action review, where an assessment is conducted after the simulation to evaluate what has happened, why it has happened, what could happen, and what should be the response. In this section, we describe our experiments and results of prototyping and deploying AII.

The AII model was first prototyped and deployed in cooperation with Lockheed Martin's Advanced Technology Laboratories. The goal of the prototype was to provide an initial proof-of-concept for AII based on a historical scenario, the Battle of Khafji during the Persian Gulf War in 1991. Khafji was a small abandoned town in Saudi Arabia near the Kuwait border, and this battle was the Iraqis' only organized offensive during the war [18].

The objective of this Iraqi attack is now accepted to be to attempt to engage the coalition forces in a ground battle while Iraqi mechanized forces could still maneuver in the Kuwait theater of operations, especially in light of the effectiveness of coalition air attacks. Several days before the attack, Iraqi forces massed behind the nearby battle line. Increased activities were detected including the digging of berms and reinforcement of artillery positions on January 26 and 27 by the Iraqis, and the movement of armored vehicles into position on January 28. On January 29, after nightfall, Iraqi tanks approached Khafji and made contact with U.S. Marine Corps outposts along the border. The outposts fell back to preplanned positions while coalition forces responded with air strikes. The Iraqis took control of Khafji and it was then the Coalition's problem to determine Iraqi intentions, contain the offensive forces, and retake Khafji. The steady surveillance and constant availability of air power helped the Coalition stop the Iraqi attack in time to spoil their advantage of surprise.

In the simulation, working with the constructed AII model, the prototype successfully predicted as well as updated the predicted actions of the adversary over time as the events unfolded. At the beginning of the simulation, the AII model was set with the observation that an Iraqi offensive in the south was unlikely and Coalition attention and sensors were focused on the western reaches of Iraq in support of SCUD (a type of tactical ballistic missile) suppression, strikes on Iraqi Republican Guard divisions, and battle damage assessment [24]. As time passed and the simulation progressed with each new observation and intelligence report about Iraqi forces moving south, massing, trying to jam Coalition communications, and so on, the AII correctly reflected the intentions of the Iraqi forces by indicating that the probability of Iraqi forces crossing the border for a ground engagement was increasing. Because the AII was a model of Iraqi forces, the intentions of the Iraqis drove the appropriate selection of actions by the AII in the simulation and ultimately initiated the attack across the border. The selection of actions was based on choosing the highest probability actions supported by the inferred goals and intentions. The observations of events had been set as evidence into the AII, which strengthened the inferred goals and intentions over time, in this case, the Iraqi desire for a ground battle.

Later, the AII model was deployed with the Force Structure Simulations (FSS) wargaming system at the Air Force Research Laboratory, Information Directorate (AFRL/D) [14,37]. In this trial, a general adversary model was first created and then specialized to portray different adversaries. The general model contained random variables that accounted for variability in weapons capabilities, tactical/strategic strikes, and responses to the presence of Blue forces in any of the four directions. Two instances of the model with different belief systems were created with the AII, referenced as adversary A and B. Adversary A possessed a competent air force, a smaller ground force, and WMDs, whereas adversary B was lacking any WMDs, had much less air power, but had a powerful ground force.

The test was to see the effects on the wargaming simulation and how much these two adversaries would differ in countering Blue force actions. Two different sets of observations of Blue forces were created and fed into the system. In the first set of inputs for Blue, data indicated a strategic bombing campaign comprised of deploying sea forces and launching cruise missiles and air strikes at strategic targets. The second input set described a land invasion of military targets by Blue. Each step in the simulation covered a 30 minute time slice [37]. Table 1.1.1 lists some of the highly ranked actions and differences resulting from the input sets. Adversary A, while characterized by confidence in its higher technology capabilities, responded to Blue attacks with air counterstrikes and potentially employing their WMDs, whereas adversary B responded through ground actions. While the results might be obvious to a human, the goal of the simulation is to see how the automated adversary forces would act differently in different situations.

TABLE 1.1.1

Sample Results Matrix

COA Inputs	Adversary A	Adversary B
Set 1	Deliver Ultimatum	Launch Ground Assault
	Launch Air Attack	Send Forces South
	Send Forces South	Enemy Recon Probing
	Arm WMD	Forces Cross Border
	Launch WMD	Deploy Forces in Civilian Areas
Set 2	Deploy Forces in Civilian Areas	Deploy Forces in Civilian Areas
	Deliver Ultimatum	Launch Ground Assault
	Deploy Forces Along Border	Send Forces West
	Arm WMD	Send Forces North
	Conceal Assets	Enemy Recon Probing
	Launch WMD	Forces Cross Border
		Deploy Forces along Border
		Conceal Assets

(Adapted from [37])

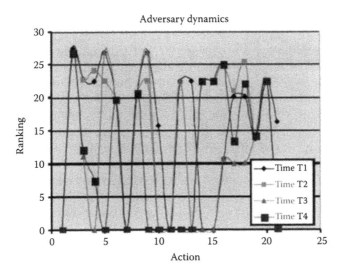

FIGURE 1.1.5
Dynamics of adversary's action behaviors (from [37]).

Figure 1.1.5 and Figure 1.1.6 are plots of the adversary actions (referenced numerically along the *x*-axis) being pursued. More than 20 Red force actions were defined in the scenario, some of these shown in Table 1.1.1. Figure 1.1.5 shows the actions of adversary A over time as the first set of Blue force COA was applied. In each time step (T_1 to T_4), adversary A chose a different set of actions in response to the Blue force actions at that moment. For example,

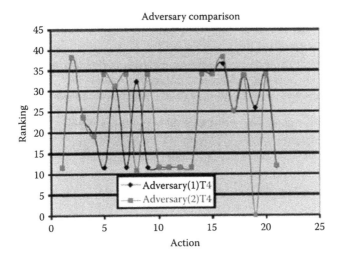

FIGURE 1.1.6
Action differences between adversaries (from [37]).

at T_2, action 5 had a high probability, but at T_4, action 5 would not be the choice of Red. The graph illustrates the dynamics in the anticipated behavior at each time interval, which shows that when the situation changes along the timeline, adversary A responded differently to Blue's attacks.

The divergence of selected actions between the two adversaries at a single time step is shown in Figure 1.1.6. Clearly at time T_4, some actions were ranked quite differently (actions 5, 7, 9, and 19) by the two adversaries. This result shows that the differences in the Beliefs of two adversaries made a noticeable difference in their behaviors. Similar results have been obtained from other time slices.

More recently, the AII model has been deployed in the Emergent Adversarial Modeling Systems (EAMS) [15]. The AII engine was supported by the EAMS ontology that describes data and semantic relationships between the domain elements. The simulation was based upon the Deny Force Scenario used in the FSS [14], as documented by AFRL/IF, with a set of predefined Blue missions. The Blue force assets included the carrier *USS Roosevelt*, FA-18s on the carrier, Nellis Air Force Base, and the F-16s at the base. On the adversarial side, the Red force has surface-to-air missiles (SAM) located at the site named Twentynine Palms, 12 Seersuckers (anti-ship missiles) at Vandenberg, airports at Vandenberg and Twentynine Palms, command posts at Pendleton, Twentynine Palms and Meadows, and so on. The possible movements — which are commands that can be issued to FSS — include moving assets along known routes, operating assets, and engaging targets.

In the scenario, the Red force faced three main threats from the Blue force: Jamming of radar by EA-6 launched from *USS Roosevelt* at Meadows, Pendleton and Twentynine Palms; attack by FA-18s from *USS Roosevelt* at Meadows and Pendleton; and attack by F-16s from Nellis AFB at Twentynine Palms and Hesperia.

According to the Deny Force Scenario, the EAMS ontology was configured with a set of Actions that was possible for Red to perform, a set of Red Beliefs, a set of Red Axioms, and a set of Red Goals. An example where we identified critical information and generated a BKB (fragment) is shown as follows and can be seen in Figure 1.1.7. (Symbols A, B, G, and X represent random variables of Action, Belief, Goal and Axiom in the AII model.)

- The Red force collected observable information, where the Blue force has attacked with FA-18s launched from the carrier *USS Roosevelt*. The Red force was based at Vandenberg airport and has 12 Seersucker missiles in inventory.

- Based on this information, Red generated a Belief that the Blue force would strike the Red site with FA-18s from the *USS Roosevelt* (B, *Air Strike by FA-18 from USS Roosevelt*).

- Next, an Axiom was generated for each Red asset concerning the status and effectiveness of the asset. In this example, they were the status of the airport (X, *Vandenberg Airport Operational*) and Seersucker missiles (X, *Have Seersucker at Vandenberg Airport*), and the chance they

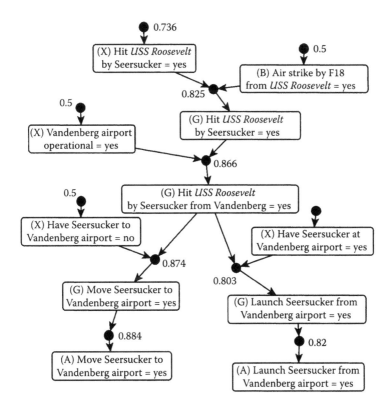

FIGURE 1.1.7
A partial rationale network (BKB) for simulation with Deny Force Scenario.

would be able use these missiles to damage the Blue carrier, which was the effectiveness of their weapon (X, *Hit USS Roosevelt by Seersucker*).

- According to the Belief that Blue's attacks were coming from the *USS Roosevelt*, Goals were then generated by pairing the Red and Blue capabilities that would be able to reach each other. One of the possible Goals was to attack the carrier with Seersuckers (G, *Hit USS Roosevelt by Seersucker*). This Goal was then detailed into a more concrete one, i.e., attack *USS Roosevelt* with Seersuckers from the Vandenberg airport (G, *Hit USS Roosevelt by Seersucker from Vandenberg*). Continuing this process, launching an attack against the *USS Roosevelt* from Vandenberg was further decomposed into two sub-Goals: To move missiles to the airport and to launch the missiles. Sub-Goals were provided by the adversary ontology, where if a weapon was to be used, it should be either already on-site or moved to the specific site.

- After the Goals have been generated, the Beliefs and Axioms were linked to Goals. Because generating Goals was a process of pairing the Red and Blue capabilities for attacking each other or one defending against the other, proper Axioms that were about Red and Beliefs about Blue could be easily assigned to related Goals.

- Finally, Actions were added for the concrete Goals — in this case, corresponding to moving missiles to Vandenberg airport (*A, Move Seersucker to Vandenberg Airport*) and launching the missile attack from Vandenberg (*A, Launch Seersucker from Vandenberg Airport*). Adding Actions and sub-Actions were supported by the ontology, where knowledge was available for what Actions were necessary for carrying out certain concrete Goals.

The probability values for this fragment came from scenario settings and theoretical calculations. During the simulation, Red started with 12 missiles and could launch all of them in a massive attack. The probability of hitting the *USS Roosevelt* by such an attack (*X, Hit USS Roosevelt by Seersucker*) would be 0.736, which is calculated based on a single-shot hit probability of 0.7 and a 0.85 probability of each missile being blocked. Later in the simulation, Red force lost 8 of their missiles in action and had only 4 Seersuckers available to them. According to this change, the AII model recalculated the probability for (*X, Hit USS Roosevelt by Seersucker*) and dropped it to 0.358. The probabilities and method for computing them are retrieved from the ontology.

In the simulation, Red commander actions were generated real-time by the AII model in response to Blue movements and thus became the executed Red missions. Two test scenarios were developed and simulated to highlight the notion that given the execution of a set of Blue missions, two adversarial commanders — differing only by their intent — will perform different sets of actions in response to the same set of Blue missions. In the experiment, one Axiom variable defined simply as "Behavior" was added into the rationale network in the AII model. It has three states: Aggressive, neutral, and passive. The three states of the variable "Behavior" simply reflect possible high, medium, and low levels of aggressiveness of Red. It is introduced as a parent node for each high-level Goal variable and the state of the "Behavior" variable influenced the probability of each Goal. Assume that the Red Goal of attacking the Blue force has a probability value of p_n that reflects a neutral commander. To automatically reflect the other commander types, we have probabilities for an aggressive commander of $p_n + 0.33 \times (1.0 - p_n)$ and, for a passive commander, $(1 - 0.33) \times p_n$.* This allows us to easily introduce different human factors into the AII model by encapsulating the behaviors in a way that permits us to automatically perturb probabilistic behaviors from a single baseline model. For the experiment, one commander was

---

* Note that in the case where $p_n = 1$, the aggressive and passive probabilities are 1.0 and 0.33, respectively. Because these are conditional probabilities representing P(G = *true* | Behavior = {*aggressive, neutral, passive*}), the respective values are probabilistically valid. Intuitively, the probability numbers will still be in a range from 0 to 1. The numerical influence of behavior is derived from the EAMS ontology reflecting the players in the battlespace.

TABLE 1.1.2

Red Commander's Actions in Simulation

Scenario 1: Commander Intent — Aggressive Attack	Scenario 2: Commander Intent — Passive Defense
Defend Initial Attack	Defend Initial Attack
Move SAMs into Meadows from Pendleton	Move SAMs to Meadows from Pendleton
React to Destruction	Continue to Defend
Launch Seersuckers to *USS Roosevelt* from Vandenberg	Move SAMs to Twentynine Palms from Pendleton
Continue to Defend	Defend with Authority
Move SAMs to Twentynine Palms from Pendleton	Operate all SAMs

selected to be "aggressive" while the second was "passive." In the two scenarios, Scenario 1 represents the aggressive Red commander and Scenario 2 represents the passive commander.

The significant events chosen for the simulation were: *Meadows Detects FA-18s, Meadows Experiences Destruction,* and *Twentynine Palms Detects F-16s.* Upon the occurrence of a significant event, the AII model was triggered to generate the list of potential Red actions that correspond to the event. Once the candidate actions were generated, EAMS generated the specific instance of a mission, which is then used by FSS to execute the mission.

Not surprisingly, the simulation demonstrated that the aggressive commander was likely to actively respond to Blue threats whereas the passive commander merely defends (Table 1.1.2). What was surprising is that the passive commander caused more serious damage to the Blue force than the aggressive commander. This outcome resulted from the fact that the passive Red commander chose to preserve assets by shutting down all equipment (SAMs, etc.), which caused targeting problems for Blue force bombers. Finally, when Red did decide to attack, Blue aircraft were already turning around and disengaging and were thus caught in a disadvantageous firing position.

The simulations above demonstrate that the AII model can support existing systems and simulation applications; descriptive elements of adversary composition can be properly classified allowing for the rapid assembly and modification of an adversary force (exploiting an ontology); and intent has great influence on the actions of an adversarial force, where soft factors such as the aggressive stance of an adversary force commander can alter adversary response and mission results.

1.1.4 Conclusions

Correctly predicting the adversary's intentions, actions, and reactions can lead to effectively responding to those actions, as well as planning ones own operations. The AII model provides a systematic approach to modeling the adversary, and predicting adversary's intentions and potential future actions in a dynamic environment, while providing explanations of adversary's goals and actions. It employs explicit representation of adversarial actions, associated goals, and their beliefs behind those goals. The inferencing results can be used as a primary driver of adversary behaviors and responses as demonstrated in our experiments. Furthermore, it provides a tool that evaluates both the adversarial capabilities and potential future movement in light of their intentions. Putting all this together, the AII model has achieved capabilities beyond the traditional goal, plan, task, or action searching and matching approaches to adversarial behavior modeling.

Acknowledgments

This work was supported in part by Air Force Research Labs, Information Directorate, Grant No. F30602-01-1-0595, Air Force Office of Scientific Research Grant No. F49620-03-1-0014, Department of Defense Grant No. FA8750-04-C-0118, and Office of the Secretary of Defense Grant No. FA8650-04-M-6435.

Thanks to Bob Hillman, Jim Hanna, Duane Gilmour, Dan Fayette, Joe Carozzoni, Al Sisti, Dawn Trevisani, and many other folks at AFRL/IF, AFRL/HE, and AFOSR; Lee Krause, Lynn Lehman, Bruce McQueary, and Tony Stirtzinger at Securboration, Inc.; Axel Anurak, Sergio Gigli, and Frank Vetesi at LM ATL; and Scott Brown, Ben Bell, Joshua Surman, Hua Wang, and Alex Negri for all their invaluable assistance in moving the ideas in this research forward. Finally, special thanks to John Graniero, Nort Fowler, and Barry McKinney for their efforts in getting all of this off the ground.

References

1. Bell, B., Santos, E. Jr., and Brown, S.M., Making adversary decision modeling tractable with intent inference and information fusion, in *Proc. of 11th Conf. Comput. Generated Forces Behav. Represent.*, Orlando, FL, 2002, 535–542.
2. Ben-Eliyahu-Zohary, R., Domshak, C., Gudes, E., Liusternik, N., Meisels, A., Rosen, T., and Shimony, S.E., FlexiMine—a flexible platform for kdd research and application development, *Ann. Math. Artif. Intell.*, 39(1-2), 175–204, 2003.
3. Benyon, D. and Murray, D., Adaptive systems: from intelligent tutoring to autonomous agents, *Knowl.-Based Syst.* 6(4), 197–219, 1993.
4. Brown, S.M., Santos, E. Jr., and Banks, S.B., Active user interface for building decision-theoretic systems, in *Proc. 1st Asia-Pacific Conf. Intell. Agent Tech.*, Hong Kong, 1999, 244–253.
5. Bratman, M.E., *Intention, Plans, and Practical Reason*, Cambridge and London: Harvard University Press, 1987.

6. Bratman, M.E., Israel, D.J., and Pollack, M.E., Plans and resource-bounded practical reasoning, *Computational Intelligence*, 4, 349–355, 1988.

7. Bushman, J.B., Mitchell, C.M., Jones, P.M., and Rubin, K.S., ALLY: an operator's associate for cooperative supervisory control systems, *IEEE Trans. Syst., Man, and Cyber.*, 23(1), 111–128, 1993.

8. Carberry, S., Modeling the user's plans and goals, *Comp. Ling.*, 14(3), 23–27, 1988.

9. Chu, R.W., Mitchell, C.M., and Jones, P.M., Using the operator function model and OFMspert as the basis for an intelligent tutoring system: towards a tutor/aid paradigm for operators of supervisory control systems, *IEEE Trans. Syst., Man, and Cyber.*, 25(7), 1054–1075, 1995.

10. Franke, J., Bell, B., Mendenhall, H., and Brown, S., Enhancing teamwork through team-level intent inference, in *Proc. Int. Conf. Artif. Intell.*, Las Vegas, NV, 2000.

11. Geddes, N.D., The use of individual differences in inferring human operator intentions, in *Proc. 2nd Ann. Aerosp. Appl. Intelli. Conf.*, Dayton, OH, 1986, 31–41.

12. Geddes, N.D., A model for intent interpretation for multiple agents with conflicts, in *Proc. of IEEE Int. Conf. Syst., Man, and Cyber.*, San Antonio, TX, 1994.

13. Georgeff, M., Pell, B., Pollack, M., Tamble, M., and Wooldridge, M., The belief-desire-intention model of agency, in Muller, J. P., Singh, M., and Rao, A., Eds., *Intelligent Agents V, Lec. Notes in AI, Vol. 1365*, Berlin: Springer-Verlag, 1999.

14. Gilmour, D.A., Hanna, J., Koziarz, W., McKeever, W., and Walter, M., High-performance computing for command and control real-time decision support, *AFRL Technol. Horizons*, 2005, http://www.afrlhorizons.com/Briefs/Feb05/IF0407.html

15. Gilmour, D.A., Krause, L.S., Lehman, L.A., Santos, E., Jr., and Zhao, Q., Intent driven adversarial modeling, *10th Intl. Command and Control Res. and Tech. Symp., The Future of C2*. McLean, VA, 2005.

16. Good, N., Schafer, J.B., Konstan, J.A., Borchers, A., Sarwar, B., Herlocker, J., and Riedl, J., Combining collaborative filtering with personal agents for better recommendations, in *Proc. 1999 Conf. Am. Assoc. Artif. Intell. (AAAI-99)*, 1999, 439–446.

17. Goodman, B.A. and Litman, D.J., Plan recognition for intelligent interfaces, in *Proc. of 6th IEEE Conf. on Artif. Intell. Appl.*, Santa Barbara, CA, 1990, 297–303.

18. Grant, R., The epic little battle of Khafji, *Air Force Mag. Online*, 81(2), 1998, http://www.afa.org/magazine/Feb1998/0298epic.asp

19. Halpern, J., *Reasoning About Uncertainty*, Cambridge, MA: MIT Press, 2005.

20. Headquarters, Department of the Army, Field Manual, No. 101-5. Staff Organization and Operations, 1997, http://www.dtic.mil/doctrine/jel/service_pubs/101_5.pdf

21. Lemmer, J.F. and Gossink, D. E., Recursive noisy OR—a rule for estimating complex probabilistic interactions, *IEEE Trans. on Syst., Man, and Cyber., Part B*, 34(6), 2252–2261, 2004.

22. Lesh, N., Rich, C., and Sidner, C.L., Using plan recognition in human-computer collaboration, in *Proc. 7th Int. Conf. User Modelling*, Banff, Canada, 1999, 23–32.

23. Nguyen, H., Saba, M.G., Santos, E., Jr. and Brown, S.M., Active user interface in a knowledge discovery and retrieval system, in *Proc. 2000 Int. Conf. Artif. Intell. (IC-AI 2000)*, Las Vegas, NV, 2000, 339–344.

24. Palmer, P.S., Scott, D.J., and Toolan, J.A., The battle of Khafji: an assessment of air power, *Research Report AU/AWC/192/1998-04*, Air War College, Air University, Maxwell Air Force Base, AL, 1998.

25. Pearl, J., *Probabilistic Reasoning in Intelligent Systems: Networks of Plausible Infer-ence*, San Mateo, CA: Morgan Kaufman, 1988.
26. Phister, P.W., Jr. and Plonisch, I.G., Military applications of information tech-nologies, *Air Space Power J.*, 18(1), 77–90, 2004.
27. Rubin, K.S., Jones, P.M., and Mitchell, C.M., OFMspert: inference of operator intentions in supervisory control using a blackboard architecture, *IEEE Trans. Syst., Man, and Cybern.*, 18(4), 618–637, 1988.
28. Santos, E., Jr., Verification and validation of knowledge-bases under uncertain-ty, *Data Knowl. Eng.*, 37, 307–329, 2001.
29. Santos, E., Jr., A cognitive architecture for adversary intent inferencing: structure of knowledge and computation, in *Proc. SPIE 17th Ann. Int. Symp. on Aerospace/ Defense Sensing and Controls: AeroSense 2003*, Orlando, FL, 2003, 182–193.
30. Santos, E., Jr. and Negri, A., Constructing adversarial models for threat intent prediction and inferencing, in *Proc. SPIE Defense and Security Symp.*, 5423, Orlando, FL, 2004.
31. Santos, E., Jr., Nguyen, H., Zhao, Q. and Pukinskis, E., Empirical evaluation of adaptive user modeling in a medical information retrieval application, in Brusilovsky, P., Corbett, A., and de Rosis, F., Eds., *Lecture Notes in Artif. Intelligence 2702: User Modeling 2003*, Johnstown, PA: Springer, 2003, 292–296.
32. Santos, E., Jr., Nguyen, H., Zhao, Q. and Wang, H., User modelling for intent prediction in information analysis, in *Proc. 47th Annu. Meet. for Hum. Factors and Ergonomics Soc. (HFES-03)*, Denver, CO, 2003, 1034–1038.
33. Santos E., Jr., Zhao, Q., Nguyen, H. and Wang, H., Impacts of user modeling on personalization of information retrieval: an evaluation with human intelli-gence analysts, in *4th Workshop Eval. of Adaptive Syst.*, in conjunction with *UM'05*, 2005, 27–36.
34. Santos, E., Jr. and Santos, E.S., A framework for building knowledge-bases under uncertainty, *J. Exp. Theor. Artif. Intell.*, 11, 265–286, 1999.
35. Santos, E., Jr., Santos, E.S., and Shimony, S.E., Implicitly preserving semantics during incremental knowledge-base acquisition under uncertainty, *Int. J. Approx. Reas.*, 33(1), 71–94, 2003.
36. Schmitt, C., Dengler, D., and Bauer, M., The MAUT machine: an adaptive recommender system, in *Online Proc. ABIS Workshop*, 2002, http://www.kbs.uni-hannover.de/henze/lla02/abis_proceedings.html
37. Surman, J., Hillman, R., and Santos, E., Jr., Adversarial inferencing for gener-ating dynamic adversary behavior, in *Proc. SPIE 17th Ann. Int. Symp. Aerosp./ Defense Sensing and Controls: AeroSense 2003*, Orlando, FL, 2003, 194–201.

1.2

Human Factors in Opponent Intent

Paul E. Nielsen, Jacob Crossman, and Randolph M. Jones

CONTENTS

Representing an opponent's beliefs and desires as well as emotional and physiological phenomena — such as fear, anger, and fatigue — are among the most important and complex aspects of adversarial reasoning. This chapter discusses knowledge-based models of such human factors for reasoning about adversarial intent. We discuss abductive reasoning (building a hypothesis from observations) to find the potential premises (beliefs, desires, goals, and intentions) that explain the motivation behind the observed behaviors. We further discuss the representations of knowledge for reasoning about an opponent's possible plans. These representations require the ability to reason about actions, spatial features, and intentions. Human factors include both the deliberate rational decision-making aspects of an adversarial task, such as a choice to defend or attack, as well as the emotional and physiological aspects, such as running away out of fear.

The primary domain of application discussed in this chapter is military wargaming. Wargaming offers a rich space of problems in determining an opponent's intent, including highly skilled adversaries, complex interactions, imperfect knowledge, time-critical information, and real-time decision making. Wargaming can bring to bear a broad range of human emotional and psychological effects. With the exception of a few very sophisticated models [1], computer-generated forces commonly used in simulation-based wargaming are not emotional. However, emotional behaviors can be introduced by human operators controlling the actions of the simulated forces. A significant body of research exists on the importance of emotions on the battlefield [2,3] and our objective in modeling these human factors of an opponent's intent is to recognize emotional states in our predictions of opponent actions.

Useful models of an opponent's intent in wargaming should make specific predictions about the future state of the world. This might involve predicting their troop movements, objective locations, targets, courses of action, and emotional states. We discuss an example system, the Knowledge-Based Intention Projection (KIP) module, that addresses the problem of determining the objectives and intentions of opponent troops.

The predictions are necessarily imprecise. Even when presented with exactly the same information about an opponent's actions, two different human experts can identify very different intentions behind these actions. This problem arises from a number of sources. First is the underlying complexity of the environment. Each small decision, such as an opponent's choice of turning left or right to avoid an obstacle, can have large consequences in the overall outcome of the battle. Second is the complexity of possible intentions and their relative importance. Each opponent holds a number of desires, some of which may be contradictory, such as the desire to attain an objective and the desire to survive. These desires vary from opponent to opponent and the relative importance of these desires to a given opponent may change over time. Third is the complexity of the information gathering process. Sensor coverage is sparse and subject to interpretation. Ten observations of a unit could indicate ten different units or the same one observed multiple times. Finally, the complexity of human adaptation must be considered. Humans learn from experience and deliberately adapt their behavior to either exploit a perceived weakness or (as discussed in later chapters) for the purposes of deception.

1.2.1 Intent Recognition in Human Opponents

One method of determining an opponent's intentions is to pretend to be the opponent and try to imagine what you would do in these circumstances. The TacAir-Soar behavior generation system [4] uses this approach to reason about air-to-air combat maneuvers. TacAir-Soar generates autonomous behaviors for military aircraft in synthetic combat. For example, knowing whether a missile has been fired by the opponent aircraft is important, but an immediate and clear indication that the firing has occurred may not always be evident. To help with this problem, TacAir-Soar uses its knowledge of aircraft, weapons, and tactics to create a speculation space where it assumes the role of the opponent.

It uses the knowledge of air tactics and emulates the reasoning of the opposing pilot whether to fire the missile. If it would have fired a weapon in the speculation space, the TacAir-Soar system assumes the opposing pilot would do so also and begins to take evasive actions.

Another method of determining an opponent's intention is to use a game theoretic approach. Several chapters in this book discuss such techniques. For example, Chapter 3.3 treats the problem as an abstract board game. The pieces move within the constraints of the battlespace and linguistic geometry [5] is used to construct optimized move sequences.

The basis for our own work on recognition of an opponent's intent is Kautz' theory of plan recognition [6]. This theory classifies plan recognition in terms of whether the opponent is aware of being observed, *intended recognition*, or unaware of the observer, *keyhole recognition*. He further distinguishes between situations with complete and accurate world knowledge and those with knowledge that might be inaccurate and incomplete. Kautz presents a formalism for dealing with the situation where knowledge is complete and accurate.

Charniak [7] extended Kautz' work with a Bayesian representation of uncertainty. This approach offers a more robust approach to plan recognition where knowledge is incomplete and inaccurate. We build on Charniak's representation with a richer opponent model using knowledge-based techniques to account for a wider range of human behavior.

Our technique of inferring goals from observations of behaviors and world state is similar to that of Huber [8,9] but we use domain-specific compositional templates, which contrast with their use of procedural models. Albrecht [10] also performs intention recognition in a complex domain, albeit with a very simple location/action/goal model.

To capture ongoing activity based on prior evidence, we use a dynamically expanding belief network model that has previously been employed by a number of authors [11–14]. Kaminka's approach to capturing ongoing activity [15] performs probabilistic inference, but with observations restricted to communications within a cooperating team, not general behaviors in an adversarial setting.

Our approach requires models of geographic reasoning and abstraction to capture the likely attack and defense zones within the area of concern. Mengshoel and Wilkins [16,17] use continuous and discrete grid representations of space. The work by Zukerman and Albrecht [17] encodes and aggregates the discrete location/places of their simulated domain world. In particular, it addresses a domain in which the complexity makes an exhaustive enumeration computationally intractable; as a result, they explore a number of abstraction and aggregation schemes.

Finally, a great deal of work exists related to opponent's intent in traditional games. Klinger [18] completed a Ph.D. thesis on adversarial reasoning in a game of Go. Billings [19] addressed the game of poker. These situations serve as compelling case studies of the importance of creating a credible opponent model rather than relying on brute force search techniques.

1.2.2   A Cognitive Approach to Modeling Opponents

The technique we discuss in this chapter builds on three cognitive science and artificial intelligence (AI) approaches and extends them to create a solution to the goal prediction problem. It employs the Soar cognitive architecture based on classic symbolic AI, [20,21] a belief-desire-intention (BDI) model of context-sensitive rational reasoning [22], and Bayesian belief networks (BBN) for reasoning over uncertainty [23].

The basis for our approach to cognitive modeling is the Soar architecture, proposed by Alan Newell [21] as a unified theory of cognition and applied to a large number of human reasoning problems including behavior generation, language understanding, student error recognition, and other cognitive tasks [24]. Soar views intelligence as symbol manipulation, embodied in the "Physical Symbol System Hypothesis" of Newell and Simon [25]. Soar provides methods for managing complex software systems and for rapid prototyping. It combines deductive pattern matching with automatic subgoaling. Soar offers the ability to translate raw observations into higher-level information and derive additional implications of a prediction once a prediction has been made. It does this through a truth-maintenance system combined with knowledge representations gleaned from subject matter experts.

BDI incorporates the assumptions that opponents are rational, have intentions and desired outcomes, and that high-level trends are more important than details. *Beliefs* are statements about the agent's environment, *desires* specify goals, and *intentions* are plans for achieving goals. Daniel Dennet [26] argues that predicting and explaining behavior in terms of beliefs, desires, and intentions is successful and that it cannot be fundamentally wrong to characterize cognition in these terms.

BDI is associated with an abstract architecture that describes the manipulation of data structures representing beliefs, desires, and intentions as the theoretical representation for discussing an opponent's mental state, as shown in Figure 1.2.1. In addition to the beliefs, desires, and intentions, such an architecture consists of a *belief revision function*, which uses input and previous beliefs to create new beliefs; a method to *create options*, which provides available alternatives; a *filter*, which selects intentions based on beliefs, desires, and previous intentions; and an *action selection function*, which determines which actions to perform [27].

BDI helps organize knowledge about entities and communicate hypothesized knowledge more effectively with humans. It is silent on the concrete formalisms required to realize these semantics [28,29], but is consistent with Soar's model of cognition and memory. With application to the wargaming domain, BDI's desires can include such potential goals as attacking, defending, retreating, and evading the opponent. These high-level desires can involve plans or subgoals such as stopping an

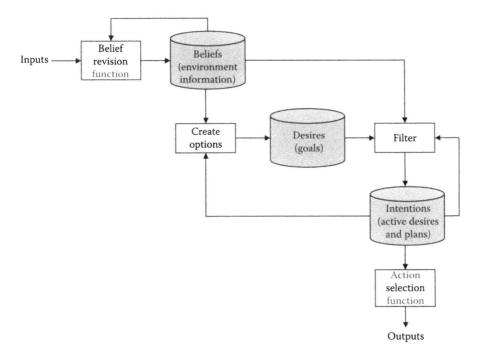

FIGURE 1.2.1
Abstract BDI architecture showing the data structure interactions.

opponent, occupying an area, or protecting a high-value friendly unit. Beliefs are created and elaborated by processing inputs derived from the sensor system.

Finally, as described in Chapter 1.1, BBNs are quantitative representations of the causal relationships between values. They provide an explicit representation of causality, manage non-monotonic information updates, and are based on a well-founded theory of Bayesian probability. The kind of cause-and-effect reasoning reflected in the belief network model is fundamental to human reasoning [23,30–33].

As a simple example, Figure 1.2.2 shows a causal diagram illustrating the relationship between achieving a military objective and having the necessary vehicles and weapons to do so. In this example, the only known way the opponent can achieve their objective is to attack. An attack can be brought about through appropriate weapons and transportation. Motorized vehicles can meet the transportation needs but they have a secondary effect of also causing fuel consumption. By disrupting the opponent's ability to consume fuel (e.g., cutting their supply lines), one can prevent their ability to attack and neutralize their ability to achieve their objective.

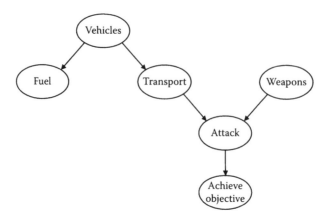

FIGURE 1.2.2
A network showing causal relationships between achieving an objective and having appropriate vehicles and weapons.

1.2.3   Knowledge-Based Abduction

Our focus is on deriving an opponent's intent from observed actions. A process called abduction is used to construct explanations for observed events and is central to tasks such as diagnosis and plan and intent recognition. *Abduction* is the process of forming an explanatory hypothesis or forming causes to explain effects [34]. Contrast this idea with *deduction*, which draws logical consequences from causes, and *induction*, which is the process of inferring general rules from specific data and is the primary task of machine learning [35].

Abduction is a complex process because many possible explanations of an observed behavior can exist. Bylander, et al. [36] have shown that, in general, abduction is NP-hard. For example, abduction is commonly observed in diagnostic medicine. A patient might go to a doctor complaining of a headache. The doctor begins to form a differential diagnosis consisting of such alternative explanations as tension, migraine, and brain tumor as shown in Figure 1.2.3. As the examination proceeds, the doctor asks questions and performs tests in an attempt to rule out alternative explanations for the pain. When only one possibility remains, it is assumed to be the cause.

Similarly, in the military wargaming domain, the system assumes a set of opponent's intentions as the potential explanations of the observed opponent's actions. From these intentions, it derives a set of possible behaviors that might be observed if the unit were engaged in each of these actions. An opponent that is not exhibiting the expected behaviors of a given intent is not likely to have that intent. Once enough behavior has been observed to eliminate all but one intent, it is assumed to be the cause.

Unlike deduction, abduction is not necessarily logically sound. Many possible causes might be found for a given observation and observing behaviors

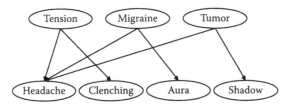

FIGURE 1.2.3
The cause of a headache can be determined by ruling in or out other symptoms that share the same cause. If the other symptoms associated with a potential cause are not present, the belief that this is the actual cause of the headache is reduced until only one possible cause remains.

long enough to eliminate all alternative explanations may not be possible. What makes abduction-based approaches feasible is that some causes are more likely than others. In the case of a headache, the doctor might consider tension as a much more likely cause and simply recommend aspirin. Similarly, in a battle, when someone fires at you, that the shooter is trying to destroy you rather than simply cleaning their weapon seems highly likely. In any case, you would take cover before considering any other alternatives.

Humans are good at assigning likelihoods from possible explanations to the resultant observable behaviors, and they improve their estimates of likelihood with experience. However, they are not very good at combining multiple observations, nor are they very good at reasoning backward from effects to causes. In contrast, computers have limited experience and cannot assign likelihoods based on their experience except in very narrow domains. However, computers are very good at combining the probabilities from multiple observations to compute the most likely goal under varying circumstances, and they can use conditional probabilities to determine the most likely cause given a collection of observations.

As described in Chapter 1.1, a BBN can compute the relative probability of explanations of a collection of observations. A BBN is a causal model with an explicit representation of the probability of observing each piece of evidence given a cause. The BBN is constructed by working with subject matter experts to capture their expertise in reasoning from causes to effects. For example, they might list what happens during an opponent's maneuver and the likelihood of each of these actions. The computer can then use Bayes' law to reverse the direction of causality and compute, for example, the probability the opponent is executing a particular tactical maneuver given a collection of observed behaviors. The tactic with the highest probability of accounting for the actual observed behaviors is selected as the opponent's intent.

It is not necessary for all the effects to be observed to determine the most probable cause. Normally, much of the information is missing or incorrect. However, in a probabilistic approach, observations that are missing or incorrect cause performance to degrade but not break the system. Further, once an explanation is inferred, the causal links can be followed forward to determine what the missing values could be.

1.2.4   Creating a Model of Opponent's Intent

Constructing a model of an opponent's intent is a top-down process. Let us explore this process using an example, a model of an intent to perform an attack (Figure 1.2.4). If our opponent intends to attack, we might make the following observations:

Troops to Be Targeted: This observation is that units are somewhere in the area where the opponent can attack them. Because an attack cannot exist without somebody to be attacked, the belief that troops exist to be targeted, given that the opponent is attacking, is nearly 100% certain.

Superior Numbers of Forces: This observation is that significantly more attacking troops should exist than defenders. Historically, in successful attacks, the attackers outnumber defenders by at least three to one. Depending on culture, doctrine, and emotional state, this parameter may not necessarily be the case, but one generally expects to attack with superior forces.

Effective Weapons: This observation is that the opponent has weapons that will be effective against the units it will be attacking. The probability here should be very high. An opponent that knows he is outgunned should rarely attack.

Moving: This observation is that the opponent is moving toward a position suitable for an attack and should be near 100% certain. (The exception is an ambush, which can be better modeled as an entirely separate hypothesis.) The overall movement trend should be toward the opponent, though an attempt may be made to move in a way that disguises the intended target.

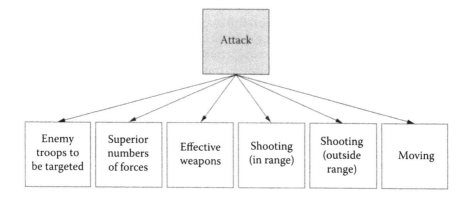

FIGURE 1.2.4

BBN illustrating some of the observable information that might be associated with an opponent's attack.

Shooting: This observation is that the opponent is deploying their weapons. When the opponent's forces are within range of their target, this should be a highly certain belief. Outside of their range, it will drop according to the level of training of the troops. One would expect untrained troops to be much more likely to shoot outside of their range.

Even though all of these actions are consistent with an attack, each individually can be consistent with another military behavior. For example, "Moving" could also be consistent with a retreat; "Troops to Be Targeted" could also be consistent with a defense; and "Shooting" is consistent with many offensive and defensive actions. Yet the combination of all these occurring together provides strong support that an attack is occurring. As these factors combine, they establish a strength of belief in the opponent's intent to attack. Intuitively, the strength of belief in the intention is a function of the number of factors that are present, the number of factors present that have little in common with other intentions, the prior belief in the intention, and the lack of evidence supporting other intentions.

Lack of an observation is different from the negation of that observation. For example, not knowing whether the opponent is carrying effective weapons would not significantly affect the belief that an attack is taking place. However, knowing for certain that the opponent does not have effective weapons would reduce the probability of an attack significantly.

In the BBN approach, the Bayesian probability is used to compute the most likely of the opponent's intents given an opponent model like the one in the example above. However, modifying and tuning the BBN is necessary based on observations and on additional domain-specific knowledge. For example, people usually run away from gunfire, but as described in the novel *Blackhawk Down* [37], "whenever there was a disturbance in Mogadishu, people would throng to the spot: men, women, children — even the aged and infirm. It was like some national imperative to bear witness." Therefore, modeling the reaction to gunfire as running away with high probability may not be correct. A better approach would be to represent running from gunfire as a conditional probability based on whether the agent is situated in a place like Mogadishu. This would complicate the representation excessively. Instead, our approach is to create a customized network based on the specific background knowledge of the situation. We describe the details in later sections.

Finally, validating such a model is difficult. The following three approaches can be used:

Validating with Respect to a Human Expert: In this approach, both the human expert and the computer watch events (e.g., in a simulation-based wargame) as they unfold and both make and record predictions at the same time. These predictions are then compared, using the human expert as the ideal standard. This approach is most useful during the model construction phase when tuning the system. It helps highlight missing information and suggests ways to improve the system.

Validating with Respect to an Opponent's Recorded Intentions: In this approach, participants are asked to record their intentions as they take part in the exercise. At the conclusion of the exercise, these records are compared with the computer-predicted intent. This practice gives a better insight into the actual intent. Our experience with this method is that a human participant often misreports or fails to report their intent because all their attention is consumed by the task of directing the units in the simulation.

Validating with Respect to Actual Events: This last approach bypasses the intent entirely and instead focuses on actual events. For example, the computer infers the intent of a unit and then uses this estimated intent to predict its movements. The predictions are then compared with the actual movements. Thus, the model is validated not with respect to its ability to divine the opponent's intent but rather to predict observable behaviors that should occur. The drawback to this approach is that even if an opponent intended to go to a given location, they might go elsewhere if strong resistance is encountered along the way. The predicted intent may have been accurate but the actual way that events unfolded does not reflect that intent.

1.2.5 Knowledge-Based Intention Projection

We now discuss a particular instance of an intent recognition mechanism called the *Knowledge-Based Intention Projection* (KIP) module [38]. KIP was developed as part of the Defense Advanced Research Projects Agency (DARPA) RAID project [41–43]. It predicts an opponent's goals using heuristics to narrow the goal search space and BBNs to determine which goals are most likely. KIP is a subcomponent of a larger system that predicts the emotional state and courses of actions of opponents [39,40]. (See also Chapter 1.3.) Testing in simulations has shown that KIP is able to determine an opponent's movement goals 84% of the time within 128 meters — a relatively small error for the purposes of the specific application in question. Goal predictions were generated an average of 90 seconds after the goal was undertaken. In the military problem addressed by RAID, Blue (U.S.) forces battle Red (opponent) forces in an urban environment. KIP's job is to help the commander of the Blue forces infer the intent of the Red forces.

Unlike most previous related work in opponent modeling [44–46], KIP explicitly represents the cognitive aspects of the opponent, with beliefs,

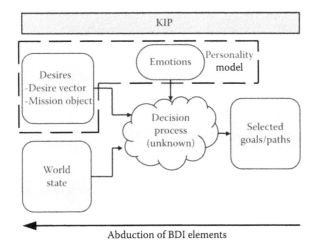

FIGURE 1.2.5
BDI model structure of KIP.

desires, intentions, and emotions. By explicitly modeling the beliefs, desires, intentions, and emotions of the opponent, KIP can perform an efficient pruning of the search space, predicting the opponent's goals with limited computational resources.

Figure 1.2.5 illustrates the BDI framework used in KIP. The belief set for each Red unit consists of observable information (such as unit type, location, time, weapon) and derived information (such as movement direction, path). The desires are represented as a vector of eight desire types, the values of which indicate the importance of each desire to the Red unit. Additionally, KIP models the team mission objectives as obligations. The intentions consist of a goal and a predicted path to achieve this goal. The model is augmented with an emotion model to account for battlefield behavior driven primarily by emotions — specifically fear and anger, as suggested by military subject matter experts. (Emotion-driven behaviors are discussed further in Chapter 1.3.)

The desires and the emotions together form a unit's *personality model*. This model represents the general behavioral influences driving the unit. The goals and mission objectives are jointly referred to as the *intentional model*; these are abduced by KIP using a combination of heuristics and evidence evaluation. Note that the computational model of KIP is roughly the opposite of most BDI models. Typical BDI models (see [47–49]) attempt to generate intentions (plans of action) from desires and beliefs, while KIP attempts to determine desires, in the form of goals, from past actions.

An example of a model instance is given in Figure 1.2.6. Here we see a Red unit named R09. The personality model of this unit is shown in the rectangle. In this case, the personality model indicates that the unit's primary desire is

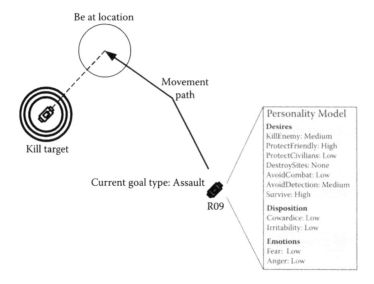

FIGURE 1.2.6

Example intentional model of an opponent. Depicted are the opponent's desires, the derived goal position, and the opponent's target.

to "Protect Forces that are Friendly" (other Red forces). However, the desires to "Destroy the Enemy" and "Avoid Detection by the Enemy" are moderate, so these desires will also impact the Red unit's behavior. For this unit, the emotional factors are low, indicating that KIP believes this unit is likely to act rationally (rather than emotionally) and to follow a plan or intention.

The intentional model generated by KIP consists of the unit's main goal and its subgoals. A "Be at Location" subgoal indicates the location that KIP believes the unit is attempting to reach. A "Destroy Target" subgoal indicates the Blue unit that KIP believes the Red unit intends to destroy. Finally, the model includes a description of the Red unit's overall goal, given as "Assault." So the KIP's intentional model describes the intent of the Red unit as being to conduct an assault by going to the given location and destroying the indicated Blue unit. This intentional model is used as input by other systems to generate detailed predictions of the movement paths of the unit.

1.2.6   KIP Architecture

The KIP architecture is depicted in Figure 1.2.7. The primary purpose of the KIP architecture is to determine the most likely goals and objectives for each opponent it observes. The core inputs to the KIP are real-time updates of unit positions (including opponent, friendly, and neutral force positions), fire events, and any updates to Blue mission objectives. The terrain database provides information about buildings, roads, and other geographic information

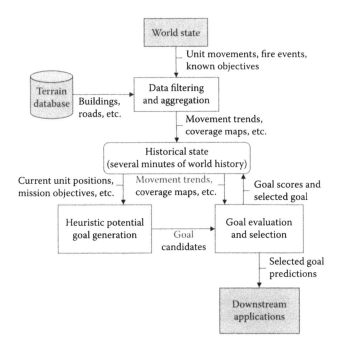

FIGURE 1.2.7
Overview of KIP's architecture.

in the area. The KIP processes this data to form a world state, which includes unit position, unit movement, and terrain cover information.

The analysis process of KIP consists of two steps. The first step is to generate a set of goal candidates based on heuristics. These heuristics narrow the set of all possible unit goals to a smaller set of reasonable goals consistent with commonly observed tactics. The second step is to evaluate this set of candidate goals more deeply using evidence derived from unit activities (e.g., movement and firing) and terrain (e.g., the cover offered by the terrain features and potential kill zones). The output is a single most-probable goal (together with its subgoals), which is sent to other applications for use in generating movement predictions. The next two sections describe these two steps in detail.

1.2.7 Heuristics for Reducing the Number of Opponent Goals

The abductive reasoning process of KIP begins with a set of heuristics derived from observing Red unit behaviors during simulated battles and from domain knowledge provided by human subject matter experts regarding the typical tactics and techniques of real-world Red forces. The purpose of these heuristics is to reduce the set of possible Red goals to a number that KIP can reason over in a short time frame. Because KIP must provide goal estimates in near real-time, it must generate new goals relatively frequently (about once every 40 seconds) as it detects changes in the intentional model. Without a pruning process, the space of possible goals for Red units is very large. For example, given a 10×10 location grid, four types of potential Red goals (e.g., Assault, Defend, Exploit, and Withdraw) and 20 possible targets, the possible combinations of goals number 8000 for a single Red unit. This number increases linearly with the number of locations being considered, the types of intentions being considered, or the number of Blue units.

KIP heuristics are algorithms that take as input the current and historical states of the world and generate as output a set of possible goals. Currently, KIP heuristics generate four types of goals for Red units:

> *Defend/Delay*: This goal type means that the Red unit wants to protect a mission objective or a location from a Blue attack. Defend implies that the unit wishes to get to a defensible location and hold that position against Blue forces. Defend also implies that Blue is not yet in the area of the defense location, and the Red unit can get to the location before Blue.
>
> *Assault/Attack*: The Red unit wants to attack either a building or Blue units within a certain region. Assault implies that the Red unit will move toward the target area and attempt to take Blue's position or inflict significant damage.
>
> *Exploit Target of Opportunity (ETO)*: The Red unit wants to limit Blue mobility and to destroy targets of opportunity, e.g., the valuable armored vehicles of the Blue force. ETO implies that Red will tend to stay just out of the weapons range of the primary Blue force but will actively hunt high-value and straggler units.
>
> *Withdraw/Avoid Combat/Disengage*: The unit wants to move out of combat to a safe location.

The heuristics used to generate these goals take into consideration such factors as Blue and Red unit positions, observed Blue and Red movements, location of known mission objectives, and the cover offered by the terrain features. An example of the KIP heuristic "Defend" is shown in Figure 1.2.8. A commonly observed tactic of Red units is to take a position along Blue's expected line of advance and to destroy the Blue units before they reach their objectives.

The heuristic procedure begins by computing an intercept region along the potential Blue line of advance that Red can reach before Blue. It then analyzes smaller cells within this region to determine which are defensible, based on the quantity and types of cover they contain. Defense goals are created around the most defensible cells and then passed to the second evaluation step in KIP, described in the next section.

KIP contains several heuristic algorithms. Each of these algorithms is executed for each reasoning cycle. Figure 1.2.9 is a graphical example of a typical

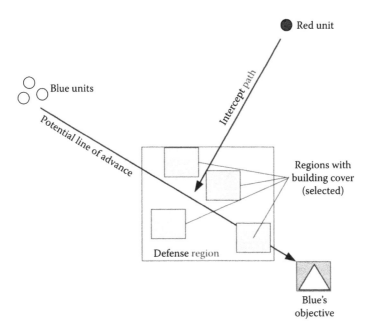

FIGURE 1.2.8
Example of the heuristic "Intercept Defend."

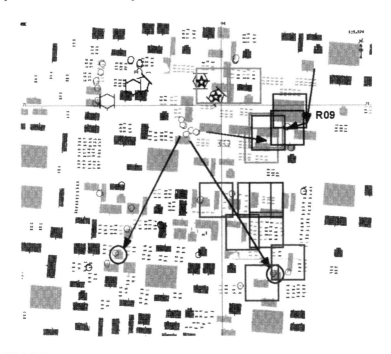

FIGURE 1.2.9
Example of potential goals KIP heuristics produce. This graphic specifically focuses on the location where an opponent might desire to take a position.

output of the KIP heuristic algorithms. The squares in the lower right indicate possible defense locations. The squares in the top center are assault locations and those in the upper right are possible ETO locations. No withdraw goals are shown in this example. The opponent unit of interest is R09, which is moving from the upper right toward the ETO locations. The actual goal of that unit is the center square of that ETO group. The arrows depict anticipated movement of friendly forces. Because KIP does not know exactly what the friendly force will do, it considers the most likely movement paths based on known mission objectives.

1.2.8 Evidence-Based Goal Selection

While the heuristic algorithms are somewhat constrained by the current world state, they are driven more by the presumed tactics of the Red force rather than by the evidence regarding the actual observed actions of the Red force. For example, a heuristic may select a "Defend" location for a Red unit despite the fact that the Red unit has a movement history more consistent with an attack on the Blue force's flank. The purpose of the goal selection step in the evaluation process is to choose the goal generated by the heuristics that is in best agreement with the available observations of the Red unit's actions and the terrain database. To accomplish this, KIP uses BBNs to calculate the likelihood of a goal based on the available evidence.

A probabilistic approach accommodates the uncertainties in the domain and performs evidence-based inference in a principled manner. Among the advantages of such an approach are the following:

- Robustness to missing or uncertain information
- Transparency of semantic interpretation
- Versatility in making inferences (both top-down and bottom-up)
- Support for learning and adaptation of structure and probabilities
- Hierarchical composability and reusability of network fragments, with guaranteed consistency

Figure 1.2.10 shows the general process. For each goal, KIP constructs a BBN that links this goal to any related subgoals (e.g., "Be at a Location") and composite observables (e.g., "Attacking Blue Unit"). Finally, physical observables (e.g., movement and weapon firing) are linked at the bottom of the tree. Based on a BDI model of behavior, they are the final outcomes of the reasoning process.

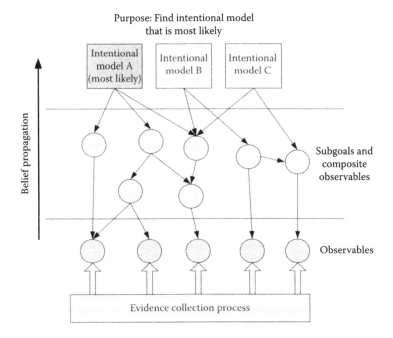

FIGURE 1.2.10
General approach to intention evaluation.

KIP's BBNs are constructed dynamically at runtime. One reason for the dynamic construction is that many of the nodes relate to spatio-temporal data, such as specific unit locations, relative unit and terrain locations, and velocities. Specific instances of this data are known only at runtime. Another reason is that dependencies between portions of the BBN must be determined at runtime. For example, whether an "Attack" location and a "Defend" location are independent of each other cannot be determined until they are generated and checked for their relative locations.

Figure 1.2.11 shows KIP's BBN instantiation and computation process. It starts with a set of templates, each for a different type of intention or for different contexts for the same type of intention. Next, the template appropriate to a given intentional model is selected and instantiated. That is, the template's nodes are constructed and bound to specific world data (e.g., specific positions of units). The third step merges networks that have dependent nodes to produce larger networks representing the mapping of all candidate intentional models onto observables. Fourth, evidence is collected from observables. Finally, the BBNs are updated and the most likely intentional model is selected as the opponent's intent.

A particularly challenging aspect of this process is the selection of conditional probabilities. Using fixed conditional probabilities for each template

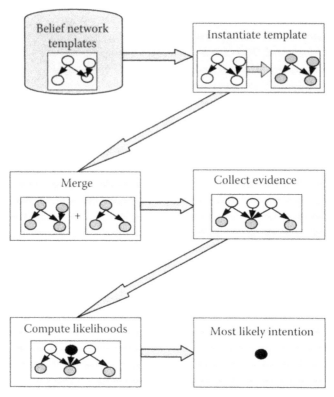

FIGURE 1.2.11
Dynamic BBN construction.

is not always desirable. For example, a Red unit might have the goal of defending a particular location. To achieve that goal, the unit may create a subgoal to destroy an approaching unit. However, the likelihood of creating this subgoal can vary with the distance between the two units or between other opponents in the vicinity. Several approaches can be used to resolve this problem. First, the given dependencies can be explicitly entered into the BBN if an appropriate BBN substructure is apparent. Second, the conditional probabilities can be instantiated based on context, specifying different conditional probabilities for different classes of situations. Third, the conditional probabilities can be learned dynamically.

Figure 1.2.12 is an example of a KIP BBN template similar to those used in the KIP implementation. This particular template is for the "Defend" goal. Here the network is shallow, directly linking the goal to various observables. Observables include movement variables such as distance and velocity, cover, support from nearby friendly units, and opponent density and position.

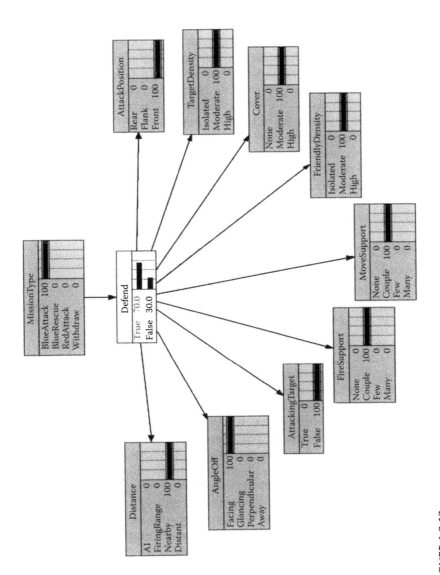

FIGURE 1.2.12
Example of a BBN template showing a "Defend" goal.

1.2.9   Experimental Results

Though the KIP implementation makes several simplifying assumptions, results show that it has proven sufficient for the most critical task of determining an opponent's movement goals. KIP was tested in an experiment executed in the RAID project [42,43]. The experiment consisted of about 20 simulated military exercises. Each exercise was a simulated battle in urban terrain with a Blue force consisting of three small-arms platoons and five armored vehicles and a Red force consisting of 20 loosely formed fire teams. In these exercises, KIP generated and logged an intentional model for each Red fire team approximately every 40 seconds. Given that the simulated battles typically lasted 60 to 120 minutes, KIP generated between 500 and 3000 intentional models during each experiment. Each of these intentional models represents KIP's best guess of the goal of a given unit at that instant in time.

The actual goals of a subset of the Red units were recorded by the support staff of the Red commander. Three Red unit controllers (military experts) were given forms (shown in Figure 1.2.13) on which they recorded the current goal of one* of their units. The specific items they recorded were as follows:

> Time at which the goal was recorded.
>
> Approximate current location of the unit being recorded.
>
> A circle with a letter inside indicating the target location and intention description. (This description matched the KIP intention types: Defend, Attack, Exploit, and Withdraw.)
>
> A path connecting the current location of the unit with the target location.

These goals were recorded at regularly scheduled simulation pauses, approximately every 15 minutes. At each pause, the controller indicated whether the actual path and target location had varied from the previously recorded goal path and target location before entering in the next goal of the Red unit. If the Red unit was destroyed, a unit was selected for recording.

Our analysis compared the goals predicted by KIP with the goals recorded by the Red unit controllers. To do this, we manually entered the data from the intention forms to a text format that could be easily read into our analysis program. For this text format, we numbered the cells given on the form and entered the path and target locations using these cell numbers.

Table 1.2.1 summarizes KIP's performance in 15 simulated battles. Altogether, human controllers recorded 84 intentions for 60 units for an average of 1.4 goals per unit. Actual goals as recorded by the controllers lasted an average of 28 minutes, implying that they often did not change their intention for a unit at the 15 minute pause periods. KIP generated a new

---

* Each Red unit controller only recorded the goals for one of his units at a time to keep the bookkeeping burden to a minimum.

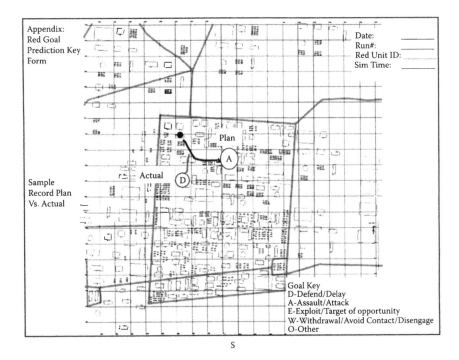

FIGURE 1.2.13
Example form on which Red unit controllers recorded the actual goals of Red units.

goal every 40 seconds, thus generating an average of 42 goals for each goal recorded by the human controller.

We also measured the distance of the KIP goal target location to the actual goal target location. This distance was computed as the two-dimensional Euclidean distance between the center of KIP's target location cell and the center of the actual target location cell. The KIP cell size is 64 square meters and the overall size of the battlefield was on the order of 1 km². We see in Table 1.2.1(b) that KIP produced target locations that were on average within two cells of the actual target locations. During a time window of 2 to 10 minutes after the battle started, KIP produced target locations that were on average within 2.4 cells of the actual target locations. This initial window was an especially important time period because the primary elements of the Red plan would unfold early in the battle, with the remaining battle time typically consisting of managing the details of the engagement.

In Figure 1.2.14, we show the cumulative density function for this distance measurement. The x-axis is the distance from the KIP target location to the actual target location (binned by KIP's cell size) and the y-axis is the percentage of KIP target locations that were at least as close as the given distance. The first bar in each group indicates the cumulative density based on all goals generated by KIP. The second bar indicates the cumulative density based on KIP goals generated in the initial stages of the battle (as discussed above).

TABLE 1.2.1

Summary of KIP Performance Over Several Runs

	Summary	
Number of Units	**Number of Actual Intentions**	**Average Intention Timeframe (minutes)**
60	84	27.83

(a)

	Whole Run	
Number of Intentional Models	**Mean Distance Difference (m)**	**Standard Deviation (m)**
41.8	123.4	61.0

(b)

	Initial	
Number of Intentional Models	**Mean Distance Difference (m)**	**Standard Deviation (m)**
8.5	151.0	60.7

(c)

The third bar shows the cumulative density that would result if goal locations were chosen at random.

KIP was able to generate target locations within one cell — overlapping the actual target location cell — 35% of the time. KIP was able to predict within two cells 70% of the time and within three cells 84% of the time. The numbers

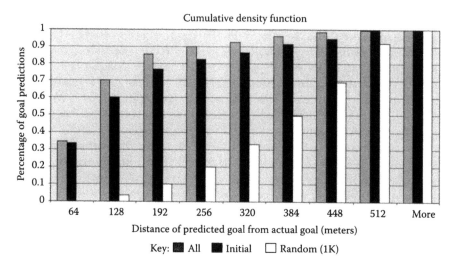

FIGURE 1.2.14

Distance errors for all goals, initially generated goals, and a random model used for comparison. KIP was able to predict an opponent's goal location within a single cell 35% of the time and within three cells (192 meters) 84% of the time.

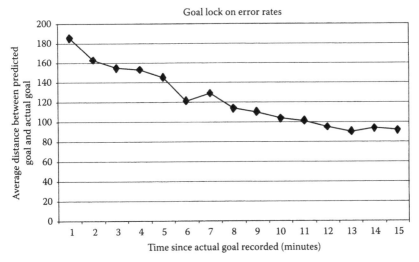

FIGURE 1.2.15
Accuracy of KIP target location predictions over time.

for the initial time window are about 10% lower. These results are significantly better than randomly picking target locations and indicate that KIP gives a good estimate of the Red goals.

Another useful metric is the time KIP takes to specify a target location within two or three cells of the actual target location. KIP is constantly adjusting its predictions based on the evidence it collects, and therefore we would expect that KIP's predictions would become more accurate as a Red unit proceeds toward achieving its goal. As shown in Figure 1.2.15, this is indeed the case. The *x*-axis is time in minutes since the Red unit controller initiated the actual goal, and the *y*-axis is the average distance of KIP's target locations from the actual target locations. A general downward trend exists and within five minutes after the start of the battle, the average KIP target location is within two cells of the actual goal. This plot is biased by the cases when KIP never predicts the correct target location. For 87% of all goals, KIP's prediction is within two cells of the actual target location, and in these cases, it takes an average of only 94 seconds to make this prediction.

Table 1.2.2 shows the percentage accuracy and time for both two-cell accuracy and three-cell deviations in prediction accuracy. When KIP gets within two or three cells of the actual target location, we call this *lockon*. The time KIP takes to achieve lockon we call *lockon time*.

TABLE 1.2.2

Summary of the Time KIP Takes to Lock onto a Target Location

Percentage Lockon 2-Cells	Lockon Time 2-Cells	Percentage Lockon 3-Cells	Lockon Time 3-Cells
87%	94	89%	28

TABLE 1.2.3

Accuracy of KIP's Predicted Intention Types
Compared with Those Recorded by the Human
Controller

	Correct Intention Types		
	Whole Run	**Initial**	**Random**
Percentage correct	61	60	25

Table 1.2.3 shows the comparison of KIP's predicted goal type to the goal type recorded by a human controller. KIP predicts the correct intention type correctly 61% of the time over all goals, and 60% of the time during the initial 2 to 10 minute window. Whereas this result is significantly better than a random prediction (25%), ample room exists for improvement. Further analysis shows that the primary reason for the apparent errors in KIP's predictions is often a problem with terminology used by the human controllers. For example, a controller recorded an intention as "Attack" when KIP expected a "Defend." In that case, Blue forces were distant from the target location. KIP assumed the assault of Blue on an existing Red position should be called "Defend" from Red's perspective. This result was different from the definition used by the controller, and the differences seemed to vary from controller to controller.*

Overall, KIP's performance was sufficient for its primary purpose: Guiding other downstream applications in making movement predictions. The downstream applications were able to make useful predictions given KIP target locations. KIP was also able to correctly abduce certain complex opponent intentions such as hook maneuvers and pullbacks to defensive positions.

References

1. Biddle, E., Henninger, A., Franceschini, R., and Jones, R., Emotion modeling to enhance behavior representation: a survey of approaches, '03 *Interservice/Ind. Train. Sim. Educ. Conf. (I/ITSEC)*, Orlando, FL, 2003.
2. Daddis, G.A., Understanding fear's effect on unit effectiveness, *Mil. Rev.*, 2004.
3. Horn, C.B., The worm revisited: the examination of fear and courage in combat, *Can. Mil. J.*, 2004.
4. Jones, R.M., Laird, J.E., Nielsen, P.E., Coulter, K.J., Kenny, P.G., and Koss, F., Automated intelligent pilots for combat flight simulation, *AI Mag.*, 1999, 27–41.
5. Stilman, B., *Linguistic Geometry: From Search to Construction*, Boston: Kluwer, 2000.
6. Kautz, H.A., A formal theory of plan recognition and its implementation, in Allen, J.F., Kautz, H.A., Pelavin, R.N., and Tenenberg, J.D., Eds., *Reasoning about Plans*, San Mateo, CA: Morgan Kaufmann Publishers, 1991.
7. Charniak, E. and Goldman, R.P., A Bayesian model of plan recognition, *Artif. Intell.*, 64(1), 53–79, 1993.

---

* In later runs, performance improved to the 80 to 90% range. Our theory is that the human controllers were improving their consistency in recording goals.

8. Huber, M.J., Durfee, E.H., and Wellman, M.P., The automated mapping of plans for plan recognition, in *Tenth Conf. on Uncertainty in Artif. Intelligence*, Seattle, WA, 1994, 344–351.

9. Huber, M.J. and Simpson, R., Recognizing the plans of screen reader users, in *AAMAS 2004 Workshop on Modeling Other Agents from Observation (MOO 2004)*, New York, 2004.

10. Albrecht, D., Zukerman, I., and Nicholson, A., Bayesian models for keyhole plan recognition in an adventure game, *User Mod. User-Adap. Interac.* 8, 1998, 5–47.

11. Mengshoel, O.J. and Wilkins, D.C., Visualizing uncertainty in battlefield reasoning using belief networks, *ARL Advanced Displays and Interactive Displays Fed. Lab. First Ann. Symp.*, Adelphi, MD, 1997, 15–22.

12. Forbes, J., Huang, T., Kanazawa, K., and Russell, S., The BATmobile: towards a Bayesian automated taxi, *Intl. Joint Conf. on Artif. Intelligence (IJCAI)*, 1995, 1878–1885.

13. Hanks, S. and Madigan, D., Probabilistic temporal reasoning, *Handbook of Temporal Reasoning in Artificial Intelligence*, Boston, MA: Elsevier, 2005, 239–261.

14. Thomas, D. and Kanazawa, K., Probabilistic temporal reasoning, *Am. Assoc. of Artif. Intelligence (AAAI)*, 1998, 524–528.

15. Kaminka, G., Pynadath, D., and Tambe, M., Monitoring deployed agent teams, *Autonomous Agents '01*, Montreal, Canada, 2001, 308–315.

16. Mengshoel, O.J. and Wilkins, D.C., Abstraction and aggregation in Bayesian networks, in Geib, C., *Abstractions, Decisions, and Uncertainty: Papers from the 1997 AAAI Workshop*, Providence, RI: AAAI Press. Technical Report WS-97-08, 1997, 53–58.

17. Zukerman, I., Albrecht, D., Nicholson, A., and Doktor, K., Trading off granularity against complexity in predictive models for complex domains, *6th Intl. Pacific Rim Conf. on Artif. Intelligence*, 2000.

18. Klinger, T., Adversarial reasoning: a logical approach for computer Go, Ph.D. thesis, New York University, 2001.

19. Billings, D., Davidson, A., Schaeffer, J., and Szaron, D., The challenge of poker, *Artif. Intell. J.*, 134(1-2), 2002, 201–240.

20. Laird, J.E., Newell, A., and Rosenbloom, P.S., Soar: an architecture for general intelligence, *Arti. Intell. J.*, 33(1), 1987, 1–64.

21. Newell, A., *Unified Theories of Cognition*, Cambridge, MA: Harvard University Press, 1990.

22. Bratman, M.E., *Intentions, Plans, and Practical Reason*, Cambridge, MA: Harvard University Press, 1987.

23. Pearl, J., *Causality: Models Reasoning and Inference*, Cambridge, MA: Cambridge University Press, 2000.

24. Rosenbloom, P.S., Laird, J.E., and Newell, A., *The Soar Papers: Research on Integrated Intelligence*, Cambridge, MA: MIT Press, 1993.

25. Newell, A. and Simon, H.A., Computer science as empirical inquiry: symbols and search, *Comm. of the ACM*, 19(3), 1976, 113–126.

26. Dennet, D.C., *The Intentional Stance*, Cambridge, MA: MIT Press, 1987.

27. Wooldridge, M., *Introduction to Multi Agent Systems*, New York: John Wiley & Sons, 2002.

28. Cohen, P.R. and Levesque, H., Communication actions for artificial agents, in Bradshaw, J.M., Ed., *Software Agents*, Menlo Park, CA: AAAI Press, 1995.

29. Rao, A.S. and Georgeoff, M.P., Modeling rational agents within a BDI architecture, in *The Knowledge Representation '91*, Morgan Kaufman, San Mateo, CA, 1995, 473–484.

30. Rasmussen, J., Skills, rules and knowledge: signals, signs, and symbols, and other distinctions in human performance models, *IEEE Trans. on Syst., Man, and Cyber.*, 13(3), 1983, 257–266.

31. Moray, N., A lattice theory approach to the structure of mental models, *Phil. Trans. Royal Soc. London B*, (327), 1990, 577–583.

32. Burns, K., Mental models and normal errors in naturalistic decision making, *5th Conf. on Naturalistic Decision Making*, Trammsvik, Sweden, 2000.

33. Wolpert, L., Causal belief and the origins of technology, *Phil. Trans.: Math., Phys. and Eng. Sci.*, 361(1809), 2003, 1709–1719.

34. Peirce, C.S., Pragmatism as a principle and method of right thinking, in Turrisi, P.A., Ed., *The 1903 Harvard Lectures on Pragmatism*, Albany, NY: State University of New York Press, 1997.

35. Mooney, R.J., Integrating abduction and induction in machine learning, *Working Notes of the IJCAI-97 Workshop on Abduction and Induction in AI*, Nagoya, Japan, 1997.

36. Bylander, T., Allemang, D., Tanner, M.C., and Josephson, J.R., The computational complexity of abduction, *Artif. Intelligence*, 49, 1991, 25–60.

37. Bowden, M., *Black Hawk Down: A Story of Modern War*, Atlantic Monthly Press, New York, 1999.

38. Nielsen, P., Crossman, J., Frederiksen, R., and Huber, M., *A Conceptual Representation of the Knowledge-based Intention Projection (KIP) Module.* Technical report, of Soar Technology, Inc., Ann Arbor, MI, 2005.

39. Parunak, H.V.D., Brueckner, S., Matthews, R., Sauter, J., and Brophy, S., *Characterizing and Predicting Agents via Multi-Agent Evolution.* Technical report of the Altarum Institute, Ann Arbor, MI, 2005.

40. Parunak, H.V.D., Bisson, R., Brueckner, S., Matthews, R., and Sauter, J., Representing dispositions and emotions in simulated combat, *Workshop on Defense Applications of Multi-Agent Systems (DAMAS05, at AAMAS05)*, Utrecht, The Netherlands, 2005.

41. Kott, A. and Ownby, M., Adversarial reasoning: challenges and approaches, in Trevisani, D.A. and Sisti, A.F., *Proceedings of SPIE, Volume 5805, Enabling Technologies for Simulation Science IX*, 2005, 145–152.

42. Kott, A., DARPA, RAID Program Website, http://dtsn.darpa.mil/ixo/programs.asp?id=43, 2005.

43. Kott, A. and Ownby, M., Tools for real-time anticipation of enemy actions in tactical ground operations, *10th Intl. Command and Control Res. and Tech. Symp.*, McLean, VA, 2005.

44. Kearns, M., Computational game theory: a tutorial, *Neural Information Processing Systems (NIPS)*, Vancouver, Canada, 2002.

45. Sycara, K.P., Multiagent systems, *AI Mag.* 19(2), 1998, 79–92.

46. Heise, S.A. and Morse, H.S., The DARPA JFACC program: modeling and control of military operations, *39th IEEE Conf. on Decision and Control*, Sydney, Australia, 2000, 2551–2555.

47. Georgeff, M., Pell, B., Pollack, M., Tambe, M., and Wooldridge, M., The belief-desire-intention model of agency, in Müller, J.P., Singh, M.P., and Rao, A.S, Eds., *Lecture Notes in Computer Science*, Springer-Verlag, Berlin 2000, 1–10.

48. Rao, A. and Georgeff, M., BDI agents: from theory to practice, *First Intl. Conf. on Multiagent Systems*, San Francisco, 1995.

49. Wooldridge, M., *Reasoning about Rational Agents*, Cambridge, MA: MIT Press, 2000.

1.3

Extrapolation of the Opponent's Past Behaviors*

Sven A. Brueckner and H. Van Dyke Parunak

CONTENTS

* This material is based in part upon work supported by the Defense Advanced Research Projects Agency (DARPA) under Contract No. NBCHC040153. Any opinions, findings, conclusions, or recommendations expressed in this material are those of the authors and do not necessarily reflect the views of DARPA or the Department of Interior-National Business Center (DOI-NBC). Distribution Statement "A" (Approved for Public Release, Distribution Unlimited). The material in this chapter draws extensively from technical reports at the Altarum Institute [1,2], which has kindly given permission for its use.

Reasoning about agents that we observe in the world must integrate two disparate levels. Our observations are often limited to the agent's external behavior, which can frequently be summarized numerically as a trajectory in space-time (perhaps punctuated by actions from a fairly limited vocabulary). However, this behavior is driven by the agent's internal state, which (in the case of a human) can involve high-level psychological and cognitive concepts such as intentions and emotions. A central challenge in many application domains is reasoning from external observations of agent behavior to an estimate of their internal state. Such reasoning is motivated by a desire to predict the agent's behavior.

This problem has traditionally been addressed under the rubric of "plan recognition" or "plan inference." Chapter 1.4 discusses this approach in more detail, and the use of Bayesian reasoning over sets of possible agent goals there and in Chapter 1.1 and Chapter 1.2 is one of the most mature approaches to recognizing an agent's plans. Work to date focuses almost entirely on recognizing the rational state (as opposed to the emotional state) of a single agent (as opposed to an interacting community) and frequently takes advantage of explicit communications between agents (as in managing conversational protocols). Many realistic problems deviate from these conditions.

- The agents often are trying to hide their intentions — and even their presence — rather than intentionally sharing information.

- Increasing the number of agents leads to a combinatorial explosion of possibilities that can swamp conventional analysis. Chapter 1.2 reasons about an adversary that consists of multiple discrete agents, and Chapter 1.1 uses extensions to the standard Bayes net formalism to address some of the combinatorial problems, but the challenge of computational complexity is pervasive with symbolic approaches to representing and reasoning about cognition.

- The agents' emotional state can be at least as important as their rational state in determining behavior. Most plan recognition work ignores the impact of agent emotion. Chapter 1.2, which describes a component of the same system as this chapter, is a notable exception.

- The dynamics of the environment can frustrate the intentions of an agent. Analysis of the agents' possible thought processes is a necessary step to recognizing a agents' plans but hardly sufficient because the agents might be unable to generate outward behavior that completely corresponds with their plan.

The last issue is particularly important because it is so widely overlooked in the plan recognition community. The frustration of deliberate plans by a hostile environment is commonplace in human experience, attested over at least three millennia: "Do not boast about tomorrow; for you do not know what a day may bring forth" (Solomon, Proverbs 27:1); "The best laid schemes o' Mice an' Men, Gang aft agley" (Robert Burns, "To a Mouse"); "No battle plan ever survives contact with the enemy" (attributed to Field Marshall Helmuth von Moltke). Yet logical calculi for plan recognition leave the environment's impact out of the equation. The only known tractable mechanism for reasoning about the interaction of deliberate plans and an active environment is simulation, and such an approach offers significant benefits in dealing with the other issues that we have identified as well.

Behavioral evolution and extrapolation (BEE) is a novel approach to addressing the recognition of the rational and emotional state of multiple interacting agents based solely on their behavior, without recourse to intentional communications from them and taking into account the nonlinear interactions of the agents with their environment. It thus addresses all of the issues identified above. It is inspired by techniques used to predict the behavior of nonlinear dynamic systems, which continually fit a representation of the system to its recent past behavior. In such analysis of nonlinear dynamic systems, the representation takes the form of a closed-form mathematical equation. In BEE, it takes the form of a set of parameters governing the behavior of software agents representing the individuals being analyzed.

1.3.1 Standing on the Shoulders of Giants

Previous approaches to the problem of predicting an agent's future behavior include plan recognition in artificial intelligence (AI), real-time fitting in nonlinear systems, and game theory. BEE draws from, integrates, and extends key insights from each of these areas.

1.3.1.1 Plan Recognition in AI

It is increasingly common in agent theory to describe the cognitive state of an agent in terms of beliefs, desires, and intentions — the BDI model [3,4]. The agents' beliefs are propositions about the state of the world that they consider true based on their perceptions. Their desires are propositions about the world that they would like to be true. Desires are not necessarily consistent with one another: The agents might desire both to be rich and to not work at the same time. The agents' intentions, or goals, are a subset of their desires that they have selected, based on their beliefs, to guide their future actions. Unlike desires, goals must be consistent with one another — or at least believed to be consistent by the agent.

The agents' goals guide their actions. Thus, one should be able to learn something about an agent's goals by observing his past actions, and knowledge of the agent's goals in turn enables conclusions about what the agent may do in the future.

A considerable body of work is found in the AI and multi-agent community on reasoning from an agent's actions to the goals that motivate them. This process is known as "plan recognition" or "plan inference." Chapter 1.4 discusses plan recognition in more detail, and a recent survey is available [5]. This body of work is rich and varied. It covers both single-agent and multiagent (e.g., robot soccer team) plans, intentional vs. nonintentional actions, speech vs. nonspeech behavior, adversarial versus cooperative intent, complete vs. incomplete world knowledge, and correct vs. faulty plans, among other dimensions.

Plan recognition is seldom pursued for its own sake. It usually supports a higher-level function. For example, in human-computer interfaces, recognizing a user's plan can enable the system to provide more appropriate information and options for user action. In a tutoring system, inferring the student's plan is a first step to identifying buggy plans and providing appropriate remediation. In many cases, the higher-level function is predicting likely future actions by the entity whose plan is being inferred.

We focus on plan recognition in support of prediction. We must take three components into account: A *rational model* of the agent's beliefs, desires, and intentions; the *external influence* of the environment, and *internal non-rational influences* such as emotions.

A rational analysis of an agent's goals can enable us to predict what he will attempt. Chapter 1.1 and Chapter 1.2 describe how belief networks can be used to conduct this analysis. Such an analysis is an essential foundation for prediction, but it is not enough. The external influence is the dynamics of the environment, which can include other agents. The dynamics of the real world impose significant constraints.

- The environment is autonomous (it may do things on its own that interfere with the desires of the agent) [6,7].
- Most interactions among agents, and between agents and the world, are nonlinear. When iterated, these can generate rapid divergence of trajectories (e.g., "chaos," sensitivity to initial conditions).

Any nontrivial plan with several steps will depend sensitively at each step to the reaction of the environment, and our prediction must take this into account as well. Actual simulation of futures is one way (the only one we currently know) to deal with these.

In the case of human agents, an internal nonrational influence also comes into play. The agents' emotional state can modulate his decision process and his focus of attention — and thus his perception of the environment. In extreme cases, emotion can lead an agent to choose actions that from the standpoint of a logical analysis can appear irrational.

Current work on plan recognition for prediction focuses on the rational plan and does not take into account either external environmental influences or internal emotional biases. BEE integrates all three elements into its predictions. In Chapter 1.2, we described a cognitive approach that feeds directly into BEE.

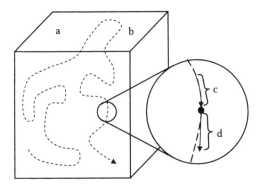

FIGURE 1.3.1
Tracking a nonlinear dynamical system: (a) System state space; (b) system trajectory over time;
(c) recent measurements of system state; (d) short-range prediction.

1.3.1.2 Real-Time Fitting in Nonlinear Systems

Many systems of interest can be described in terms of a vector of real
numbers that changes as a function of time. The dimensions of the vector
define the system's state space. Notionally, one typically analyzes such sys-
tems as vector differential equations, e.g., $\frac{d\bar{x}}{dt} = f(\bar{x})$. When f is nonlinear, the
system can be formally chaotic, and starting points arbitrarily close to one
another can lead to trajectories that diverge exponentially rapidly and
become uncorrelated. Long-range prediction of the behavior of such a system
is impossible in principle. However, anticipating the system's behavior a
short distance into the future is often useful. To do so, one common technique
is to fit a convenient functional form for f to the system's trajectory in the
recent past and then extrapolate this fit into the future (Figure 1.3.1) [8]. This
process is repeated constantly as the system is running, providing the user
with a limited look-ahead into the system's future.

While this approach is robust and widely applied, it requires systems that
can efficiently be described in terms of mathematical equations that can be
fit using optimization methods, such as least squares.

1.3.1.3 Game Theory

Game theoretic approaches [9–11] explicitly model adversarial conflict. They
deal with distinct strategy choices on each side, making them more relevant
than purely numerical methods. They define a space of utilities, not just a
single outcome.

In its classical form, game theory requires enumeration of all possible
strategies and so is not adequately constrained. It also treats the entire
engagement as a one-time comparison of utilities over the space of Red
and Blue strategy options when, in fact, engagements evolve through time.

Some recent developments in game theory — which we discuss in Chapter 2.4, Chapter 3.2, and Chapter 3.3 — overcome these limitations, iterating a game-theoretic analysis through successive phases of the conflict and aggressively pruning the tree of possible contingencies.

The major distinction between game theory and BEE is that game theory seeks to reason *a priori* about the utility of a particular choice, whereas BEE takes the approach of trying out multiple choices to evaluate their outcomes *a posteriori*. BEE can incorporate the results of game-theoretic reasoning, just as it currently incorporates statistical and cognitive analyses, and our current implementation takes advantage of the output of the algorithms described in Chapter 2.4. Its distinctive characteristic is a greater reliance on simulation than analysis to evaluate alternative futures and produce predictions and recommendations.

1.3.1.4   BEE's Hybrid Approach

Our approach, BEE, takes its main inspiration from the nonlinear systems approach. Nonlinear prediction uses statistical methods to fit a representation (an equation) to recent past behavior and extrapolates it into the future. BEE differs in the representation that it fits and the method it uses to do the fitting.

- The representation is not an analytic equation but a software agent that embodies a vector of psychological variables that guides its behavior.

- The fitting is done not by statistical methods but by evolving the agents' psychology with a genetic algorithm, using as fitness a comparison of the agents' simulated behavior with the recently observed behavior of the entity under study.

BEE can integrate information from multiple other reasoners both in fitting agents' internal models to past observations and in extrapolating their future behavior, and our current implementation demonstrates this integration with game-theoretic, cognitive, and statistical reasoners.

1.3.2   Ant-Like Agents with Humanistic Behavior

The agents in BEE are inspired by two bodies of work. The first is our own previous work on fine-grained agents that coordinate their actions with mechanisms similar to insect stigmergy through digital pheromones in a shared environment [12–16]. The second inspiration is the success of previous agent-based combat modeling in EINSTein and MANA, extended by research on computational emotions. Thus, BEE agents manifest their decidedly humanoid personalities through insect-like coordination. In spite of the wide separation

TABLE 1.3.1

Pheromone Flavors in BEE

Pheromone Flavor	Description
RedAlive	Emitted by a living or dead entity of the appropriate group
RedCasualty	(Red = enemy, Blue = friendly, Green = neutral)
BlueAlive	
BlueCasualty	
GreenAlive	
GreenCasualty	
WeaponsFire	Emitted by a firing weapon
KeySite	Emitted by a site of particular importance to Red
Cover	Emitted by locations that afford cover from fire
Mobility	Emitted by roads and other structures that enhance agent mobility
RedThreat	Determined by external process (see "Playing Together")
BlueThreat	

between ants and humans on the biological spectrum, a growing body of research shows that stigmergy is a prevalent and important mechanism for coordination among humans [17].

Digital pheromones are scalar variables that agents deposit at their current location in the environment and that they can sense. Agents respond to the local concentrations of these variables tropistically, typically climbing or descending local gradients. Their movements in turn change the deposit patterns. This feedback loop, together with processes of evaporation and propagation in the environment, can support complex patterns of interaction and coordination among the agents [18]. Table 1.3.1 shows the pheromone flavors currently used in the BEE. In addition, agents take into account their distance from distinguished static locations, a mechanism that we call "virtual pheromones" because it has the same effect as propagating a pheromone field from such a location but with lower computational costs. A later section describes the BEE's pheromone infrastructure in more detail.

Our use of agents to model combat is inspired by EINSTein and MANA. EINSTein [19] represents an agent as a set of six weights, each in the interval [−1, 1], describing the agents' response to six kinds of information. Four of these describe the number of alive friendly, alive enemy, injured friendly, and injured enemy troops within the agents' sensor range. The other two weights relate to the model's use of a childhood game, "capture the flag," as a prototype of combat. Each team has a flag and seeks to protect it from the other team while seeking to capture the other team's flag. The fifth and sixth weights describe how far the agent is from its own and its adversary's flag. A positive weight indicates that the agent is attracted to the entity described by the weight, whereas, a negative weight indicates that they are repelled.

MANA [20] extends the concepts in EINSTein. Friendly and enemy flags are replaced by the waypoints being pursued by each side. MANA includes four additional components: Low, medium, and high threat enemies, and a set of triggers (e.g., reaching a waypoint, being shot at, making contact with the enemy, being injured) that shift the agent from one personality vector to another. A default state defines the personality vector when no trigger state is active.

The personality vectors in MANA and EINSTein reflect both rational and emotive aspects of decision-making. The notion of being attracted or repelled by friendly or adversarial forces in various states of health is an important component of what we informally think of as emotion (e.g., fear, compassion, aggression), and the use of the term "personality" in both MANA and EINSTein suggests that the system designers are thinking anthropomorphically, though they do not use the term "emotion" to describe the effect they are trying to achieve. The notion of waypoints to which an agent is attracted reflects goal-oriented rationality.

BEE embodies an integrated rational-emotive personality model. A BEE agents' rationality is modeled as a vector of seven desires, which are values in the interval $[1, +1]$: *ProtectRed* (the adversary), *ProtectBlue* (friendly forces), *ProtectGreen* (civilians), *ProtectKeySites, AvoidCombat, AvoidDetection,* and *Survive*. Negative values reverse the sense suggested by the label. For example, a negative value of *ProtectRed* indicates a desire to harm Red. Table 1.3.2 shows which pheromones A(ttract) or R(epel) an agent with a given desire and how that tendency translates into action.

The emotive component of a BEE agents' personality is based on the *Ortony-Clore-Collins* (OCC) framework [21] and is described in detail elsewhere [22]. OCC define emotions as "valenced reactions to agents, states, or events in the environment." This notion of reaction is captured in MANA's trigger states. An important advance in BEE's emotional model with respect to MANA and EINSTein is the recognition that agents can differ in how sensitive they are to triggers. For example, threatening situations tend to stimulate the emotion of fear, but a given level of threat will produce more fear in a new recruit than in a seasoned combat veteran. Thus, our model includes not only *Emotions*, but *Dispositions*. Each Emotion has a corresponding Disposition. Dispositions are relatively stable and considered constant over the time horizon of a run of the BEE, whereas Emotions vary based on the agents' dispositions and the stimuli to which they are exposed.

Based on interviews with military domain experts*, we identified the two most crucial emotions for combat behavior as Anger (with the corresponding disposition Irritability) and Fear (whose disposition is Cowardice). Table 1.3.3 shows which pheromones trigger which emotions. Emotions are modeled as agent hormones (internal pheromones) that are augmented in the presence of the triggering environmental condition and evaporate over time.

---

* We are particularly grateful to Colonel Joseph Moore, U.S. (Ret), for helping identify the most crucial emotions to model and discussing how they would manifest themselves in combat behavior.

TABLE 1.3.2

Interactions of Desires and Pheromones

DESIRES

Num	Environment Info Type	Environment Info	Protect Red		Protect Blue		Protect Green		Protect Key Sites		Avoid Combat		Avoid Detection		Survive	
		Desire Value	+1	1	+1	1	+1	1	+1	1	+1	1	+1	1	+1	1
		Desire Sense	Protect	Kill	Protect	Kill	Protect	Kill	Protect	Destroy	Avoid	Seek	Avoid	Seek	Survive	Suicide
1	pheromone	RED-ALIVE	A	A									R	A		
2	pheromone	RED-CASUALTY	A								R	A	R	A		
3	pheromone	BLUE-ALIVE			A	A							R	A		
4	pheromone	BLUE-CASUALTY			A						R	A	R	A		
5	pheromone	GREEN-ALIVE					A	A								
6	pheromone	GREEN-CASUALTY					A				R	A				
7	pheromone	COVER											A	R		
8	pheromone	MOBILITY	A		A		A		A		A	A	A	A		
9	pheromone	WEAPONS-FIRE		A		A		A		A	R	A	A	A		
10	pheromone	KEY-SITES							A							

Num	Action Type	Action	Protect Red		Protect Blue		Protect Green		Protect Key Sites		Avoid Combat		Avoid Detection		Survive	
1	move	Move-In Direction	A/R	driven	A/R	driven	A/R	driven	A/R	driven	A/R	driven	A/R	driven	tbd	
2	move	Move-At Speed	max	max	max	max	max	max	max	max	max	max	max	vertically	tbd	tbd
3	fire	Fire Weapon In Direction		@ Red		@ Blue		@ Green		@ KeySites					tbd	tbd
4	posture	Change Posture											hiding	exposing	tbd	tbd

TABLE 1.3.3

Interactions of Pheromones and Dispositions/Emotions

| | Dispositions/Emotions | | | | | |
| | Red Perspective | | Blue Perspective | | Green Perspective | |
Pheromone	Irritability /Anger	Cowardice /Fear	Irritability /Anger	Cowardice /Fear	Irritability /Anger	Cowardice /Fear
RedAlive			X	X		
RedCasualty	X	X				
BlueAlive	X	X			X	X
BlueCasualty			X	X		
GreenCasualty	X	X			X	X
WeaponsFire	X	X	X	X	X	X
KeySites	X				X	

The effect of a nonzero emotion is to modify actions. An elevated level of Anger will increase movement likelihood, weapon firing likelihood, and tendency toward an exposed posture. An increasing level of Fear will decrease these likelihoods.

Figure 1.3.2 summarizes the BEE's personality model. The two left columns are a straightforward BDI model (where we prefer the term "goal" to "intention"). The right column is the emotive component, where an appraisal of the agents' beliefs — moderated by the disposition — leads to an emotion that in turn influences the BDI analysis.

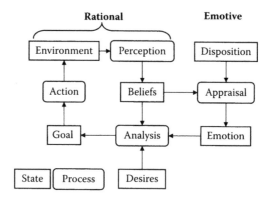

FIGURE 1.3.2

Integrated personality model. The personality of a BEE ghost includes both rational and emotional factors.

1.3.3 Exploring Possible Worlds

BEE's major innovation is an extension of the nonlinear systems technique to characterize agents based on their past behavior and extrapolate their future behavior based on this characterization. This process requires a novel agent modeling concept (the polyagent) and the synchronization of several different notions of time.

1.3.3.1 Polyagents and Possible Futures

Agent-based modeling is a powerful tool for systems modeling. Instantiating each domain entity with an agent permits us to capture many aspects of system dynamics and interactions that other modeling techniques do not support. However, the software agent representing an entity can execute only one trajectory in each run of the system and so does not capture the alternative trajectories accessible to the entity in the evolution of any realistic system. This weakness is shared with other techniques, such as those of Chapter 3.3, that follow the trajectory of a system through time. One can average over the results of multiple runs, but this technique still does not capture the range of individual interactions involved.

We address these problems with a new modeling entity, the *polyagent*, that represents each entity with a collection of agents. The leader of this collection is a single persistent *avatar*. The avatar is supported by a swarm of transient *ghosts*. Each ghost follows its own trajectory through time and space, effectively exploring an alternative possible behavior for the avatar. The avatar interacts with the ghosts of all other avatars through digital pheromone fields, thus sampling many possible interactions in a single run of the system. The avatar generates ghosts based on what it needs to learn about the future and integrates the information that they return to form an assessment of its most likely future.

Polyagents offer an intriguing parallel with quantum physics. Just as a quantum wave function captures many possible behaviors of the corresponding particle, a polyagent's ghosts represent a bundle of possible behaviors of the entity it represents. Just as the wave function is collapsed upon observation, the polyagent's avatar collapses the multiple ghost trajectories into a single picture.

1.3.3.2 Evaluating Alternatives with Evolution

A polyagent's ghosts explore alternative possible behaviors of the entity being modeled. We can use this multiplicity in two ways: To *characterize* individual agents and to *project* their behavior into the future.

In the future, the ghosts' different trajectories sample different ways that the world might evolve. If they are close together, the avatar can make a

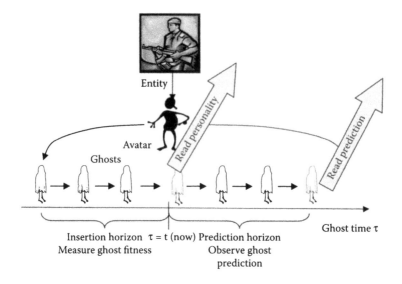

Entity

Avatar

Ghosts

Insertion horizon τ = t (now) Prediction horizon
Measure ghost fitness   Observe ghost
                                                            prediction

Ghost time τ

FIGURE 1.3.3

Behavioral emulation and extrapolation. Each avatar generates a stream of ghosts that sample the personality space of the entity they represent. They evolve against the observed behavior of the entity in the recent past, and the fittest ghosts then run into the future to generate predictions.

fairly reliable prediction. If they diverge widely, the nonlinear dynamics of interactions between agents and the environment require more modest projections.

The past offers us a history of what actually happened, so we do not need to generate multiple predictions. However, if the ghosts represent an adversary, this outward history is all that we know. Importantly, we do not have access to the adversary's internal mental and emotional state. In the past, an avatar generates ghosts with a range of different personalities and compares their behavior with the history that it actually observes. The ghosts whose behavior best matches the actual history are then used to estimate likely future events.

Figure 1.3.3 is an overview of the BEE process. Each active entity in the battlespace has an avatar that continuously generates a stream of ghost agents representing itself. Ghosts live on a timeline indexed by τ that begins in the past at the insertion horizon and runs into the future to the prediction horizon. The variable τ is offset with respect to the current time t in the domain being modeled. The timeline is divided into discrete maps of the world, or "pages," each representing a successive value of τ. The avatar inserts the ghosts at the insertion horizon. In our current system, the insertion horizon is at $\tau - t = 30$, meaning that ghosts are inserted into a page representing the state of the world 30 minutes ago. At the insertion horizon, each ghost's behavioral parameters (desires and dispositions) are sampled from distributions to explore alternative personalities of the entity it represents.

Each page between the insertion horizon and $\tau = t$ ("now," the page corresponding to the state of the world at the current domain time) records the historical state of the world at the point in the past to which it corresponds. As ghosts move from page to page, they interact with this past state based on their behavioral parameters. These interactions mean that their fitness depends not just on their own actions but also on the behaviors of the rest of the population, which is also evolving. Because τ advances faster than time in the real world, eventually $\tau = t$ (domain time). At this point, each ghost is evaluated based on its location compared with the actual location of its corresponding real-world entity. The fittest ghosts have three functions:

- The personality of the fittest ghost for each entity is reported to the rest of the system as the likely personality of the corresponding entity. This information enables us to characterize individual warriors as unusually cowardly or brave.

- The fittest ghosts are bred genetically and their offspring are reintroduced at the insertion horizon to continue the fitting process.

- The fittest ghosts for each entity form the basis for a population of ghosts that are allowed to run past the avatar's present into the future. Each ghost allowed to run into the future explores a different possible future of the battle, analogous to how some people plan ahead by mentally simulating different ways that a situation might unfold. Analysis of the behaviors of these different possible futures yields predictions.

A review of this process shows that BEE has three distinct notions of time, all of which can be distinct from real-world time (the time frame occupied by real humans). *Domain time*, indicated by t, is the current time in the domain being modeled. This time can be the same as real-world time if BEE is being applied to a real-world situation. In our current experiments, we apply BEE to a battle taking place in a simulator, the OneSAF Test Bed (OTB), and domain time is the time-stamp published by OTB. During actual runs, OTB is often paused, so domain time runs slower than real-world time. When we replay logs from simulation runs, we can speed them up so domain time runs much faster than the battle would evolve in the real world.

BEE time, indicated by τ, pertains to a specific page of the pheromone book and records the domain time corresponding to the state of the world represented on that page. It is computed as an offset from the current domain time. *Shift time* is incremented every time the ghosts move from one page to the next. The relation between shift time and real-world time depends on the processing resources available.

1.3.3.3 Under the Hood: Managing the Book of Pheromones

BEE must operate very rapidly to keep pace with the ongoing evolution of the battle. Thus we use simple agents coordinated using pheromone mechanisms. We have described the basic dynamics of our pheromone infrastructure elsewhere [15]. This infrastructure runs on the nodes of a graph-structured environment — in the case of BEE, a rectangular lattice. Each node maintains a scalar value for each flavor of pheromone and provides three functions:

- It aggregates deposits from individual agents, fusing information across multiple agents and through time.
- It evaporates pheromones over time. This dynamic is an innovative alternative to traditional truth maintenance in artificial intelligence. Traditionally, knowledge bases remember everything they are told unless they have a reason to forget something, and expend large amounts of computation in the NP-complete problem of reviewing their holdings to detect inconsistencies that result from changes in the domain being modeled. Our agents immediately begin to forget everything they learn, unless it is continually reinforced. Thus inconsistencies automatically remove themselves within a known period.
- It diffuses pheromones to nearby places, disseminating information for access by nearby agents.

The distribution of each pheromone flavor over the environment forms a scalar field that represents some aspect of the state of the world at an instant in time. Each page of the timeline discussed in the previous section is a complete pheromone field for the world at the BEE time τ represented by that page. The behavior of the pheromones on each page depends on whether the page represents the past or the future.

In pages representing the future ($\tau > t$), the usual pheromone mechanisms apply. Ghosts deposit pheromones each time they move to a new page, and pheromones evaporate and propagate from one page to the next. In pages representing the domain past ($\tau < t$), we have an observed state of the real world. This situation has two consequences for pheromone management. First, we can generate the pheromone fields directly from the observed locations of individual entities, so the ghosts do not need to make deposits. Second, we can adjust the pheromone intensities based on the changed locations of entities from page to page, so we do not need to evaporate or propagate the pheromones. Both of these simplifications reflect the fact that in our current system, we have complete knowledge of the past. When we introduce noise and uncertainty, we will probably need to introduce dynamic pheromones in the past as well as the future.

Execution of the pheromone infrastructure proceeds on two time scales, running in separate threads. The first thread updates the book of pages each time the domain time advances past the next page boundary. At each step:

- The former "now + 1" page is replaced with a new current page, whose pheromones correspond to the locations and strengths of observed units.
- An empty page is added at the prediction horizon.
- The oldest page is discarded as it has passed the insertion horizion.

The second thread moves the ghosts from one page to the next, as fast as the processor allows. At each step:

- Ghosts reaching the $\tau = t$ page are evaluated for fitness and removed or evolved.
- New ghosts from the avatars and from the evolutionary process are inserted at the insertion horizion.
- A population of ghosts based on the fittest ghosts are inserted at $\tau = t$ to run into the future.
- Ghosts that have moved beyond the prediction horizon are removed.
- All ghosts plan their next actions based on the pheromone field in the pages they currently occupy.
- The system computes the next state of each page, including executing the actions elected by the ghosts, and (in future pages) evaporating pheromones and recording new deposits from the recently arrived ghosts.

Ghost movement based on pheromone gradients is a very simple process, so this system can support realistic agent populations without excessive computer load. In our current system, each avatar generates eight ghosts per shift. Because about 50 entities exist in the battlespace (about 20 units each of Red and Blue and about five of Green), we must support about 400 ghosts per page, or about 24,000 over the entire book.

How fast a processor do we need? Let p be the real-time duration of a page in seconds. If each page represents 60 seconds of domain time and we are replaying a simulation at 2 × domain time, $p = 30$. Let n be the number of pages between the insertion horizon and $\tau = t$. In our current system, $n = 30$. A shift rate of n/p shifts per second will permit ghosts to run from the insertion horizon to the current time at least once before a new page is generated. Empirically, we have found this level a reasonable lower bound for reasonable performance and easily achievable on stock Wintel platforms.

1.3.4 Playing Together with Other Approaches

The flexibility of the BEE's pheromone infrastructure permits the integration of numerous information sources as input to our characterizations of entity personalities and predictions of their future behavior. Our current system draws on four sources of information, but others can readily be added. Observations from the real world are encoded into the pheromone field each increment of BEE time, as a new "current page" is generated. Table 1.3.1 identifies the entities that generate each flavor of pheromone.

An independent process developed by Rafael Alonso and Hua Li at Sarnoff Corporation [23] uses statistical techniques to estimate the level of threat to each force (Red or Blue) based on the topology of the battlefield and the known disposition of forces. For example, a broad open area with no cover is particularly threatening, especially if the opposite force occupies its margins. The results of this process are posted to the pheromone pages as *RedThreat* pheromones (representing a threat to Red) and *BlueThreat* pheromones (representing a threat to Blue).

BEE is motivated by the recognition that prediction requires analysis not only of an entity's intentions, but also of its internal emotional state and the dynamics it experiences externally in interacting with the environment. While plan recognition is not sufficient for effective prediction, it is a valuable input. In our current system, a Bayes net is dynamically configured based on heuristics to identify the likely goals that each entity might hold. We describe the system actually used with BEE in Chapter 1.2. The system described in Chapter 1.1, based on an enhancement of Bayes nets, could also generate these goals. The destinations of these goals function as "virtual pheromones." Ghosts include their distance to such points in their action decisions, achieving the result of gradient following without the computational expense of maintaining a pheromone field.

Finally, the game-theoretic mechanisms discussed in Chapter 2.3 generate information about likely deceptive moves on the part of the enemy that we translate into pheromone fields to guide the movements of the BEE's polyagents.

1.3.5 Experimental Experience

We have tested BEE in a series of experiments in which human wargamers make decisions that are played out in a real-time battlefield simulator. The commander for each side (Red and Blue) has at his disposal a team of pucksters, human operators who set waypoints for individual units in the simulator. Each puckster is responsible for four to six units. The simulator moves the units, determines firing actions, and resolves the outcome of conflicts.

Our experience in these experiments shows that BEE is able both to fit the internal personalities of agents based on their past behavior and to derive accurate predictions of future behavior by simulating the fitted agents.

1.3.5.1 Fitting Personalities from Past Behavior

To test our ability to fit personalities based on behavior, one Red puckster responsible for four units was designated the "emotional" puckster. His instructions were to select two of his units to be cowardly ("Chickens") and two to be irritable ("Rambos"). He did not disclose this assignment during the run. His instructions were to move each unit according to the commander's orders until the unit encountered circumstances that would trigger the emotion associated with the unit's disposition. He would then

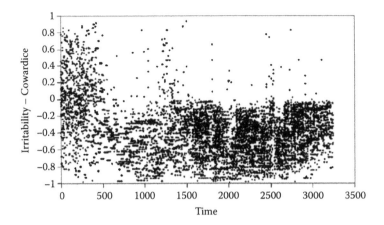

FIGURE 1.3.4
Delta Disposition for a Chicken's ghosts. The ghosts whose behavior most closely matches that of a Chicken have a much higher Cowardice than Irritability.

manipulate Chickens as though they were fearful (typically avoiding combat and moving away from Blue) and move Rambos into combat as quickly as possible.

We found that the difference between the two disposition values (Irritability to Cowardice) of the fittest ghosts is a better indicator of the emotional state of the corresponding entity than either value by itself. Figure 1.3.4 shows the Delta Disposition for each of the eight fittest ghosts at each time step, plotted against the time step in seconds, for a unit played as a Chicken in an actual run. The values clearly trend negative. Figure 1.3.5 shows a similar plot for a Rambo.

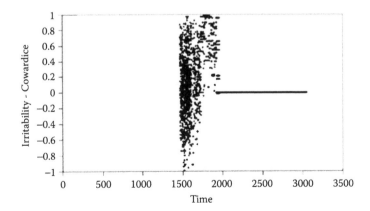

FIGURE 1.3.5
Delta Disposition for a Rambo. Rambos rush into combat and usually die young, but when they survive long enough for ghosts to evolve against their behavior, those ghosts develop a stronger disposition to Irritability than to Cowardice.

Units played with an aggressive personality tend to die very soon and often do not give their ghosts enough time to evolve a clear picture of their personality but, in this case, the positive Delta Disposition is clearly evident before the unit's demise.

To distill such a series of points into a characterization of a unit's personality, we maintain an 800-second exponentially weighted moving average of the Delta Disposition and declare the unit to be a Chicken or Rambo if this value passes a negative or positive threshold, respectively. Currently, this threshold is set at 0.25. In addition to passing this threshold, we are exploring additional filters. For example, a rapid rate of increase enhances the likelihood of calling a Rambo; units that seek to avoid detection and combat are more readily called Chicken.

Table 1.3.4 shows the percentages of emotional units detected in a recent series of experiments. We never called a Rambo a Chicken, and examination of the logs for the one case where we called a Chicken a Rambo shows that the unit was being played aggressively, rushing toward oncoming Blue forces. Because the brave die young, we almost never detect units played intentionally as Rambos. BEE detects about as many intentional Chickens as does a human observer, but BEE detects them about 15 minutes faster than does the human (Figure 1.3.6, where "cowards" are the Chickens discussed above).

In addition to these results on units intentionally played as emotional, we have a number of cases where other units were detected as cowardly or brave. Analysis of the behavior of these units shows that these characterizations were appropriate: Units that flee in the face of enemy forces or weapons fire are detected as Chickens whereas those that stand their ground or rush the adversary are denoted as Rambos.

The whole question of detecting emotional states from external behavior is complicated by the possibility of deliberate deception on the part of a unit. A unit might deliberately behave in a way that appears cowardly to mislead its adversary into a false sense of confidence. We discuss various ways to detect such deception in Chapter 1.2. BEE assigns the emotional state that is most consistent with the observed behavior of the unit, whether that behavior is sincere or feigned. Recognizing a unit's outward behavior as cowardly is the first step in the process of reasoning about whether that cowardice is genuine or feigned. Analyses such as Figure 1.3.6 show that

TABLE 1.3.4

Experimental Results on Fitting Disposition (16 Runs)

	Called Correctly	Called Incorrectly	Not Called
Chickens	68%	5%	27%
Rambos	5%	0%	95%

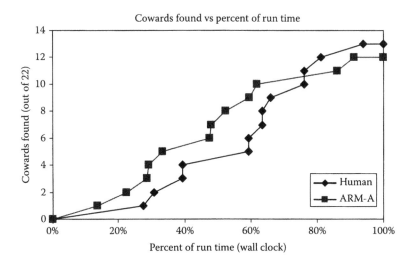

FIGURE 1.3.6

BEE vs. human. BEE detects about as many units that are intentionally played as cowards as does a human observer, but does so about 15 minutes earlier in the wargame than the human.

BEE's ability to detect emotion on the part of a combatant is comparable to that of a human observer, which is already a strong accomplishment for a computer system.

1.3.5.2 Predicting Future Behaviors

Each ghost that runs into the future generates a possible future path that its unit might follow. The set of such paths for all ghosts embodies a number of distinct predictions, including the most or least likely future, the future that poses the greatest or least risk to the opposite side, the future that poses the greatest or least risk to one's own side, and so forth. In the experiments reported here, we select the future whose ghost receives the most guidance from pheromones in the environment at each step along the way. In this sense, it is the most likely future.

Assessing the accuracy of these predictions requires a set of metrics and a baseline against which they can be compared. We have explored two sets of metrics. One set evaluates predictions in terms of their individual steps, and the other examines several characteristics of an entire prediction. The step-wise evaluations are based on the structure summarized schematically in Figure 1.3.7. Each row in the matrix is a successive prediction and each column describes a real-world time step. A given cell records the distance between where the row's prediction indicated the unit would be at the column's time and where it actually was. The figure shows how these cells

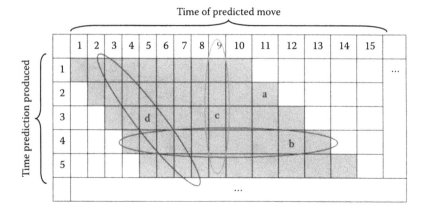

FIGURE 1.3.7

Evaluating predictions. Each row corresponds to a successive prediction for a given unit and each column to a time in the real world that is covered by some set of these predictions. The shaded cells show which predictions cover which time periods. Each cell (a) contains the location error, that is, how far the unit is at the time indicated by the column from where the prediction indicated by the row said it would be. We can average these errors across a single prediction (b) to estimate the prospective accuracy of a single prediction, across a single time (c) to estimate the retrospective accuracy of all previous predictions referring to a given time, or across a given offset from the start of the prediction (d) to estimate the horizon error, how prediction accuracy varies with look-ahead depth.

can be averaged meaningfully to yield three different measures: The prospective accuracy of a single prediction issued at a point in time, the retrospective accuracy of all predictions concerning a given point in time, or the offset accuracy showing how predictions vary as a function of look-ahead depth.

The second set of metrics is based on characteristics of an entire prediction. Figure 1.3.8 summarizes three such characteristics of a path (whether real or

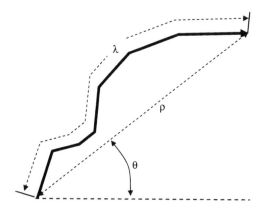

FIGURE 1.3.8

Path characteristics. Angle θ, straight-line range ρ, and actual length λ.

predicted): The overall angle θ it subtends, the straight-line radius ρ from start to end, and the actual length λ integrated along the path. A fourth characteristic of interest is the number of time intervals τ during which the unit was moving. Each of these four values provides a basis of comparison between a prediction and a unit's actual movement (or between any two paths).

Let θ_p be the angle associated with the prediction and θ_a the angle associated with the unit's actual path over the period covered by the prediction. Let $\Delta\theta = |\theta_p - \theta_a|$. The angle score is (with angles expressed in degrees)

$$A_{Score} = 1 - \text{Min}(\Delta\theta, 360 - \Delta\theta)/180$$

If $\Delta\theta = 0$, $A_{Score} = 1$. If $\Delta\theta = 180$, $A_{Score} = 0$. The average of a set of random predictions will produce an A_{Score} approaching 0.5.

Let ρ_p be the straight-line distance from the current position to the end of the prediction and ρ_a the straight-line distance for the actual path. The range score is

$$R_{Score} = 1.0 - |\rho_p - \rho_a|/\text{Max}(\rho_p, \rho_a)$$

If the prediction is perfect, $\rho_p = \rho_a$ and $R_{Score} = 1$. If the ranges are different, R_{Score} gives the percentage that the shorter range is of the longer one. Special logic returns an R_{Score} of 0 if just one of the ranges is 0, and 1 if both are 0.

Let λ_p be the sum of path segment distances for the prediction and λ_a the sum of path segment distances for the actual path. The length score is

$$L_{Score} = 1.0 - |\lambda_p - \lambda_a|/\text{Max}(\lambda_p, \lambda_a)$$

If the prediction is perfect, $\lambda_p = \lambda_a$ and $L_{Score} = 1$. If both lengths are nonzero, L_{Score} indicates what percentage the shorter path length is of the longer path length. Special logic returns an L_{Score} of 0 if just one of the lengths is 0, and 1 if both are 0.

Let τ_p be the number of minutes that the unit is predicted to move and and τ_a the number of minutes that it actually moves. The time score is

$$T_{Score} = 1.0 - |\tau_p - \tau_a|/\text{Max}(\tau_p, \tau_a)$$

If the prediction is perfect, $\tau_p = \tau_a$ and $T_{Score} = 1$. If both times are nonzero, T_{Score} indicates what percentage the shorter path length is of the longer path length. Special logic returns a T_{Score} of 0 if just one of the times is 0, and 1 if both are 0.

As a baseline for comparison, we use a random-walk predictor. This process starts at a unit's current location and then takes 30 random steps. A random step consists of picking a random number uniformly distributed between 0 and 120, indicating the next cell to move to in an 11 × 11 grid with the current position at the center. (The grid is of size 11 because the BEE

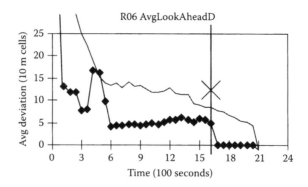

FIGURE 1.3.9
Stepwise metrics: Average prospective error.

movement model allows the ghosts to move from 0 to 5 cells in the x and y directions at each step.) The random number r is translated into x and y steps Δx and Δy using the equations $\Delta x = r/11 - 5$, $\Delta y = (r \bmod 11) - 5$. To compile a baseline, the random prediction is generated 100 times, and each of these runs is used to generate one of the metrics discussed above. The baseline that we report is the average of these 100 instances.

Figure 1.3.9 through Figure 1.3.11 illustrate the three stepwise metrics for a single unit in a single run. In each figure, the thin line represents the average of 100 random walks and the vertical line shows where the unit dies. These are error curves, so being lower than the thin line indicates better than baseline performance. In the case of this unit, BEE was able to formulate good predictions that are superior to the baseline in all three

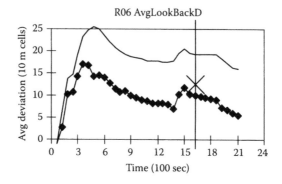

FIGURE 1.3.10
Stepwise metrics: Average retrospective error.

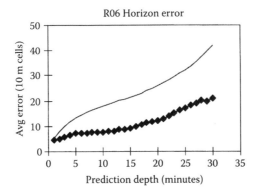

FIGURE 1.3.11
Stepwise metrics: Average horizon error.

metrics. It is particularly encouraging that the horizon error increases so gradually. In a complex nonlinear system, trajectories might diverge at some point, making prediction physically impossible. We would expect to see a discontinuity in the horizon error if we were reaching this limit. The gentle increase of the horizon error suggests that we are not near this limit.

Figure 1.3.12 through Figure 1.3.15 illustrate the four component metrics for the same unit and the same run. Again, the thin line is the random baseline. Because these metrics indicate the degree of agreement between prediction and baseline, higher is better. In general, these metrics support the conclusion that our predictions are superior to the baseline and make clear which characteristics of the prediction are most reliable.

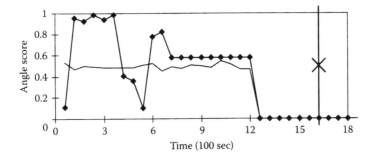

FIGURE 1.3.12
Component metrics: Angle.

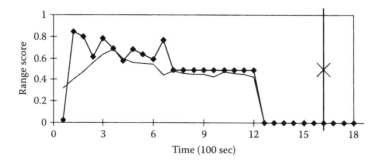

FIGURE 1.3.13
Component metrics: Range.

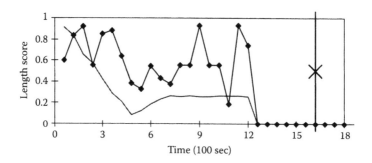

FIGURE 1.3.14
Component metrics: Length.

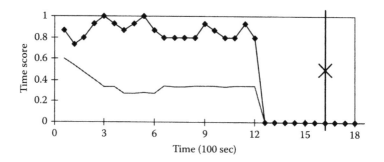

FIGURE 1.3.15
Component metrics: Time.

1.3.6   Looking Ahead

In many domains, it is important to be able to reason from an entity's observed behavior to an estimate of the entity's internal state and then to extrapolate that estimate into a prediction of the entity's likely future behavior. BEE performs this task using a faster-than-real-time simulation of lightweight swarming agents, coordinated through digital pheromones. This simulation integrates knowledge of threat regions, a cognitive analysis of the agent's beliefs, desires, and intentions, a model of the agent's emotional disposition and state, and the dynamics of interactions with the environment. By evolving agents in this rich environment, we can fit their internal state to their observed behavior. In realistic wargame scenarios, the system successfully detects deliberately played emotions and makes reasonable predictions about the entities' future behavior.

An important qualification for BEE is that it can only model internal state variables that impact the agent's external behavior. It cannot fit variables that the agent does not manifest externally because the basis for the evolutionary cycle is a comparison of the outward behavior of the simulated agent with that of the real entity. This limitation is serious if our purpose is to understand the entity's internal state for its own sake. If our purpose of fitting agents is to predict their subsequent behavior, the limitation is much less serious. State variables that do not impact behavior — while invisible to a behavior-based analysis — are irrelevant to a behavioral prediction.

The BEE architecture lends itself to extension in several promising directions:

- The various inputs being integrated by the BEE are only an example of the types of information that can be handled. The basic principle of using a dynamic simulation to integrate a wide range of influences can be extended to other inputs as well, requiring much less additional engineering than other more traditional ways of reasoning about how different knowledge sources come together in impacting an agent's behavior.

- Our initial limited repertoire of emotions is a small subset of those that have been distinguished by psychologists and that might be useful for understanding and projecting behavior. We expect to extend the set of emotions and supporting dispositions that BEE can detect.

- The mapping between an agents' psychological (cognitive and emotional) state and his outward behavior is not one-to-one. Several different internal states might be consistent with a given observed behavior under one set of environmental conditions, but might yield distinct behaviors under other conditions. If the environment in the recent past is one that confounds such distinct internal states, we will be unable to distinguish them. As long as the environment stays in this state, our predictions will be accurate no matter which of the internal states we assign to the agent. If the environment then shifts to one under which the different internal states lead to different behaviors, using the previously chosen internal state will yield inaccurate predictions. The degree of inaccuracy will depend on the variations among the behaviors evoked by the environment from the various states. One way to address these concerns is to probe the real world, perturbing it in ways that would stimulate distinct behaviors from entities whose psychological state is otherwise indistinguishable. Such probing is an important intelligence technique. We will explore how BEE's faster-than-real-time simulation could enable us to identify appropriate probing actions, greatly increasing the effectiveness of intelligence efforts.

- BEE has been developed in the context of adversarial reasoning in urban warfare. We expect that it will be applicable in a much wider range of applications including computer games, business strategy, and sensor fusion, and are exploring such alternative applications for it.

References

1. Parunak, H.V.D. and Brueckner, S., Technical Report, Ann Arbor, MI: Altarum Institute, 2005.
2. Parunak, H.V.D., Brueckner, S., Matthews, R., Sauter, J., and Brophy, S., Technical Report, Ann Arbor, MI: Altarum Institute, 2005.
3. Rao, A.S. and Georgeff, M.P., Modeling rational agents within a BDI architecture, in Allen, J., Fikes, R., and Sandwall, E., Eds., *Intl. Conf. on Principles of Knowledge Representation and Reasoning (KR-91)*, San Mateo, CA: Morgan Kaufman, 1991, 473–484.
4. Haddadi, A. and Sundermeyer, K., Belief-desire-intention agent architectures, in O'Hare, G.M.P. and Jennings, N.R., *Found. Distr. Artif. Intell.*, New York: John Wiley, 1996, 169–185.
5. Carberry, S., Techniques for plan recognition, *User Mod. User-Adapt. Interac.*, 11(1-2), 2001, 31–48.
6. Ferber, J. and Müller, J.-P., Influences and reactions: a model of situated multiagent systems, *Second Intl. Conf. on Multi-Agent Systems (ICMAS-96)*, Kyoto, Japan, 1996, 72–79.
7. Michel, F., Formalisme, méthodologie et outils pour la modélisation et la simulation de systèmes multi-agents, Doctorat Thesis, Université des Sciences et Techniques du Languedoc, 2004.
8. Kantz, H. and Schreiber, T., *Nonlinear Time Series Analysis*, Cambridge, UK: Cambridge University Press, 1997.
9. Rosenschein, J.S. and Zlotkin, G., *Rules of Encounter: Designing Conventions for Automated Negotiation among Computers*, Cambridge, MA: MIT Press, 1994.
10. Vane, R. and Lehner, P., Using hypergames to increase planned payoff and reduce risk, *Auton. Agents Multi-Agent Syst.*, 5(3), Sept. 2002, 365–380.

11. Stirling, W.C., *Satisficing Games and Decision Making*, Cambridge, UK: Cambridge University Press, 2003.

12. Parunak, H.V.D., Brueckner, S.A., and Sauter, J., Digital pheromone mechanisms for coordination of unmanned vehicles, *First Intl. Conf. on Autonomous Agents and Multi-Agent Systems (AAMAS 2002)*, Bologna, Italy, 2002, 449–450.

13. Parunak, H.V.D., Brueckner, S., and Sauter, J., Digital pheromones for coordination of unmanned vehicles, in Weyns, D., Parunak, H.V.D., and Michel, F., Eds., *Workshop on Environments for Multi-Agent Systems (E4MAS 2004)*, New York: Springer, 2004, 246–263.

14. Parunak, H.V.D. and Brueckner, S., Ant-like missionaries and cannibals: synthetic pheromones for distributed motion control, *Fourth Intl. Conf. on Autonomous Agents (Agents 2000)*, Barcelona, Spain, 2000, 467–474.

15. Brueckner, S., Return from the ant: synthetic ecosystems for manufacturing control, Dr.rer.nat. thesis, Humboldt University, Berlin, 2000.

16. Sauter, J.A., Matthews, R., Parunak, H.V.D., and Brueckner, S., Evolving adaptive pheromone path planning mechanisms, *Autonomous Agents and Multi-Agent Systems (AAMAS02)*, Bologna, Italy, 2002, 434–440.

17. Parunak, H.V.D., A survey of environments and mechanisms for human-human stigmergy, in Weyns, D., Michel, F., and Parunak, H.V.D., Eds., *Proc. of E4MAS 2005*, Utrecht, the Netherlands: Springer, 2006.

18. Parunak, H.V.D., Brueckner, S., Fleischer, M., and Odell, J., A design taxonomy of multi-agent interactions, in *Agent-Oriented Software Engineering IV*, Melbourne, Australia: Springer, 2003, 123–137.

19. Ilachinski, A., *Artificial War: Multiagent-based Simulation of Combat*, Singapore: World Scientific, 2004.

20. Lauren, M.K. and Stephen, R.T., Map-aware non-uniform automata (MANA) — a New Zealand approach to scenario modelling, *J. Battlefield Tech.*, 5(1), March, 2002, 27ff.

21. Ortony, A., Clore, G.L., and Collins, A., *The Cognitive Structure of Emotions*, Cambridge, UK: Cambridge University Press, 1988.

22. Parunak, H.V.D., Bisson, R., Brueckner, S., Matthews, R., and Sauter, J., Representing dispositions and emotions in simulated combat, in Thompson, S., Ghanea-Hercock, R., Greaves, M., Meyer, A., and Jennings, N., Eds., *Workshop on Defence Applications of Multi-Agent Systems (DAMAS05, at AAMAS05)*, Utrecht, Netherlands, 2005 (forthcoming).

23. Alonso, R. and Li, H., Analyzing the Adversary's Context, Technical Report, Princeton, NJ: Sarnoff Corporation, 2005.

1.4

Plan Recognition

Christopher Geib

CONTENTS

All chapters in this section share a common theme: Only by understanding the intentions of adversaries are we able to correctly respond to them. The identification and understanding of the adversaries' intentions make possible the prediction of their actions. Correct prediction of the enemy's next actions makes possible the planing of an effective response.

The first three chapters have all made the point that inferring an opponent's intent involves looking at a number of factors, including recognizing high-level objectives, situational features, the opponent's cognitive state, and the plans they are executing. The focus of this chapter is specifically on the last of these problems, the recognition of an adversary's plans on the basis of observations of his actions without considering his beliefs or emotional state. Previous work in this area has left a number of open research questions that must be solved before existing computational approaches can be used to infer an adversary's plans. To address this need, we discuss previous approaches to plan recognition and their limitations. We then discuss a specific algorithm for plan recognition called the Probabilistic Hostile Agent Task Tracker (PHATT) that combines the strengths of logical and probabilistic reasoning. We show PHATT does not have the limitations of earlier work and show how it addresses the needs of adversarial domains. Finally, we discuss theoretical and pragmatic issues and lessons learned from the application of PHATT in adversarial cybersecurity problems.

1.4.1   An Example of Plans and Plan Recognition

In this chapter, we define a *plan* as a complex series of partially ordered actions designed to achieve a *root goal*. The actions are hierarchically decomposed from the root goal into simpler lower-level actions. For example, the high-level root goal of stealing data from a computer could be broken down into the substeps of performing reconnaissance on the target machine, getting administrative-level access to the machine, and finding the data. Reconnaissance of the target could be further broken down into steps like scanning an IP address range for the machine and then scanning the machine to identify which services are available on the machine to attack. Notice that the actions in this example are at multiple levels of granularity, from a very high level down to a very low level. Further, the action sequences can have ordering requirements. The reconnaissance actions must be done before attempting to gain access, which must be done before attempting to find the data. Finally, plans might have choice points that allow the tailoring of the plan to the situation.

Plan recognition is the identification of these highly complex, ordered sequences of actions on the basis of observations of the agent's actions. The approach that we explore in detail here does not explicitly model the opponent's beliefs or emotional state, but rather performs a very specific type of pattern recognition to group observed adversary actions into complex plans that indicate high-level goals. In the past, work in this area has gone by a number of names, including "intent recognition" and "task tracking." Subtle distinctions are found between these areas and it is worth briefly noting the differences.

One can distinguish *intent recognition* [12] from plan recognition as the process of recognizing only the root goal or intent of the agent without developing a hypothesis about the plans being followed or the methods chosen to achieve those plans. For example, if we observed a man being mugged, we could infer his desire to obtain help even without being able to identify any specific plan he was considering to achieve that end. While in some specialized applications identifying the root goal of an agent without knowledge of his plans is possible, in practice, disentangling these two problems is usually difficult. Systems that do this often make strong assumptions about the application [12] or the goals of the agent based on situational features [1].

Recognizing the plans of an agent and tracking the development of the these plans usually requires the production of a hypothesis of the agent's root goal. In some applications, the root goal is called the "intention" of the plan to distinguish it from other subgoals or substeps within the plan. Because determining and tracking an agent's plans without understanding the root goal is difficult, this process is sometimes referred to as intent recognition. However, this term is ambiguous because some systems do not conflate a plan's root goal and the agent's intention. This chapter is about plan recognition or task tracking rather than the larger question of intent recognition. While this does more narrowly define the scope of our discussion, clearly recognizing that the plans being followed by an adversary is a critical part of understanding and correctly reacting to them.

To discuss the details of plan recognition, an example problem is helpful. Almost all plan recognition systems require as input a set of plans to be recognized. For this discussion representing these plans as a set of simple hierarchical plans is most convenient [7]. Figure 1.4.1 shows hierarchical plans for a computer network security application represented as partially ordered and-or trees. In this case, the agent is motivated by one of three top level goals: Bragging (*Brag*, being able to boast of his success to others); theft of information (*Theft*); or denial of service (*DOS*).

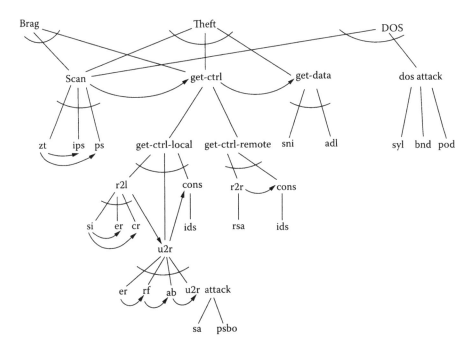

FIGURE 1.4.1

An example set of plans: In this figure, and-nodes are represented by an undirected arc across the lines connecting the parent node to its children. Or-nodes do not have this arc. Ordering constraints in the plans are represented by directed arcs between the ordered actions. For example, the scan action must be executed before *get-ctrl*, which must be executed before *get-data*.

Children of an and-node represent those steps that must be taken to achieve the parent node. Arrows between siblings represent ordering constraints. For example, an agent who wishes to achieve bragging rights must first scan the target network for vulnerabilities (*scan*) and then attempt to gain administrative-level control of the machine (*get-ctrl*). Such agents are not motivated to exploit the control they gain. On the other hand, agents who wish to steal information will perform these same two steps and then exploit their control of the machine to steal data (*get-data*). Finally, an agent whose root goal is the *DOS* of the target machine need only scan to identify a vulnerability and then carry out a specific attack designed to take the machine offline (*dos-attack*).

Children of an or-node represent a choice for the agent within the plan. For example, *syl, bnd,* and *pod* all denote different ways of performing a *dos-attack*. However, the agent only needs to perform one of them to achieve the parent goal.

Note that this plan library, while displaying a variety of the phenomena that we are interested in discussing, is not a complete set of plans for this application. It reflects both the plans that we are interested in as well as specific problem features of interest and is presented as an example to facilitate discussion.

1.4.1.1 Early Work in Plan Recognition

A great deal of artificial intelligence research has been done on plan recognition using a range of algorithms: Traditional Bayesian nets, parsing of probabilistic (and nonprobabilistic) context-free grammars, graph covering, and even marker passing. Much of this work has made the assumption of a single observed agent pursuing a single goal. Further, that the observed agent is either cooperative or at least agnostic about the inference of his goals is usually assumed. This assumption has left a number of issues critical for adversarial domains unexplored in the literature. For example, previous work has almost exclusively assumed the actions of the agent are fully observable. In adversarial situations, one of the first things agents will do is attempt to mask the actions they are executing to make the inference of their goals more difficult. We discuss plan recognition under partial observability in the second half of this chapter. Some previous approaches to plan recognition have also ignored the question of what can be inferred from missing observations, even though this is critical for adversarial reasoning. For example, consider Sherlock Holmes' famous case that hinged on the fact that the dog did not bark [6]. Finally, for any real-world agent to be engaged in only a single task at a time is rare. Multiple concurrent and interleaved plans for different goals are the norm, not the exception, and yet previous research has not addressed the issue. We discuss previous work in the light of these issues.

The earliest work in plan recognition [17,20] was rule based; researchers attempted to develop inference rules that would capture the nature of plan recognition. Cohen, Perrault, and Allen [4] distinguish between two types of plan recognition, keyhole and intended plan recognition. In keyhole recognition, the recognizer is simply watching normal actions by an ambivalent agent. In intended recognition, the agent is cooperative; his actions are done with the intent that they be understood. In neither case is the agent actively hostile to the process of plan recognition.

We believe Charniak was the first to argue that plan recognition was best understood as a specific form of the general problem of *abduction*, or reasoning to the best explanation [2]. In 1986, Kautz and Allen published an article, entitled "Generalized Plan Recognition," [14] that framed much of the following work in plan recognition. Kautz and Allen defined the problem of keyhole plan recognition as the problem of identifying a minimal set of top-level actions sufficient to explain the set of observed actions. Plans were represented in a plan graph, with top-level actions as root nodes and expansions of these actions into unordered sets of child actions representing plan decomposition. To a first approximation, the problem of plan recognition was then a problem of graph covering. Kautz and Allen formalized this view of plan recognition in terms of McCarthy's circumscription. Kautz and Allen's model of plan recognition treated the problem as one of computing minimal explanations in the form of vertex covers based on the plan graph.

While Kautz and Allen's work does not take into account differences in the *a priori* likelihood of different plans, Charniak and Goldman [3] argued that because plan recognition involves abduction, it could best be done as Bayesian (probabilistic) inference. Bayesian inference supports the preference for minimal explanations in the case of hypotheses that are equally likely, but also correctly handles explanations of the same complexity but different likelihoods.

Unfortunately, neither Kautz and Allen nor Charniak and Goldman address the problem of evidence from failure to observe actions. Consider the plan library in Figure 1.4.1. What would happen if one observed actions consistent with *scan* and *get-ctrl*? Assuming that their *a priori* probabilities are the same, a plan recognition system should conclude that *Brag* or *Theft* are equally good explanations. However, as time progresses, if the system sees other actions without seeing actions that contribute to *get-data*, the system should become more and more certain that *Brag* is the correct explanation and not *Theft*.

Systems like those of Charniak and Goldman and Kautz and Allen do not consider plan recognition as a problem that evolves over time. As a result, they cannot represent the fact that an action has not been observed yet. They can only be silent about whether an action has occurred — which means the system has failed to notice the action, not that the action has not occurred — or they assume that an action has not and will not occur.

Vilain [19] presented a theory of plan recognition as parsing, based on Kautz and Allen's theory.* Vilain does not actually propose parsing as a

---

* This was not the first attempt to cast plan recognition as parsing [85].

solution to the plan recognition problem. Instead, he uses the reduction of limited cases of plan recognition to parsing to investigate the complexity of Kautz and Allen's theory. The major problem with parsing as a model of plan recognition is that it does not treat partially ordered plans or interleaved plans well. Both partial ordering and interleaving of plans can result in an exponential increase in the size of the required grammar.

More recently, Wellman and Pynadath have proposed a plan recognition method that is both probabilistic and based on parsing. They represent plan libraries as *probabilistic context free grammars* (PCFG) and extract Bayesian networks from the PCFGs to interpret observation sequences. Unfortunately, this approach suffers from the same limitations on plan interleaving as Vilain's. Wellman and Pynadath also propose that probabilistic context sensitive grammars (PCSG) might overcome this problem, but defining a probability distribution for a PCSG is difficult [16].

Huber et al. [13] present an approach to keyhole plan recognition for coordinating teams of Procedural Reasoning System (PRS) based agents. They developed an approach for automatically generating belief networks for plan recognition from PRS knowledge areas (hierarchical reactive plans). However, they do not address the interleaving of multiple plans and the development of plans over time.

Finally, Bui [1] has proposed a model of plan recognition based on a variant of hidden Markov models (HMM). While this work does recognize the plan recognition problem as evolving through time, it does not address the case of multiple goals. Like Wellman and Pynadath, to address multiple concurrent root goals, Bui faces the problem of defining a probability distribution over the set of all possible root goal sets.

Thus, to effectively address plan recognition in adversarial settings, we must discard the assumption that the observed agents will be amenable to our observations and inference and look critically at the simplified models this method has produced. We must abandon algorithms based on plans as formal models and look to models of plan generation for the inspiration for our algorithms. The information provided by understanding the order in which actions are executed provides crucial information about the goals of the agent.

1.4.2   PHATT System Basics

Given the limitations of previous work, we have taken a very different approach in building the PHATT. The central realization of the PHATT approach is that plans are executed dynamically and as a result, the actions that an agent takes at each step depend critically on the actions he has previously taken. That is, at any given moment, the agent is able to execute any one of the actions that contribute to his plans that have been enabled by previous actions. We call the set of actions that contribute to the agent's current plans, and are enabled by his previous actions, a *pending set*. These are the actions that are "pending" execution by the agent.

With this idea in mind, we can build a model of plan execution. First, an agent chooses or has chosen a set of goals. On the basis of these goals, he chooses a set of plans to achieve them. Before the agent has acted, a subset of actions are in the plan that have no prerequisite actions. These actions form the initial pending set for the agent. From this initial set, the agent chooses his first action for execution.

After this action has been performed, the agent's pending set is changed. Some actions might be removed from the pending set (the action that was just executed, for example) and other actions might be added to the pending set (those actions that are enabled by the execution of the previous action). The agent will choose his next action from the new pending set and the process of choosing an action and building new pending sets repeats until the agent stops performing actions or completes his plans. This process is illustrated graphically in Figure 1.4.2.

If we probabilistically model the selection of goals, plans, and actions for execution, the pending sets are a Markov chain and this model of plan execution is a hidden Markov model. As such, a number of algorithms exist that we could use to infer the state of this Markov process including traditional Bayesian nets or Bui's work. However, given the limitations of these methods already discussed, we have developed a new algorithm tailored to this specific model of plan recognition.

Notice that we can probabilistically simulate the process of plan execution by sampling the agent's goals and plans, then repeatedly choosing elements from the resulting pending sets, thus generating future pending sets. This practice provides a simple model for the generation of execution traces, and for each such execution trace, a unique corresponding sequence of pending sets is generated.

Given this model, PHATT takes a Bayesian approach to perform probabilistic plan recognition. To compute $Pr(g|obs)$, the conditional probability of

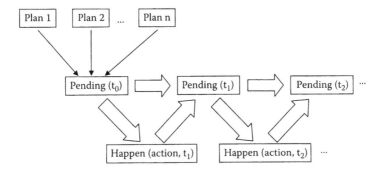

FIGURE 1.4.2
A simple model of plan execution.

a particular goal g given the set of observations *obs*, it computes $Pr(exp|obs)$, the conditional probability of a particular explanation *exp* given a set of observations, *obs*. Bayes' rule:

$$Pr\,(exp|obs) = Pr(exp \wedge obs)/\,Pr\,(obs)$$

provides a simple way of computing $Pr(exp|obs)$. Like many practical Bayesian systems, PHATT exploits the equivalent formulation:

$$Pr\,(exp_0|obs) = Pr\,(exp_0 \wedge obs)/\sum_i Pr(exp_i \wedge obs)$$

where the conditional probability of a specific explanation exp_0 is computed by dividing the probability of that explanation and the observations by the sum of the probability mass associated with all of the possible explanations.

To make use of this approach, PHATT uses the model of plan execution to build the complete set of explanations for the observations. It then establishes the probability of each of the explanations and observations and then, on the basis of this information, it can compute the conditional probability of any particular explanation and, from that, the conditional for a particular goal.

As an approach, this method raises the question of the practicality of generating the set of all explanations for a given set of observations. The answer to this issue is problem specific. In some applications, building the complete set of explanations for a given set of observations is a trivial exercise and in others, it is exponential in the length of the observation stream. We will discuss the results of some empirical studies about the effectiveness of this approach later. For a more theoretical analysis of the complexity of these methods, we refer the reader to [8].

1.4.2.1 Building the Set of Explanations

Given our model of plan execution, we define an explanation for a set of observations $\sigma_1 \ldots \sigma_n$ as a pair consisting of the set of minimally expanded instances of trees from the plan library, sufficient to associate each observation with at least one step within the plan trees, and the pending sets required for its construction. For example, given the plan library shown in Figure 1.4.1, one possible explanation* for the sequence of observations (zt, t_1), (ips, t_2), (ps, t_3), (pod, t_4), is shown in Figure 1.4.3.

In the pending sets, each pair refers to the use of a particular primitive action to contribute to the achievement of a specific method within the existing plan. For example, the pair (zt, DOS) in the initial pending set $(PS(t_0))$ represents the possibility of a zt action contributing to a plan for a *DOS*, while $(ips, Scan)$ in $PS(t_1)$ represents the possibility of the action labeled *ips*

---

* We use an integer time notation throughout this chapter.

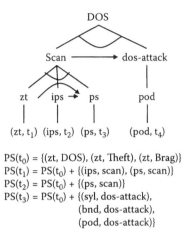

$$PS(t_0) = \{(zt, DOS), (zt, Theft), (zt, Brag)\}$$
$$PS(t_1) = PS(t_0) + \{(ips, scan), (ps, scan)\}$$
$$PS(t_2) = PS(t_0) + \{(ps, scan)\}$$
$$PS(t_3) = PS(t_0) + \{(syl, dos\text{-}attack),$$
$$(bnd, dos\text{-}attack),$$
$$(pod, dos\text{-}attack)\}$$

FIGURE 1.4.3
An example explanation.

in the plan library, contributing to the *scan* method in the previously hypothesized *DOS* plan explaining (zt, t_1).

PHATT uses a breadth-first search directed by the observed actions to search the space of possible explanations. If at any point the next observation does not fit as the next action within an explanation, PHATT prunes that portion of the search space. If the search exhausts the given observations, the resulting explanation is added to the set of possible explanations and PHATT continues to collect the complete and covering set of such explanations. More details of this search and PHATT's method for performing it can be found in [9–11].

1.4.2.2 Computing an Explanation's Probability

PHATT computes the probability of an explanation based on three probabilistic features of the explanations. First, it considers the prior probability of each of the root goals being adopted by the actor. We assume these are given to PHATT in the plan library. In many applications, these types of priors can be learned or approximated from previous performance. In adversarial domains, such estimates are likely to be inaccurate. However, previous research has shown that inaccuracies in such prior assessments are often not significant because the effect of evidence from observations outweighs the priors. We denote these probabilities by $Pr(G_i)$, where i ranges over all the root goals in the explanation.

Second, for each subgoal in the explanation that is represented by an or-node in the plan library, PHATT must have a probability distribution over the set of the agent's choices. For example, if an agent could use a *bnd*, *syl*, or *pod* for a *dos-attack*, PHATT must have a distribution over how likely each of these possible attacks are given that the agent will commit a *dos-attack*. We call such subgoals within the explanation *choice-points*.

Typically, we have assumed that each possible expansion of a choice-point is equally likely. Following this assumption, if J choice-points are within a given explanation and $|Ch_j|$ represents the number of alternative expansions that could be used to expand a particular choice-point, then $1/|Ch_j|$ represents the probability of the agent choosing a particular expansion. However, this uniformity assumption is not required by the framework. Any distribution over the alternative expansions could be used in its place.

Third, for each pending set, PHATT computes the probability that the observed action is the one chosen next for execution. We again assume that all of the actions within the pending set are equally likely. Thus, for a particular pending set at time k, the probability of any specific element of the set is given by $1/|PS_k|$. Again, the uniformity assumption made here is not required; any distribution could be used. This distribution could be conditioned on the state of the world, hypothesized root goals, or even the plans of the agent.

Using these three features of an explanation, PHATT computes the prior probability of a given explanation by multiplying together the priors for each goal, the probability of the specific expansion of the choice-points, and the probability of the observed actions being chosen. More formally:

$$Pr(exp, obs) = \prod_{i=0}^{I} Pr(G_i) \prod_{j=0}^{J} (1/|Ch_j|) \prod_{k=0}^{K} (1/|PS_k|)$$

where the first term is the probability of the agent's root goal set, the second term is the probability that the agent chose the particular expansions for the choice-points to achieve the goals, and the final term captures the probability that the given observations occurred in the specified order.

Using these computed probabilities and Bayes' rule, PHATT computes the conditional probability of a root goal by summing the probability mass for those explanations that contain the goal and dividing by the total probability mass associated with all the explanations. That is:

$$Pr(g|Obs) = \sum_{e}^{Exp_g} Pr(e, Obs) / \sum_{e}^{Exp} Pr(e, Obs)$$

where the denominator sums the probability of all explanations for the observations and the numerator sums the probability of the explanations in which the goal g occurs.

A common misconception is that the denominator in this step should always be 1, making this division unnecessary. In fact, the probability mass of the covering set of explanations almost never sums to 1 as a result of multiple independent root goals and the choices within an explanation.

This method also allows more general conditional queries to be computed for a given set of observations. All that is required is to select the set of explanations that satisfy the condition, sum their probability mass, and divide by the total. For example, to compute the conditional probability that an agent used a plan that called for achieving *get-ctrl-local* (as opposed to *get-ctrl-remote*), PHATT can sum the probability mass of the explanations that have a *get-ctrl-local* in them and divide by the total probability mass.

The use of three different probabilities differentiates PHATT from other work in probabilistic grammars [16,19]. Most probabilistic context-free (and sensitive) grammar (PCFG/PCSG) research has included the use of a single probability for each grammar rule to capture how likely the given nonterminal is expanded using that grammar rule. As a structural relation, this conflates the probabilities that we have identified as the root priors and the choice-point terms in the above equation. This also completely leaves out the term for the pending sets, and makes it harder for these approaches to effectively handle partial observability, partially ordered plans, or multiple concurrent plans.

With this model of plan recognition couched in terms of plan execution, PHATT is able to handle a number of problems critical to application in the real world, including multiple interleaved goals, partially ordered plans, the effect of negative evidence or failure to observe ("the dog didn't bark"), and observations of "failed actions."

Beyond simply allowing multiple root goals, this approach to plan recognition also allows for multiple instances of the same root goal to be active at the same time. This attribute is unusual for plan recognition systems. In fact, most other approaches do not allow a user to have more than one goal at a time, let alone multiple instances of the same goal. For many real-world adversarial domains, this assumption is simply unacceptable.

Consider intent recognition in cybersecurity applications. In the real world, a determined cyberattacker commonly launches multiple different attacks against a single host, or even multiple instances of the same attack, to achieve a single goal. This is done for a number of reasons — diversity of target susceptibility, attack success likelihood, and to create confusion, among others. In this application, seeing multiple instances of the same goal being pursued by different, very similar, or even identical instances of plans is very common.

1.4.3   Algorithmic Complexity and Scalability

One of the chief criticisms of this type of approach to plan recognition and probabilistic reasoning in general is the argument that building the complete set of explanations for a given set of observations is computationally impractical. The argument claims that so many explanations for a given set of observations must exist that no matter the complexity of the algorithm used to generate them, the runtime of the system will be excessive. To address these concerns, we have completed scalability studies on the PHATT algorithm to look at the factors that have the most significant impact on the algorithm's runtime. We summarize the results here.

TABLE X

Experimental Factors

Factor	Description	Levels
Order	Types of ordering constraints between actions	Total, one, partial, unord, last
Depth	Plan depth	3, 4, 5, 6
BF	Method and choice node branching factor	3, 4
Roots	Number of root goals in the plan library	10, 100, 200, 400, 600, 800, 1000

While some aspects of PHATT are amenable to theoretical analysis, a complete theoretical analysis of the algorithm is very difficult. However, key issues with the algorithm's complexity can be recognized by empirical analysis. Therefore, we have conducted a series of exploratory experiments designed to identify the critical factors determining the runtime of the PHATT algorithm. Our initial hypothesis was that whereas the number of roots in the plan-library might be intuitively assumed to have a large effect on the runtime of the algorithm, other features of the plan library would have more impact.

Our experiments measuring the runtime for the PHATT algorithm were conducted entirely *in situ* on a Sun Sunfire-880 with 8 GB of main memory and four 750 MHz CPUs, which afforded a large number of replications (1000). Note that measured CPU time (msec) was exclusive of any time used by the operating system or by other processes on the computer.

We identified five features of plan libraries that we believed might have a significant affect on the runtime of the PHATT algorithm: The type of inter-action ordering constraints in the plans, the depth of the plans in the plan library, the number of intendable roots in the plan library, the branching factor for methods (and nodes), and the branching factor for choice points. The experimental factors and levels used in the experiments are summarized in Table X.

The definitions and possible values for each of these factors is given below. For each experimental condition, a single plan library was generated. The discussion of each experiment documents which of the features was a tested factor and which were held constant.

- *Order*: This factor is an indication of how many and what type of ordering constraints exist between the actions in the and-nodes in the plan library.
    - *Total*: All of the actions are totally ordered. Each action has a single ordering constraint with the action that precedes it.
    - *One*: Each plan has a designated first action. All other actions in the plan are ordered after it but are unordered with respect to each other.

- *Partial*: Each action can have a single ordering constraint. This constraint orders the action after one other randomly chosen action in the definition. Cyclic orderings are prevented at generation. This means that an and-node's children can vary from being totally ordered to completely unordered and was specifically included to approximate real-world plan libraries. In most cases, actions will be neither totally ordered nor completely unordered. Such a plan will never have more ordering constraints than the totally ordered case.

- *Unord*: All of the actions are unordered with respect to each other.

- *Last*: Each plan has a designated last action. All other actions in the plan are ordered before it but are unordered with respect to each other.

- *Plan Library Depth*: This factor is a measure of the depth of the plan trees. In these plan trees, or-nodes (choice-points) and and-nodes alternate levels. In all cases, the root is defined as an or-node and levels alternate as they descend.

- *Method BF*: This factor determines the number of child actions (branching factor) at an and-node.

- *Choice BF*: This factor determines the number of child actions (branching factor) at an or-node.

- *Number of Roots*: This factor measures the number of plan root nodes in the plan library at 10, 100, 200, 400, 600, 800, and 1000 roots, respectively.

Note that all the actions in the plan libraries are unique. Thus, once an action is observed, no actual ambiguity exists about what root intention the action must contribute to. This practice does not inherently reduce the runtime of the algorithm and does not rule out the possibility of more than one instance of a given plan. However, this does allow us to make several inferences about the affect of various factors on the algorithm's runtime. We return to this discussion later.

For each experimental condition, 1000 test cases were generated. To generate a test case, three unique root goals were selected at random from the relevant plan library. For each of these root goals, a legal plan and linearization of the plan was generated following the plan library. The three component plans were then randomly interleaved, maintaining the ordering constraints of the individual plans. For each test case, the internal clock was started and PHATT was presented with the observed action sequence; after processing the sequence, PHATT computed the probability distribution over the root goals. At this point, the clock was halted and the CPU time measured. This time was recorded for the condition. An increment of 1 msec was added to any runtime that registered as 0.

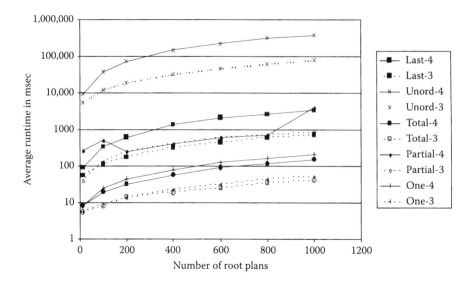

FIGURE 1.4.4
Average runtimes.

We collected runtimes in a full factorial experiment for the Order and Roots features holding Choice BF fixed at 3, Method BF fixed at 4, and varying the Depth feature between 3 and 4. Figure 1.4.4 plots average runtime on a log scale against the number of root goals for each of the test conditions.

The first thing one notices about this data is that the algorithm is scaling linearly in the number of plan roots in the plan library. This behavior is validated across three orders of magnitude and is very encouraging for its use in large problems. Note that, though the results for the order partial, depth 4 runtimes do have a dip between 200 and 800 root plans, the overall trend is still linear. We believe this dip in the runtimes to be caused by the natural variability of the complexity of the partially ordered plans, and at the time of this writing, we are still examining this effect. The graph also shows that the type of ordering constraint has a profound effect on means. Unordered plans exhibit the highest means; partially ordered plans also have relatively high means.

Reconsidering the PHATT algorithm in light of these results suggests that the difference between the "one" and "total" order levels is caused by maintaining larger pending sets. In order "one" cases, after the initial action for a plan is seen, all the other actions are enabled and are added to the pending set, making a very large pending set. In "total" cases, only a single action is always in the pending set. This means that whereas multiple explanations are not a possibility for either case, the size of the average pending set will be larger for order "one" cases than for order "total" cases. Computing and maintaining these larger pending sets causes the increase in runtime.

In summary, the following are the major conclusions drawn from this set of experiments.

- The algorithm's average runtime scales linearly with the number of roots in the plan library.
- The feature of the plan library that has the most significant effect on the algorithm's runtime is the ordering constraints within the plan library, followed by the number of roots in the plan library, followed by the actual depth of the plan trees.
- Ordering constraint organization has a significant impact on the algorithm's runtime.
- Ordering constraints — even at the end of plans — significantly reduce the algorithm's runtime.
- Plan libraries without ordering constraints significantly increase the algorithm's runtime and are the worst case for the ordering factor.
- Maintaining a large number of possible explanations is the most significant cost for the algorithm.

These results are very promising for the application of the PHATT algorithm, especially in adversarial domains. However, to be effective against adversarial agents, the system must be able to deal with domains that are only partially observable.

1.4.4 Handling Partial Observability

PHATT's foundation in plan execution makes possible a relatively simple treatment of partial observability. All that must happen is to extend the model of plan execution with actions that are performed but not observed. This entails quantifying the probability that the action was not observed. To do this, the probability that the observed agent has actually performed some action that was not observed is quantified. Then, a term is added to the formula for computing the probability of a given explanation to capture this probability. Next, we modify the algorithm for generating explanations to eliminate any explanation in which the probability of unobserved actions exceeds a user-defined threshold. We discuss each of these steps in more detail.

1.4.4.1 Quantifying the Probability of Not Observing

We are rarely equally likely to observe all performed actions. Relative to the sensors available, some actions are harder to detect than others. In the literature, this idea has been captured by the "false negative rate" for a given sensor. This feature of the sensor can be learned by watching its long-term performance and noting when it fails to report an actual occurrence. We assume that for each possible observed action, we can learn the long-term false negative rate of the sensor and use this value as the prior probability that the action could occur and not be observed. This will allow us to explicitly model the possibility that an action has been performed and not observed.

Note that a number of limitations exist to this approach. For example, significant changes in the underlying problem or observed agent's capabilities can affect the false negative rates and will force the system to relearn them. Meanwhile, error will be introduced in the system's probability computations. Further, we have chosen to use the false negative rate as an unconditional prior probability. We could have modeled it as a conditional, and when situational factors affect the false positive rate, it would be more accurate to do so. This would be a straightforward extension to the model but would increase the computational cost of the resulting algorithm. Therefore, for simplicity and to establish a baseline cost for these additions to the algorithm, we have used an unconditional prior. Finally, note that in this treatment, we are not modeling the possibility that the sensor observed the action but, for some other reason, failed to report it (for example, communication problems). We are only concerned with the case of the sensor actually failing to observe the action.

Having an explicit model of the probability that a particular action could be performed and not observed makes computing the probability of a given explanation and observations relatively easy. The following new definition for the probability of a single explanation and observations extends the previous definition with a final term to explicitly model the probability that all unobserved actions in the explanation are executed and not observed:

$$Pr\,(exp,\,obs) = \prod_{i=0}^{I} Pr\,(G_i)\prod_{i=0}^{J}(1/\,|Ch_j|\,)\prod_{k=0}^{K}(1/\,|PS_k|\,)\prod_{l=0}^{L}(Pr\,(Unobs_l))$$

Without loss of generality, we have assumed that the explanation has L actions that have been performed and not observed and that $Pr(Unobs_l)$ represents the false negative rate for sensing the unobserved action l. This addition is the only change to the computation of probabilities for the algorithm. No change in the formula for computing the conditional probability for a specific goal is necessary once we have the probabilities for each explanation.

Extending the definition of the probability of an explanation to cover unobserved actions is not sufficient. We must also address the question of how to generate explanations that make use of unobserved actions. We previously described an algorithm for building explanations that incrementally processes each of the observations to advance PHATT's pending set. We can extend the algorithm for generating explanations to explicitly consider the possibility that actions were not present in the observation stream but were actually executed.

Note that assuming rational, goal-driven agents that only engage in actions that contribute to their goals, even unobserved actions must be within the pending set of the observed agents. This significantly constrains the set of actions that can be executed even unobserved. Thus, even the extended algorithm we now present does not consider the possibility of unobserved actions that are inconsistent with the current pending set of the agents. Note that this does not prevent the observation of actions that would introduce new goals, as these actions would be within the pending set.

To produce a complete and covering set of explanations for the observations, explanation generation must be extended to consider the possibility that every action in the pending set can be executed next and not observed. This results in a two-stage explanation generation algorithm. First, the algorithm considers the possibility that each of the actions in the pending set is performed and not observed. Second, following the original algorithm, it generates those explanations in which no unobserved action was performed but instead the next action in the observation stream was performed. This results in a significant expansion of the space of explanations.

1.4.4.2 Thresholding the Production of Explanations

Without further mechanisms, the algorithm just given will not terminate the process of building explanations. Whereas the original algorithm naturally terminates at the end of the observation stream, nothing in the extended algorithm dictates when the system must stop considering the possibility of adding still more unobserved actions. This will result in ever more unlikely explanations.

To address this issue, we require the user to provide a threshold value that determines how unlikely an explanation they are willing to accept relative to the unobserved actions. Specifically, the algorithm removes any explanation where:

$$\prod_{l=0}^{L} Pr(Unobs_l) < Threshold$$

This value allows the users to specify, for example, they are willing to accept only those explanations where the unobserved actions could have been performed and not noticed 90% of the time. Because the algorithm is generating explanations incrementally, thresholding the acceptable explanations provides a natural method for limiting the search for explanations and provides a stopping criteria for the algorithm. At some point, the addition of another unobserved action will drive the current explanation below the threshold. This will force the process of addition of unobserved actions to stop. If all the observations have been explained, this explanation can be kept. If observations still remain, the algorithm must attempt to explain the remainder without considering unobserved actions.

Notice that this approach allows the system to differentially consider actions on the basis of their false negative rates. At the same threshold value, the system will consider explanations with more instances of actions with high false negative rates. For example, the system would more easily consider an explanation with multiple stealthy scans of a computer (low probability of observation) than an explanation with even a single unobserved successful denial of service on one of its critical domain name servers (high probability of observation).

A critical relation exists between the threshold value and the size of the search space. As the threshold value is lowered, the user is allowing the system to consider more and more unlikely streams of actions. However, this is done at a significant computational cost.

1.4.4.3 Impact on the Algorithm's Runtime

Considering problems that are only partially observable can result in a significant increase in the algorithm's runtime. By considering the possibility of unobserved actions, the algorithm moves from considering only those elements in the pending set that are consistent with the next observed action to considering all of the elements in the pending set. The search space of possible explanations has significantly increased.

While the user-defined threshold clearly has an affect on the size of the explanation search space, a simple relation does not exist between them. The branching factor of the search space at each explanation critically depends on how many and what kind of unobserved actions have already been hypothesized. For completely observable problems, in the worst case, [8] shows that the branching factor of the search space for this sort of algorithm can be exponential. Consider such a case in a partially observable problem where the user-defined threshold is sufficient to allow the initial actions to be performed unobserved. The exponential branching factor of the search space caused by the initial unordered actions will always be present if the threshold does not allow significant pruning.

Conversely, in the best case, very high threshold values will all but prevent the algorithm from considering unobserved actions, thereby adding to the algorithm's runtime. Thus, setting the threshold parameter is critical to achieving reasonable runtimes.

1.4.5 Limitations of the PHATT Algorithm

Two significant limitations exist to the PHATT algorithm: PHATT has a limited qualitative model of time, and the central factor in the runtime of the algorithm is the number of explanations that must be maintained, which has implications for the types of problems that can be solved with PHATT.

The plans in PHATT's plan library allow for ordering constraints on the actions. That is, the substeps of the plans can be partially ordered. As each explanation is created, the actions of the plan are placed on a timeline in a total order that obeys the partial ordering in the plan specification. This timeline represents the only significant model of time that PHATT has.

Thus, PHATT is limited in its ability to represent certain types of temporal relationships. While it can reason about action ordering, no quantitative reasoning about time can be accomplished. This restriction rules out plans that require reasoning about specific interaction temporal intervals, for example, reasoning that a plan step is done within a specific time period after another action.

PHATT's language for representing the temporal relationships between plan steps could be straight-forwardly extended. Doing so would require adding temporal constraints between action start and end times to the plan library and adding a temporal constraint engine [5] to verify the constraints. Because enforcing temporal constraints in the plan library only requires simple checks at the time of explanation generation, such an extension should not have a significant impact on the runtime of the algorithm. Remember, such a system is not doing temporal projection — a very time consuming process — but rather is just verifying the specified temporal relationships held between the start and end times of the actions. While PHATT's simple temporal model might seem like a significant limitation, in practice, this has not presented a significant problem for our work in computer network security.

As we have seen, the runtime of the PHATT algorithm depends critically on the number of possible explanations for a given set of observations. We can look at the PHATT algorithm as searching through the space of partially constructed explanations. From this perspective, the number of possible explanations and the size of the search for them depends critically on how many of the forward branches from a given partial explanation can result in a complete explanation of the observations. Any increase in the branching factor of this search space increases the number of consistent explanations and is directly related to the PHATT algorithm's runtime. Unfortunately, most increases in the expressive power of the system increase at least the number of consistent explanations, if not the branching factor of this search directly. For example, PHATT's handling of partially ordered plans, multiple active concurrent goals, observed action failures, and partially observable action streams all increase the branching factor and the number of consistent explanations and therefore the runtime of the algorithm.

The worst cases for the algorithm results when a long, partially ordered prefix is common to more than one goal in the plan library. If two plans with this common prefix are interleaved, alternating one action from each plan, the number of possible explanations is quite large and they must all be maintained by the system.

Rather than saying that the runtime of the algorithm depends on the branching factor of the space of explanations, a more accurate statement would be that the runtime of the algorithm is affected by the number of explanations that must be considered as possibly leading to a complete explanation. That is, if we can rule out explanations (i.e., conclude that an explanation cannot cover all of the observations), then we can eliminate that explanation from consideration and improve the runtime of the algorithm.

This result leads us to an important lesson about designing an effective problem representation for PHATT. We want to represent the plans so the system can identify as quickly as possible when a particular explanation will not result in a complete solution and can be eliminated. This can be accomplished in a number of ways:

- Isolate common action prefix sequences as separate goals that can be identified on their own without hypothesizing a higher level root goal.

- Require identifying or distinguishing actions early in a plans definition.

- Design the plan library to eliminate the need to consider unobserved actions.

With such optimizations to the plan library, while the worst case runtime for the algorithm might be exponential, the application specific runtime will be much closer to $O(n \log(n))$.

1.4.6   Lessons Learned: Computer Network Security

We have completed some preliminary work applying PHATT to computer network security. Computer security can be divided into at least two different levels of abstraction to which PHATT can be applied. However, before we can discuss the application of PHATT, we first must define these levels and differentiate between the two.

A typical computer network administrator has the responsibility of the operation and security of a collection of computers enumerated by IP address. We will call this collection of computers the *IP domain* of the administrator. The administrator will use a collection of software tools called *intrusion detection systems* (IDS) to monitor network traffic and individual computer states to identify when attackers are active within an IP domain and the actions the attackers have taken. As such, IDSs act as the administrator's sensors for hostile actions.

We will define *single domain security plan recognition* (SDPR) as the problem of inferring the goals and actions of an attacker given direct (possibly clustered) inputs from traditional IDSs. Thus, we are interested in providing the administrator a level of analysis on top of the reports of IDSs about attacker plans and goals.

Abstracted inputs to PHATT for SDPR might look like:

- IDS1 and IDS2 both report a scan of IP addresses in the range X to Y from time T1 to T2.
- IDS3 and IDS4 both report a land attack at time T3 to T5 on host Z.

While the output we would like PHATT to produce might look like:

- A hostile agent is attempted a denial of service on logistics database server Z from time T1 to T5.

As the name might suggest, *cross-domain security plan recognition* (CDPR) is plan recognition at the next abstraction level up from a SDPR. Some computer network attacks take place across multiple administrative IP domains. A relatively common example of this is distributed denial of service attacks where multiple machines (in possibly multiple IP domains) all conspire to flood a particular machine. While a single administrator would see part of the attack, no administrator would see all of the attack as it crosses multiple IP domains.

While an instance of PHATT working on the SDPR problem will get its inputs directly from an IDSs for an individual IP domain, an instance of PHATT working on the CDPR problem would get its inputs from processing engines working on the SDPR problem (PHATT instances or other analysis tools). Thus, the inputs to PHATT for CDPR could look like:

- Logistics database server Z in IP domain D1 experienced DOS from T1 to T5.
- Lost contact with IP domain D3 from T0 to T3.

While the output of this level might look like:

- Procurement process disrupted from T0 to T5.

Note that the distinction we are making here has to do with the level of the processing and types of conclusions that we would expect the system to draw, not with the number or type of resources that are being managed.

Most of our empirical work in applying PHATT to network security has been done in SDPR. This work has had very positive results and has even motivated further improvements in the details of the PHATT algorithm. Given some of the algorithmic limitations of PHATT discussed above, many of the observations that we make here should sound familiar.

Surprisingly, PHATT's limited temporal model has not proven to be a problem in SDPR. The work that we have done has focused above the level of abstraction that would require reasoning about action durations. PHATT's partially ordered plans have proved sufficient.

The largest single challenge in SDPR was long runtimes as a result of a common plan prefix. In this application, almost all plans are initiated by a reconnaissance step. The intruder first scans the network to be attacked to determine host IP addresses and vulnerabilities. This scanning activity is a common prefix for almost all of the plans in the library. As mentioned, these types of shared prefixes do not differentiate between root goals and require the system to maintain a large number of possible explanations, thereby slowing the system. This problem is intensified because the substeps of the reconnaissance activities are partially ordered with respect to one another. That is, IP sweeping and machine-port scanning are unordered with respect to each other. This results in a very large number of possible explanations that must be maintained by the system. In fact, this represents the worst case for the PHATT algorithm and results in slow runtimes.

This common prefix can also speak to a fundamental difference between the kinds of plans that PHATT is designed to recognize and the inherent features of the SDPR problem. Hacking plans are often very short, or even a single step. In contrast, PHATT is designed to recognize multistep, goal-directed plans. While PHATT can be used to recognize these plans, other "lighter weight" methods might be more applicable. This suggests that PHATT might be better suited to conventional military applications or extended game playing that involve multistep plans.

The SDPR also presents rapidly changing goals based on opportunistic features of the problem. For example, an attacker driven by *Brag* may shift to *Theft* when he sees intriguing file names, and may even further shift to *DOS* if his activities are successfully thwarted by the system administrator. PHATT is not designed for applications where agents adopt and abandon goals rapidly and opportunistically. In these problems, previous actions are not strong indicators of the goals of the agents and their future actions. The rapid changing of the agent's goals and the opportunistic execution of actions will fail to create sequences of actions long enough for PHATT to recognize.

To the degree that the plans in the plan library are short, single-step, we are asking PHATT to do something that it was not designed to do. Our experience suggests the SDPR problem is not inherently this way; however, there are plan libraries for it that do have these properties. Therefore, building a plan library for SDPR requires careful design.
Au:
clarify [1]
this
stateme

Unlike our empirical work on SDPR, our work on CDPR has been more exploratory: Talking to current security professionals, learning how a task is done now, and identifying potential applications for PHATT. Cyberattacks that cross IP domains represent a new family of vulnerabilities. We define a *distributed-process denial of service* as an attack directed at a particular distributed work process. Imagine a military logistics planning process that needs access to three different databases and is maintained by different people. A coordinated attack against all three databases is far more likely to disrupt the logistics process than an attack against any single database. Such a process-centered attack requires the coordination of different types of attacks across IP domains.

The most obvious parallel in the single IP domain case would be attacks where one machine is crashed or suppressed so that the attacker's machine can impersonate it to other machines in the IP domain. We have also seen a particularly simple form of these attacks in the distributed denial of services attacks that are so common on the internet today. However, as attackers increase in sophistication and begin to operate at the cross-IP domain level, we will see much more stealthy attacks where an attacker does not *DOS* a machine or IP address, but cripples a specific work process at multiple points while leaving the rest of the IP domains unharmed.

Using PHATT to recognize these types of attacks will place new requirements both on the sensors for detecting the attacks as well as PHATT itself. This will require more analysis of the possible attacks and the generation of new PHATT plan libraries. Further, for PHATT to recognize these types of attacks in time for effective response, PHATT will need timely detailed reporting of SDPR events. Daily or weekly summary statistics will not be sufficient. Finally, and most troublesome for PHATT, CDPR will require a more powerful temporal model. One of the central features of cross-IP domain attacks is their coordination. Recognizing this fact requires both a knowledge of the types of attacks and the timing requirements across IP domains. For example, recognizing a coordinated denial of service against all the suppliers of a specific commodity requires reasoning about the simultaneity of the attacks against the distributed suppliers.

Yet another class of challenges exist that PHATT will face when dealing with more sophisticated attacks. Because PHATT does not model an attacker's mental state, it is unable to distinguish feints, bluffs, and other forms of obscured attacks. For example, if a single high-impact attack can be made to resemble a series of separate high-likelihood but low-impact attacks, PHATT might report the low-impact attacks as the most likely explanation, and the human operator might miss the unified high-impact attack. This leads us to the next large topic of this book — deception.

References

1. Bui, H.H., Venkatesh, S., and West, G. Policy recognition in the abstract hidden Markov model, *Technical Report 4/2000 School of Computer Science*, Curtin University of Technology, Bentley, Australia, 2002.
2. Charniak, E. and McDermott, D. *Introduction to Artificial Intelligence*, Reading, MA: Addison-Wesley, 1987.
3. Charniak, E. and Goldman, R. A Bayesian model of plan recognition, *Artificial Intelligence*, vol. 64, no. 1, 1993, 53–79.
4. Cohen, P.R., Perrault, C.R., and Allen, J.F. Beyond question answering, in Lehnert, W. and Ringle, M. Eds. *Strategies for Natural Language Processing* Hillsdale, NJ: Lawrence Erlbaum Associates, 1981, 245–274.

5. Dechter, R., Meiri, I., and Pearl, J. Temporal constraint networks, *Artificial Intelligence*, 49, 1991, 61–95.
6. Doyle, A.C. The Adventure of the Silver Blaze, *Memoirs of Sherlock Holmes*, Oxford University Press, USA, 1995.
7. Erol, K., Hendler, J., and Nau, D.S. UMCP: a sound and complete procedure for hierarchical task network planning, *Proc. of the Second Int. Conf. on Artificial Intelligence Planning Systems (AIPS 94)*, Chicago, IL, 1994, 249–254.
8. Geib, C.W. Assessing the complexity of plan recognition, *Proceedings of the AAAI, 2004*, San Jose, CA, 2004.
9. Geib, C.W. and Goldman, R.P. Probabilistic plan recognition for hostile agents, *Proc. of the FLAIRS 2001 Conf.*, Key West, FL, 2001.
10. Geib, C.W. and Goldman, R.P. Recognizing plan/goal abandonment, *Proc. of the AAAI 2002 Fall Symp. on Intent Inference for Users, Teams, and Adversaries*, North Falmouth, MA, 2002.
11. Geib, C.W. and Goldman, R.P. Recognizing plan/goal abandonment, *Proc. of IJCAI 2003*, Acapulco, Mexico, 2003.
12. Horvitz, E., Breese, J., Heckerman, D., Hovel, D., and Rommelse, K. The Lumiere project: Bayesian user modeling for inferring the goals and needs of software users, *Proc. of the 14th Conf. on Uncertainty in Artificial Intelligence*, Madison, WI, 1998.
13. Huber, M.J., Durfee, E.H., and Wellman, M.P. The automated mapping of plans for plan recognition, *Proc. of the Tenth Conf. on Uncertainty in Artificial Intelligence (UAI)*, Seattle, WA, 1994.
14. Kautz, H. and Allen, J.F. Generalized plan recognition, *Proc. of the Conf. of the Am. Assoc. of Artif. Intelligence (AAAI-86)*, Philadelphia, PA, 1986, 32–38.
15. Lesh, N., Rich, C., and Sidner, C. Collaborating with focused and unfocused users, *Proc. of the 8th Int. Conf. on User Modeling*, Sonthofen, Germany, 2001.
16. Pynadath, D. and Wellman, M. Probabilistic state-dependent grammars for plan recognition, *Proc. of the Conf. on Uncertainty in Artificial Intelligence (UAI-'00)*, Stanford, CA, 2000, 507–514.
17. Schmidt, C., Sridharan, N. and Goodson, J. The plan recognition problem: an intersection of psychology and artificial intelligence, *Artificial Intelligence*, 11, 1978, 45–83.
18. Sidner, C.L. Plan parsing for intended response recognition in discourse, *Computational Intelligence*, 1, 1, 1985, 1–10.
19. Vilain, M. Deduction as parsing, *Proc. of the Conf. of the Am. Assoc. of Artif. Intelligence (1991)*, Anaheim, CA, 1991, 464–470.
20. Wilensky, R. *Planning and Understanding*, Reading, MA: Addison-Wesley, 1983.

2.1

Detecting Deception

Christopher Elsaesser and Frank J. Stech

CONTENTS

Deception is characteristic of most adversarial situations [1]. Descriptions and historical accounts of deception abound and theories from a variety of disciplines have been developed to analyze deception. However, almost no historical accounts of detecting deception and few theories of detecting deception are to be found [2–6].

In this chapter, we present a process to aid counter-deception* reasoning. First, we describe how deceptions exploit cognitive biases that result from common reasoning heuristics. Next, we review prior work on processes that can help people recognize organized deceptions. With this review as background, we describe a counter-deception process that is suitable as the central component of a system to assist analysts detect deception. We illustrate our process by demonstrating how it might detect two of the most important military deceptions of the 20th century.

---

* We use the term *counter deception* interchangeably with *deception detection*. We use the term *deception* to include both misleading about key information and hiding key information. *Hiding* is also known as *denial*.

2.1.1   Why Deception Works

Deception is ubiquitous, ranging from the common (magic, financial fraud, scams) to the famous (D-Day, Indian nuclear tests) [7]. Complex stratagems, even though they have many opportunities to fail, often fool even those on guard against deception. Magicians, extremely skilled at deception, are often misled by other magicians [4]. Tactics used to hide key information (denial) and to present misleading information (deception) are shown in Table 2.1.1, with brief descriptions why they work [5,8].

These tactics work by exploiting reasoning errors, cognitive limitations, and concomitant biases. The most important reasoning errors contributing to susceptibility to deception are

- Reasoning causally from evidence to hypotheses.
- Failure to entertain a deception hypothesis.
- Biased estimates of probabilities.
- Failure to consider false positive rates of evidence.

The first two involve considering too few alternative hypotheses due to incomplete generation or premature pruning, which can involve misestimates of probabilities. The sources and effects of biases arising from mental estimates of probabilities are well-known [9]. We are particularly concerned with bias due to making conclusions that support preconceptions, assuming a piece of evidence is consistent with too few hypotheses [10], and mirror imaging — assuming an adversary is likely to choose a course of action that appeals to the observer.

2.1.2   Detecting Deception

To recognize deception, one must consider alternatives and overcome biases that lead to inappropriately weighing evidence that seems to support one of only a few alternatives. Elsaesser investigated several techniques to reduce bias in probabilistic assessments [11]. The most promising method is to require a subject to perform and document a systematic analysis of evidence [12]. However, this method sometimes makes one more susceptible to deception if not carefully applied.*

Johnson et al. [3] observed forensic accountants while they examined questionable business records. Protocol analysis indicated accountants who were

---

* Personal communication between Elsaesser and Fischoff.

TABLE 2.1.1

Denial and Deception Tactics

Denial Tactics	Features of Denial Tactics	Psychological Consequences of Denial
Masking	Conceal key characteristics (cues); eliminate characteristic patterns, blend characteristics with background patterns	Lack of cues for appropriate concepts and schema cause perceptual inattention and blindness to cues for the correct concept and a search for additional confirming cues for incorrect concept.
Repackaging	Add and change key characteristics; modify characteristic patterns, match an alternative component's characteristic pattern	Misleading cues create incorrect concepts and schemas, causing concept-formation around incorrect, misleading schema, and a search to confirm incorrect conclusions.
Dazzling	Obscure key characteristics, saturate perception by adding over-powering characteristics; blur characteristic patterns to increase observer uncertainty	Reduces perceptual effectiveness and lengthens time required for perception, reaction, concept formation, and situation assessment, while a search shifts to perceptual and information channels not subject to dazzle.
Red Flagging	Display key characteristics ostentatiously, make high information value patterns conspicuous ("wave a red flag"); generate observer suspicions	By attracting attention, creates and then exploits doubt and suspicions to mislead target about truth and falsehood. Depends on target doubting the veracity of the information because of the ease of the information collection.

Deception Tactics	Features of Deception Tactics	Psychological Consequences of Deception
Mimicking	Recreate or imitate familiar characteristic patterns; copy alternative characteristics; create fictitious entities	Stimulates incorrect concept formation for the mimic; making the unique cues of a real object harder to perceive.
Inventing	Create new characteristic patterns with high information value; synthesize realistic indicators; invent key components	Initiates and sustains incorrect concept formation; making the cues identifying the real character of the object harder to perceive.
Decoying	Create parallel characteristic patterns, forming immaterial entities or indicators; provide realistic characteristic patterns to increase observer certainty	Stimulates incorrect concept formation for the decoy; leading perception away from the cues identifying the real object; making the real object impossible to perceive (out of the field of view) or harder to perceive.
Double Play	Weakly and suspiciously suggest correct interpretation to reinforce incorrect interpretation; maintain or display real but suspicious characteristics to decrease observer acceptance	By suspiciously providing the correct interpretation, the double play creates and then exploits doubt and suspicions to mislead target about information truth and falsehood. Depends on target confusing the real veracity of the information with the doubtful veracity of the information source and channel.

best able to detect fraudulent information in financial statements used the following four processes sequentially:

- *Activation*: Detect inconsistencies between expectations and observations.
- *Detection*: Produce hypotheses about possible deceptive manipulations of the environment and adjust the assessments of evidence to reflect possible deception tactics.
- *Editing*: Modify initial hypotheses based on the deceptive manipulations and reassess observations.
- *Reevaluation*: Decide on appropriate actions to test the deception hypotheses.

Recent suggestions for training intelligence analysts to detect deception are consistent with Johnson's model. Whaley and Busby's *congruity theory and ombudsman method* [4] identifies information that must be collected to reveal inconsistencies and other cues to deception. R. V. Jones's *theory of spoof unmasking* [2] describes how to check the validity of evidence, highlight inconsistencies, and develop deception hypotheses.

One of the best-known intelligence analysis procedures is Heuer's *analysis of competing hypotheses* (ACH) [13]. ACH specifies how to consider inconsistent and anomalous information, develop competing hypotheses — including deception hypotheses — and test hypotheses in a manner that reduces susceptibility to cognitive limits and biases. ACH consists of the following steps:

1. Identify hypotheses to be considered.
2. List the significant evidence and assumptions for and against each hypothesis.
3. Draw tentative conclusions about the relative likelihood of each hypothesis.
4. Analyze the sensitivity of the conclusion to critical items of evidence.
5. Identify future observations that would confirm one of the hypotheses or eliminate others.

ACH is the basis of the decision aid we report in this paper. However, as outlined by Heuer, ACH is not specific enough to use for counter deception [5,6]. In the process of implementing a counter-deception decision process, we have filled in the gaps. We call this extended process ACH-CD, for *analysis of competing hypotheses-counter deception*.

Summarizing prior work, we know the basic cognitive biases and heuristics that cause deception to succeed and which reasoning procedures seem to offset them to help individuals detect deception. Because teaching elements of these procedures to analysts does not produce consistently effective deception detectors, a decision support system seems necessary. The next section describes the key part of such a system.

2.1.3   Implementing ACH-CD

This section describes how we use state-based plans, converted to Bayesian belief networks, to implement ACH-CD. Recall that the first step of ACH is to list alternative hypotheses. As implemented in ACH-CD, this is accomplished by generating alternate courses of action the adversary might use to accomplish his goal. Generating multiple courses of action compels the analyst to consider alternatives and avoid prematurely settling on one hypothesis because of a few salient observations or preconceptions. We use a domain independent task decomposition planning system called *Adversarial Planner* (AP) [14] to automate hypothesis generation.* Here we describe the parts of AP that relate directly to ACH-CD.

AP uses a task decomposition strategy that is consistent with many types of planning, including much of military planning. Figure 2.1.1 shows a typical action template used by AP.** These action templates are instantiated and fit together in sequences to make plans. AP starts with an abstract goal, refines it into successively more concrete (less abstract) subgoals, and terminates when a sequence of actions that accomplish each subgoal is found. In ACH-CD, alternate hypotheses can either be alternate goals or alternate plans to accomplish a given goal.

During plan generation, if an effect of a template unifies with the current subgoal, that template's expansion tells the planner what to do to accomplish the effect, but not how those subgoals are to be accomplished. Thus, the planner can consider alternative methods of accomplishing the subgoals. AP attempts to expand each alternative, creating a contingency plan when more than one action can fulfill a subgoal. This method is intended to help the user consider all the alternatives (Figure 2.1.2).

AP computes a temporal model of the plans it generates. The model consists of temporal constraints and numerical time points for each action's earliest and latest start and end times based on estimates of action duration. Temporal constraints among subgoals are specified in each abstract action's expansion. For example, the expansion in the template in Figure 2.1.1 has two temporal relations. "Series" means the subgoals that follow must be accomplished in the order listed. "Parallel" means that the enclosed subgoals may be accomplished in any order.*** Temporal reasoning is required when generating hypotheses in a situation where deception is possible. For example, a diversionary action might mask the beginning of an attack. When AP

---

* Later in this chapter, we give an example of what we call *strategic deception*, where automated course of action generation is not practical. Addressing such cases relies on elicitation of alternative hypotheses and the potential indicators of each. Further research on hypothesis generation of strategic intentions is essential to the continued development of counter-deception support methods [35,38].
** Symbols starting with a question mark ("?") denote variables that the planning algorithm must instantiate.
*** Any of the temporal relations in [36] may be used.

```
(define (durative-action transport)
    :parameters (?cargo - resource
                 ?dest - location)
    :vars (?td - TransportationDevice)
    :constraints (not (instance-of ?cargo 'TransportationDevice))
    :precondition (located ?td (located ?cargo))
    :expansion (series
                (parallel (contains ?td ?cargo)
                          (adequate_fuel ?td))
                (located ?td ?dest)
                (not (contains ?td ?cargo)))
    :effect (located ?cargo ?dest)
    :duration transport-duration)
```

FIGURE 2.1.1
A task decomposition action template.

generates contingency subplans, the temporal information is also used to determine if alternate hypotheses are mutually exclusive alternatives.

AP allows variables to designate resources. For example, the action in Figure 2.1.1 stipulates that some *Transportation Device* be available to transport the given object. Depending on the resources available, settling on a particular

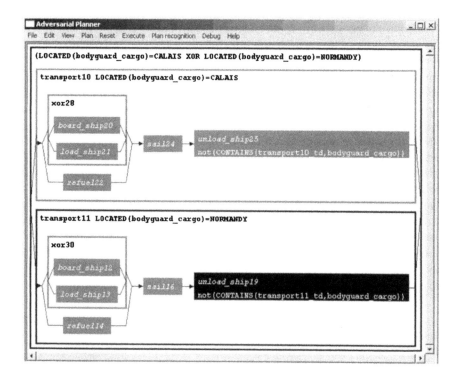

FIGURE 2.1.2
Contingency plan for D-Day invasion logistics. Highlight on the node representing unloading at Normandy indicates that it depends on an assumption that there are port facilities.

resource assignment is often not necessary until the plan is prepared for execution. As we are concerned with what might transpire rather than planning a specific course of action, the plan must represent all the possible assignments.

In contrast to classical planning systems, AP does not require that specific resources be enumerated to fulfill all plan parameters. This specification is necessary for counter deception because the observer is probably not aware of all the resources available to the adversary. In such cases, AP simply notes that resources of particular types are required.* In a counter deception, observing such a resource increases the probability that an alternative is viable. For example, if an adversary is developing nuclear weapons, a necessary precondition is to have raw materials such as uranium yellowcake. Whether the adversary possesses such resources might not be known with certainty to the analyst.

Typical state-based planning systems cannot generate plans unless all the preconditions required either hold in the initial situation or can be accomplished by a planned action. This condition is problematic when one is uncertain about the disposition and capacities of an adversary. To address ignorance, AP can assume preconditions not listed in the input situation,** allowing AP to develop competing hypotheses with incomplete knowledge and alternatives a user might not consider. Such precondition assumptions — if confirmed — tend to be key indicators to the adversary's true course of action, i.e., the key information the adversary is attempting to hide through denial.

With the capabilities listed above, AP is able automatically to generate competing hypotheses, fulfilling Steps 1, 2, and 3 of ACH. Figure 2.1.2 shows a very simple example that we will discuss later in the first application.

2.1.3.1 Converting Plans to Belief Networks

Recall Steps 3, 4, and 5 of ACH:

3. Draw tentative conclusions about the relative likelihood of each hypothesis.
4. Analyze the sensitivity of the conclusion to critical items of evidence.
5. Identify future observations that would confirm one of the hypotheses or eliminate others.

Heuer does not specify how to perform these steps, but Bayesian inference must be used to deal with uncertainty to avoid the errors we outlined in the first section of this chapter [6,10,15]. Unaided, Bayesian analysis sufficient for

---

* A number of heuristics are invoked to ensure that this requirement does not result in an intractable combinatorial explosion.
** As with assumed resources, this feature must be used parsimoniously.

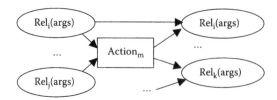

FIGURE 2.1.3
Segment of a belief network from a plan.

ACH-CD borders on impossible [16]. Therefore, we determined that automating the generation and analysis process would be necessary.

A *plan* is a partially ordered sequence of actions. In state-based planning, each action has an input situation and subsequent output situation. Situations are represented by sets of *propositions*.* To create a belief network from a plan, propositions that represent the preconditions of an action are the predecessor nodes of the node representing the action. The states of these nodes are the possible values of the proposition on the arguments at the time of the situation. For example, a precondition to your driving home this evening is that the proposition *has_fuel(<your automobile>)* is true during the time you will be driving.

When we convert a plan to a belief network, each action is represented by a node with two states: Succeed and fail. Action node beliefs are computed based on the states of the action's precondition nodes and a user-specified estimate of the probability of success of the action. Action nodes are predecessors of nodes representing their effects. Under typical persistence assumptions [17], a proposition's value persists until an action changes it. Thus, failure of an action means that the value of the proposition after the action was scheduled to execute would be the same as its value at the latest corresponding node before the action. Hence, a typical propositional node has two parents.** A representative segment of a belief network made from a plan is depicted in Figure 2.1.3.

AP's ACH-CD extensions are not difficult to represent in a belief network. Contingency nodes are treated as disjunctions. Designators that represent possible assignments become parent nodes of the actions where they originate. Designator nodes are treated the same way as action preconditions: They must take on legal combinations of values for the action to execute. The domain and range of these nodes is determined by constraints imposed by the actions that use the resources. For example, if you want to transport troops, the conveyance should not be a petroleum tanker. Finally, assumptions are treated like propositions without predecessors and have a default probability. Setting the default to a low probability, say 0.01, ensures that analysis will indicate all but the most trivial assumption as crucial to the hypothesized outcome.

---

* Thus, a situation specifies an equivalence class of states where the listed propositions hold.
** We allow the possibility of decay into a state of ignorance for propositions with a range of unknown cardinality.

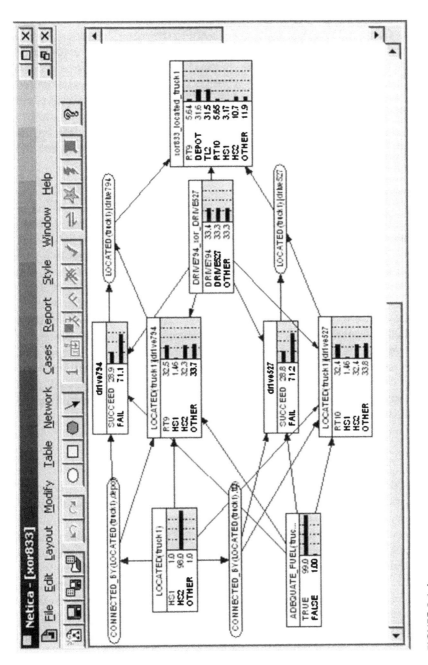

FIGURE 2.1.4
A Bayesian belief network for a simple contingency plan.

Figure 2.1.4 demonstrates what a Bayesian belief network from a very simple contingency plan generated by AP looks like. The plan consists of two alternatives: Drive *truck 1* from *HS2* via *RT10* to *TL2*, or, alternately, via *RT9* to *DEPOT*. The nodes on the left side of the figure represent the propositions in the initial situation that are relevant to the plan. The nodes labeled *drive734* and *drive527* represent the alternate actions in this very simple contingency plan. The nodes directly below the action nodes represent the possible locations of *truck1* during the respective actions. The node labeled *DRIVE734_xor_DRIVE527* represents the adversary's choice of actions and is the ultimate hypothesis to be tested. Note that it includes the possibility labeled *OTHER*, allowing for ignorance as to the choices available to the adversary. Finally, the node on the far right of the diagram represents the location of *truck1* after the plan is (or is not) executed.

2.1.3.2 Identifying Key Indicators

Steps 4 and 5 of ACH require identifying indicators of an adversary's intention. This point is where ACH is susceptible to bias when people — as they often do — fail to weigh the impact of evidence by its false positive rate [6,10] or misestimate prior probabilities. To avoid such errors, we treat each state in the network as a potential two-category dicotomizer [18]. A *dicotomizer* is a numerical criterion for determining if a data point is more likely to be in or out of a given set. In our case, the data point is an observation (i.e., evidence), and the "set" is a given hypothetical course of action. Whenever some uncertainty exists about the association of evidence with hypotheses, which is usually the case when considering a potential deception, some probability exists that the judgment will be incorrect. In pattern classification terminology, this is called the *error rate* of the dicotomizer. The minimum error rate discriminant for a two-category dicotomizer is

$$g(e_i) = \ln \frac{P(e_i \mid \omega)}{P(e_i \mid \varpi)} + \ln \frac{P(\omega)}{P(\varpi)}$$

In this formula, e_i is a possible observation of evidence (e.g., Iraq has purchased anodized aluminum tubes made to precise specifications), ω is a given hypothesis (e.g., Iraq has restarted its nuclear weapons development program), and g is a unitless real number in the interval [1,1]. In classical pattern classification, each time some evidence is observed, one should compute $g(e_i)$ and apply the decision rule that if $g(e_i) > 0$, then hypothesis ω is more likely than not (or the converse). We observed that the first component of the formula — the log likelihood of observing the evidence — is a way to rank the relative impact of observing any bit of evidence, either for or against a given hypothesis. Importantly, it also could indicate that certain evidence might be meaningless. As we will see in subsequent sections of this chapter, making an adversary misapprehend meaningless evidence is an important tool of a deceiver.

Note that in our implementation of ACH-CD, we do not compute the second term of the discriminant, the prior log likelihood of hypothesis ω. This decision is because the prior probabilities of the hypotheses are not necessary for focusing attention on the most important evidence of the alternatives. An important benefit of ignoring prior probabilities is that our algorithm avoids potentially biased prior assumptions about what is actually happening.

Including hypothesis generation, the ACH-CD consists of the following steps:

1. Generate a contingency plan representing one or more hypotheses about the possible course of action of an adversary (e.g., the Allies are invading France at Pas de Calais or at Normandy; Figure 2.1.2).

2. Create a belief network from the plan (Figure 2.1.4).

3. Enter a finding ω — typically the goal state of a plan or one of the branches of a contingency plan (e.g., the invasion will come at Normandy).

4. Record the conditional probability of all network states for those nodes that precede the hypothesized outcome ω, i.e., $P(e_i \mid \omega)$. This action is done because we are trying to identify evidence that will indicate the adversary's intent before they can accomplished it.

5. Remove the finding ω and enter a finding of its complement, $\overline{\omega}$ (e.g., the invasion will not come at Normandy).

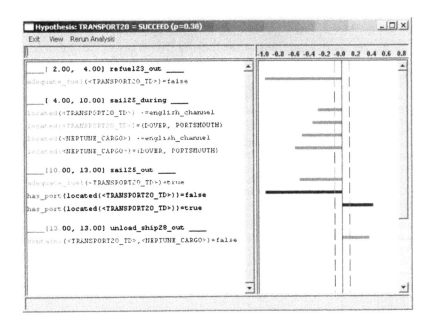

FIGURE 2.1.5
Diagnostic analysis of Normandy as the objective of D-Day. The most informative state is that Normandy must have port facilities.

6. For each state e_i, compute the log likelihood ratio, $\ln[P(e_i | \omega)/P(e_i | \varpi)]$

7. Apply a threshold to eliminate states that provide little evidence to distinguish between w and ϖ. On a $(-1.0, 1.0)$ scale, a threshold of ± 0.05 is typical.

8. Display the results, as in Figure 2.1.5.

The closer a state's (scaled) log likelihood is to 1.0 (−1.0), the more diagnostic that state is of $\omega (\varpi)$. These are the information states the deceiver must hide, as revealing them should lead the deceived to recognize the true course of action. Conversely, the counter-deceiver must look for just these states. Less diagnostic states are indicative of more hypotheses, often including the adversary's deceptive cover story.

The process outlined in this section addresses the main sources of bias that interfere with people's ability to recognize deception. The next section gives an example to illustrate how the process might be used for counter deception.

2.1.4   Applying Automated ACH-CD to D-Day

The D-Day invasion of France via Normandy was the turning point in World War II. A key factor in its success was the Allied campaign of deception that played on Germany's predisposing that the invasion would come via the Dover Straits in the vicinity of Pas de Calais. Pas de Calais was considered a favorable landing site for the invasion because it was on the most direct route to Germany, minimized flying time for Allied air cover, and would help the Allies defeat the German threat of V-1 flying bombs. An important consideration influencing the German assessment was that such an invasion requires port facilities to offload troops and supplies. The Pas de Calais region had several major ports; Normandy had none [19].

Allied planners knew they could not break through Germany's defensive forces if the German Army concentrated where the Allies landed. Therefore, the Allies had to convince the Germans to defend some point other than the true Allied objective. Pas de Calais was the obvious invasion objective, so the Allies had either to convince the Germans of another objective, or find an alternative to Pas de Calais and deceive the Germans so that they would not consider the true destination the primary objective. As we know from history, the latter is what happened.

Allied planners embarked on a deception campaign called BODYGUARD whose sub-plan FORTITUDE-SOUTH was to reinforce the German preconception of an Allied landing at Pas de Calais [20]. FORTITUDE-SOUTH was designed to convince the Germans that Normandy was a large-scale feint, a secondary assault designed to lure the German 15th Army to the west, to reinforce the 7th Army in Normandy, and away from the "primary objective" of Pas de Calais. The Allies carefully disguised the key fact that they would not need to capture a major port for over a month to support the Normandy invasion forces. This was feasible because the Allies had prepared transportable port facilities, called MULBERRY, to use on the Normandy beaches [20–22].

Special basins were excavated along the Thames and elsewhere to construct the enormous MULBERRY caissons which, measuring 60 by 200 feet wide and having the height of a five-story building, were far too massive to camouflage from German aerial observation. The Allied deception plan was designed to mislead the Germans about the purpose of these massive structures.

The Allies also hid their development of the first undersea oil pipelines, *PipeLines Under The Ocean* (PLUTO), that could supply adequate fuel to the Allied forces until deep-water French ports could be liberated [23]. Under a veil of secrecy, the PLUTO pump works were camouflaged as bungalows, gravel pits, and garages, and all critical activities were conducted at night. The 780-mile pipe system was always referred to by a cover term, as a "cable," and the RAF flew regular photographic control missions to ensure no visible traces of the PLUTO project were collected by German reconnaissance [23,24].

An entire Appendix of the FORTITUDE-SOUTH deception plan covered gambits to mislead the Germans about MULBERRY [20]. British-controlled double agents provided reports that hinted the massive constructions might be flood-control systems [22,25]. If the British code-breakers determined that Germans had detected the massive structures, a cover story would be put about that MULBERRY would be used at Pas de Calais. Despite Allied security, MULBERRY's existence leaked; by March 1944, over a dozen attempts had been made to communicate MULBERRY and PLUTO information to unauthorized persons [26]. Shown aerial photographs of MULBERRY, Hitler concluded they would replace the quays in the Pas de Calais channel ports that the Germans would destroy in the event of an invasion.

In April 1944, German propaganda alluded to MULBERRY: "We know exactly what you intend to do with these concrete units. You think you are going to sink them on our coasts in the assault...When you come to get underway, we're going to sink them for you." This compromise dismayed Allied planners until the code-breakers determined the Germans had erroneously concluded the MULBERRY structures were giant anti-aircraft gun towers [27]. On the eve of the D-Day landings, the Germans continued to focus on the need for deep-water ports and estimated "the first operational aim of the enemy must be to win large and capacious harbors. Le Harve and Cherbourg are primarily to be considered for this purpose" [21].

MULBERRY and PLUTO headed the Allied list of "important items which it is undesirable" for the enemy to see and were deemed "the greatest single factor of surprise" in the D-Day operation by Allied security authorities [26]. Following the June 6th D-Day landings, the British code-breakers assessed

```
(define (durative-action unload_ship)
    :ako unload
    :parameters (?td - Watercraft
                 ?cargo - object)
    :precondition (and (contains ?td ?cargo)
                       (has_port (located ?td)))
    :effect (not (contains ?td ?cargo))
    :probability-of-success 0.95
    :duration 3.0)
```

FIGURE 2.1.6
Unload action from transportation domain.

the Germans' views: "Though the area chosen for the landings (Normandy) comes as no surprise to Rommel and his senior as C-in-C West, von Rundstedt, as a result of the success of the deception programme both Rommel and von Rundstedt are convinced still larger ones in the Pas de Calais will follow these Normandy landings" [28].

After D-Day, PLUTO pipelines pumped 112 million gallons of fuel across the English Channel. The MULBERRYs landed over 2.5 million men, 500,000 vehicles, and 4 million tons of supplies (up to 11,000 tons daily) until December 1944, when Antwerp and Cherbourg were secured and repaired by the Allies [20,29,30]. For almost 2 months after D-Day, the German High Command continued to expect the Allied main effort would seize the channel ports. The German command kept the 15th Army in place, leaving it out of the battle for Normandy [21]. One historian concluded, "Few, if any, deception schemes have been more spectacularly put over" [31].

We implemented a simple version of BODYGUARD/FORTITUDE-SOUTH to illustrate our ACH-CD process. We started with an existing planning domain description for the transportation of supplies. The key action represents unloading a ship at a destination, depicted in Figure 2.1.6. We created an initial situation with the relevant facts of BODYGUARD. From these parts, we planned the transportation of invasion supplies from the south of England to alternate destinations in France.

The first plans we generated were from the Allied point of view and indicated nothing remarkable; with port facilities, you can supply an invasion at either Normandy or Pas de Calais, sensitive only to the usual mundane items such as availability of sufficient transport. But the Germans did not know about MULBERRY or PLUTO, so we deleted the proposition *has_port(Normandy)* from the initial situation* to represent the German preconception. The result was a single feasible plan with Pas de Calais as the destination — the upper branch of the contingency plan in Figure 2.1.2 — just as the Germans concluded.

The German High Command did not have our tool. If they had, their next step would be to allow AP to make assumptions for preconditions that cannot be accomplished with actions. The relevant part of the analysis on

---

* Alternately, we could have set its probability to 0.0.

the plan in Figure 2.1.2 is shown in Figure 2.1.5. The top two lines indicate the decisive factor that would make an invasion at Normandy feasible is port facilities. This fact is what the Allies knew to hide from the Germans or deceive them as to their purpose. The Germans should have entertained this deception hypothesis and tried to determine if the Allies could establish its key precondition.

2.1.5   Application without Automation: The Battle of Midway

Here we illustrate how ACH-CD addresses military counter deception by examining the Japanese planning for the Battle of Midway from the viewpoint of the *Imperial Japanese Navy* (IJN). We did not use automated planning in this example because the alternative hypotheses considered by the IJN are documented and the belief networks were easily developed by hand.

In planning for the attack on Midway, the IJN conducted war plan reviews, table-top exercises, and naval exercises using the same steps as Heuer's ACH but as disjointed planning episodes, not as an integrated analytic process.* Many of the tactical and operational problems that contributed to the defeat of the IJN at Midway were identified and discussed during these ACH-like exercises, but the Japanese planners ultimately dismissed the problems or met them with inadequate halfmeasures or inappropriate countermeasures. As it became apparent that IJN planning assumptions were incorrect during the early phases of the operation, the IJN failed to replan or adjust its operations. With the benefit of historical hindsight, we can see if arraying the intelligence for deception and other courses of action against the same hypotheses the IJN considered during its planning using ACH-CD would have alerted the IJN to the possibility of a U.S. Navy deception and ambush.

IJN planning hypotheses that surfaced before the battle in the IJN's ACH-like exercises were

- ω_1: U.S. Pacific Fleet would respond to the IJN invasion of Midway, sending its remaining aircraft carriers to attempt to retake Midway.

- ω_2: U.S. Pacific Fleet would not respond to the IJN invasion of Midway, letting Japan extend its naval base perimeter to mid-Pacific.

- ω_3: U.S. Pacific Fleet aircraft carriers will be waiting near Midway to attack the IJN Carrier Battle Group (*Kido Butai*).

The IJN received considerable intelligence and had operational and tactical experience before the Battle of Midway that was relevant to assessing these three hypotheses. Historical accounts show the IJN surfaced these hypotheses explicitly in its ACH-like exercises. However, the record is clear that the

---

* See [5] for historical sources and references.

IJN never integrated all the evidence and all of the hypotheses as advocated by Heuer. The three hypotheses above were raised and considered episodically and evidence was then dismissed piecemeal. The IJN planners never considered all the evidence against the three hypotheses as they assessed the strengths and weaknesses of their planning assumptions. Much of the evidence reflecting IJN tactical and operational weaknesses (e.g., in intelligence, reconnaissance, and surveillance, or ISR) was largely ignored in the design of their invasion of Midway, "Operation MI." In short, the IJN neither organized an assessment of all the intelligence and evidence in planning Operation MI nor acknowledged the impact of important evidence that reflected potential problems in executing the Operation MI plan.

Had the IJN drawn tentative conclusions using ACH and assessed the relative likelihood of each hypothesis based on the evidence they had available, $P(\omega_j \mid e_i)$, the IJN might have estimated that the U.S. Pacific Fleet carriers could as likely be waiting to ambush the *Kido Butai* (ω_3), or that the U.S. carriers would not respond as the IJN intended to Operation MI (ω_2), as was the hypothesis that the U.S. would respond as the IJN assumed to the invasion of Midway (ω_1).

Had the IJN assessed the evidence using ACH-CD, assessing the relative likelihood that the evidence would be observed given each of the hypotheses — $P(e_i \mid \omega_j)$ and $P(e_i \mid \overline{\omega}_j)$, the IJN might have concluded that ω_2 and ω_3 were as likely as ω_1, and that the evidence did not strongly support the IJN favored course of action, ω_1.

In other words, the IJN might have done much to overcome the first two major hurdles impairing their counter-deception analysis: *Poor anomaly detection* (missing anomalies or prematurely dismissing anomalies as irrelevant or inconsistent) and *misattribution* (attributing inconsistent or anomalous events to collection gaps or processing errors rather than to deception). Using ACH-CD to review the IJN planning assumptions against the available evidence, the IJN planners would have had reason to re-examine the soundness of their plan for Operation MI.

Furthermore, the IJN might have been able to overcome a major impediment to effective counter deception: Failure to *link deception tactics to deception hypotheses* (failure to recognize anomalous evidence as indicators of deception). The events and evidence available to the IJN before the Battle of Midway might have been assessed as possible indicators that the U.S. Pacific Fleet was using denial and deception tactics to conceal its true response to Operation MI. Evidence reflecting specific denial and deception tactics used to conceal ω_2 or ω_3, and inconsistent with ω_1, are shown in Table 2.1.2 and Table 2.1.3 (these tactics are described in Table 2.1.1). Note that these indicators included negative evidence (e.g., *No U.S. aircraft carrier sightings in South Pacific after 17 May 1942; No apparent objectives for U.S. carriers in South Pacific, late May 1942*).

We put this evidence of possible deception into a Bayesian belief network and linked the evidence to the relevant events. We set the prior probabilities at $\omega_1 = 0.70$, $\omega_2 = 0.20$, $\omega_3 = 0.09$, and ω_4 (other) $= 0.01$. We linked the events and hypotheses to the evidence using the ACH-CD procedures described

TABLE 2.1.2

Counter-Denial Indicators Available to IJN before the Battle

Denial Tactics	General Indicators of Denial Tactics	Indicators from Battle of Midway, May–June 1942
Masking	Key components missing, incomplete, or unaccounted High information value components unobserved where expected	U.S. aircraft carriers undetected in North Pacific vicinity of Hawaii or Midway, until 1–3 June 1942 Aerial surveillance aircraft in vicinity of Midway all shot down
Repackaging	Excessive, inconsistent, or unexpected alternative components detected Too many of the wrong things	U.S. aircraft carriers radio traffic prevalent in South Pacific Operation K thwarted Midway defenses and reconnaissance greatly enhanced, 3–4 Jun 1942 Aleutian, other North Pacific defenses not enhanced
Dazzling	Unexpected perceptual stimuli Atypical or uncommon patterns Unusual intensity, density, frequency	Apparent U.S. carrier losses, e.g., Battle of Coral Sea No apparent objectives for U.S. carriers in South Pacific, late May 1942.
Red flagging	Some, but not all, expected key components on obvious display Significant key components missing or unaccounted	U.S. submarines and scout aircraft at Midway deployed beyond normal operational limits, 1–3 June 1942. U.S. aircraft carriers undetected in North Pacific vicinity of Hawaii or Midway until 1–3 June 1942

TABLE 2.1.3

Counter-Deception Indicators Available to IJN before the Battle

Deception Tactics	Indicators of Deception Tactics	Indicators from Battle of Midway, May–June 1942
Mimicking	Observations inconsistent with expected numbers, patterns, configurations Insufficient fidelity, inexplicable anomalies Too many of the wrong things	U.S. aircraft carriers radio traffic prevalent in South Pacific No U.S. aircraft carriers sightings in South Pacific after 17 May 1942 No apparent objectives for U.S. carriers in South Pacific, late May 1942
Inventing	Insufficient history, resolution, fidelity Multi-dimensional "thinness" Inappropriate consistencies Exploitation of expectations, conditioning, reflexive control	U.S. aircraft carriers radio traffic prevalent in South Pacific No U.S. aircraft carriers sightings in South Pacific after 17 May 1942 "Midway short on water," "AF" short on water
Decoying	Insufficient history or contiguity Configuration and correlation anomalies Multi-spectral anomalies or resolution "thinness" Inconsistencies in spectral or dimensional resolution	No apparent objectives for U.S. carriers in South Pacific, late May 1942 U.S. aircraft carriers undetected in North Pacific vicinity of Hawaii or Midway until 1–3 June 1942
Double play	Inconsistent history or timing of discrediting information Discontinuous volume or intensity of disconfirming information Inconsistent selectivity of information Artificial consistency or uniformity of discrediting information	U.S. radio traffic in North Pacific of vicinity Hawaii, 1–3 June 1942

above, using intermediate probabilities representative of a counter-deception analyst's expectation of events (e.g., *U.S. aircraft carriers in South West Pacific*) and associated intelligence evidence items (*U.S. aircraft carrier radio inter-cepts*), given those events and those hypotheses (Intercepted, Not Inter-cepted). The likelihoods connecting the intelligence evidence to the relevant events and to the hypotheses reflect the possibility of American denial and deception. That is, the IJN counter-deception analyst should reason that, if ω_3 were true but event *U.S. CVs in SW Pacific* is false, the evidence *U.S. CVs SIGINT INTERCEPTED* would be very likely (P = 0.80) because such American radio deception would be highly consistent with ω_3.

Next, the evidence indicating possible denial and deception tactics is instantiated. For example, radio intercepts indicated the U.S. aircraft carriers (CVs) in the South West Pacific (SW Pac). IJN sighted U.S. aircraft carriers in the South West Pacific on May 17th but not after. Midway Island aerial and submarine reconnaissance ranges were increased from 500 to 700 miles (*MI_Recce_Expanded*). The impact of these denial and deception indicators on the hypotheses reflecting the enemy courses of action is dramatic. The probability of ω_1 drops from 0.70 to about 0.14, whereas ω_3 jumps from 0.09 to over 0.85.

2.1.5.1 The Role of ω_4: Other

The parameter ω_4: *other* in these models provides an index of noise versus signal in the interpretation of the intelligence. All the intelligence relative to ω_4 is coded as $P(e_i \mid \omega_4) = P(e_i \mid \varpi_4) = 0.50$. That is, because the evidence cannot discriminate between ω_4 and its opposite, ϖ_4, the likelihood of ω_4 represents a baseline of complete ignorance relative to hypotheses $\omega_1 - \omega_3$. When all the intelligence is noise, the likelihood of ω_4 approaches 1.0. Our model has the benefit of hindsight, so all the intelligence evidence is "pure signal" and can be interpreted to have discriminatory significance for hypotheses $\omega_1 - \omega_3$. Had noisy intelligence been added to the model, the strength of ω_4 would increase, but the likelihoods of $\omega_1 - \omega_3$ relative to each other would remain in the same relative proportions. The models would still reflect that the "pure signals" would indicate the possibility of American denial and deception tactics and the possibility of ω_2 and ω_3 as well as ω_1.

While the effect is powerful, it merely shows the impact of isolating the intelligence evidence that was most indicative of possible American denial and deception tactics and then determining how that evidence could impact beliefs in possible enemy courses of action (COAs). That is, the model might have been used by an IJN counter-deception analyst to make the case that the success of Operation MI was highly sensitive to indicators that IJN intelligence had observed. Such indicators strongly support the possibility of course of action ω_3, an American ambush. Although IJN intelligence had observed the indicators of American denial and deception tactics, the Japanese lacked the framework and business process that links indicators to hypotheses of deceptive courses of action.

TABLE 2.1.4

Probabilities for Enemy Courses of Action before and after Evidence

Enemy (U.S. Pacific Fleet) Courses of Action	Notional Prior Probability	Probability after Evidence is Considered
ω_1: U.S. Pacific Fleet would be surprised and would respond to the IJN invasion of Midway, sending its remaining aircraft carriers to attempt to retake Midway.	0.70	< 0.02
ω_2: U.S. Pacific Fleet would be surprised and would not respond to the IJN invasion of Midway, letting Japan extend its naval base perimeter to the mid-Pacific.	0.20	< 0.01
ω_3: U.S. Pacific Fleet would not be surprised and its carriers will be waiting near Midway to attack the IJN Carrier Battle Group (*Kido Butai*).	0.09	0.98
ω_4: Other	0.01	< 0.01

In making an overall assessment of the IJN intelligence, all key intelligence items should be weighed along with these denial and deception indicators, in keeping with the ACH-CD procedure. When all these evidence items are instantiated, as they might have been on the eve of the battle, the probabilities for the enemy (U.S. Pacific Fleet) courses of action change dramatically (Table 2.1.4). If the evidence available to the IJN in April, May, and through 3 June 1942 is instantiated in the belief network, the probabilities in Table 2.1.5 show how the accumulating intelligence might have shifted IJN beliefs in the various enemy courses of action in response to Operation MI.

TABLE 2.1.5

Probabilities for Enemy Courses of Action Based on Evidence Available to IJN in April, May, and up to 3 June 1942

Enemy (U.S. Pacific Fleet) Courses of Action	April 1942	May 1942	3 June 1942
ω_1: U.S. Pacific Fleet would be surprised and would respond to the IJN invasion of Midway, sending its remaining carriers to attempt to retake Midway.	0.69	0.29	< 0.02
ω_2: U.S. Pacific Fleet would be surprised and would not respond to the IJN invasion of Midway, letting Japan extend its naval base perimeter to the mid-Pacific.	0.20	0.01	< 0.01
ω_3: U.S. Pacific Fleet would not be surprised and its carriers will be waiting near Midway to attack the IJN Carrier Battle Group (*Kido Butai*).	0.10	0.70	0.98
ω_4: Other	0.01	< 0.01	< 0.01

The pattern in Table 2.1.5, the possible IJN appreciation of alternative U.S. Navy COAs, is symmetrical with the growing understanding of Japanese plans and intentions by the Pacific Fleet intelligence officers and commanders in Hawaii. By the end of May 1942, they had pieced together 90% of the plans for Operation MI, had successfully portrayed the remaining U.S. carriers as being in the South West Pacific through radio deception, and had planned their ambush for the Japanese carriers. When the *Kido Butai* arrived at Midway, the rest, as the saying goes, is history. Had the Japanese had a better counterdeception process, their situation assessment might not have been so far inferior to that of their opponent and the outcome might not have been so one-sided.

In summary, the IJN operational planners and intelligence analysts could have conceivably used an analysis and assessment akin to Heuer's ACH or our ACH-CD to review the available evidence and the planning assumptions underlying Operation MI, as well as the other COA hypotheses that were surfaced in the IJN ACH-like exercises. Using the ACH technique, they might have noted that the evidence available before the Battle of Midway becomes increasingly consistent with H_3, the deception hypothesis (the U.S. Pacific Fleet would ambush the IJN attack) and less consistent with H_1, the hypothesis on which Operation MI was based (that the Pacific Fleet would be surprised by Operation MI and would respond on the IJN timetable).

Had the IJN planners used tools such as we developed to support counterdeception, they would have been able to isolate those items of evidence that were most significant in supporting the various possible U.S. courses of action. These sensitivities can reinforce reconnaissance operations and counter planning, e.g., they could have aided the IJN in the design of planned or natural operational-intelligence "experiments," as recommended by Jones's [2] "theory of spoof unmasking," to force the U.S. Pacific Fleet to reveal more evidence of its intentions and dispositions. For example, a realistic IJN feint in the Coral Sea towards New Guinea or Australia in late May 1943 might have forced the U.S. Navy to react and thus have uncovered the key element of Nimitz's radio deception.

2.1.6 Future Applications of ACH-CD

We have described a process that extends Heuer's ACH as the basis of a counter-deception analysis. The key extensions of ACH to make ACH-CD are:

1. Denial and deception hypotheses as possible courses of action
2. Include hypothesis "Other" to assess the adequacy of the model as evidence is collected
3. Include explicit denial or deception events with other events
4. Include evidence or indicators of denial or deception tactics

The most difficult components for counter-deception analysis are Steps 3 and 4. Counter-deception analysts must understand denial and deception tactics (Table 2.1.1) and how these might occur in their situation (e.g., Table 2.1.2 and Table 2.1.3). Analysts must form clear expectations and anticipate the possible tactical situations, both with and without denial and deception tactics, and must be able to express expectations about denial and deception tactical events as observable and collectible indicators. Less demanding but still challenging is the analysts need to hypothesize how possible denial and deception courses of action serves the opponent's goals (Step 1).

Historically, most denial and deception goals and courses of action are relatively straightforward (simulate an attack on Pas de Calais, simulate U.S. aircraft carriers still in the South Pacific). Should the analyst select denial and deception goals inconsistent with the observed denial and deception tactics, the second component in the ACH-CD model (hypothesis "Other") tends to indicate the mismatch, which should motivate the analyst to reconsider the hypotheses and re-examine the evidence. We continue conducting experiments to assess how well our counter-deception process can reliably plan deceptions [32] and detect deceptions. Assessments of Iranian nuclear intentions and Iraqi denial and deception and nuclear weapons developments show the applicability of ACH-CD to contemporary cases.

We have developed a software system that automates ACH-CD for some problems. We are reviewing algorithms that detect anomalies to incorporate in our counter-deception process and tools [3,33–35]. We are creating a system to suggest deception tactics to keep an adversary from recognizing the true plan (dissimulation) and ways to give the adversary a false apprehension of reality (simulation). The temporal model generated with the alternate courses of action will be an important input to this process. After we complete a deception planning system, we will continue to extend it to counter-deception planning using AP's counter-planning process.

References

1. Hespanha, J.P., Atekan, Y., and Kizilocak, H.H., Deception in non-cooperative games with partial information, *Proc. of the 2nd DARPA-JFACC Symp. on Adv. in Enterprise Control*, San Diego, CA, July 2000.
2. Jones, R.V., Enduring principles: some lessons in intelligence, *CIA Stud. Intell.*, 38, 5, 1995.
3. Johnson, P.E., Grazioli, S., Jamal, K., and Berryman, R.G., Detecting deception: adversarial problem solving in a low base-rate world, *Cognit. Sci.* 25(3), May-June 2001.
4. Whaley, B. and Busby, J., Detecting deception: practice, practitioners, and theory, in Godson, R. and Wirtz, J.J. (Eds.), *Strategic Denial and Deception: The Twenty-First Century Challenge*, New Brunswick: Transaction Publishers, 2002.

5. Stech, F.J. and Elsaesser, C., Midway revisited: detecting deception by analysis of competing hypothesis, *72nd MORS Symposium*, Naval Postgraduate School, Monterey, CA, June 22–24, 2004.

6. Pope, S. and Jøsang, A., Analysis of competing hypotheses using subjective logic, CRC for Enterprise Distributed Systems Technology (DSTC Pty Ltd), The University of Queensland, Australia, 2005.

7. Central Intelligence Agency, *Press Release: Indian Nuclear Testing*, 1998, http://www.cia.gov/cia/public_affairs/press_release/archives/1998/pr051298.html

8. Whaley, B. and Bell, J.B. *Cheating: Deception in War and Magic, Games and Sports, Sex and Religion, Business and Con Games, Politics and Espionage, Art and Science*, New York: St. Martin's Press, 1982.

9. Gilovich, T., Griffin, D., and Kahneman, D., *Heuristics and Biases*, Cambridge, UK: Cambridge University Press, 2002.

10. Dawes, R.M. *Everyday Irrationality: How Pseudo Scientists, Lunatics, and the Rest of Us Systematically Fail to Think Rationally*, Boulder, CO: Westview Press, 2001.

11. Elsaesser, C., Explanation of probabilistic inference, in Kanal, L. N., Levitt, T. S., and Lemmer, J. F. (Eds.), *Uncertainty in Artificial Intelligence 3*, Amsterdam, The Netherlands: Elsevier Science Publishers B.V., 1989, 387–400.

12. Fischhoff, B., Debiasing, in Kahneman, D., Slovic, P., and Tversky A. (Eds.), *Judgment under Uncertainty: Heuristics and Biases*, Cambridge, UK: Cambridge University Press, 1982, 422–444.

13. Heuer, R.J. *Psychology of Intelligence Analysis*, Washington, DC: Central Intelligence Agency Center for the Study of Intelligence, 1999.

14. Applegate, C., Elsaesser, C., and Sanborn, J., An architecture for adversarial planning, *IEEE Trans. on Syst., Man, Cyberne.*, 20, 2, January 1990.

15. Schum, D.A. *The Evidential Foundations of Probab. Reasoning*, New York: John Wiley & Sons Inc., 1994.

16. Valtorta, M., Dang, J., Goradia, H., Huang, J., and Huhns, M., Extending Heuer's analysis of competing hypotheses method to support complex decision analysis, *Intl. Conf. on Intelligence Analysis*, McLean, VA, May 2005.

17. Shoham, Y., *Reasoning about Change*. Cambridge, MA: MIT Press, 1988.

18. Duda, R.O., Hart, P.E., and Stork, D.G., *Pattern Classification*, 2nd edition, New York: John Wiley & Sons Inc., 2001.

19. Blumenson, M., The emergence of infrastructure as a decisive strategic concept, *Parameters*, Winter 1999-2000, 39–45.

20. Hesketh, R., *Fortitude: The D-Day Deception Campaign*, New York: Overlook Press, 2000.

21. Howard, M., *Strategic Deception in the Second World War*, New York: Norton, 1995.

22. Masterman, J. C., *The Double-Cross System in the War of 1939 to 1945*, New Haven, CT: Yale University Press, 1972.

23. Anonymous, Code name: Operation Pluto, *Surveyor* (Quarterly Magazine from the American Bureau of Shipping), Spring 2001, 12–13.

24. Thomas, D., PLUTO, *Canadian Military Engineers Throughout History*, 1999, updated January 16, 2005, http://mypage.uniserve.ca/~echo2/Don.htm

25. Seaman,M., *Garbo: The Spy Who Saved D-Day*, Kew, UK: The National Archives, 2004.

26. Hinsley, F.H. and Simkins, C.A.G., *British Intelligence in the Second World War, Vol. 4: Security and Counter-Intelligence*, New York: Cambridge University Press, 1990.

27. Brown, A.C., *Bodyguard of Lies*, New York: Harper and Row, 1975.

28. Bletchley Park, History: June 1944, Accessed April, 2006, http://www. bletchleypark.org.uk/content/archive/jun1944.rhtm.

29. Alper, C., ARMADA: the D-Day landing fleet marks the largest invasion in history, *Military History Online*, 2004, http://www.militaryhistoryonline.com/wwii/dday/armada.aspx

30. Imperial War Museum, *Commemorative Visit Historical Background, Operation Overlord and the D-Day Landings in Normandy*, 2005, http://www.theirpastyourfuture.org.uk/upload/doc/D-Day_Historical_Word.doc

31. Holt, T., *The Deceivers: Allied Military Deception in the Second World War*, New York: Scribner, 2004.

32. Stech, F.J., Outguessed and one-behind: the real story of *The Man Who Never Was, Sixty Years On (Revisiting World War II): An International Conference*, Conflict Studies Research Group, History and Governance Research Institute, University of Wolverhampton, U.K., July 1–3, 2004.

33. Dragoni, A.F., Maximal consistency: theory of evidence and Bayesian conditioning in the investigative domain, *Proc. of the Fifth Iberoamerican Conf. on Computer Science and Law*, Havana, Cuba, 1996.

34. Santos, E., Jr. and Johnson, G., Toward detecting deception in intelligent systems, to appear in *Proc. of the SPIE: Defense and Security Symp.*, 5423, Orlando, FL, 2004.

35. Adsit, D.J., Effects of hypothesis generation on hypothesis testing in rule-discovery tasks, *J. Gen. Psych.*, January 1997.

36. Allen, J.F., A general model of action and time, *Artif. Intelligence* 23, 2, July 1984.

37. Siegel, N., Shepard, B., Cabral, J., Witbrock, M., Hypothesis generation and evidence assembly for intelligence analysis, *Intl. Conf. on Intelligence Analysis*, McLean, VA, May 2005.

2.2

Deception as a Semantic Attack

Paul Thompson

CONTENTS

Large-scale deceptions unfolding over relatively long time periods, like those described in Chapter 2.1, allow an extensive involvement of an experienced human analyst. In such cases, decision aids such as analysis of competing hypotheses-counterdesign (ACH-CD) are intended to support the human reasoning process. But what about other domains, such as information security on the Internet, where deceptions can be extremely frequent, numerous, and unfold within very short periods of time? Such deceptions require computational countermeasures that can act on very large volumes of information very rapidly and with minimal human involvement.

Attacks on computer and other networked systems can be categorized as physical, syntactic, and semantic [1]. *Physical attacks* are those that seek to destroy hardware. *Syntactic attacks,* such as worms and viruses, target the computer network infrastructure. *Semantic attacks* are directed against a decision making process, whether of an autonomous agent or of a human user of a computer system. Libicki described autonomous agents being fed misinformation in the battlespace as a primary example of a semantic attack. As an example of a semantic attack against the mind of a computer system user, consider a false or misleading discussion group posting that induces the user to become the victim of a "pump-and-dump" scheme whereby the price of a company's stock is manipulated. Semantic attacks specifically against the user of a system have also been referred to as *cognitive attacks,* or *cognitive hacking* [2,3]. As is the case with all deceptions described in this book, semantic attacks are directed at the mind of the system user, in contrast to physical and syntactic attacks, which operate against hardware or software systems. In this chapter, we use the more general term semantic attack to refer to attacks in the contexts of computer security, intelligence analysis, and military operations.

We describe two types of countermeasures against semantic attacks: Linguistic countermeasures and information trajectory modeling [2]. Linguistic countermeasures can be used in situations where either single or multiple sources of information exist. They can be used to determine the identity of an attacker or the fact that certain information is likely to be misinformation. Information trajectory modeling requires building a model of a source of information based on statistical historical data or an analytic understanding of how the information relates to the real world. For example, weather data coming from a single source (a website or environmental sensor) could be calibrated against historical databases (from previous years) or a predictive model (extrapolating from previous measurements). A large deviation would suggest that the information might be manipulated by an adversary. This chapter provides a hypothetical analysis of how information trajectory modeling could be used for financial fraud auditing.

Finally, we describe semantic attacks in the context of the proposed new scientific discipline of intelligence and security informatics. The National Science Foundation (NSF) and the National Institute of Justice have been holding an annual conference on the topic of intelligence and security informatics since 2003 [4]. The goal of this conference is to help establish a new science of intelligence and security informatics modeled after existing fields, such as bioinformatics. Misinformation and deception play a much more significant role in intelligence and security informatics than in other informatics disciplines, such as those concerned with scientific, medical, and legal publications. Accordingly, such a new science must concern itself with semantic attacks and countermeasures.

2.2.1 Semantic Attacks in Relation to Other Topics in This Book

As we discussed in Chapter 2.1, deception is characteristic of most adversarial situations. In Chapter 1.1, we described how inferences can be made about an adversary's intent based on observations and background knowledge about the adversary. Here we are less concerned with inferring an adversary's specific intent than with realizing that an adversarial situation exists in the first place, i.e., that a semantic attack is underway. As we discuss in Chapter 2.3, these adversarial situations are where opponents have partial information, but semantic attacks generally cannot be modeled as games. By contrast, some areas of computer security, such as honeynets [5], are adversarial environments similar to those of the military operations and games that we describe throughout this book. A *honeynet* is an environment that simulates an operational computer network. The actions taken by a hacker breaking into a honeynet are monitored by the honeynet so the intent of the hacker can be learned, much as we described in Chapter 1.1.

In Chapter 2.1, we described the ACH-CD model for detecting deception. ACH-CD has already been applied to financial fraud detection. In this chapter, we describe a technique for financial fraud detection, information trajectory modeling, which is a more autonomous approach rather than a tool to aid a human analyst. The information trajectory modeling approach that we describe is a hypothetical one that has not yet been implemented, although several applications have been built with the Process Query System [6], the framework in which the approach would be implemented. The hypothetical implementation that we describe in this chapter also has much in common with the dynamic game problems with uncertainties that we discuss in Chapter 3.3. Finally, although we do not discuss the matter further here, Thompson et al. [3] have described an information-theoretic value of information analysis similar to our discussion in Chapter 2.3.

2.2.2 Changing the Behavior of Humans

Computer and network security present great challenges to our evolving information society and economy. The variety and complexity of cybersecurity attacks that have been developed parallel the variety and complexity of the information technologies that have been deployed. Physical and syntactic attacks operate totally within the fabric of the computing and networking infrastructures [2]. For example, the well-known Unicode attack against older, unpatched versions of Microsoft's® Internet Information Server (IIS) can lead to root/administrator access [7]. Once such access is obtained, the attacker can engage in any number of undesired activities. For example, files containing private information such as credit card numbers can be downloaded and used by an attacker. Such an attack does not require any intervention by users of the attacked system. By contrast, a semantic attack requires some change in users' behavior, accomplished by manipulating their perception of reality. The attack's desired outcome cannot be achieved unless human users change their behaviors in some way. Users' modified actions are a critical link in a semantic attack.

Provision of misinformation, the intentional distribution or insertion of false or misleading information intended to influence reader's decisions or activities, is a semantic attack. The Internet's open nature makes it an ideal arena for the dissemination of misinformation. Semantic attacks differ from social engineering, which (in the computer domain) involves a hacker's psychological tricking of legitimate computer system users to gain information, e.g., passwords, to launch an autonomous attack on the system.

Most analyses of computer security focus on the time before misinformation is posted, i.e., on preventing unauthorized use of the system. Semantic attacks take place when a user's behavior is influenced by misinformation. At that point, the focus is on detecting that a semantic attack has occurred and on possible legal action. Our concern is with developing tools to prevent semantic attacks, that is, tools that can recognize and respond to misinformation before a user acts based on the misinformation (Figure 2.2.1).

As we said, users' modified actions are a critical link in a semantic attack's sequencing. For a concrete example of a semantic attack, consider the following news report [8]:

"Friday morning, just as the trading day began, a shocking company press release from Emulex (Nasdaq: EMLX) hit the media waves. The release claimed that Emulex was suffering the corporate version of a nuclear holocaust. It stated that the most recent quarter's earnings would be revised from a $0.25 per share gain to a $0.15 loss in order to comply with Generally Accepted Accounting Principles (GAAP), and that net earnings from 1998 and 1999 would also be revised. It also said Emulex's CEO, Paul Folino, had resigned and that the company was under investigation by the Securities and Exchange Commission. Trouble is, none of it was true. The real trouble was that Emulex shares plummeted from their Thursday close of $113 per share to $43 — a rapid 61% haircut that took more than $2.5 billion off of the company's hide — before the shares were halted an hour later. The damage had been done: More than 3 million shares had traded hands at the artificially low rates. Emulex vociferously refuted the authenticity of the press release, and by the end of the day the company's shares closed within a few percentage points of where they had opened."

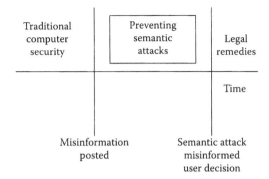

FIGURE 2.2.1
Countermeasures can detect misinformation before user behavior is altered.

A 23-year-old individual named Mark Jacob fraudulently posted the bogus release on Internet Wire, a Los Angeles press release distribution firm. The release was picked up by several business news services and widely redistributed without independent verification. The speed, scale, and subtlety with which networked information propagates have created a new challenge for society outside the domain of classical computer security, which has traditionally been concerned with ensuring that all use of a computer and network system is authorized.

The use of information to affect the behavior of humans is not new. Language, or more generally, communication, is used by one person to influence another. Propaganda has long been used by governments or by other groups to influence populations, particularly in times of war. Although the message conveyed by propaganda or other communication intended to influence might be believed to be true by the propagator, it usually is presented in a distorted manner so as to have maximum persuasive power and is often deliberately misleading or untrue. Propaganda is a form of perception management. Other types of perception management include psychological operations in warfare, consumer fraud, and advertising. Deception detection has long been a significant area of research in the disciplines of psychology and communications.

2.2.3 Perception Management

Perception management is pervasive in contemporary society. Its manifestation on the Internet is one aspect of the broader phenomenon. Not all perception management is negative (e.g., education can be considered a form of perception management) nor is all use of perception management on the Internet a semantic attack. Clearly, the line between commercial uses of the Internet such as advertising — which would not be considered a type of semantic attack — and manipulation of stock prices by the posting of misinformation in news groups — which would be so considered — is a difficult one to draw.

For example, the integrity of a system would include correctness or validity of the information the user gets from the system. In this context, the integrity of a computer system can be defined more broadly than the definition implicit in Landwehr's classic definition of computer security in terms of confidentiality, integrity, and accessibility [9]. Breaches in computer security can be viewed as violations of the semantics of the computer system, i.e., the intended operation of the system. In this sense, the World Wide Web itself can be seen as a computer system used for communication, e-commerce, and so on. As such, activities conducted over the Web that violate the norms of communication or commerce — for example, fraud and propaganda — are considered to be instances of semantic attacks even if they do not involve illegitimate access to a computer. A person might maintain a website that presents misinformation with the intent of influencing viewers of the information to engage in fraudulent commercial transactions with the owner of the website.

2.2.4   Semantic Attacks and Information Warfare

A definition of semantic attacks closely related to ours has been described by Schneier [10], who characterizes semantic attacks as "attacks that target the way we, as humans, assign meaning to content." He goes on to note, "Semantic attacks directly target the human/computer interface, the most insecure interface on the Internet."

Denning's [11] discussion of *information warfare* overlaps our concept of semantic attacks. Denning describes information warfare as a struggle over an information resource by an offensive and a defensive player. The resource has an exchange and an operational value. The value of the resource to each player can differ depending on factors related to each player's circumstances. The outcomes of offensive information warfare are: Increased availability of the resource to the offense, decreased availability to the defense, and decreased integrity of the resource. Applied to the Emulex example, described above, Jakob is the offensive player and Internet Wire and the other newswire services are the defensive players. The outcome is a decreased integrity of the newswires' content. Viewed as a semantic attack, while the above analysis would still hold, the main victims of the attack would be the investors who were misled. In addition to the decreased integrity of the information, an additional outcome would be the money the investors lost.

2.2.5   Deception Detection

Deception of detection in interpersonal communication has long been a topic of study in the fields of psychology and communications [12]. The majority of interpersonal communications are found to involve some level of deception. Psychology and communications researchers have identified many cues that are characteristic of deceptive interpersonal communication. Most of the this research has focused on the rich communication medium of face to face communication, but more recently other forms of communication have been studied such as telephone communication and computer-mediated communication [13]. A large study is underway [14] to train people to detect deception in communication. Some of this training is computer-based. Most recently, a study has begun to determine whether psychological cues indicative of deception can be automatically detected in computer-mediated communication (e.g., e-mail) so that an automated deception detection tool might be built [13].

2.2.6   Semantic Attacks and Intelligence
and Security Informatics

The NSF has supported the development of a new science of intelligence and security informatics [4] over the past several years by holding an annual conference on the topic. Intelligence and security informatics is seen by the NSF as a science analogous to bioinformatics, or medical informatics, i.e., as a science addressing information processing related to security and intelligence analysis. Based on the papers presented at these conferences, a consensus view exists that data mining, visualization, and link analysis technology are essential ingredients of this new science. However, considering the role of semantic attacks in intelligence and security informatics is important. Intelligence and security analysts should also be provided with an analysis environment supporting mixed-initiative interaction with both raw and aggregated data sets [15]. Because analysts need to defend against semantic attacks, this environment should include a toolkit of countermeasures against semantic attacks. For example, if faced with a potentially deceptive news item from the Foreign Broadcast Information Service (FBIS) [16], a U.S. government news service with an automated countermeasure might provide an alert using adaptive fraud detection algorithms or through a retrieval mechanism allowing the analyst to quickly assemble and interactively analyze related documents bearing on the potential misinformation.

Information or document retrieval, developed historically to serve the needs of scientists and legal researchers, among others. Despite occasional hoaxes and falsifications of data in these domains, the overwhelming expectation is that documents retrieved are honest representations of attempts to discover scientific truths or to make a sound legal argument. This assumption does not hold for intelligence and security informatics. Most information retrieval systems are based either on an exact match with Boolean logic, by which the system divides the document collection into those documents matching the logic of the request and those that do not, or on *ranked retrieval*. With ranked retrieval, a score is derived for each document in the collection based on a measure of similarity between the query and the document's representation, as in the vector space model [17] or based on a probability of relevance [18].

Although not implemented in existing systems, a utility-theoretic approach to information retrieval [19] shows promise for a theory of intelligence and security informatics. In information retrieval, predicting relevance is hard enough. Predicting utility, although harder, would be more useful. When information contained in, say, a FBIS document, might be misinformation, then the notion of utility-theoretic retrieval becomes more important. The provider of the content might have believed the information to be true or false, aside from whether it was true or false in some objective sense. The content might be of great value to the intelligence analyst, whether it is true or false, but in general, knowing not only whether it was true or false but also whether the provider believed it to be true or false would be important. Current information retrieval algorithms would not take any of these complexities into account in calculating a probability of relevance.

Predictive modeling using the concepts of semantic attacks and utility-theoretic information retrieval can be applied in two intelligence and security informatics settings that are mirror images of each other, i.e., the user's model of the system's document content and the system's model of the user as a potential malicious insider. Consider an environment where an intelligence analyst accesses sensitive and classified information from intelligence databases. The accessed information itself might represent semantic attacks coming from the sources from which it has been gathered (e.g., FBIS documents). As discussed above, each of these documents will have a certain utility for the analyst, based on the analyst's situation, on whether or not the documents contain misinformation, and — if the documents do contain misinformation — whether or not the analyst can determine that the misinformation is present. Alternately, the analyst might be a malicious insider engaged in espionage. The document system will need to have a cost model for each of its documents and will need to build a model of each user based on the user's transactions with the document system and other external actions.

Denning's theory of information warfare [11] and an information-theoretic approach to the value of information [20] can be used to rank potential risks given the value of each document held by the system. Particular attention should be paid to deception on the part of the trusted insider to evade detection. Modeling the value of information to adversaries will enable prediction of which documents are likely espionage targets and will enable development of hypotheses for opportunistic periods and scenarios for compromise. These models will be able to detect unauthorized activity and predict the course of a multistage attack so as to inform appropriate defensive actions.

Misinformation resulting from semantic attacks plays a much more prominent role in intelligence and security informatics than it has played in traditional informatics disciplines. In turn, the status of content as information or misinformation influences its utility for users. Countermeasures are needed to detect and defend against semantic attacks.

2.2.7   Current Countermeasures for Semantic Attacks

What countermeasures are used against semantic attacks in practice? The Internet Enforcement Office of the Securities and Exchange Commission (SEC) is interested in preventing fraud perpetrated via pump-and-dump schemes and some indication has been found in the press [21] that the SEC may have tools that can be used to defend against pump-and-dump schemes. Nevertheless, as far as we know, no public discussion has been documented of these tools. Academic research projects and prototypes have also been developed to detect financial and tax fraud. A research project is also currently underway in this area at MITRE [22] using the ACH-CD model that we discussed in Chapter 2.1. Additionally, as phishing, pharming, and identity theft have become increasingly major problems in recent years, commercial tools have been developed that attempt to detect these attacks.

While one might argue that pump-and-dump schemes are of relatively small significance and that the authentication-based commercial tools that address phishing, pharming, and identity theft are adequate solutions, millions of dollars are lost to pump-and-dump schemes and much larger losses are involved in financial fraud such as the Enron case. Furthermore, while the significance of the U.S. vulnerability to strategic cyberattacks remains controversial, exercises such as LIVEWIRE [23] have shown the high financial costs that could be associated with such attacks.

2.2.8   New Countermeasures for Semantic Attacks

Technologies for preventing, detecting, and prosecuting semantic attacks are still in their infancies. Given the variety of approaches to and the very nature of semantic attacks, preventing semantic attacks reduces either to preventing unauthorized access to information assets in the first place or detecting posted misinformation before user behavior is affected (that is, before behavior is changed but possibly after the misinformation has been disseminated). The latter may not involve unauthorized access to information, as in pump-and-dump schemes that use newsgroups and chat rooms. By definition, detecting a successful semantic attack would involve detecting that the user behavior has already been changed. We are not considering detection in that sense at this time.

Here, our discussion of methods for preventing semantic attacks is restricted to approaches that could automatically alert users of problems with their information source or sources (information on a webpage, newsgroup, chat room, and so on). Techniques for preventing unauthorized access to information assets fall under the general category of computer and network security and are not considered here. Similarly, detecting that users have already modified their behaviors as a result of the misinformation, namely that a semantic attack has been successful, can be reduced to detecting misinformation and correlating it with user behavior.

We discuss two approaches to countermeasures for semantic attacks in some detail: Information trajectory modeling and linguistics. Cybenko et al. [2] describe additional countermeasures. Information trajectory modeling is an example of a countermeasure against attacks with a single source of information, whereas news verification is a countermeasure for attacks with multiple sources of information. The use of linguistic techniques in computer security has been pioneered by Raskin and colleagues at Purdue University's Center for Education and Research in Information Assurance and Security [24]. However, their work has not addressed countermeasures against semantic attacks.

2.2.9   Information Trajectory Modeling

As an interesting aside, consider the storylines of many well-scripted mystery novels or films. We believe that the most satisfying and successful stories involve a sequence of small deviations from what is expected. Each twist in the story is believable but when aggregated, the reader or viewer has reached a conclusion quite far from the truth. In the context of semantic attacks, this end is achieved by making a sequence of small deviations from the truth, not one of which fails a credibility test on its own. However, the accumulated deviations are significant and surprise the reader or viewer who was not paying much attention to the small deviations one by one. Yet a small number of major "leaps of faith" would be noticed and such stories are typically not very satisfying. Modeling information sources is done on a case-by-case basis as determined by the availability of historical data and the suitability of analytic modeling.

2.2.10   Linguistic Countermeasures to Semantic Attacks

Linguistic countermeasures to semantic attacks such as pump-and-dump schemes might take at least two forms. First, a careful human reader of misinformation (e.g., exaggerated pump-and-dump scheme postings on the Web about a company's expected stock performance) can often detect the misinforming posting from other legitimate postings, even if these legitimate postings are also somewhat hyperbolic. Second, pump-and-dump schemes on the Internet are often carried out by a single or a small number of perpetrators, each with multiple user accounts. This attribute conveys the impression that perhaps hundreds of individuals are expressing similar opinions about a company. Linguistic techniques can be used to determine that the information has a few or only one author.

Authorship attribution using stylometry is a field of study within statistics and computational linguistics with a long history. Since Mosteller and Wallace's [25] seminal work on authorship attribution, statistical linguistics approaches have been used to recognize the style of different writings. In their work, this stylistic analysis was done to determine the true author of anonymous Federalist papers where the authorship was disputed. Kessler, Nunberg, and Schütze [26] developed and tested algorithms to automatically detect the genre of text using similar stylistic analysis. This approach to genre analysis is within the framework of corpus linguistics, i.e., based on a statistical analysis of general word usage in large bodies of text. The work on deception detection in the psychology and communications fields is based on a more fine-grained analysis of linguistic features, or cues. Psychological experiments have been conducted to determine which cues are indicative of deception. To date, this work has not led to the development of software tools to automatically detect deception in computer-mediated communication, but researchers see the development of such tools as one of the next steps in this line of research [13].

Burrows [27] developed a principal components analysis approach to authorship attribution in the field of literary and linguistic computing. Rao and Rohatgi [28] have shown that Burrows' techniques can be employed even more successfully with text taken from the Internet. Stylometry techniques can be used to determine the likelihood that two documents of uncertain authorship were written by the same author, or that a document of unknown authorship was written by an author from whom sample writings are available. Similarly, given a set of documents with several authors, partitioning the documents into subsets of documents all written by the same author is possible. Two parameters are used in such techniques: The data requirements per pseudonym and the discriminating power of the technique. Using only semantic features, Rao and Rohatgi demonstrated that anonymity and pseudonymity cannot preserve privacy. They did exploratory research to confirm that inclusion of syntactic features — e.g., misspellings or other idiosyncratic features much more prevalent in Web, as opposed to published, documents — could provide stronger results.

2.2.11 News Verification: An Instance of Multiple Source Semantic Attacks

Here we discuss possible approaches to preventing semantic attacks when multiple, presumably redundant, sources of information are available about the same subject of interest. This situation is clearly the case with financial, political, and other types of current event news coverage. Several aspects of information dissemination through digital network media, such as the Internet and the World Wide Web, make semantic attacks possible and relatively easy to perform. Obviously, enormous market pressures exist on the news media and on newsgroups to quickly disseminate as much information as possible. In the area of financial news in particular, competing news services strive to be the first to give reliable news about breaking stories that impact the business environment. Such pressures are at odds with the time-consuming process of verifying accuracy. A compromise between the need to quickly disseminate information and the need to investigate its accuracy is generally not easy to achieve. Elsewhere, we have given an information-theoretic analysis of this problem in terms of the value of information [3].

In principle, automated software tools could help people make decisions about the veracity of information they obtain from multiple networked information systems. A discussion of such tools, which could operate at high speeds compared with human analysis, follows. The problem of detecting misinformation on the Internet is much like that of detecting other forms of misinformation in newsprint or verbal discussion. Reliability, redundancy, pedigree, and authenticity of the information being considered are key indicators of the overall "trustworthiness" of the information. The technologies of collaborative filtering and reputation reporting mechanisms have been receiving much attention recently, especially in the area of online retail sales. Reputation reporting is commonly used by the many online price comparison services to inform potential customers about vendor reliability. The reliability rating is computed from customer reports. Another technology, closely related to reliability reporting, is collaborative filtering. This technique can be useful in semantic situations that involve opinions rather than hard, objective facts. Both of these approaches involve user feedback about information they receive from a particular information service, building up a community notion of reliability and usefulness of a resource. The automation in this case is in the processing of the user feedback, not the evaluation of the actual information itself.

2.2.12 Process Query Systems for Information Trajectory Countermeasures

Let us now describe how the information trajectory countermeasure to detect fraudulent financial practices could be implemented using a Process Query System (PQS). PQS [6] is a software system that has been implemented through several government contracts. It provides a generic environment to support multiple target hypothesis tracking and thus could be used to implement an information trajectory countermeasure designed to detect fraud in financial auditing. Stech and Elsaesser [22] describe an application of the ACH-CD model discussed in Chapter 2.1 to financial fraud auditing. Whereas ACH-CD is an automated aid to the human analyst, information trajectory modeling is a data mining approach that, while still requiring a final decision by a human analyst, is more automated than ACH-CD.

PQSs allow users to define processes and make queries against databases of processes using the process definitions as queries. The PQS parses the process description and executes queries against the databases of processes. An information trajectory model can be represented as processes. In the financial fraud detection application, the processes would be the expected flows of financial information.

2.2.12.1 General Architecture of a PQS

A PQS consists of three main components (Figure 2.2.2). These components are a user interface, the TRAcking and Fusion ENgine (TRAFEN), and message-

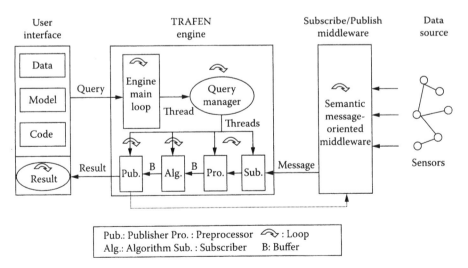

FIGURE 2.2.2
Process Query System (PQS) architecture.

oriented middleware (MOM). Distributed sensor networks sense and acquire data. In existing PQS applications, these networks are physical sensors on a battlefield or software sensors monitoring traffic flowing through computer networks. In the financial fraud auditing application, these would also be software sensors, monitoring flows of financial data.

The input from these sensors are fed through various *fuselets*, or lightweight data fusion processing nodes, that apply various signal processing or other logic to the raw sensor data. The output of the fuselets are messages that are published to the MOM, classified under various specific topic headings. In the battlefield example, such a heading might be "ground vehicle." In the financial fraud auditing example, a heading might be "earnings statement." The front-end interface allows a user or an application program to define process models using high-level abstractions such as hidden Markov models (HMM). The PQS architecture also supports a variety of other abstractions, including Petri nets and various weak sequential models. These models can be more appropriate when the strong assumptions of network topology and the availability of probabilities of HMMs are not met. The user-defined process models and the message topics are fed into the back-end TRAFEN. TRAFEN parses the process model and subscribes to the messages, available via the MOM, that match the processes specified by the user. In general, these messages could come from sensors on the battlefield, intelligent databases, human observers, or from a variety of other sources. In the financial fraud auditing application, messages would come from software sensors detecting irregularities in financial statements. Next, multiple hypothesis tracking (MHT) algorithms are used with the user-defined processes to uncover the hidden relationships among the observations and to construct hypotheses regarding the true state of the system being observed. Hypothesis results and predictions are used to support decision making. These results and predictions can also be published back to the MOM as message sources for other fusion engines. The sensor networks themselves, hardware or software, can subscribe to the hypotheses and predictions as a form of feedback with which to optimize their sensing.

Users can browse and select message subscription topics using the user interface. They can also define process models using high-level abstractions, such as HMMs. *Process models* describe the state transitions of tracked targets, which evolve according to the model-based constraints. For physical objects, these constraints might be known kinematic laws. The state-transition models and their corresponding process definitions can be described with abstractions including, among others, state equations, HMMs, and rule-based models. For example, the PQS graphical user interface provides standard templates with which the user can define the states and transitions of an HMM. The process model and its parameters along with the event subscription topics are then formulated as a process query that is submitted to the TRAFEN engine.

MOM is a communication mechanism that permits loosely coupled applications to communicate asynchronously in a connectionless manner. The applications only need to know the message format to communicate. MOM uses a publish-subscribe architecture for messaging that allows delivery to more than one subscriber at a time. Messages are clustered according to specific topic groups in the MOM. PQS uses a semantic MOM based on Sun's Java Messaging Service and DARPA Agent Markup Language (DAML) for message topics and content. Sensor fuselets publish observation messages using specific topic headings. TRAFEN receives all messages on a given topic from the MOM and begins the multiple hypothesis tracking process. This clustering of messages into topics divides the set of targets and measurements into small independent groups, so that these smaller tracking problems can be solved in parallel instead of trying to solve a single large tracking problem. This structure helps manage the size of the hypothesis space and the complexity of the MHT algorithms.

2.2.12.2 Tracking and Fusion Engine (TRAFEN)

TRAFEN is designed to be a general fusion engine capable of implementing a variety of multiple hypothesis tracking/fusion processes. For example, when tracking physical objects (e.g., vehicles), TRAFEN uses Reid's multiple hypothesis tracking algorithm [29] and Bayesian analysis to determine the possible associations of observations to tracked targets. Each association is a unique hypothesis whose probability is calculated. Reid's algorithm is recursively used to calculate the likelihood that each new observation is associated with each of the existing hypotheses. For physical objects, a Kalman filter is used to predict the object's state at a future time.

The main components of TRAFEN are MHT algorithms, prediction models, hypothesis management and storage, and event subscription and publication. A PQS has MHT algorithms implemented as modules as well as standard prediction-model implementations. The process query, sent to TRAFEN by the user, includes parameters that are inputs to the prediction models. The MHT algorithms are run with the instantiated process model and messages from the MOM. Hypothesis management includes assigning observations to tracks, where possible. An observation that is not assigned to an existing track becomes the start of a tentative new track. If the new tentative track passes quality tests, it then becomes a confirmed track. As observations continually update the system, low-quality tracks are deleted.

2.2.12.3 Multiple Hypothesis Tracking

PQS includes a Kalman filter, a recursive solution for the discrete-data linear filtering problem [29]. At any point during the execution of the recursive algorithm, the MHT algorithm retains the hypotheses with the highest likelihoods. As each new observation is recorded, the algorithm generates all possible hypotheses that can explain the observation. Three possible situations can occur:

- The observation is added to one of the existing tracks based on a calculation of the distance of the observation from the predicted next observation for that track.
- The observation is determined to represent a new target and a new track is initiated.
- The observation is determined to be noise and is discarded.

Thus, every time a new observation is added, each hypothesis from the set of current hypotheses generates several more hypotheses. To cut down on the explosion of hypotheses, pruning is performed after each observation is added to remove less likely hypotheses.

An early computer security application of PQS was to automatically detect a propagating worm on the Internet by monitoring Internet Control Message Protocol-Destination Unreachable (or ICMP-T3) messages [6]. An ICMP-T3 message is sent by a router that has been configured to do so when an attempt is made to reach a nonexistent Internet Protocol (IP) address. This message can be a sign of a worm, which randomly scans an address space as part of its strategy for propagating itself. Figure 2.2.3 shows the percentage of vulnerable machines infected when the PQS system detects a simulated worm. The x-axis is the number of addresses in the simulated network (in thousands) and the y-axis is the percentage of vulnerable machines that the worm infects before being detected. In this simulation, 25% of the address space was reachable (meaning that a machine exists at that address), 1% of the address space was both reachable and vulnerable to being infected by the

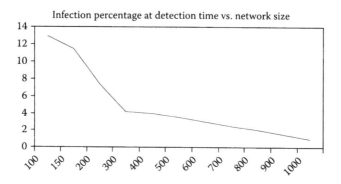

FIGURE 2.2.3
The percentage of vulnerable machines infected at the time PQS detects a simulated worm. (From Berk, V. et al., Proceedings of the 7th World Multiconference on Systematics, Cybernetics, and Informatics, 2003. With permission.)

worm, and 2% of routers were configured to send ICMP-T3 messages. As shown by the graph in Figure 2.2.3, detection performance increases as the size of the simulated Internet increases. For example, under these assumptions, with a network size of 1 million addresses, PQS would detect a worm before 1% of vulnerable machines were infected.

2.2.13   Tracking Hypotheses in the Financial Fraud Domain

In Chapter 2.1, we discussed the ACH-CD model for deception detection. There, ACH-CD was applied to analyzing deception in two military operations. Stech and Elsaesser have also applied ACH-CD to financial fraud auditing with a system called Turbo-Fraud [22]. Turbo-Fraud has a three layer Bayesian belief network model. The top level is a node that provides a score for an auditor alert. The middle level is a network based on Schilit's [30] seven corporate manipulation tactics. For example, one such tactic would be "shifting current expenses to a later or earlier period." The bottom layer consists of 31 of Schilit's red flag warning sign indicators of deception. These bottom layer nodes are set to be true or false. For example, one warning sign is "long-term debt increased, yet interest expense decreased." Stech and Elsaesser note that their model is a relatively simple, robust implementation. With PQS, building a more complicated process model of financial fraud would be possible, based on the expert knowledge of accountants. An empirical question yet to be determined is whether a more complicated process model might yield significantly improved performance over a simpler model, such as Turbo-Fraud. With the ACH-CD approach, an analyst would apply his expertise to the interpretation of results provided by the Bayesian belief network model. The key difference between the PQS and ACH-CD approaches is that PQS approach would be more autonomous and capable of detecting fraud in real time.

As an example of how PQS might be used in this domain, consider the case study of accounting fraud at MiniScribe discussed by Shilit [30]. A total of 22 warning signs are used in this analysis. The 22 warning signs are broken down into four categories based on how the signs were found: Using vertical analysis, using horizontal analysis, in footnotes to financial reports, and in statements of cash flow. Vertical analysis provides a way to find structural changes between the balance sheet and statement of operation accounts. For example, two warning signs from this category, reflecting changes from 1985 to 1986 that applied in the MiniScribe case, are "receivables represent a much larger percentage of total assets" and "inventories represent a much larger percentage of total assets." Horizontal analysis highlights growth in sales relative to growth in key asset and expense accounts. Warning signs found in footnotes, the third category, would not be found by information trajectory modeling but could be found using information extraction techniques. We do not consider these warning signs further here as this is outside the scope of our discussion. Finally, the warning sign found in the MiniScribe case from the statement of cash flow was "cash flow from operations (CFFO) materially lagged behind net income."

Shilit did not describe these 22 warning signs applying to the MiniScribe case as being anything other than independent indicators but, undoubtedly, a human accounting fraud analyst would learn to recognize the occurrence of patterns of these indicators, whether through manual analysis or through the use of a tool based on a technique such as ACH-CD. An information trajectory model implemented in PQS would allow an analyst to represent these patterns as processes and further automate the detection of accounting fraud.

References

1. Libicki, M., The mesh and the net: speculations on armed conflict in an age of free silicon, National Defense University McNair Paper 28, 1994, http://www.ndu.edu/ndu/inss/macnair/mcnair28/m028cont.html
2. Cybenko, G., Giani, A., and Thompson, P., Cognitive hacking: a battle for the mind, *IEEE Computer*, 35, 50, 2002.
3. Thompson, P., Cybenko, G., and Giani, A. Cognitive hacking, in Camp, J.L. and Lewis, S. (Eds.), *Economics of Information Security*, Boston: Kluwer Academic Publishers, 255, Ch. 19, 2004.
4. Chen, H. et al. (Eds.), Lecture notes in computer science, *Proc. NSF/NIJ Symp. on Intelligence and Security Informatics*, Berlin: Springer-Verlag, 2003.
5. Bakos, G. and Bratus, S., Ubiquitous redirection as access control response, *Proc. of Third Annual Conf. on Privacy, Security and Trust*, New Brunswick, Canada: St. Andrews, 2005.
6. Berk, V. et al., Process query systems for surveillance and awareness, in *Proc. Systemics, Cybernetics and Informatics (SCI2003)*, Orlando, Florida, July 2003.
7. SANS, 2005, http://www.sans.org/resources/malwarefaq/wnt-unicode.php
8. Mann, B., Emulex fraud hurts all, *The Motley Fool*, 2000, http://www.fool.com/news/foolplate/2000/foolplate000828.htm
9. Landwehr, C.E., Formal models of computer security, *Comp. Surveys*, 13, 1981.
10. Schneier, B., Semantic attacks: the third wave of network attacks, *Crypto-gram Newsletter*, October 15, 2000, http://www.counterpane.com/crypto-gram-0010.html
11. Denning, D., *Information Warfare and Security*, Reading, MA: Addison-Wesley, 1999.
12. Buller, D.B. and Burgoon, J.K., Interpersonal deception theory, *Comm. Theory*, 6, 203, 1996.
13. Zhou, L. et al., An exploratory study into deception in text-based computer-mediated communications, *Proc. 36th Hawaii Intl. Conf. on Systems Science*, 2003.
14. George, J. et al. Training professionals to detect deception, in Chen et al. (Eds.), *Proc. NSF/NIJ Symp. on Intelligence and Security Informatics, Lecture Notes in Computer Science*, Berlin: Springer-Verlag, 2003, 366.

15. Thompson, P., Semantic hacking and intelligence and security informatics, in Chen et al. (Eds.), *Proc. NSF/NIJ Symp. on Intelligence and Security Informatics, Lecture Notes in Computer Science*, Berlin: Springer-Verlag, 2003, 390.

16. Foreign Broadcast Information Service, https://www.fbis.gov, 2005.

17. Salton, G. and McGill, M., *Introduction to Modern Information Retrieval*, New York: McGraw-Hill, 1983.

18. Maron, M.E. and Kuhns, J.L., On relevance, probabilistic indexing and information retrieval, *J. ACM*, 7, 216, 1960.

19. Cooper, W.S. and Maron, M.E., Foundations of probabilistic and utility-theoretic indexing, *J. Assoc. Comp. Machinery*, 25, 67, 1978.

20. Cover, T.A. and Thomas, J.A., *Elements of Information Theory*, New York: John Wiley & Sons, 1991.

21. Salierno, D., SEC fights internet fraud — United States Securities and Exchange Commission investigates Internet securities fraud — Brief Article, 2000, http://findarticles.com/p//articles/mi_m4153/is_5_57/ai_67590512#continue

22. Stech, f. and Elsaesser, C., Turbo-fraud: counter deception support for forensic auditing, MITRE Technology Program briefing, 2005.

23. *The Dartmouth*, Expert: U.S. at risk of cyberterrorism, April 19, 2004, http://www.thedartmouth.com/article.php?aid=2004041901010k

24. Atallah, M.J. et al., Natural language processing for information assurance and security: an overview and implementations, in *Proc. 9th ACM/SIGSAC New Security Paradigms Workshop (NSPW 00)*, Ballycotton, Cork County, Ireland, 2001, 51.

25. Mosteller, F. and Wallace, D.L., *Inference and Disputed Authorship: The Federalist*, Reading, MA: Addison-Wesley, 1964.

26. Kessler, B., Nunberg, G., and Schütze, H., Automatic detection of text genre, *Proc. Thirty-Fifth Annual Meeting of the Assoc. Comput. Ling.* and *Eighth Conf. of the European Chapter of the Assoc. Comp. Ling.*, Madrid, Spain, 1997, 32.

27. Burrows, J.F., Word patterns and story shapes: the statistical analysis of narrative style, *Literary and Linguistic Computing*, 2, 61, 1987.

28. Rao, J.R. and Rohatgi, P., Can pseudonymity really guarantee privacy? in *Proc. 9th USENIX Security Symposium*, Denver, Colorado, 2000, 85.

29. Reid, D.B., An algorithm for tracking multiple targets, *IEEE Trans. on Automatic Control*, 24, 843, 1979.

30. Schilit, H., *Financial Shenanigans*, 2nd ed., New York: McGraw-Hill, 2002.

2.3

Application and Value of Deception

João Pedro Hespanha

CONTENTS

The two previous chapters stressed those aspects of deception that relate to human cognition. However, one can ask whether deception is a purely human phenomenon and question if deception can arise in the solution to mathematical games played by strictly rational players that are not affected by human emotions. In this chapter, we argue that the answers to these questions are no and yes, respectively. We also illustrate how the framework of noncooperative games provides answers to the questions of how to use deception optimally and how to guard against it.

In mathematical game theory, several alternative notions exist for what is meant by the "optimal policy for a rational player." Some of the most common are as follows:

1. The *Stackelberg leader's policy* is based on the assumption that a player will select a course of actions and advertise it to the other players (followers), who will then select their policies. It implicitly assumes that the leader will not deviate from the advertised policy and that the followers will know this to be true.

2. The *Stackelberg follower's policy* is the best response to an advertised leader's policy.

3. *Security policies* refer to a situation in which players choose a course of action that maximizes their reward, assuming that other players are taking the least favorable courses of actions.

4. A *Nash set of policies* is a collection of policies, one for each player, chosen so that if a single player deviates from the assigned policy, that player will do worse (or at least no better).

Stackelberg policies are inherently based on trust, so they are clearly the wrong framework for deception — the first thought of a human Stackelberg leader would be to advertise the wrong policy. Security policies generally lead to very conservative decisions because players guard themselves against decisions the opponents' worst-case actions, even if these actions are also harmful for the opponents.* These policies can potentially lead to deception but generally they lead to poor rewards. This leaves us with Nash policies which, as we shall see, can indeed exhibit deception and counter deception.

For simplicity, in this chapter we restrict our attention to zero-sum, two-player games. In this case, Nash policies are also called *saddle-point policies* and are defined formally as follows: Consider a game between players A and B, and let $J(\alpha, \beta)$ denote the value of a criterion that player A would like to minimize and player B would like to maximize. The criteria depends on the policies α and β utilized by players A and B, respectively. A particular pair of policies (α^*, β^*) is called a *saddle-point equilibrium* for the game if

$$J(\alpha^*, \beta) \leq J(\alpha^*, \beta^*) \leq J(\alpha, \beta^*), \quad \forall \alpha, \beta$$

The left inequality shows that β^* is the best policy for player B (who is the maximizer) in case player A decides to play α^*. Conversely, the right inequality shows that α^* is the best policy for player A (who is the minimizer) in case player B decides to play β^*. In view of this, the players have no incentive to deviate from their saddle-point policies, justifying the use of the word "equilibrium." Of course, this assumes that no collusion exists among players (i.e., that we are in a noncooperative setting). The reader is referred to [1] for the formal definitions of other types of solutions to mathematical games.

2.3.1 Information, Computation, and Deception

Mathematical games are usually classified as either having full or partial information. In *full-information* games, both players know the whole state of the game as they make their decisions. By "state," we mean all information that is needed to completely describe the future evolution of the game, when the decision rules used by both players are known. Examples of full information

---

* In some zero-sum games, security policies are also Nash policies, in which case these statements do not apply.

games include chess, checkers, and Go. *Partial-information* games differ from these in that at least one of the players does not know the whole state. Poker, bridge, and hearts are examples of such games because each player does not know the hand of the others.

From a formal point of view, full- and partial-information games differ in what types of policies are acceptable. In full-information games, a policy should be understood as a function that selects one particular action for each possible state of the game. In partial-information games, policies are also functions, but now they select one action for each set of (past) observations collected by the player. The definition of saddle-point equilibrium in the above equation is valid for both types of games provided that we restrict our attention to the appropriate sets of policies.

In full information games, as players plan their next moves, they only need to hypothesize about their own and their opponent's future moves to predict the possible outcomes of the game. This is key to using dynamic programming [2] to solve full-information games. Partial-information games are especially challenging because this reasoning can fail. In many partial-information games, to predict the possible outcomes of the game, players must hypothesize not only about the future moves of both players, but also about the past moves of their opponent. Note that when the state of the game is known, hypothesizing over the opponent's past moves is pointless, but when the state is not known, the past actions of the opponent are key to constructing an estimate of the current state and of the eventual outcome of the game based on past observations.

The need to take the past into account when trying to decide on future actions leads to a tremendous increase in complexity. In general, partial-information games are poorly understood and the literature is relatively sparse. Notable exceptions are games which lack information for one of the players [3,4] and games with particular structures such as the Duel game [5], the Rabbit and Hunter game [6], the Searchlight game [7,8], and so on.

The existence of Nash equilibrium in behavioral (i.e., feedback) policies for finite games was established in [9], but the procedure used to construct the Nash policies suffers from an exponential complexity growth in the size of the game. Chapter 2.4 presents a more efficient construction for saddle-point policies based on dynamic programming, which can be used when a zero-sum finite game has a *nested information structure*, i.e., when one of the players has access to all observations of the opponent (and perhaps some additional observations). This provides a worst-case scenario for the player with information inferiority, allowing one to investigate how to avoid potential deceptions. Chapter 3.1 discusses yet another technique to find solutions for finite-games — a tree search. This technique is applicable to deterministic games of sequential moves, i.e., when players alternate in taking actions. Tree searches for partial-information games also suffer from an exponential complexity growth, but the approaches discussed in Chapter 3.1 can alleviate this problem to some extent.

Infinite games with partial information are especially challenging. Chapter 3.2 considers one such zero-sum game subject to linear dynamics and a quadratic cost on the state. The information structure is a variation on the nested case discussed above, in which one player has perfect access to the state of the game, whereas the observations of the opponent are partial and noisy. This scenario is also useful to study how the player with information inferiority can avoid potential deceptions.

Partial information games are particularly interesting because a player can obtain future rewards by either one of the two following mechanisms:

1. Choosing an action that will take the game to a more favorable state.

2. Choosing an action that will make the other player believe that the game is in a state other than the actual one. Moreover, this should lead the opponent to act in our own advantage.

The latter corresponds to a deception move that is only possible in partial-information games because it relies on the fact that the perception of one player can be manipulated by the other. Later in this chapter, we will see that this type of move can occur in saddle-point solutions to mathematical games.

Most of this chapter is focused on deception due to partial information. However, deception can also arise due to *limited computation* and is not restricted to partial-information games. To understand how, consider a deterministic game of full information and suppose that player A has sufficient computational power to explore all possible game outcomes for all possible choices of the players' actions. However, assume that player B can only evaluate the possible evolution of the game for N steps into the future. In this scenario, the player with computational superiority (player A) can select actions that will prompt a response by player B that appears good when the preview horizon is limited to N steps but that will prove damaging in the long term. This type of move also reveals deception, which is now caused by an asymmetry in the computational power available to the players. This asymmetry was widely used by human players against early chess-playing computers, and gave the former a significant advantage until raw computing power and advanced board evaluation metrics tilted the balance in favor of computers.

Deception due to limited computation can reveal itself in numerous ways. In the scenario described above, we assume that player B can only explore the game's decision tree N steps into the future. If instead the tree exploration is limited in terms of the total number of tree-nodes explored, one can imagine that player B may decide to explore a few tree branches more exhaustively than others based on some heuristics. Player A can take advantage of this by creating "diversions" that bias player B's search away from the tree branch that player A ultimately plans to follow. This type of deception can be recognized in humans playing board games, who sometimes try to draw the attention of their opponents away from the areas in which they plan to make decisive attacks. In the context of games played by humans, one should understand "limited computation" to mean "limited attention span."

In military operations, deception due to limited computation (or more precisely, limited attention span) is often combined with partial information to maximize its efficiency. A notable historical event was Operation Overlord during the Second World War, which culminated with the D-Day invasion of France in June 1944 by the allied forces. As discussed in Chapter 2.1, multiple diversions were used to attract the attention of the German command to the Pas de Calais area, making them believe that the Normandy incursion was a diversionary landing and that the true seaborne assault would take place in Pas de Calais several days later. This led Hitler to delay sending several of his divisions to fight the Allies on the Normandy coast, a move that eventually came too late for the Germans. This example reveals the tremendous benefits (and risks) that can arise when the effect of limited attention span is amplified by limited access to information. The use of deception in the context of military operations has been documented and studied by several authors [10–15]. For example, also widely recognized is that by the end of the Cold War, the trend in Soviet naval electronic warfare was changing toward an independent type of combat action instead of a purely supportive role. This new role emphasized radio deception and misinformation at all levels of command [11]. The detection of false targets or decoys is now an important area of research in radar systems [12,14].

The potential use of deception has been recognized in several other areas, such as price negotiation [16,17], multiobject auctioning [18], pursuit-evasion [10,19], human relations [20], and card games [21]. In [16,17], the authors analyze a negotiation where the players do not know each other's payoffs but receive estimates from their opponents. To increase their gain, each player may bias the estimate given. In [17], an advising scheme is proposed to make deception mostly useless. In [18], how a bidder can use deception to lower the price of an item sold in a multiobject auction is analyzed. A pursuit-evasion game is analyzed in [10] where the evader corrupts the information available to the opponent to gain an advantage. The authors assume that the evader can jam the pursuer's sensor and therefore induce measurement errors, produce false targets, or interrupt the observations. The use of deception in abstract games was also reported in [22–24]. In these papers, the authors analyze games in which one of the players is forced to make a decision based on information that has been tampered with by the opponent.

2.3.2 Games of Deception

In the beginning of this chapter, we claimed that deception could naturally arise in saddle-point solutions to mathematical games. We will now use a series of games to demonstrate this idea. In the process, we will also see how "rational" players deal with deception. The games considered are inspired by military air-strike operations. These games are sufficiently simple that they can be solved in closed form, but they are still sufficiently rich to exhibit deception and counter-deception policies. These games were first introduced in [25]. We refer the reader to the technical report [26] for all the relevant mathematical derivations.

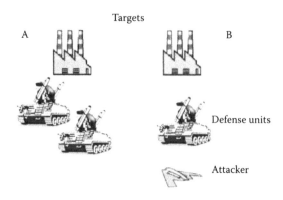

Targets

A

B

Defense units

Attacker

FIGURE 2.3.1
The air-strike game.

2.3.2.1 A Prototype Noncooperative Game

Consider the air-strike game represented schematically in Figure 2.3.1. The *attacker* must choose one of two possible targets (A or B), and the *defender* must decide how to better defend them. We assume that the defender has a finite number of assets available that can be used to protect the targets. To make these defense assets effective, they must be assigned to a particular target and the defender must choose how to distribute them among the targets. To raise the stakes, we assume that the defender only has three defensive units and is faced with the decision of how to distribute them among the two targets. We start by assuming that both players make their decisions independently and execute them without knowing the choice of the other player. Although convenient to regard the players as "attacker" and "defender," this type of game also arises in nonmilitary applications. For example, the "attacker" could be trying to penetrate a consumer market that the "defender" currently dominates.

The game described above can be played as a zero-sum game with the following criterion, which the attacker tries to minimize and the defender tries to maximize:

$$J := \begin{cases} c_0 & \text{no units defending the target attacked} \\ c_1 & \text{one unit defending the target attacked} \\ c_2 & \text{two units defending the target attacked} \\ c_3 & \text{three units defending the target attacked} \end{cases}$$

This cost is shown schematically in Figure 2.3.2. Without loss of generality, we can normalize the constants c_i to have $c_0 = 0$ and $c_3 = 1$. The values for the constants c_1 and c_2 are domain-specific, subject to the reasonable constraint

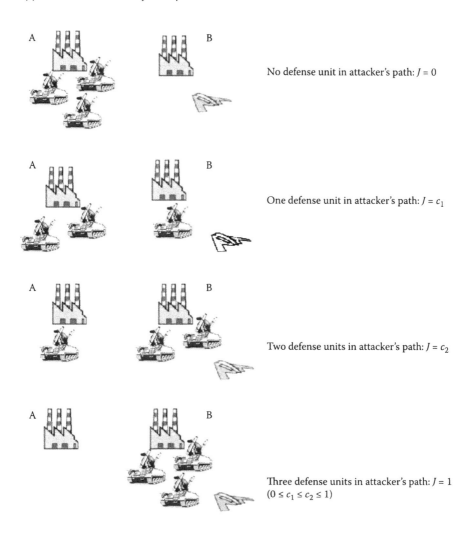

No defense unit in attacker's path: $J = 0$

One defense unit in attacker's path: $J = c_1$

Two defense units in attacker's path: $J = c_2$

Three defense units in attacker's path: $J = 1$
$(0 \leq c_1 \leq c_2 \leq 1)$

FIGURE 2.3.2
Cost structure for the air-strike game.

that $0 < c_1 \leq c_2 < 1$. Implicit in the above cost is the assumption that both targets have the same strategic value. We only make this assumption for simplicity of presentation.

As formulated above, the attacker has two possible choices (attack target A or attack target B) and the defender has a total of four possible ways of distributing the defensive units among the two targets. Each choice available to a player is called a *pure policy* for that player. We will denote the pure policies for the attacker by α_i, $i \in \{1, 2\}$, and the pure policies for the defender by δ_j, $j \in \{1, 2, 3, 4\}$. These policies are enumerated in Table 2.3.1. In Table 2.3.1b, each "o" represents one defensive unit. The defender

TABLE 2.3.1

Pure Policies

(a) Attacker Policies		(b) Defender Policies		
Policy	Target Assigned	Policy	Target A	Target B
α_1	A	δ_1	ooo	
α_2	B	δ_2		ooo
		δ_3	oo	o
		δ_4	o	oo

polices δ_1 and δ_2 will be called *3-0 configurations* because they correspond to situations in which the defender assigns all the units to a single target. The policies δ_3 and δ_4 will be called *2-1 configurations* and correspond to situations in which two units are assigned to one target and one unit to the other.

The game under consideration can be represented in its *extensive form* by associating each policy of the attacker and the defender with a row and column, respectively, of a 2×4 matrix G. The entry g_{ij}, $i \in \{1, 2\}$, $j \in \{1, 2, 3, 4\}$, of G corresponds to the cost J when the attacker chooses policy α_i and the defender chooses policy δ_j. The matrix G for this game is given by

$$\begin{array}{cccc} \delta_1 & \delta_2 & \delta_3 & \delta_4 \end{array}$$
$$G := \begin{bmatrix} 1 & 0 & c_2 & c_1 \\ 0 & 1 & c_1 & c_2 \end{bmatrix} \begin{array}{c} \alpha_1 \\ \alpha_2 \end{array}$$

We are interested in saddle-point policies for the game. A *saddle-point equilibrium* in pure policies is a pair of policies $\{\alpha_{i^*}, \delta_{j^*}\}$, one for each player, for which

$$g_{i^*j} \le g_{i^*j^*} \le g_{ij^*}, \quad \forall i, j$$

As mentioned before, saddle-point policies are chosen by rational players because they guarantee a cost no worse than $g_{i^*j^*}$ for each player, no matter what the other player decides to do. As a consequence, playing at a saddle-point is "safe" even if the opponent discovers our policy of choice. They are also reasonable choices because a player will never do better by unilaterally deviating from the equilibrium. However, no saddle-points exist in pure policies for the game described by the matrix G. In fact, all the pure policies violate the "safety" condition mentioned above. For example, suppose that the attacker plays policy α_1 (i.e., always attack target A). This choice is not safe in the sense that if the defender guesses it, this player can choose the policy δ_1 (i.e., assign all units to target A), which subjects the attacker to the highest possible cost. Similarly, α_2 is not safe and therefore cannot also be in a saddle-point policy.

To obtain a saddle-point, one needs to enlarge the policy space by allowing each player to randomize among the available pure policies. In particular, suppose that the attacker chooses policy α_i, $i \in \{1, 2\}$, with probability a_i and the defender chooses policy δ_j, $j \in \{1, 2, 3, 4\}$, with probability d_j. When the game is played repeatedly, the expected value of the cost is then given by

$$E[J] = \sum_{i,j} a_i g_{ij} d_j = a'Gd$$

Each 2-vector $a := \{a_i\}$ of probabilities is called a *mixed policy for the attacker*, whereas each 4-vector $d := \{d_j\}$ of probabilities is called a *mixed policy for the defender*. It is well known that at least one saddle-point equilibrium in mixed policies always exists for finite matrix games (cf. Minimax Theorem [1, p. 27]). In particular, a pair of mixed policies $\{a^*, d^*\}$ always exists for which

$$a^{*\prime} Gd \leq a^{*\prime} Gd^* \leq a' Gd^*, \quad \forall a, d$$

Assuming that both players play at the saddle-point, the cost will then be equal to $a^{*\prime}Gd^*$, which is called the *value of the game*. Showing that for this game, the unique saddle-point equilibrium for the matrix G is given by

$$a^* := \begin{bmatrix} \dfrac{1}{2} & \dfrac{1}{2} \end{bmatrix}',$$

$$d^* := \begin{cases} \begin{bmatrix} \dfrac{1}{2} & \dfrac{1}{2} & 0 & 0 \end{bmatrix}' & c_1 + c_2 \leq 1 \\[2em] \begin{bmatrix} 0 & 0 & \dfrac{1}{2} & \dfrac{1}{2} \end{bmatrix}' & c_1 + c_2 > 1 \end{cases}$$

with a value equal to

$$a^{*\prime}Gd^* = \max\left\{ \frac{c_1 + c_2}{2}, \frac{1}{2} \right\}$$

This equilibrium corresponds to the intuitive solution that the attacker should randomize between attacking targets A or B with equal probability (i.e., randomize between α_1 and α_2), and the defender should randomize between placing most of the defensive units next to A or next to B, also with equal probability. The optimal choice between 3-0 or 2-1 configurations (policies δ_1/δ_2 vs. δ_3/δ_4) depends on the parameters c_1 and c_2. We conclude that 3-0 configurations are optimal when $c_1 + c_2 \leq 1$, otherwise the 2-1 configurations are preferable. Figure 2.3.3 shows the saddle-point policies when $c_1 + c_2 \leq 1$.

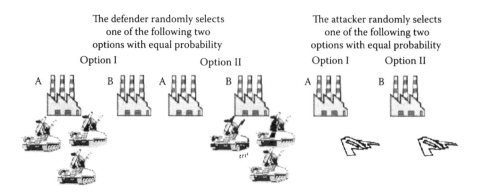

The defender randomly selects one of the following two options with equal probability
Option I   Option II

The attacker randomly selects one of the following two options with equal probability
Option I   Option II

FIGURE 2.3.3
Saddle-point equilibrium in mixed policies for the game defined by G with $c_1 + c_2 \le 1$. In this case, two units do not provide adequate defense, so 3-0 configurations are always chosen.

In the game described so far, deception is not possible because the players are forced to make a decision without any information. We will change that in the next section.

2.3.2.2 Full Manipulation of Information

Suppose now that the game described above is played in two steps. First, the defender decides how to distribute the defensive units. The defender may also disclose the position of some of the units to the attacker. On the second step, the attacker decides which target to strike. To do this, the attacker might use the information provided by the defender. For now, we assume that this is the only information available to the attacker, therefore the defender completely controls the information that the attacker uses to make a decision. This game is represented schematically in Figure 2.3.4.

The rationale for the defender to voluntarily disclose the position of the defensive units is to deceive the attacker. For example, suppose that the attacker uses two units to defend target A and only one to defend B (as in Figure 2.3.4). By disclosing that units were placed next to B, the defender might expect the opponent to attack A and, consequently, suffer a heavier cost.

In this new game, the number of admissible pure policies for each player is larger than before. The attacker now has eight distinct pure policies available because for each possible observation (no unit detected, unit detected defending target A, or unit detected defending target B), one has two possible choices (strike A or B). These policies are enumerated in Table 2.3.2(a).

In policies α_1 and α_2, the attacker ignores any available information and always attacks target A or target B, respectively. These policies are therefore called *blind*. In policies α_3 and α_4, the attacker never selects the target where he detects a defense unit was detected. These policies are called *naive* because they reflect the belief that the target where defense units are visible is better defended. In policies α_5 and α_6, the attacker chooses the target where a

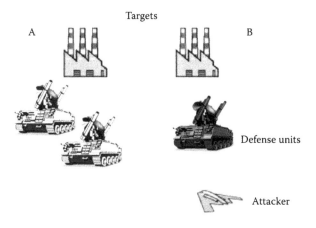

Targets

FIGURE 2.3.4
The air-strike game with manipulation of information. The two "transparent" defensive units near target A are assumed invisible to the attacker, whereas the "solid" unit near target B can be seen by the attacker.

defensive unit was detected. These policies are called *counter deception* because they presume that a unit is being shown close to the least defended target. These policies are represented schematically in Figure 2.3.5b.

The defender has ten distinct pure policies available, each one corresponding to a particular configuration of the defensive units and a particular choice of which units to disclose (if any). These are enumerated in Table 2.3.2b, where "•" represents a defense unit whose position has been disclosed and

TABLE 2.3.2

Pure Policies for the Air-Strike Game with Manipulation of Information

(a) Attacker Policies				(b) Defender Policies		
	Target Assigned When			Policy	Target A	Target B
Policy	No Obs.	Unit Detected at A	Unit Detected at B	δ_1	ooo	
α_1	A	A	A	δ_2		ooo
α_2	B	B	B	δ_3	oo	o
α_3	B	B	A	δ_4	o	oo
α_4	A	B	A	δ_5	oo•	
α_5	A	A	B	δ_6		oo•
α_6	B	A	B	δ_7	o•	o
α_7	A	B	B	δ_8	o	o•
α_8	B	A	A	δ_9	oo	•
				δ_{10}	•	oo

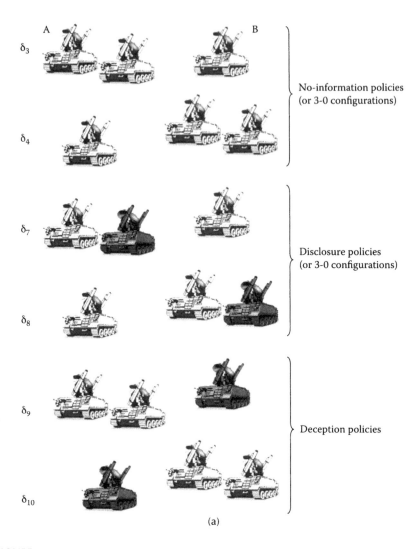

FIGURE 2.3.5
Qualitative description of the pure policies in Table 2.3.2.

"o" a defense unit whose position has not been disclosed. Here we are assuming that the defender will — at most — disclose the placement of one unit because more than that would never be advantageous. In policies δ_1 through δ_4, nothing is disclosed about the distribution of the units. These are called *no-information* policies. In policies δ_9 and δ_{10}, the defender shows units placed next to the target that has fewer defenses. These are *deception* policies. Policies δ_5 through δ_8 are *disclosure* policies, in which the defender is showing a unit next to the target that is better defended. These policies are represented schematically in Figure 2.3.5a.

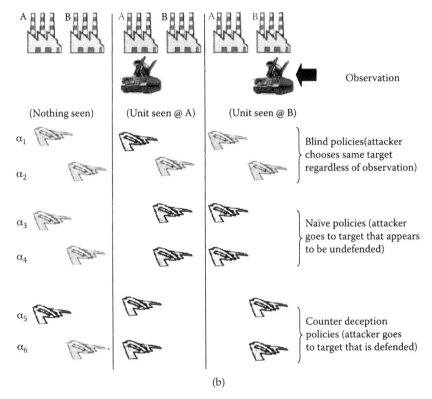

(b)

FIGURE 2.3.5 (Continued).

This game can be represented in extensive form by the following 8×10 matrix:

$$
G :=
\begin{array}{cccccccccc}
\delta_1 & \delta_2 & \delta_3 & \delta_4 & \delta_5 & \delta_6 & \delta_7 & \delta_8 & \delta_9 & \delta_{10}
\end{array}
$$

$$
G := \begin{bmatrix}
1 & 0 & c_2 & c_1 & 1 & 0 & c_2 & c_1 & c_2 & c_1 \\
0 & 1 & c_1 & c_2 & 0 & 1 & c_1 & c_2 & c_1 & c_2 \\
0 & 1 & c_1 & c_2 & 0 & 0 & c_1 & c_1 & c_2 & c_2 \\
1 & 0 & c_2 & c_1 & 0 & 0 & c_1 & c_1 & c_2 & c_2 \\
1 & 0 & c_2 & c_1 & 1 & 1 & c_2 & c_2 & c_1 & c_1 \\
0 & 1 & c_1 & c_2 & 1 & 1 & c_2 & c_2 & c_1 & c_1 \\
1 & 0 & c_2 & c_1 & 0 & 1 & c_1 & c_2 & c_1 & c_2 \\
0 & 1 & c_1 & c_2 & 1 & 0 & c_2 & c_1 & c_2 & c_1
\end{bmatrix}
\begin{array}{c}
\alpha_1 \\
\alpha_2 \\
\alpha_3 \\
\alpha_4 \\
\alpha_5 \\
\alpha_6 \\
\alpha_7 \\
\alpha_8
\end{array}
$$

Just as before, for this game to have saddle-point equilibria, one needs to consider mixed policies. However, this particular game has multiple equilibria, one of them being

$$a^* := \begin{bmatrix} \dfrac{1}{2} & \dfrac{1}{2} & 0 & 0 & 0 & 0 & 0 & 0 \end{bmatrix}'$$

$$d^* := \begin{cases} \begin{bmatrix} \dfrac{1}{2} & \dfrac{1}{2} & 0 & 0 & 0 & 0 & 0 & 0 & 0 & 0 \end{bmatrix}' & c_1 + c_2 \leq 1 \\[4mm] \begin{bmatrix} 0 & 0 & \dfrac{1}{2} & \dfrac{1}{2} & 0 & 0 & 0 & 0 & 0 & 0 \end{bmatrix}' & c_1 + c_2 > 1 \end{cases}$$

with a value equal to

$$a^{*\prime} G d^* = \max \left\{ \frac{c_1 + c_2}{2}, \frac{1}{2} \right\}$$

This shows that:

1. The attacker can ignore the information available and simply randomize among the two blind policies α_1 and α_2 with equal probability.
2. The defender gains nothing from disclosing information and can therefore randomize among the no-information policies, also with equal probability.

Saddle-point equilibria do exist that utilize different policies. For example, when $c_1 + c_2 > 1$, an alternative Nash equilibrium is

$$\bar{a}^* := \begin{bmatrix} 0 & 0 & \dfrac{1}{4} & \dfrac{1}{4} & \dfrac{1}{4} & \dfrac{1}{4} & 0 & 0 \end{bmatrix}'$$

$$\bar{d}^* := \begin{bmatrix} 0 & 0 & 0 & 0 & 0 & 0 & \dfrac{1}{4} & \dfrac{1}{4} & \dfrac{1}{4} & \dfrac{1}{4} \end{bmatrix}'$$

In this case, the defender randomizes between deception and disclosure policies with equal probability and the attacker between the naive and counter-deception policies. However, in zero-sum games all equilibria yield the same value, so the players have no incentive to choose this equilibrium that is more complex in terms of the decision rules. Finally, because of the equilibrium interchangeability property for zero-sum games, the pairs $\{a^*, \bar{d}^*\}$ and $\{\bar{a}^*, d^*\}$ are also saddle-point equilibria [1, p. 28]. This means that one still gets an equilibrium, e.g., if the defender plays $\bar{d}^*$ (randomization between deception and disclosure) and the attacker plays a^* (randomization between blind policies).

We have just seen that in this version of the game, the attacker gains nothing from using the observations available, even though these observations give precise information about the position of some of the defensive units. At an intuitive level, this is because the information available to the attacker is completely controlled by the opponent. If the defender chooses to disclose the position of some of the defensive units, this is done solely to get an advantage. For example, this can be seen in the equilibrium given by the values of mixed policies $\bar{a}^*$ and $\bar{d}^*$. We shall consider next a version of the game where the defender no longer has complete control over the information available to the attacker. For the new game, the attacker can sometimes improve the cost by using the available information.

2.3.2.3 Partial Manipulation of Information

Suppose that when the defender decides to "show" one of the defensive units, the unit is simply not camouflaged, making it easy to find by the surveillance sensors used by the attacker. In the previous game, we assumed that uncamouflaged units are always detected by the attacker and camouflaged ones are not. We will now deviate from this ideal situation and assume that (i) noncamouflaged units may not be detected and, more importantly, (ii) camouflaged units may sometimes be detected by the attacker. We consider a generic probabilistic model for the attacker's surveillance, which is characterized by the conditional probability of detecting units next to a particular target given a specific total number of units next to that target and how many of them are being shown:

$$\text{Prob (defenses detected near target A} \mid n_A = n, s_A = s) = \chi(n, s)$$

where $\chi(n, s)$ is the *sensor characteristic function*, $n_A \in \{0, 1, 2, 3\}$ is the total number of units defending target A, and s_A is the number of these that are shown. Because no incentive exists for the defender to show more than one unit, s_A is restricted to the set $\{0, 1\}$. For simplicity, we assume that the surveillance of target B is identical and independent, i.e.,

$$\text{Prob (defenses detected near target B} \mid n_B = n, s_B = s) = \chi(n, s)$$

where the symbols with the subscript B refer to the defensive units assigned to target B.

For most of the discussion that follows, the sensor characteristic function $\chi(n, s)$ can be arbitrary, provided that it is monotone nondecreasing with respect to each of its arguments (when the other is held fixed). The monotonicity is quite reasonable because more units (shown or not) should always

In this configuration, a reliable sensor is more likely to detect the two camouflaged defenses next to A than the noncamouflaged one next to B

FIGURE 2.3.6
Trustworthy sensors.

result in a higher probability of detection. A few particular cases should be considered:

- When $\chi(n, s) = 0$, $\forall\, n, s$, we have the first game considered in this chapter because the defense units are never detected.
- When

$$\chi(n, s) = \begin{cases} 1, & s > 0 \\ 0, & s = 0 \end{cases} \quad \forall n \in \{0, 1, 2, 3\}, \quad s \in \{0, 1\}$$

the defense units are detected if and only if they are shown. This corresponds to the second game considered here, where the defender has full control over the information available to the attacker.

- Another interesting situation occurs when the probability of detecting two camouflaged units is still larger than the probability of detecting one uncamouflaged unit, i.e.,

$$\chi(2, 0) \geq \chi(1, 1)$$

When this happens, we say that the attacker's sensors are *trustworthy* because the probability of detecting camouflaged defense units near the better-defended target is still larger than the probability of detecting a single uncamouflaged unit by the less-defended target (cf. Figure 2.3.6).

We will see shortly that when the sensors are trustworthy, the attacker should choose naive policies. A special case of trustworthy sensors arises when $\chi(n, s)$ is independent of s for all values of n. In this case, we have sensors that cannot be manipulated by the defender because the detection is independent of the number of units "shown" to the defender.

In terms of the policies available, the game considered in this section is fairly similar to the one in the previous section. The only difference is that, in principle, the attacker can now detect defensive units next to both targets. In practice, this means that Table 2.3.2a should have a fourth column entitled, "units detected at A and B," which would result in 16 distinct pure policies. Not detecting any unit or detecting units next to both targets is essentially the same. Therefore, we shall consider for this game only the eight policies in Table 2.3.2a, with the understanding that when units are detected next to both targets, the attacker acts as if no units were detected. Showing that this introduces no loss of generality is not hard. The defender's policies are the same as in the previous section and are given in Table 2.3.2b.

This game can also be represented in extensive form by an 8×10 matrix. The reader is referred to [26] on how to construct this matrix. As before, the game has saddle-point equilibria in mixed policies but now the equilibrium policies depend on the sensor characteristic function $\chi(n, s)$. The saddle-point policies for this game were computed in [26] and are as follows:

1. When the sensors are trustworthy [i.e., when $\chi(2, 0) \geq \chi(1, 1)$], a saddle-point solution is given by

$$a^* := \begin{bmatrix} 0 & 0 & \dfrac{1}{2} & \dfrac{1}{2} & 0 & 0 & 0 & 0 \end{bmatrix}'$$

$$d^* := \begin{cases} \begin{bmatrix} \dfrac{1}{2} & \dfrac{1}{2} & 0 & 0 & 0 & 0 & 0 & 0 & 0 & 0 \end{bmatrix}' & c_1 + c_2 \leq 1 - \chi(3,0) + \eta_1 \\[3mm] \begin{bmatrix} 0 & 0 & 0 & 0 & 0 & 0 & 0 & 0 & \dfrac{1}{2} & \dfrac{1}{2} \end{bmatrix}' & c_1 + c_2 > 1 - \chi(3,0) + \eta_1 \end{cases}$$

where $\eta_1 = (c_2 - c_1)(\chi(2, 0) - \chi(1, 1))$. In this case, the attacker randomizes among the naive policies and the defender either randomizes among the deception policies or the 3-0 no-information configurations. The latter occurs when the attacker only incurs significant cost when three units are in its path and therefore 2-1 configurations are not acceptable for the defender. The value of the game is

$$a^{*\prime}Gd^* = \frac{\max\{1 - \chi(3,0), c_1 + c_2 - \eta_1\}}{2} \leq \frac{c_1 + c_2}{2}$$

which is smaller than the one obtained in the previous two games. This game is therefore more favorable to the attacker, who is now able to take advantage of the surveillance information.

2. When the sensors are not trustworthy [i.e., $\chi(2, 0) < \chi(1, 1)$] and $c_1 + c_2 \geq 1$, a saddle-point solution is given by

$$a^* := \begin{bmatrix} \dfrac{1}{2} & \dfrac{1}{2} & 0 & 0 & 0 & 0 & 0 & 0 \end{bmatrix}'$$

$$d^* := \begin{bmatrix} 0 & 0 & \dfrac{n_2}{2} & \dfrac{n_2}{2} & 0 & 0 & 0 & 0 & \dfrac{1-n_2}{2} & \dfrac{1-n_2}{2} \end{bmatrix}'$$

where $n_2 := \dfrac{\chi(1,1) - \chi(2,0)}{\chi(1,1) - \chi(1,0)}$

In this case, the attacker randomizes among his blind policies and the defender randomizes between deception and no-information in 2-1 configurations. The probability distribution used by the defender is a function of the several parameters. However, the value of the game is always

$$a^{*\prime}Gd^* = \frac{c_1 + c_2}{2}$$

which is the same as in the previous two games. This means that the surveillance sensors of the attacker are effectively rendered useless by the defender's policy. This result happens because the sensors are not trustworthy, and therefore the defender can significantly manipulate the information available to the attacker.

3. When the sensors are not trustworthy [i.e., $\chi(2, 0) < \chi(1, 1)$] but $c_1 + c_2 < 1$, a saddle-point solution is given by

$$a^* := \begin{bmatrix} \dfrac{1-n_3}{2} & \dfrac{1-n_3}{2} & \dfrac{n_3}{2} & \dfrac{n_3}{2} & 0 & 0 & 0 & 0 \end{bmatrix}'$$

$$d^* := \begin{bmatrix} \dfrac{1-n_4}{2} & \dfrac{1-n_4}{2} & 0 & 0 & 0 & 0 & 0 & 0 & \dfrac{n_4}{2} & \dfrac{n_4}{2} \end{bmatrix}'$$

where $n_3 := \dfrac{1-c_1-c_2}{\chi(3,0)-n_1}$ $n_4 := \dfrac{\chi(3,0)}{\chi(3,0)-n_1}$

In this case, the attacker randomizes between his blind and naive policies, whereas the defender randomizes between deception and no-information in 3-0 configurations. The value of the game is

$$a^{*\prime}Gd^* = \frac{1}{2} - \frac{(1-c_1-c_2)\chi(3,0)}{2(\chi(3,0)-n_1)} \leq \frac{1}{2}$$

which is smaller than the one obtained in the previous two games. Therefore, the attacker can attain a cost smaller than $\frac{1}{2}$, which would be obtained by only using blind policies.

Both in case 2 and case 3, the sensors are not trustworthy and the defender has sufficient power to manipulate the information available to the attacker so as to make it effectively useless. However, in case 3, the 2-1 configurations required for deception are very costly to the defender, and deception is no longer an attractive alternative. Because of this fact, the defender will avoid it, giving an advantage to the attacker.

2.3.3 The Rational Side of Deception

The games considered above reveal several interesting facts about the rational use of deception in partial information games.

Deception can occur in saddle-point policies. For some parameters of the game with partial manipulation of information, the equilibrium policy for the defender attempts to make the attacker believe that the least-defended target was the best-defended one. This is achieved by disclosing the position of defensive units near a poorly defended target and hiding the presence of other units near a better-defended one. This confirms our original claim that deception can arise naturally in saddle-point solutions to mathematical games played by strictly rational players. We have thus shown that deception is not limited to the phenomena arising out of human cognitive limitations.

Deception provides a mechanism to remove information content from the observations. In the games with full and partial manipulation of information, the attackers had access to sensor data, which was not available in the initial game, yet this player was not able to fully utilize this data. In fact, in the game with full manipulation of information — as well as with partial manipulation of information, $c_1 + c_2 \geq 1$, and non-trustworthy sensors — the use of deception by the defender essentially forced the attacker to completely ignore the available observations. In both cases, the attackers could not improve their chances of success by using observations. This result is perhaps not surprising with full manipulation of information, in which case the defender completely controlled the information available to the attacker. However, even when the sensors allowed the attacker to "see through" the defender's camouflage, blind policies would still be optimal if the sensor's trustworthiness fell below a particular threshold.

The potential rewards collected by deception must be weighted against its cost. When $c_1 + c_2 < 1$ in the game with partial manipulation of information, the attacker is biased towards the naive policies and never uses the counter-deception ones. This means that the observations still provide useful information even when the sensors can be substantially manipulated by the defender (including the case of nontrustworthy sensors). The explanation for this apparent paradox is that when $c_1 + c_2 < 1$, the use of 2-1 configurations does not provide sufficient defense, even for the target with two defensive units. It is therefore costly for the defender (in terms of protecting the targets) to use the 2-1 configurations, which are the only ones for which deception is possible. The defender thus chooses to limit the use of the 2-0 deception policies to the extent that, even for nontrustworthy sensors, this player no longer removes all information content from the observations available to the attacker, even for nontrustworthy sensors.

At a qualitative level, the opening statements of the three paragraphs above seem intuitive and even "common sense." The role of the analysis presented in this chapter — based on the concept of saddle equilibrium — was to provide the specific policies for the defender that optimize the use of deception and the corresponding policies for the attacker that are most robust against manipulation of information. We believe that this is a key contribution that game theory has to offer to adversarial reasoning.

References

1. Basan, T. and Olsder, G.J., *Dynamic Noncooperative Game Theory*, No. 23 in Classics in Applied Mathematics, 2nd ed., Philadelphia: SIAM, 1999.
2. Bellman, R., *Dynamic Programming*. Princeton, NJ: Princeton University Press, 1957.
3. Sorin, S. and Zamir, S., "Big Match" with lack of information on one side (III), in Raghavan et al.*Theory and Decision Library, Series C, Game Theory, Mathematical Programming and Operations Research*. Dordrecht: Kluwer Academic Publishers, 1991.
4. Melolidakis, C., Stochastic games with lack of information on one side and positive stop probabilities, in Raghavan et al. *Theory and Decision Library, Series C, Game Theory, Mathematical Programming and Operations Research*. Dordrecht: Kluwer Academic Publishers, 1991.
5. Kimeldorf, G., Duels: an overview, in Schubik, M., (Ed.), *Mathematics of Conflict* Amsterdam: North-Holland, 1983, 55–72.
6. Bernhard, P., Colomb, A.L. and Papavassilopoulos, G.P., Rabbit and hunter game: two discrete stochastic formulations, *Comp. Math. App.*, 13, 1–3, 205–225, 1987.
7. Olsder, G.J. and Papavassilopoulos, G.P., About when to use a searchlight, *J. Math. Anal. Appl.* 136, 466–478, 1988.
8. Olsden, G.J. and Papavassilopoulos, G.P., A Markov chain game with dynamic information, *J. Opt. Theo. Appl.* 59, 467–486, December 1988.
9. Hespanha, J.P. and Prandini, M., Nash equilibria in partial-information games on Markov chains, *Proc. of the 40th Conf. on Decision and Contr.*, Orlando, FL, December 2001.

10. Yavin, Y., Pursuit-evasion differential games with deception or interrupted observation, *Comp. Math. Appl.* 13, 1–3, 191–203, 1987.
11. Vego, M., Soviet naval electronic warfare, *Signal*, 44, 4, 96–99, 1989.
12. Oliveira, C.L.C., Grivet, M.A. and Pantoja, E.R., Brazil, Radar-ECM simulation system, *Proc. of the Int. Microwave Conf.*, Brazil, 1, 255–260, 1993.
13. Tambe, M., San Francisco Recursive agent and agent-group tracking in real-time dynamic environment, *Proc. of the Int. Conf. on Multi-agent Syst.*, San Francisco, 368–375, 1995.
14. Yanglin, S.Z., Identification of false targets in bistatic radar system, *Proc. of the IEEE National Aerospace and Electronics Conf.*, 2, Dayton, OH, 878–883, July 1997.
15. Burns, R.W., Deception technology and the D-Day invasion, *Engineering Science and Education J.*, 4, 81–88, April 1995.
16. Greenberg, I., The effect of deception on optimal decisions, *Op. Res. Lett.*, 1, 144–147, September 1982.
17. Matsubara, S. and Yokoo, M., Negotiations with inaccurate payoff values, *Proc. of the Int. Conf. on Multi-agent Syst.*, Paris, France, 449–450, 1998.
18. Hausch, D.B., Multi-object auctions: sequential vs. simultaneous sales, *Management Science*, 32, 1599–1610, December 1986.
19. Hespanha, J.P., Prandini, M. and Sastry, S., Probabilistic pursuit-evasion games: a one-step Nash approach, *Proc. of the 39th Conf. on Decision and Contr.*, 3, 2272–2277, December 2000.
20. Reimbold, C., Games of deception, *Proc. of the Int. Prof. Comm. Conf.*, Sydney, Australia, 96–101, 1989.
21. Billings, D., Papp, D., Schaeffer, J., and Szafrone, D., Poker as a testbed for machine intelligence research, *Adv. in Artif. Intelligence: Proc. of the 12th Biennial Conf. of the Canadian Soc. for Computational Studies*, Vancouver, British Columbia, 228–238, 1998.
22. Spencer, J., A deception game, *Am. Math. Monthly*, 416–417, 1973.
23. Baston, V.J. and Bostock, F.A., Deception games, *Int. J. Game Theory*, 17, 2, 129–134, 1988.
24. Inohara, T., Takahashi, S. and Nakano, B., Impossibility of deception in a conflict among subjects with interdependent preference, *Appl. Math. Computation*, 81, 2–3, 221–244, 1997.
25. Hespanha, J.P., Ateskan, Y.S., and Kizilocak, H.H., Deception in non-cooperative games with partial information, *Proc. of the 2nd DARPA-JFACC Symp. on Advances in Enterprise Control*, Minneapolis, MN, July 2000.
26. Hespanha, J.P., Ateskan, Y.S., and Kizilocak, H.H., Deception in non-cooperative games with partial information, Technical Report, EE-Systems, University of Southern California, Los Angeles, February 2001. This report supersedes two previous reports with the same title, dated April 2000 and June 2000.
27. Raghavan, T.E.S., Ferguson, T.S. and Parthasarathy, T. (Eds.), *Stochastic Games and Related Topics: In Honor of Professor L. S. Shapley*, Vol. 7 of *Theory and Decision Library, Series C, Game Theory, Mathematical Programming and Operations Research*. Dordrecht: Kluwer Academic Publishers, 1991.

2.4

Robustness against Deception

William M. McEneaney and Rajdeep Singh

CONTENTS

As we have seen in the chapters of this section, estimation of ground-truth in the presence of deception is quite difficult. At best, one might obtain a measure of the likelihood (loosely defined) that a deception is being employed. However, this does not imply that one cannot determine an effective course of action regardless of the lack of certainty with regard to whether the opponent is employing deception. How should one act if a deception is suspected but cannot be ascertained? In this chapter, we consider how one can reduce the susceptibility to deception, i.e., how one can choose one's actions so that the impact of a deception is minimized. We refer to this reduction in susceptibility to deception as deception robustness.

To study this problem properly and to produce rigorously supported technology for deception robustness, we must have some mathematical model of adversarial conflict. This model must encompass both the inputs of an intelligent adversary and the necessarily unpredictable outcomes of low-level actions in a conflict. Thus, the natural framework for study of this problem is that of stochastic games. We will be interested only in *dynamic* games (i.e., time-dependent systems) rather than static games. We will be discussing deceptions that critically rely on the lack of perfect observations of the system. Thus, we are led to the realm of stochastic games under imperfect information (also referred to in the literature as stochastic games under partial information). The theory in support of deception robustness will be developed in this realm. The bulk of the theory will be independent of whether the system state takes values in a discrete space or in the continuum. However, to develop tractable algorithms, we will concentrate on the case of systems with a finite number of discrete states. We will also assume that these systems operate in discrete time. This implies that the underlying models of the state dynamics will be discrete-time Markov chains. We will suppose that there are two players are in these games. Consequently, the transition probabilities for the Markov chains will be controlled by the actions of the two players. The player who we attempt to assist with our solution is designated as Blue and their opponent is designated as Red.

As noted above, the classes of deceptions we study here will rely on Blue's imperfect knowledge of the state of the system. This implies that we must model the Blue player (for which we are developing our deception-robust controller) as obtaining their information from an observation process, which will also be combined with some initial estimates. Alternately, we choose not to model the Red player as also obtaining their information from their own observation process. One of the reasons for this simplification is the presence of serious mathematical roadblocks to the solution of such games in the case where the information available to each of the players is different and where one player's knowledge does not necessarily completely subsume the other's. Further, the case where the opponent has perfect knowledge of the system is clearly the most demanding. If the opponent has partial and corrupted knowledge, then the achieved results will be more favorable than predicted.

Lastly, we will consider only zero-sum games. This is the case when the opponent is choosing their actions to maximize whatever criterion it is that we wish to minimize. One can make a compelling argument that the opponent will generally not have a diametrically opposite goal. However, if the opponent is choosing their actions based on a goal other than the diametrically opposite goal, then the expected outcome of the game (from our perspective) will be no worse than what we predict under the zero-sum assumption. We will also refer to this formulation as a *minimax formulation* because we will be minimizing the maximum (worst-case) expected outcome.

Further, the theory on non-zero-sum games is significantly less well developed than that of zero-sum/minimax games, and because the theoretical developments in support of deception robustness are already substantial (and difficult) extensions of the previously existing theory, the minimax case is perhaps at the current limit of tractability for this class of problems.

2.4.1 In Search of Antideception

Game theory underwent significant development in the 1950s and 1960s, but application of the theory to problems of interest was severely limited due to the limited computational power available at the time. The theory did continue to progress, particularly in the arena of the observational/informational aspects of the games, and notable references are [2,3,27]. Interest was heightened in the late 1980s and early 1990s as it became clear that nonlinear H_∞ control under imperfect information took the form of a dynamic game [1,15,17–19]. More details on these recent developments will follow below.

In the last 10 years, a substantial effort has been made in the application of automated reasoning techniques to problems in the military command and control arena. In these efforts, it has become increasingly clear that the lack of perfect information and deception play critical roles in the development of useful command and control strategies. (Of course, these play important roles in many other areas. However, a command and control application happened to provide the impetus for the work to be described in this chapter.) Although these issues had arisen earlier (c.f. [2,3,27]), the substantial growth in computational power in the intervening years has allowed one to address these problems much more satisfactorily.

In Chapter 2.3, it was demonstrated that deception can be a useful strategy. In the game considered there, a single observational event was followed by a single dynamic event. In this chapter, we extend this reasoning to a multi-step problem. We also follow a slightly different (but related) approach to deal with the scenario of partial information. In particular, we provide a general mathematical framework from the viewpoint of the player who lacks perfect information. Also in contrast to Chapter 2.3, which deals with mixed strategies for a given problem, in this chapter we build a theoretical framework using pure strategies dependent on the information patterns of the players. This framework is applied to a problem that is similar in nature to the problem of Chapter 2.3 in that the events and states of the system take values in finite sets. One other notable variation in the application used here is that we now add decoys and false-alarm observations to the problem as well.

Chapter 3.2 will take a somewhat similar game-theoretic approach. However, the theory built in that chapter will be for a system taking values in the continuum rather than in a discrete set. The theory developed there will be restricted to linear systems. That restriction allows one to obtain certain elegant results that are not generalizable to the problem form considered here. There is a similarity in that the controls obtained there are specifically constructed to handle potential deception, but in that chapter, there are tremendous problem-complexity reductions that are induced by the linearity.

Some of the issues dealt with in this chapter — particularly the computation of the value function (described below) — are also considered in Chapter 1.3. In some sense, the relation of the techniques developed there and the value function discussion below is analogous to the relation of a Particle Filter to a Kalman or Zakai/Kushner filter, and is also analogous to the relation between diffusion process realizations and the associated second-order partial differential equation.

Lastly, we note that the theoretical underpinning of the methods developed in this chapter have origins in a particular branch of game theory and nonlinear, risk-sensitive, stochastic control. Fleming [6], Friedman [13], and Elliott & Kalton [4] developed the notion of value for dynamic games in the 1960s and early 1970s. In the 1980s, nonlinear H∞ control was developed. Most importantly, a representation in terms of dynamic games was formed (c.f. [1]). Soon after, in the early 1990s, risk-sensitive control was developed (subsuming stochastic control and robust/H∞ control), and was found to have an equivalent representation as a stochastic, dynamic game [8–10,17,28]. These were first developed as state-feedback control. James et al. (c.f. [18,19]) extended this to observation-feedback. Basar & Bernhard [1] also obtained a similar result. In the robust/H∞ limit approach to observation-feedback, the concept of information state as a worst-case cost over potential opponent inputs was a critical breakthrough [1,15]. The risk-sensitive approach in this chapter is a direct descendent of the above referenced risk-sensitive control theory. The deception-robust approach significantly generalizes the above information state from a class of problems with only deterministic noise inputs to the stochastic game realm.

2.4.2 Modeling the Game

We model the state dynamics as a discrete-time Markov chain. The state will take values in a finite set, χ. A state value, $i \in \chi$, can represent a complex game state. For instance, in a military example, state i might correspond to "Blue entity B7 is at position 84, and is in health state 'damaged;' Red entity R9 is at position 117, and in health state 'Okay'." Time will be denoted by $t \in \{0, 1, 2 \ldots T\}$. We will consider only the problem with two players, and we will denote these players as Blue and Red. Blue controls will take values in a finite set, U, and Red controls will take values in a finite set, W. Given Blue and Red controls and a system state, probabilities of transitioning to other possible states are found. We let $P_{i,j}(u, w)$ denote the probability of transitioning from state i to state j in one time step given that the Blue and Red controls are $u \in U$ and $w \in W$, respectively. Also, $P(u, w)$ will denote the matrix of such transition probabilities. We must allow for feedback controls, that is, the control can be state-dependent. For technical reasons, we will find that we specifically need to consider Red feedback controls because we will know what controls we (the Blue player) are employing. Suppose the size of χ is n, i.e., that n possible states of the system exist. Then we can represent a Red feedback control as $\bar{w} \in W^n$, an n-dimensional vector with components having values in W. Specifically, $\bar{w}_i = w \in W$ implies that Red plays w if the state is i. Define matrix $\tilde{P}(u, \bar{w})$ by

$$\tilde{P}_{i,j}(u, \bar{w}) = P_{i,j}(u, \bar{w}_i), \quad \forall i, j \in \chi$$

Let ξ_t denote the (stochastic) system state at time t. Let q_t be the vector of length n whose ith component is the probability that the state is i at time t, that is, the probability that $\xi_t = i$. If Blue plays u and Red plays $\bar{w}$ at time t, the probability propagates as

$$q_{t+1} = \tilde{P}'(u, \bar{w})q_t$$

where the prime notation indicates transpose. This completely defines the game dynamics.

We suppose a terminal cost exists for the game that is incurred at terminal time, T. Let the cost for being in terminal state $\xi_T = i \in \chi$ be $\in (i)$, which we will also sometimes find convenient to represent as the ith component of a vector, $\bar{\in}$ (where we note the abuse of notation due to use of $\in$ for two different objects). Suppose that at time $T - 1$, the state is $\xi_{T-1} = i_0$, and that Blue plays $u_{T-1} \in U$ and Red plays $\bar{w} \in W^n$. The expected cost would then be

$$E[\in (\xi_T)] = q_T' \bar{\in}$$

where $q_T = \tilde{P}'(u, \bar{w})q_{T-1}$ with q_{T-1} being 1 at i_0 and 0 in all other components.

We also need to define the observation process. We suppose that Red has perfect state knowledge but that Blue obtains their state information through observations. Let the observations take values $y \in Y$. We will suppose that this observation process can be influenced not only by random noise but also by the actions of both players. For instance, again in a military example, Blue can choose where to send sensing entities, and Red can choose to have some entities act stealthily while having some other entities exaggerate their visibility for the purposes of deception. We let $R_i(y, u, w)$ be the probability that Blue observes y given that the state is i and Blue and Red employ controls u and w. We will also find it convenient to think of this as a vector indexed by $i \in \chi$.

We suppose that at each time, $t \in \{0, 1 \ldots T - 1\}$, first an observation occurs and then the dynamics occur. We let q_t be the *a priori* distribution at time t, and $\hat{q}_t$ be the *a posteriori* distribution. With this, the dynamics update is rewritten as

$$q_{t+1} = \tilde{P}'(u_t, \vec{w}_t)\hat{q}_t$$

with controls u_t and $\vec{w}_+$ at time t. The observation, say $y_t = y$, at time t updates q_t to $\hat{q}_t$ via Bayes rule,

$$[\hat{q}_t]_i = \frac{P(y_t = y \mid \xi_t = i, u, w)[q_t]_i}{\sum_{k \in \chi} P(y_t = y \mid \xi_t = k, u, w)[q_t]_k}$$

which yields

$$[\hat{q}_t]_i = \frac{R_i(y, u, w)[q_t]_i}{\sum_{k \in \chi} R_k(y, u, w)[q_t]_k}$$

Alternatively, letting $\tilde{R}(y, u, w)$ be the vector of elements $R_i(y, u, w)$ and letting $D(y, u, w)$ be the matrix with diagonal elements $R_i(y, u, w)$ and off-diagonal elements zero, one has

$$\hat{q}_t = \frac{1}{\tilde{R}'(y, u, w)q_t} D(y, u, w)q_t$$

Then q_{t+1} and $\hat{q}_t$ define the dynamics of the conditional probabilities.

2.4.3 Deception-Rejection Machines

Control under partial information involves three components. The first consists of the accumulation of observational data up to the current moment and the construction of an abstract object that condenses this data into a form useful to the controller. The second consists of the determination of the effects of control choices on the expected (broadly defined) future costs. The third is the component that combines the output of the other two components in a way that yields the optimal (again, broadly defined) choice of control at the current moment. The object obtained by the first component is generally referred to as the *information state*. It depends only on the past. The object obtained by the second component is generally referred to as the *value function* and maps current states into future costs. Thus, the third component combines these past and future objects to obtain the best decision in the present.

One very natural way to address the control problem under partial information (and here we also use the term "control" broadly to also indicate the decision process in a game problem) is to estimate the current state of the system and then apply the optimal control that one has determined for that state. In linear, stochastic problems with quadratic cost measures (most notably, the linear/quadratic regulator), this does in fact yield the optimal control given the current available observational data. However, very few problems are found outside of that example for which this approach yields the optimal control decision. Alternately, the computations required to obtain the mathematically demonstrable optimal controller have until recently been too excessive for real-time applications for most problems. Further, for problems that are not "too" nonlinear, the above heuristic approach has yielded an acceptable (and often quite good) controller.

Unfortunately, most real-world adversarial problems do not fit within the category of problems that are well-handled by this heuristic approach. Rather, the problems are often strongly nonlinear and, importantly, have an opponent who might be attempting to cause you to make an incorrect decision through their influence on your observation process. (Interestingly, for a class of linear adversarial problems, one might find that a very low-complexity information state can still obtain the optimal control; see Chapter 3.2.) In such problems, an information state that is simply a single state estimate cannot contain enough information to make an optimal control decision. One must be able to evaluate the alternatives based on the (past) data up to the moment and the (future) measures of the total cost. States that may "seem" unlikely based on the observations but that pose large benefits for the opponent can be important in deciding which action to take.

We will consider two new approaches to handling this class of problems. These will be referred to as risk-averse control and deception-robust control. The concentration will be mainly on the latter approach.

2.4.3.1 Risk-Averse Controller Theory

If Blue were to model the (unseen) Red control actions as a stochastic process, then using q_{t+1} and $\hat{q}_t$, along with its model of the Red control process, Blue can propagate forward a conditional probability representing its lack of knowledge of the state of the system. Of course, the unseen Red controls will very likely not be randomly chosen. To safeguard itself against those possibilities that are most dangerous, Blue needs to somehow emphasize those possible states when deciding what action to take. In this section, we consider one approach to that method, which we will refer to as the *risk-averse controller* (for Blue). This method will combine the likelihood of each possible state with the dangerousness of that state to obtain a state estimate. This estimate will be averse to risk in the sense that it will tend toward those states that are likely to lead to undesirable outcomes from the Blue perspective. This approach will employ a heuristic that is based on an equivalence between risk-sensitive stochastic control and stochastic games. Proving such an equivalence is technically challenging. This equivalence has been obtained for some problem classes, but is not proven for our problem class. Nonetheless, we will apply the resulting theory (assuming equivalence) to our problem.

In linear control systems with quadratic cost criteria, the control obtained through the *separation principle* is optimal. That is, the optimal control is obtained from the state-feedback control applied at the state given by

$$\bar{x} = \arg\max_i [q_t(i)]$$

A different principle, the *certainty equivalence principle*, is appropriate in robust control. We have applied a generalization of the controller that would emanate from this latter principle. This generalization allows us to tune the relative importance between the likelihood of possible states and the risk of misestimation of the state. Let us motivate the proposed approach in a little more detail.

In deterministic games under partial information, the certainty equivalence principle indicates that one should use the state-feedback optimal control corresponding to the state given by

$$\bar{x} = \arg\max_x [I_t(x) + V_t(x)]$$

where I is the information state and V is the value function [11] (assuming uniqueness of the argmax, of course). In this problem class, the information state is essentially the worst-case cost-so-far, and the value is the minimax cost-to-come. Heuristically, this is roughly equivalent to taking the worst-case possibility for total cost from the initial time to the terminal time. For instance, see James et al. [15,18,19] and McEneaney [25,26].) The next three paragraphs discuss the mathematics that lead to the heuristic for the algorithm described below.

The deterministic information state is very similar to the logarithm of the observation-conditioned probability density in stochastic formulations for terminal/exit cost problems. (In fact, this is exactly true for a class of linear/quadratic problems.)

In the stochastic linear/quadratic problem formulation, the information state at any time t is characterized as a Gaussian distribution, say

$$p_t(x) = k(t) \exp\left\{ -\frac{1}{2}(x - \bar{x}(t))^T C^{-1}(t)(x - \bar{x}(t)) \right\}$$

In the deterministic game formulation, the information state at any time t is characterized as a quadratic cost,

$$I_t(x) = -\frac{1}{2}(x - \hat{x}(t))^T Q(t)(x - \hat{x}(t)) + r(t)$$

Interestingly, Q and C^{-1} satisfy the same Riccati equation (or, equivalently, Q^{-1} and C satisfy the same Riccati equation). The values of $\hat{x}$ and $\bar{x}$ satisfy identical equations as well. Therefore, $I_t(x) = \log[p_t(x)] + $ "time-dependent constant" [5, 26].

This motivates the algorithm proposed. Apply state-feedback control at

$$x^* = \arg\max_i \{\log[\hat{q}_t(i)] + \kappa V_t(i)\}$$

where $\hat{q}$ is the probability distribution based on the conditional distribution for Blue given previously and a stochastic model of Red control actions, and V is a state-feedback stochastic game value function [11]. Here $\kappa \in (0, \infty)$ is a measure of risk aversion. Note that $\kappa = 0$ implies that one is employing a maximum likelihood estimate in the state-feedback control (for the game), i.e.,

$$\arg\max_i \{\log([\hat{q}_t]_i)\} = \arg\max_i \{[\hat{q}_t]_i\}$$

Note also (at least in the linear-quadratic case where $\log[\hat{q}_t]_i = I_t(i)$ modulo a constant), $\kappa = 1$ corresponds to the deterministic game certainty equivalence principle [15, 18], i.e., $\arg\max\{I_t(i) + V_t(i)\}$. As $\kappa \to \infty$, this converges to an approach that always assumes the worst possible state for the system when choosing a control, regardless of observations.

We should note that the state-feedback value function can be computed using dynamic programming with various numerical approaches. Specifically, one has

$$V_T(i) = \in (i)$$

and for $t < T$,

$$V_t(i) = \min_{u \in U} \max_{\omega \in W} \mathbf{E}[V_{t+1}(\xi_{t+1})]$$

where, given that $\xi_t = i$, ξ_{t+1} is distributed by q_{t+1} with

$$[q_{t+1}]_j = P_{i,j}(u, w)$$

and so

$$V_t(i) = \min_{u \in U} \max_{\omega \in W} \sum_{j \in \chi} P_{i,j}(u, w) V_{t+1}(j)$$

(See [24] for further discussion of the value function in a similar game problem.)

2.4.3.2 Deception-Robust Controller Theory

We now turn to another approach to handling deception. The above approach was cautious (risk-averse) when choosing the state estimate at which to apply state-feedback control. In this section, we consider a controller that explicitly reasons about deception. This approach typically handles deception better that the risk-averse approach, but this improvement comes at a substantial computational cost. For a given, fixed computational limit (depending on the specific problem), the additional approximations that must be made for the deception-robust controller to be computed can reduce its effectiveness, and which approach will be more successful is not obvious.

Here we find that the truly proper information state for Red is $I_t: Q(\chi) \to \mathbf{R}$, where $Q(\chi)$ is the space of probability distributions over state space χ; $Q(\chi)$ is the simplex in $\mathfrak{R}^n$ such that all components are nonnegative and such that the sum of the components is 1. We let the initial information state be $I_0(\cdot) = \phi(\cdot)$. Here, ϕ represents the initial cost to obtain or obfuscate initial state information. The case where this information cannot be affected by the players can be represented by a max–plus delta function, that is, ϕ taking the form

$$\phi(q) = \delta_{q_c}(q) = \begin{cases} 0 & \text{if } q = q_c \\ -\infty & \text{otherwise} \end{cases}$$

This will be the case we will concentrate on here.

Notation will be reduced and the presentation will be simplified if we consider first the case without observations; the observation process will be included further below. Note that although the dynamics map into $Q(\chi)$, it is not necessarily onto. Consequently, it will be necessary to keep track of the set of feasible conditional probabilities at time t, denoted as Q_t.

Now let $\vec{w}_{[0,t-1]} = \{\vec{w}_0, \vec{w}_1 \ldots \vec{w}_{t-1}\}$ where each $\vec{w}_t \in W^n$ denotes a vector of state-dependent controls for Blue. One now sees that (in the absence of an observation process) the feasible set at time t should be given by

$$Q_t(u_{[0,t-1]}) = \{q \in Q(\chi): \exists \vec{w}_{[0,t-1]} \in [W^n]^t \text{ such that } q_0 \in Q(\chi) \text{ where}$$
$$q_0 \text{ is given by backward propagation with } q_t = q\}$$

where

$$q_{r-1} = \tilde{P}^{-1}(u_{r-1}, \vec{w}_{r-1})q_r$$

Here we assume throughout, that $\tilde{P}^{-1}$ exists in the standard sense and let superscript $-'$ denote the transpose of the inverse.

Recall that the observations occur at each time step just before the dynamics, and we continue to denote the *a priori* by q_t and the *a posteriori* by $\hat{q}_t$. Also, as noted earlier,

$$\hat{q}_t = \left(\frac{1}{\tilde{R}'(\bar{y}, u_t, \vec{w})q_t} \right) D(\bar{y}, u_t, \vec{w})q_t$$

The possible set of posteriori distributions, $\hat{Q}_t$, is the set of all $\hat{q}_t$ given by the above equation for some $q_t \in Q_t$. We suppose that D is full rank; i.e., that $\tilde{R}_i \neq 0$ for all i. Otherwise, some additional technical analysis is necessary which we do not include here. Inverting this, one finds with a little work that each component $q_{t_i} = [1/(\sum_i \tilde{R}_i^{-1} \hat{q}_{t_i})] \tilde{R}_i^{-1} \hat{q}_{t_i}$.

With the addition of the observation process, the feasible set now becomes

$$Q_t(u_{[0,t-1]}, y_{[0,t-1]}) = \{q \in Q(\chi) : \exists \vec{w}_{[0,t-1]} \in [W^n]^t\} \text{ such that } q_0 \in Q(\chi)$$
$$\text{where } q_0 \text{ is given by backward propagation}$$
$$\text{with } q_t = q$$

where

$$q_{r-1} = G^{-1}(q_r, u_{r-1}, \vec{w}_{r-1}, y_{r-1})$$

$$= \frac{1}{\hat{R}'(y_{r-1}, u_{r-1}, \vec{w}_{r-1}) q_r} D^{-1}(y_{r-1}, u_{r-1}, \vec{w}_{r-1}) \tilde{P}^{-'}(u_{r-1}, \vec{w}_{r-1}) q_r$$

where

$$\hat{R}_i(y_{r-1}, u_{r-1}, \vec{w}_{r-1}) \doteq 1/[\tilde{R}_i(y_{r-1}, u_{r-1}, \vec{w}_{r-1})]$$

The information state definition becomes

$$I_t(q; u_{[0,t-1]}, y_{[0,t-1]}) \doteq \begin{cases} \sup_{q_0 \in Q_0^{q, u_{[0,t-1]}}} \sup_{\vec{w}_{[0,t-1]} \in [W^n]^t} I_0(q_0) & \text{if } q \in Q_t \\ -\infty & \text{otherwise} \end{cases}$$

where

$$Q_0^{q, u_{[0,t-1]}} \doteq \{\tilde{q} \in Q(\chi) : \exists \vec{w}_{[0,t-1]} \in [W^n]^t\} \text{ such that } q_t = q \text{ given}$$
$$q_0 = \tilde{q} \text{ and the previous propagation. Note that we}$$
$$\text{will often suppress the dependence of } Q_t \text{ on } u_{[0,t-1]}, y_{[0,t-1]}.$$

The information state at time t maps conditional probability distributions (conditioned on the observation process) to costs ($\in \Re \cup \{-\infty\}$). It indicates the maximal cost (optimal from Red perspective) to generate conditional distribution q in a Bayesian estimator given the Blue observations up to time t. For the case we concentrate on here, the initial information state $I_0 = \phi$ take the form of a max-plus delta function $\phi(q)$. (The general case appears in [22,23].) This corresponds to the situation where Red controls do not affect the initialization. This can be generalized by taking a sum of max-plus delta functions as the initialization. For each (known) u_0 and (unknown) $\vec{w}_0$, the dynamics and observation propagation discussed above takes q_0 into some q_1. The set of all possible q_1's that can be generated by feasible $\vec{w}_0$s is Q_1

(as indicated mathematically above). Note that the size of Q_1 is no larger than the size of W^n. Further,

$$I_1(q) = \begin{cases} 0 & \text{if } q \in Q_1 \\ -\infty & \text{otherwise} \end{cases}$$

This defines the propagation of the information state forward in time by one time-step for this particular class of initial information states. More generally,

Theorem 1: If ϕ is a max-plus delta function, then $I_t(q) : Q(\chi) \to \{-\infty, 0\}$ is a max-plus sum of at most $(\#W^n)^t$ max-plus delta functions.

The proof is quite trivial [22].

Various methods are used to reduce the potentially exponential growth in the size of Q_t including pruning (whereby various methods are used to remove elements on Q_t, see the section on pruning below) and assumptions of time-consistency of Red strategies (reducing the number of potential Red controls at each time step). Also, additional theory in support of a somewhat more general propagation can be found in [22].

We now turn to the second component of the theory, computation of the state-feedback value function. This value function will be combined with the above information state to obtain the optimal Blue control. In this context, the term *value function* refers to the minimax expected payoff as a function of the current time and current "state" of the system. Our value function is a generalized value function in that it is a function not only of the physical state of the system, but also of what probability distribution Blue believes reflects its lack of knowledge of this true physical state. More specifically, the full generalized state of the system is now described by the true state taking values $x \in \chi$ and the Blue conditional probability process taking values $q \in Q(\chi)$. We denote the terminal cost for the game as $\epsilon : \chi \to \mathbf{R}$ (where this does not depend on the internal conditional probability process of Blue). Thus the state-feedback value function at the terminal time is

$$V_T(x, q) = \epsilon(x).$$

The value function at any time $t < T$ takes the form $V_t(x, q)$. It is the minimax expected payoff where Blue assumes that q is the "correct" distribution for x at time t, that at each time Blue will know the correct q, and that Red will know both the true physical state and this distribution, q. In particular, q will propagate according to $\tilde{P}'$ and the state will propagate stochastically, governed by $\tilde{p}$. Loosely speaking, this generalized value function is the minimax expected payoff if Blue believes the state to be distributed by q_r at each time $r \in (t, T]$ starting from $q_t = q$), while Red knows the true state (as well as q_r). A rigorous mathematical definition can be found in [22].

As with the information state, we must specify how one can compute $V_t(x, q)$. Ideally, this is done through backward dynamic programming, starting from the above equation. From V_T, one obtains V_{T-1}, and from this, one obtains V_{T-2}. In theory, one can propagate this backward to $t = 0$ if needed. (There are computational complexity issues here, which will be discussed further below.) Suppose one has already computed V_{t+1}. The steps that one performs to obtain V_t are as follows:

1. First, let the vector-valued function $\vec{M}_t$ be given component-wise by

$$[\vec{M}_t]_x(q, u) = \max_{\tilde{w} \in W^n} \left[\sum_{j \in \chi} \tilde{P}_{xj}(u, \tilde{w}) V_{t+1}(j, q'(q, u, \tilde{w})) \right]$$

where

$$q'(q, u, \tilde{w}) = \tilde{P}'(u, \tilde{w}) q$$

and the optimal $\tilde{w}$ is

$$[\tilde{w}_t^0] = \tilde{w}_t^0(x, q, u) = \operatorname*{argmax}_{\tilde{w} \in W^n} \left\{ \sum_{j \in \chi} \tilde{P}_{xj}(u, \tilde{w}) V_{t+1}(j, q'(q, u, \tilde{w})) \right\}$$

2. Then, define L_t as

$$L_t(q, u) = q' \vec{M}_t(q, u),$$

and note that the optimal u is

$$u_t^0 = u_t^0(q) = \operatorname*{argmin}_{u \in U} L_t(q, u) = \operatorname*{argmin}_{u \in U} q' \vec{M}_t(q, u)$$

3. With this, one obtains the next iterate from

$$V_t(x, q) = \sum_{j \in \chi} \tilde{P}_{xj}(u_t^0, \tilde{w}_t^0) V_{t+1}(j, q'(q, u_t^0, \tilde{w}_t^0)) = [\vec{M}_t]_x(q, u_t^0)$$

and the best achievable expected result from the Blue perspective is

$$V_t^1(q) = q' \vec{M}_t(q, u_t^0)$$

Consequently, for each $t \in \{0, 1 \dots T\}$ and each $x \in \chi$, $V_t(x, q)$ is a piecewise constant function over simplex $Q(\chi)$. Due to this piecewise constant nature, propagation is relatively straightforward (more specifically, it is finite-dimensional in contradistinction to the general case). We should note that $L_t(q, u)$, given in the above steps, will be an important object, and that it represents how well Blue can do applying control u at time t, if indeed the state were distributed according to q.

The remaining component of the computation of the control at each time instant is now discussed. The control computation for such games is typically performed via the use of the certainty equivalence principle [1,15]. When the certainty equivalence principle holds, the information state and state-feedback value function can be combined to obtain the optimal controls, which can be shown to be robust in a sense to be discussed below. The chief gain is that this allows one to compute a state-feedback controller ahead of time. Then in real-time, one only propagates the information state, computes the certainty-equivalent state, and obtains the associated precomputed state-feedback control at this state. Note that this is much cheaper than computing the control as a function of the information state in real-time. The computational cost of this latter approach is prohibitive because it requires computing a control as a function of a complex object.

To simplify notation, note that for for u,

$$L_t(q,u) = \mathbf{E}_q \left[\max_{\vec{w} \in W^n} \sum_{j \in \chi} \tilde{P}_{Xj}(u,\vec{w}) V_{t+1}(j, q'(q,u,\vec{w})) \right]$$

where the notation $q'(q,u,\vec{w})$ is defined previously. Let us hypothesize that the optimal control for Blue is

$$u_t^m \doteq \underset{u \in U}{\operatorname{argmin}} \left[\max_{q \in Q(\chi)} \{ I_t(q) + L_t(q,u) \} \right]$$

To prove robustness, one must first define a partial observation value function in terms of the worst-case expected cost (from the Blue point of view). To make this more readable, we begin by writing this value function and then describing the terms within it rather than vice versa. For technical reasons, it appears best to work with the following value function. (This value function is distinct from the generalized state-feedback value function described above.) This value at any time $\bar{t}$ is

$$Z_{\bar{t}} \doteq \sup_{q_{\bar{t}} \in Q_t} \quad \inf_{\lambda_{[\bar{t},T-1]} \in \Lambda_{[\bar{t},T-1]}} \quad \sup_{\theta_{[\bar{t},T-1]} \in \Theta_{[\bar{t},T-1]}} \quad [I_{\bar{t}}(q_{\bar{t}}^-) + \mathbf{E}_{X \sim q_{\bar{t}}} \{ \mathbf{E}[\in (X_T) \mid X_{\bar{t}} = X] \}]$$

The expectation uses the (Blue) assumption that the distribution of $X_{\bar{t}}$ is $q_{\bar{t}}$ for each $q_{\bar{t}} \in Q_{\bar{t}}$ and is taken not only over $X_{\bar{t}}$ but also over all observation and dynamic noise from time $\bar{t}$ to terminal time T. The strategy set for Blue is

$$\Lambda_{[\bar{t},T-1]} = \left\{ \lambda_{[\bar{t},T-1]} : Y^{T-\bar{t}} \to U^{T-\bar{t}}, \text{nonanticipative in } y_{-1} \right\}$$

where "nonanticipative in y_{-1}" is defined as follows. A strategy, $\lambda_{[\bar{t},T-1]}$ is nonanticipative in y_{-1} if given any $t \in (\bar{t}, T-1]$ and any sequences $y_{\cdot}, \tilde{y}_{\cdot}$.

such that $y_r = \tilde{y}_r$ for all $r \in (\bar{t}, t-1]$ one has $\lambda_t[y] = \lambda_t[\tilde{y}]$. Note that because the infimum over $\lambda_{[\bar{t},T-1]}$ occurs inside the supremum over $q_{\bar{t}}$, the "optimal" choice of λ may depend on $q_{\bar{t}}$. Also note that the "optimal" choice of $\lambda_{[\bar{t},T-1]}$ may depend on $I_{\bar{t}}$. The strategy set for Red (neglecting $q_{\bar{t}}$ as a Red control, even though we take a supremum over $q_{\bar{t}}$) is naturally

$$\Theta_{[\bar{t},T-1]} = \{\theta_{[\bar{t},T-1]} : Y^{T-\bar{t}} \to W^{n(T-\bar{t})}, \text{ nonanticipative in } y_{-1}\}$$

The first step in obtaining the robustness result is to show that the value $Z_{\bar{t}}$ has the following representation [22].

Theorem 2:

$$Z_{\bar{t}} = \sup_{q_{\bar{t}} \in Q_{\bar{t}}} [I_{\bar{t}}(q_{\bar{t}}) + V_{\bar{t}}^1(q_{\bar{t}})] \quad \forall \bar{t} \in [0,T]$$

In other words, the game value $Z_{\bar{t}}$ is the supremum of the sum of the information state $I_{\bar{t}}$ and the optimal expected state-feedback value $V_{\bar{t}}^1$, from Blue's perspective. Using Theorem 2, one can show [22] that

$$Z_{\bar{t}} = \sup_{q_{\bar{t}} \in Q_t} [I_{\bar{t}}(q_{\bar{t}}) + \min_{u \in U} L_{\bar{t}}(q_{\bar{t}}, u)] = \sup_{q_{\bar{t}} \in Q_t} \min_{u \in U} [I_{\bar{t}}(q_{\bar{t}}) + L_{\bar{t}}(q_{\bar{t}}, u)]$$

To obtain the robustness/certainty equivalence result below, making the following saddle-point assumption is sufficient. We assume that for all t,

$$\sup_{q_{\bar{t}} \in Q_t} \min_{u \in U} [I_{\bar{t}}(q_{\bar{t}}) + L_{\bar{t}}(q_{\bar{t}}, u)] = \min_{u \in U} \sup_{q_{\bar{t}} \in Q_t} [I_{\bar{t}}(q_{\bar{t}}) + L_{\bar{t}}(q_{\bar{t}}, u)]$$

This type of assumption is typical in game theory. Although it is difficult to verify for a given problem, the alternative is a theory that cannot be translated into a useful result. With the above assumption (labeled A-SP), this becomes

$$Z_{\bar{t}} \min_{u \in U} \sup_{q_{\bar{t}} \in Q_t} [I_{\bar{t}}(q_{\bar{t}}) + L_{\bar{t}}(q_{\bar{t}}, u)]$$

Finally, after some work [22], one obtains the robustness result:

Theorem 3: Let $\bar{t} \in \{0, T-1\}$. Let I_0, $u_{[0,\bar{t}-1]}$, and $y_{[0,\bar{t}-1]}$ be given. Let the Blue control choice, $u_{\bar{t}}^m$ be a strict minimizer. Suppose saddle-point assumption (A-SP) holds. Then, given any Blue strategy $\lambda_{[\bar{t},T-1]}$, such that $\lambda_{\bar{t}}[y.] \neq u_{\bar{t}}^m$, there exists $\varepsilon > 0$, $q_{\bar{t}}^\varepsilon$ and $\bar{w}_{[\bar{t},T-1]}^\varepsilon$ such that

$$\sup_{q \in Q_{\bar{t}}} \{I_{\bar{t}}(q) + L_{\bar{t}}(q, u_{\bar{t}}^m)\} = Z_{\bar{t}} \leq I_{\bar{t}}(q_{\bar{t}}^\varepsilon) + \mathbf{E}_{X \sim q_{\bar{t}}^\varepsilon} \{\mathbf{E}[\varepsilon (X_{\bar{t}}^\varepsilon) \mid X_{\bar{t}}^\varepsilon = X]\} - \varepsilon$$

where X^ε denotes the process propagated with control strategies $\lambda_{[\bar{t},T-1]}$ and $\vec{w}^\varepsilon_{[\bar{t},T-1]}$.

In other words, following any such alternative strategy λ yields a poorer expected result.

2.4.4 A Seemingly Simple Game

The remainder of this chapter will be devoted primarily to application of the above methods for handling deception to a particular example game. This game will seem to be quite simple at first. However, once one introduces the partial information and deception components, determination of the best (or even nearly best) strategy becomes quite far from obvious.

We refer to this game as the Masked Attack Game. A snapshot from the game is depicted in Figure 2.4.1. In the Masked Attack Game, the Red player is attempting to take (or, equivalently from the perspective of the game, destroy) a valuable Blue asset. Red can use stealth and decoys to obscure the direction from which the attack will occur, whereas Blue will attempt to interdict the Red advances.

In particular, we consider an example where Red and Blue have only a handful of forces and the attacks can come along only two routes. This example of the Masked Attack Game is complex enough to demonstrate many of the issues that appear when applying this technology. At the same time, it is simple enough so that technical complications do not muddy the picture excessively.

The following terminology (used in the remainder of this chapter) may require a little elaboration:

- *Entity*: Controllable objects, e.g., tanks and unmanned aerial vehicles.
- *Attrition*: Damage caused by one of the sides to the entities belonging to the other.
- C^2: Command and control, the process by which the opponents guide their entities in the battle.
- *Intel*: Information that one side obtains by observing the territory and entities of the other.
- *Asset*: An object of high value. (In this example, the term *asset* will only be used to designate certain stationary Blue objects, not the Red and Blue entities.)
- *Decoy*: An inexpensive imitation of an entity without combat capability.
- *Stealth*: Use of camouflage or other means to avoid detection.
- *UCAV*: Unmanned or Uninhabited Combat Air Vehicle, capable of attacking the opponent entities.

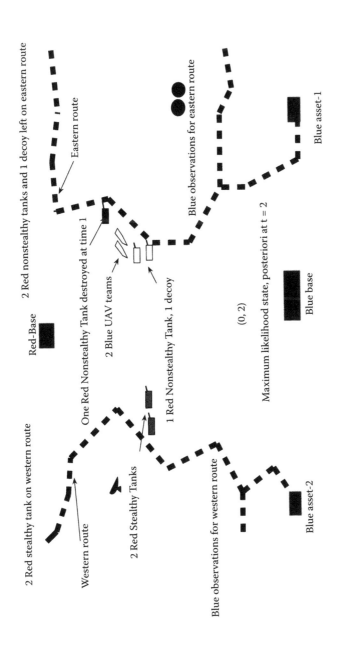

FIGURE 2.4.1
Snapshot from Masked Attack Game.

2.4.4.1 Objective

In this game, the Red player has four ground entities (tanks) and the Blue player has two UCAVs. The objective of the Red player is to capture the high-value Blue assets by moving at least one nondecoy Red entity to a Blue asset location by the terminal time, T. The Blue player uses the UCAVs to interdict and destroy the moving Red entities and prevent them from reaching the Blue assets by the terminal time.

Winning and losing are measured in terms of the total cost (equivalently, the score) at the prespecified terminal time. Blue attempts to minimize this cost whereas Red attempts to maximize it. The cost at terminal time is computed as follows: Each Red surviving entitiy costs Blue 1 point, and if Blue loses any (or both) of the high-value assets to Red (amounting to at least one nondecoy Red entity reaching the asset by the terminal time), it costs Blue 20 points. Suppose we designate the number of surviving Red entities on route i at time t as r_t^i. In the best-case scenario, Blue achieves a cost of 0 ($r_T^1 + r_T^2 = 0$), at terminal time), and in the worst-case scenario, a cost of 24 ($20 + r_T^1 + r_T^2$, where $r_T^1 + r_T^2 = 4$, at terminal time). No running cost is applied. The running cost in an example such as this would refer to the cost of specific control processes used up to the current time t, for example, the cost of using the decoys and the fuel cost when moving the UCAVs from one route to another.

2.4.4.2 Dynamics

Red entities move at the same speed independent of being stealthy or nonstealthy and independent of the route (uniform terrain) and are not allowed to switch routes during the game. Red entities do not have any attrition capability against the Blue UCAVs. Blue UCAVs require at least two time steps to travel from one route to the other.

The simulation snapshot in Figure 2.4.1 is taken between time steps 1 and 2 from the graphic for a MATLAB® simulation that runs the example game. Blue's base is at the bottom of the figure. Red is depicted with a base at the top of the figure. The two rectangular shapes on either side of the Blue base represent the positions of two high-value assets belonging to Blue. The dashed lines are meant to indicate routes that the Red entities (depicted as tanks) could take toward each of the Blue high-value assets. The Red player is moving four ground entities from the Red base toward two Blue assets. These entities move along either an eastern route or a western route depending on which Blue asset they are attacking. (Red entities may be moving along both routes, and simply two groups of Red entities, those moving along the eastern route and those moving along the western route.)

At the time of the snapshot in Figure 2.4.1, Red was in the process of nonstealthily moving one tank and one decoy tank toward the eastern Blue asset and two tanks (their gray color indicating stealthy movement) toward the western Blue asset. The black tank icon along the eastern route road indicates that at time 1, the tank on that route (which had been operating nonstealthily) was destroyed. Obviously, Red entities can move stealthily or nonstealthily.

Red entities are detected more easily when they are nonstealthy. Blue has two attack UCAVs that can be assigned to attack Red entities on either route, individually or in tandem. In the figure, the missile-shaped icons moving along the eastern road indicate Blue UCAVs that are currently attempting to intercept the Red entities moving along that route. Blue's UCAVs are typically expected to be more effective against the Red entities when they are moving in the nonstealthy mode (although for study purposes, we mainly include results where the effectiveness against stealthy and non-stealthy entities are identical once Blue has decided to attack them).

Further, a fixed travel time exists for the UCAVs to move from one route to the other. At each time step, Blue must decide how to assign its UCAVs while Red decides which Red entities to make stealthy and whether to employ a decoy. Red also initially decides how to partition its ground entities between the two routes; this partition remains in effect throughout the game. The health of the Red entities will transition as a discrete-time Markov chain where the transition probabilities depend on whether they are under attack by zero, one, or two Blue UCAVs. We should note that Red "takes" an asset by successfully moving at least one nondecoy entity to the asset, while Blue UCAVs provide resistance by intercepting the Red entities). The state transition probabilities can be affected by the actions of both players. Note that the observation probabilities can also be affected by the controls of both players. The current Blue observations are also shown for both routes in the Figure 2.4.1. In this snapshot, the annotations indicate that Blue has detected both the Red entities on the eastern route (one of which is a decoy) and detected nothing on the western route. The maximum likelihood state (MLS), i.e., the naive estimate, is also indicated. Blue can choose to apply the optimal state-feedback control corresponding to the MLS estimate as the control for the partiallyobserved game. We will refer to this Blue approach as the naive approach.

2.4.4.3 Controls

The Blue control options are simply where to send the Blue UCAVs for the next time step. As we noted above, not all possibilities are allowed. The Blue state at any time t is X_t^B, which is an index corresponding to an ordered pair indicating the positions of the two UCAVs. The first element of the pair is the position of the first UCAV and the second element is the position of the second UCAV. The position can only take the following three values: On the eastern route, on the western route, or in the middle zone. The Blue state at the next time step is the Blue control at the current time step, i.e.,

$$X_{t+1}^B = u_t$$

The state-dependent Blue control options will be given in tables further below. The following notation will be used:

- $u = 1$: Send both UCAVs to the eastern route.
- $u = 2$: Send both UCAVs to the middle/neutral zone.

- $u = 3$: Send both UCAVs to the eastern route.
- $u = 4$: Send one UCAV to the western route and move one to the middle/neutral zone.
- $u = 5$: Send one UCAV to the eastern route and move one to the middle/neutral zone.
- $u = 6$: Send one UCAV to the eastern route and one to the western route.

At any time t, the Blue control is $u_x \in U$, where $U = [1, 2, 3, 4, 5, 6]$ (or typically, a subset of U). Consequently, the state X_t^B, also takes values in U.

Recall that Red initially partitions its forces along the two routes, and because this partition remains in effect throughout the game, we do not include this in the controls at each time step. For simplicity, we also restrict Red to use a decoy on route i at time t if and only if the entities on that route at that time are operating nonstealthily. The set of Red control choices at each time step is denoted as W, where $W = \{(S, S),(S, N),(N, S),(N, N),\}$. The individual control options are as follows:

- (S,S): Red entities on both routes operate stealthily.
- (S,N): Red entities on the western route operate stealthily and those on the eastern route operate nonstealthily.
- (N,S): Red entities on the western route operate nonstealthily and those on the eastern route operate stealthily.
- (N,N): Red entities on both routes operate nonstealthily.

2.4.4.4 Notation and Parameters

The Red team state at any time has the representation $X_t^R = (r_t^1, r_t^2)$, where r_t^1 is the number of surviving Red entities on the western route and r_t^2 is the number of surviving Red entities on the eastern route at time t. Recall that in the particular example we are using here, Red moved at a fixed rate, independent of stealth, and so Red entity positions did not need to be included in the state. Also, as indicated just above, the Blue state at time t is denoted as X_t^B. Therefore, the state of the game at any time t is $\xi_t = (X_t^B, X_t^R)$.

The main parameters employed in the simulation study to follow are:

- p_2^N: Probability of a Red entity being destroyed when attacked by both UCAVs and when Red is nonstealthy.
- p_1^N: Probability of a Red entity being destroyed when attacked by one UCAV and when Red is nonstealthy.
- p_2^S: Probability of a Red entity being destroyed when attacked by both UCAVs and when Red is stealthy.
- p_1^S: Probability of a Red entity being destroyed when attacked by one UCAV and when Red is stealthy.

- $p1$: Probability of observing a nonstealthy Red entity.
- $p2$: Probability of observing a stealthy Red entity.
- pf: Probability of observing a Red decoy.
- ps: Probability of all Red entities on a route being stealthy.
- α^1: p_1^N/p_2^N or p_1^S/p_2^S, the ratio of attrition caused by one UCAV relative to attrition caused by two UCAVs.
- α^2: p_2^S/p_2^N, a parameter measuring attrition caused on stealthy Red entities relative to attrition caused on nonstealthy Red entities by two UCAVs.
- r_r: r_0^1/r_0^2, the ratio of the (asymmetrical) initial Red entity distribution on the two routes.

2.4.4.5 Notes on Strategy

In a Masked Attack Game, Red typically gains nothing by being completely open about its actions. On the contrary, one obvious strategy for Red is to attempt to lead Blue into thinking that the coming attack is completely along a certain route while, in fact, another contingent is approaching an asset along the alternate route. Because the total number of Red forces are known, one specific approach is for Red to employ almost all of its forces nonstealthily (and with a decoy) along one route and only a single stealthy entity along the alternate path. The resulting observations would look much like an entire force approaching along a single route.

The problem for Blue is how to dynamically apportion its UCAVs between the two routes, keeping in mind that a nonzero travel time exists between the two routes. A seemingly cautious approach is to simply send one UCAV along each route. However, one UCAV is substantially less effective than two, and if Red's forces are heavily asymmetrical, then this approach is suboptimal.

Upon study of automatically generated Red controllers, another approach to Red strategies was also found effective. This approach attempts to cause Blue to waste time traveling between the two routes. In particular, as Blue sends its UCAVs toward one route, Red sets the entities on the Blue-destination route to stealthy and exaggerates the size of its forces on the other route. If Blue reacts to this baiting, it tends to oscillate in its force distribution.

The optimal strategy depends on many parameters, such as the probabilities of detecting stealthy, nonstealthy, and decoy entities, as well as the various attrition probabilities.

2.4.5 Analysis of the Fully Observable Case

Prior to discussing the results of our study of this partially observed game, we look at the fully observable case, which we will also refer to as the state-feedback case. Clearly the state-feedback problem is quite simple.

TABLE 2.4.1

Blue State Dependent Control

X_b \ u_b	1	2	3	4	5	6
1	1	1	0	1	0	0
2	1	1	1	1	1	1
3	0	1	1	0	1	0
4	1	1	0	1	0	1
5	0	1	1	0	1	1
6	0	1	0	1	1	1

Model MS2

X_b \ u_b	1	2	3	4	5	6
1	1	0	0	1	0	0
2	1	1	1	1	1	1
3	0	0	1	0	1	0
4	1	1	0	1	0	1
5	0	1	1	0	1	1
6	0	1	0	1	1	1

Model MS3

Further, the optimal control choices in the state-feedback case help illuminate the partially-observed problem, which is the focus of our study.

The Blue UCAVs can be allowed to move from one route to the other in either 2 or 3 time steps. We will use the notation *MS2* for the former and *MS3* for the later. Note that in these two cases described above, the state-dependent allowable Blue controls will be different. For *MS2* and *MS3*, the state dependent Blue control tables are shown in Table 2.4.1. The table should be understood as indicating that a control is allowed in a certain state by having a 1 in that state/control entry. In other words, the entry 1 at the (i,j) position in the above tables implies that if Blue is at state i at any time, movement to state j is a feasible control option for Blue. We will sometimes refer to the cost as "value" in the simulation results or the figure captions. The strategy and the cost also depend on the terminal time, T. We would refer to the model with $T = k$ by *Tk*. Combining these two modeling issues, *MS2T5* would refer to the model where the Blue UCAVs can move from one route to the other in 2 time steps and the terminal time is 5 units (or 4 control actions allowed per UCAV).

We briefly discuss the dependence of the cost on the model choice, but we will use a single model (*MS2T5*) thereafter to study deception robustness. The first results compare *MS2T5* to *MS3T5* for exactly the same parameters. This is depicted in the upper plot of Figure 2.4.2a. Clearly, the faster Blue (being able to go from one route to the other in less time) achieves a smaller cost (the one in the left figure). The second result again simply (and intuitively) gives the effect of having more control action for Blue. Obviously, a higher T (in *MS2T5*) gives Blue more control steps and so it is able to eliminate more Red entities, leading to a lower cost as shown in lower plot of Figure 2.4.2b.

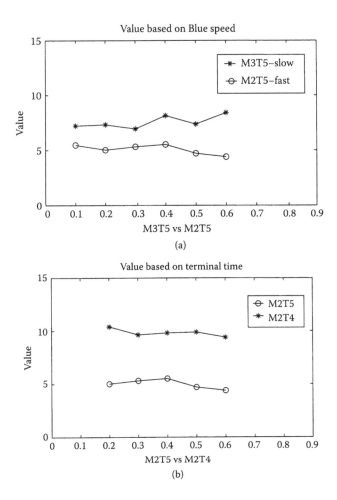

FIGURE 2.4.2
Cost dependence on Blue speed and terminal time.

In the subsequent discussion, we will use only the model *MS2T5*. We will discuss the following two scenarios:

- A_D: The case where the attrition of Red entities is dependent on the stealthiness of Red entities (or $p_2^N > p_2^S$). The Red control in this case is to choose an initial state X_0^R and controls w_t for $t \in [0, 1 \ldots T - 1]$.

- A_I: The case where the attrition probabilities are independent on the stealthiness of Red entities (or $p_2^N = p_2^S$). The Red control in this case is only to choose an initial state X_0^R.

In many state-feedback games with available control choices known for both players, one can narrow down the set of feasible controls to a smaller set of controls that are sufficient to compute the optimal control sequences. We consider the case A_l from Blue's perspective. We choose $\alpha^l \leq 0.5$, the attrition capability of one UCAV being less than half the attrition capability of two UCAVs. The best initial Red state distribution is either $X_0^R = (1,3)$ or $X_0^R = (2,2)$. The first Blue control with initial state $X_0^B = 2$, (or Blue UCAVs in the central/neutral zone) is to attack the eastern route with both UCAVs, $u_1^B = 3$. Further, the Blue control for subsequent steps depends on the outcome of the interaction at time 1 between the two UCAVs and the Red entities (three in number) on the eastern front. Recall that the Blue control depends on the current Blue state and the modeling constraints. For best results, the Blue player would like to have at least one shot at Red on both routes. With $u_0 = 3$, 108 control sequences ($u_0 = 3, u_1, u_2, u_3$) are possible for this set up. If $X_3^B = u_2$, one can easily enumerate all the sequences ($3, u_1, u_2, u_3^*$) with optimal Blue control choice u_3^* as:

- (3, 2, 1, 1), (3, 2, 2, 1), (3, 2, 4, 1), (3, 2, 5, 6), (3, 2, 6, 6)
- (3, 5, 2, 1), (3, 5, 4, 1), (3, 5, 4, 6), (3, 5, 5, 6), (3, 5, 6, 6)
- (3, 3, 2, 1), (3, 3, 5, 6)

By cross-comparing sequences, some of these control sequences will achieve better results mainly due to removing redundant steps — (3, 2, 1, 1) vs. (3, 2, 2, 1) — or by noting the existence of more efficient attack sequences — (3, 2, 6, 6) vs. (3, 2, 5, 6). Finally, only five sequences — (3, 2, 1, 1), (3, 3, 2, 1), (3, 5, 4, 1), (3, 5, 6, 6), and (3, 3, 5, 6) — need to be considered for evaluating the optimal strategy for Blue. The Blue control choice is thus fairly straightforward for the state-feedback game. Clearly with X_0^R unknown, such computational simplification is not available for the Blue player and finding an optimal control sequence for the entire time horizon is not a simple task anymore. In an adversarial environment, similar reasoning is not sufficient or does not have the structure (due to lack of information) to yield a narrower set of control choices for computing the optimal control sequence. In fact, for the state-feedback case, for given attrition parameters, the optimal control sequences can also be enumerated as a function of r, and α_1. We conclude this part of the discussion by stating that unlike state-feedback, partially observed games require a more complex algorithmic approach (like the deception-robust theory; it uses observations/estimation of the true state).

Another aspect of strategy or control formulation that is easy to analyze in the state-feedback game is the dependence of the Blue control strategy on α^l. For Red initial states (a, b), with $b > a$ and $b \neq 0$, $a \neq 0$ (as in the above example, the optimal Blue control u_{T-1}^o (with $X_{T-1}^B = 2$) changes from 3 to 6 for specific α^l as a function of (a, b) and p_2^N. The switch between the two control options is determined by simply comparing the cost using $u_{T-1} = 3$,

$$a + b(1 - p_2^N)$$

and using $U_{T-1} = 6$,

$$\sum_{k=0}^{a}\left[(p_2^N)^{a+b-k}(1-p_2^N)^k(20+k)\left[\sum_{l_1}^{l_2}\binom{a}{l}\binom{b}{k-l}\right]\right]$$

where $l_1 = max(0, k - b)$ and $l_2 = min(k, a)$. As $b \gg a$, typically a higher α^l value is required for switching the control from 3 to 6, for a fixed p_2^N. This result can be easily obtained from a brief theoretical analysis. Such change in strategy is not distinct in the partially observed game because Blue control is a function of q_t, which is dependent on the observation process. Also note that for even a fixed r_r, a higher value of α^l is required for $(a + 1, a + 1)$ compared to (a, a). For the partially observed game (using the above example) in the appropriate α^l regime (that admits attacking both routes as an optimal Blue strategy at time $T - 1$), an observation — say $(0, 3)$, due to use of decoys by Red — may give a maximum likelihood state of $(0, r_4^2)$, leading to an optimal Blue control $u_t^o = 3$ using the naive approach. However, because the true state is $(1, 3)$, this would be a suboptimal control for Blue in the partially observed game setup. Simplified analytical expressions for computing the optimal Blue control are not available in the partially observed game owing to the unknown Red states and potentially antagonistic noise.

Naturally, given lack of true state information, Blue will achieve a worse cost (higher) compared to the case where it has complete state information. This result is shown in Figure 2.4.3 where the * curves are the complete state information cases. We further point to the difference in the nature of a state-feedback game to the partially-observed game scenario (using our example problem) by comparing the performance of a symmetric Red (a, a) initial state to an asymmetric one — (a, b), with $a \neq b$ — in both scenarios. The results indicate that even when the symmetric initial Red state $(2, 2)$ is marginally better for Red in the state-feedback case, the asymmetrical Red initial state $(1, 3)$ is better for Red in the partially-observed game.

The results for this second study are shown in Figure 2.4.4. Note that the symmetric distribution $(2, 2)$ works slightly better for Red than $(1, 3)$ in the full state-feedback game. But the asymmetric layout $(1, 3)$ (skewed with an added decoy on the nonstealthy eastern route) works better for Red in the partially observed case. These results are for the model $MS2T5$ in the case A_I. Importantly the attrition is independent of stealth. Thus, the effect of the information level on the Blue control decisions is isolated to illustrate the importance of state information.

From Red's perspective, the case A_D is just minutely different. Red can still choose to make entities on each route stealthy or nonstealthy in this case. Typically, attrition for stealthy entities will never be greater than that for nonstealthy entities. Consequently, the optimal Red control is to have the entities operate stealthily on the route under attack. (Red, being

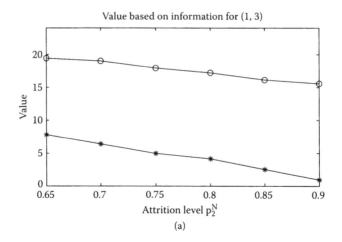

(a)

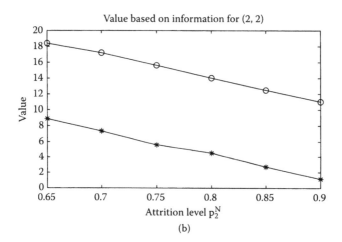

(b)

FIGURE 2.4.3
Comparing state-feedback and partial-information game scenarios.

the maximizer, is the inside player in the minimax and so makes its control decision after Blue makes its decision). More simply, Red can stay stealthy all the time as no running cost is applied. The partially observed game in the A_D case is again complex, as the Red player can use decoys to corrupt the observation process of Blue. Simply employing the state-feedback control for Red does not allow it the full potential to deceive Blue. Finally, one should note that unlike the state-feedback game, the partially observed game (with adversarial noise) is a problem with a more complex structure.

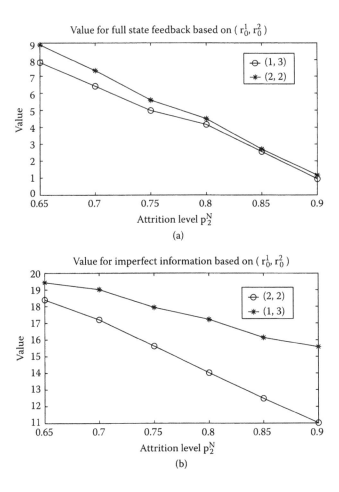

FIGURE 2.4.4
Initial Red force distribution: state-feedback and partial-information.

2.4.6 Analysis of the Partially Observed Case

So far we have analyzed our example game in the case where the Blue player has full information about the state of the Red entities. Now let us reformulate the game problem so that the Blue player has only partial information about the Red entities. This creates a problem for Blue by enabling a deceptive Red control. We would like to emphasize that the information state definition

$$I_t(q) = \begin{cases} 0 & \text{if } q \in Q_t \\ -\infty & \text{otherwise} \end{cases}$$

reduces the Blue control computation to

$$u_t^m \doteq \arg\min_{u \in U} \left[\max_{q \in Q_t} \{L_t(q, u)\} \right]$$

and so we are simply computing the maximum over the distributions in the set of feasible distributions Q_t (owing to the definition of I_{tq}). Hence, in the rest of this chapter, we represent the information state as a feasible set of observation-conditioned distributions.

Blue only has partial information and uses observation-based control strategies, so the Blue player can choose to use one UCAV on each route to "play it safe." This may not lead to the best result due to asymmetrical force distributions (e.g., one UCAV against three Red entities and one UCAV against one Red entity). As Blue updates its information using observations, it might decide to move both the UCAVs on one route if no Red entities are observed on the other route. Hence, the speed with which Blue can go from one route to the other and the observation accuracies are clearly the factors that affect Blue's performance. Blue is also aware that the observations are potentially corrupted by the Red player through the use of stealth or decoys. So Blue cannot trust the observations.

From Red's perspective, the lack of information for Blue can be used to gain potential advantages. This can be achieved through the use of stealth and decoys such that the observation process is misleading. Ideally for Red, this would lead Blue to choose a suboptimal control and incur a higher cost. (For examples, see the notes on strategy at the end of the "A Seemingly Simple Game" section.)

We now look at a specific heuristic Red approach. The Red team can start with the the following initial states : (0, 4), (1, 3), (2, 2), (3, 1), and (4, 0). The cases (0, 4) and (4, 0) are trivial in structure and (1, 3) is axially symmetric to (3, 1). As shown in the state-feedback game section, (1, 3) gives a higher cost for Red in partially observed games, so we discuss simulation results for this Red initial state (unknown to Blue). The initial Red force partition affects Blue's observations (and, consequently, its information state). Note that the use of stealth is equivalent to low values of $p2$. In particular, we set the observation probability for a Red decoy to be the same as for a non-stealthy (nondecoy) Red entity. An intuitive and reasonable Red control is to operate one entity stealthily along the western route and three entities nonstealthily along the eastern route, accompanied by a decoy. We will refer to this Red control strategy with a Red initial state of (1, 3) as RG, or the "Red game" approach.

This forms a formidable Red opponent. The low probability of detecting the single Red entity on the western route relative to the likely observations on the eastern route would tend to lure a naive Blue controller into thinking that all the Red forces are along the eastern route and to only apply UCAVs there to have the highest probability of stopping all the forces on this route. This is indeed the optimal Blue choice when using a Bayesian (naive) filter, but the deception-robust approach does not fall for this deception and provides resistance to the western Red entities as well. In this study, we use the above reasonably deceptive, hand-crafted Red *RG* strategy. With the Red *RG* approach specified, we return to Blue's control mechanism and the effect of *p2*, *ps*, and *pf* on the cost. Recall that Blue is not aware of the true initial Red state. The objective for the rest of the chapter is to explore the merits of using a complex control algorithm like the deception-robust approach over a standard Bayesian/Kalman filter approach.

2.4.6.1 Initializing the Controller

Recall that we consider only the case where the initial information state in the deception-robust controller, $I_0 = \phi$, is zero for some $q \in Q(\chi)$ and $-\infty$ elsewhere. Choosing the proper ϕ at the outset is important in ensuring good future behavior of the controller. This issue is a significant generalization over the analogous issue for standard methods where one simply must pick a reasonable initial probability distribution (covariance, for example). Here in the deception-robust case, one could imagine that very poor initial information might be represented by a ϕ that is zero only on the uniform distribution because the uniform distribution represents a total lack of knowledge. Alternatively, one might also represent this complete lack of knowledge by letting ϕ be zero on every distribution that is one at a single state and zero elsewhere. These two possibilities represent radically different concepts regarding the underlying cause of our lack of initial information of the opponent state. The first approach corresponds to a worldview, wherein all of our lack of knowledge is due to unknown random variables — as though the initial state was random. The second approach corresponds to a worldview, where one imagines the opponent carefully choosing its initial state with no randomness about the actual initial state at all. Thus, we see that the initialization issue is a good deal more complex in the deception-robust controller than it is in more typical approaches. We will present some data indicating how this decision should be made.

Recall that we are only considering ϕ that are sums of max-plus delta functions (these can alternatively be represented by sets of distributions). The decision on what is the best set of initial distributions depends on several factors, of which the information on Red's initial state plays a critical role. We first ascertain that quality of information is more important than quantity of information. Specifically, the manner in which the lack of knowledge is represented is critical. Some interesting results obtained by differentiating the quality of information contained in the initial distributions are presented here. In the first scenario Blue models the unknown Red initial state with three initial distributions, one of which is a delta function at the true Red state $(1, 3)$. Then more distributions (of delta function type) are added and the simulation is repeated for increasing numbers of initial distributions. The results are in the left plot of the Figure 2.4.5a. It shows no significant change in the value if we keep adding more spiky distributions to the original three. We now compare this to the second set of results in the right plot of Figure 2.4.5b, which

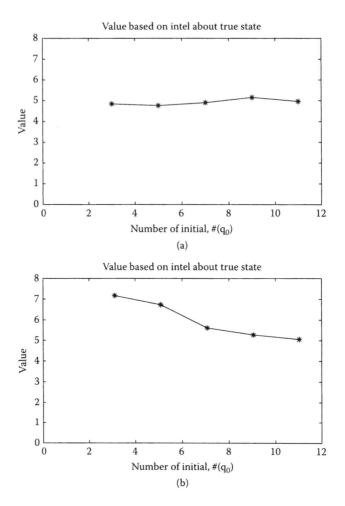

FIGURE 2.4.5
Value of intel in initial distribution: Deception-robust.

are obtained with the same parameters but with no initial distribution having a delta function at the true state (1, 3), and using relatively flatter initial distributions. As we increase the number of such distributions, one obtains a better cost for Blue and it approaches the cost Blue achieves in the first scenario. This leads to the conclusion that with the knowledge that Red is using some intelligent strategy (such as *RG*), one can use fewer initial distributions and, consequently, the computational growth factor can be reduced. This reduction is linear in the number of initial distributions.

The choice of Blue initial distributions requires more analysis. If the Red player uses a nonprobabilistic (not naive) strategy for the initial state layout on the two routes, but Blue models the Red initial state layout strategy probabilistically (or vice versa), how does such mismodeling affect Blue's performance? We discuss these questions using simulation results. We will differentiate between parameters used in the simulation by using the subscript S and the subscript B for parameters used in the Blue state estimation and control computations (e.g., k_B). We will also use the following terminology for the true initial Red state distribution strategy and the modeling used by the Blue player for the same:

- BD-RD: Blue uses probabilistic modeling of Red initial state layout strategy, and Red's initial state layout strategy is also probabilistic (naive).

- BD-RG: Blue uses probabilistic modeling of Red initial state layout strategy, and Red's initial state layout strategy is not probabilistic but potentially deceptive (RG).

- BG-RG: Blue uses multiple initial distributions of max-plus delta type (deception-robust strategy) to model Red initial state layout strategy, and Red's initial state layout strategy is not probabilistic but potentially deceptive (RG).

- BG-RD: Blue uses multiple initial distributions of max-plus delta type (deception-robust strategy) to model Red initial state layout strategy, and Red's initial state layout strategy is also probabilistic (naive).

Mismodeling in the pf parameter exists in the current model even with $pf_B = pf_S$. This happens because we allow Red to choose just one route on which it can use decoys, whereas the Blue modeling of Red assumes a potential Red decoy on both routes. In this first mismodeling result (Figure 2.4.6, $pf_B = pf_S$), by comparing the "*" plot with the "o" chart, Blue clearly achieves a lower cost by using a single probabilistic distribution (BD) when Red is using RD, as opposed to using BG when Red is using RD. However, using BG does not produce serious disadvantages, as the curves are rather close. Similar results can be deduced by comparing "x" with "∇" (or the inverted triangle) for the second case. Here Blue gets a better cost when it models the (true, potentially deceptive) intelligent Red initial state layout strategy appropriately, using multiple delta functions as initial distributions (deception-robust approach) compared to modeling the Red strategy probabilistically. The difference in this case is proportionately higher indicating that in the presence of mismodeling, Blue tends to suffer more drastically when using a naive model strategy for an intelligent Red opponent than using an intelligent modelling strategy for a naive Red opponent. The result in Figure 2.4.7 leads to very similar conclusions ($pf_B \neq pf_S$; the false alarm parameter is different in the simulation and the Blue observation update). As an aside, also note that Red always achieves better results using an intelligent strategy (potentially involving deception). This can be ascertained by comparing the plots: "∇" vs. "*" and "x" vs. "o". Blue will generally achieve better results by using multiple delta

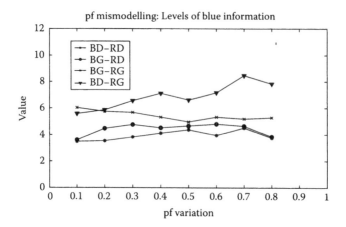

FIGURE 2.4.6
Information state initialization, deception-robust.

functions at various potential states (note that these initial distribution types are harder to prune, as we will see in the next section).

Using more distributions may not always achieve a better cost (for Blue) for a theoretical reason. With the above discussion, one can intuitively claim that a few distributions based on reliable intelligence could in fact work better (at least no worse) than using more distributions. The additional

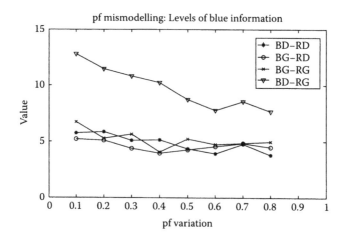

FIGURE 2.4.7
Information state initialization, $pf_B \neq pf_S$, deception-robust.

benefit with such a knowledge is that the resulting computational speeds are relatively faster. More specifically, the deception-robust approach will work no worse (and potentially better) when Blue has some "specific" information about Red control choices. In this example, the Red player is using the RG strategy. Assume that Blue knows $\underline{W} \subset W$ such that it has strong reasons to believe that Red will only use $w \in \underline{W}$. Then, one immediately has that $\underline{M} = \#\underline{W}$ is less than $M = \#W$. Correspondingly, one has $\underline{Q}_t \subset Q_t$, where $\underline{Q}_t$ is a new set of feasible distributions at time t. Clearly, one has a slower growth rate per time step by a factor of $M/\underline{M}$. Then for any $u \in U$, one has

$$\max_{q \in \underline{Q}_t}\{I_t(q) + L_t(q, u)\} \leq \max_{q \in Q_t}\{I_t(q) + L_t(q, u)\}$$

which gives

$$\min_{u \in U}\left[\max_{q \in \underline{Q}_t}\{I_t(q) + L_t(q, u)\}\right] \leq \min_{u \in U}\left[\max_{q \in Q_t}\{I_t(q) + L_t(q, u)\}\right].$$

This implies that Blue achieves a value that is no worse than using a larger set of distributions and has a potential for saving substantial computational time. For technical reasons, we will assume that no reduction in the size of set Q_t is done in this analysis. We provide a brief comparison to the naive approach using results from a simulation study (for similar information levels on the Red control set). Note that Blue uses a probabilistic model for Red control strategy in the naive approach. Let $p(xy)$ be the probability of using the (x, y) Red control in the Blue update algorithm. We enumerate the intelligence level numerically by an increasing number representing improving knowledge level of the Red control set:

- 1: $p(SS) = 0$, $p(SN) = p(NS) = p(NN) = \frac{1}{3}$.
- 2: $p(SS) = 0$, $p(SN) = p(NS) = 0.45$, $p(NN) = 0.1$
- 3: $p(SS) = 0$, $p(SN) = p(NS) = 0.5$, $p(NN) = 0$
- 4: $p(SS) = 0.03$, $p(SN) = 0.91$, $p(NS) = 0.03$, $p(NN) = 0.03$

For example, Blue may know that Red is using an asymmetrical control and hence set the probability of Red using (S, S) or (N, N) to 0. With this modeling of Red control, one can again expect Blue to do no worse than having no information about the actual Red control at all. However, as seen in Figure 2.4.8, for our example such information does not gain any advantage for Blue using the naive approach. This indicates that for this problem, such information was not able to change Blue control strategy.

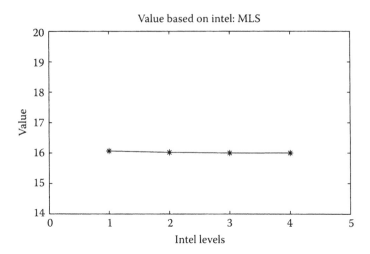

FIGURE 2.4.8
Naive Blue and Intel.

2.4.7   Pruning

We refer to the reduction in the size of the set of potential states as *pruning*. From Blue's perspective in the partially observed case, this refers to a reduction in the size of the set of feasible observation-conditioned distributions, Q_t. Pruning techniques for Blue directly affect computational speed. An important issue for this study is the relation of intelligence information about the initial Red force distributions, q_0, and about Red controls to computational speed and Blue performance. As outlined in the theory, a set of initial distributions is carried forward by Blue using each Red control to obtain the set of feasible distributions at each time. In the deception-robust approach, an argmax must be computed over such a set of feasible distributions, so we must prune these distributions sufficiently to allow computational feasibility and stay within reasonable error tolerance levels at the same time. Growth in the number of these distributions is linear in the number of initial distributions and exponential in the size of the Red control set. This provides motivation to study the effects of pruning using various initial distributions (and in different numbers) and the effect of more knowledge of the Red control set on the performance of the Blue player.

Note that given $M = \#W$ and n_i initial distributions, the set of feasible distributions Q_t^B at time t has size $n_i M^t$. This growth is exponential and must be checked to allow a practical implementation of the deception-robust approach. In practice, only a few distributions will be useful. In the computation involving argmax over $q \in Q_t^B$, a smaller size of Q_t^B will make faster computational speeds possible. We first outline the pruning algorithm that is used in the simulation results to follow. At time t, for a pair (k, l) such that $q^k \in Q_t^B$ and $q^l \in Q_t^B$, we remove any one of them from Q_t^B if

$$\left\| q^k - q^l \right\| \leq ptol$$

where *ptol* is the pruning tolerance level. Another pruning technique can use the "spikiness" of the information in the distributions. At time t, for a pair (k, l) such that $q^k \in Q_t^B$ and $q^l \in Q_t^B$,

$$\text{Let } m^{*k} \doteq \operatorname{argmax}_i [q_i^k] \quad \text{and} \quad m^{*l} \doteq \operatorname{argmax}_i [q_i^l]$$

$$\text{If } m^{*k} = m^{*l} \quad \text{and} \quad (q_{m^{*k}}^k - q_{m^{*k}}^l) \leq ptol, \quad \text{delete } q^k$$

$$\text{If } m^{*k} = m^{*l} \quad \text{and} \quad (q_{m^{*k}}^l - q_{m^{*k}}^k) \leq ptol, \quad \text{delete } q^l$$

In the second (comparatively stricter) method of pruning, we do not discard a cautious distribution (relatively flatter). Because we are able to demonstrate reasonable speed advantages with the first pruning technique for our example game, we prefer it over the second due to its simplicity. The second pruning technique (or potentially more rigorous or analytical ones) can most likely find use in larger scale problems. A Red strategy *RG* and the model *MS2T5* have been used in the following simulation results.

The effect of *ptol* on computational speed is expected to be very simple — a higher *ptol* would generally prune more distributions in comparison to a lower *ptol*. Thus, with higher *ptol* values, simulation speeds are faster compared to lower values of *ptol*. However, this intuitive relationship also depends on another factor, the actual distribution set. Because Q_t^B is obtained from Q_0^B, the choice of the initial distributions will also affect the pruning speed. When more spiky distributions (each being a delta function at a different Red initial state) are used, less distributions are pruned and simulation speed slows down considerably. However, the value in this case is not very sensitive to the tolerance level as one can see in the upper plot of Figure 2.4.9a. This can allow the use of a higher tolerance level. Initial distributions that are flater lead to faster pruning and hence better speeds. But with flatter distributions, the value is more sensitive to the *ptol* value. Consequently, such distributions might need a tighter error tolerance to achieve the desired performance specifications. The results for this case are shown in the lower plot of Figure 2.4.9b. Note that the tolerance level can be adjusted as time progresses if a learning-rate type of information is available to increase or decrease the pruning level.

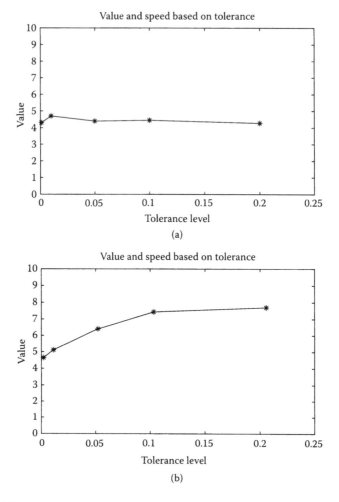

FIGURE 2.4.9
Initial distribution and effect of tolerance level: Deception-robust.

2.4.8 Comparison of the Risk-Averse and Deception-Robust Approaches

Let us briefly foray into a comparative study between the naive approach, the risk-averse algorithm, and the deception-robust approach for Blue. The critical component of the risk-averse approach is the choice of the risk level, κ. For the example studied in this chapter, we vary κ between 0 and 10 to demonstrate the nature of the risk-averse approach in general. First, for the case $\kappa = 0$, we have the risk-averse approach equivalent to the naive approach; apply the state-feedback control at the MLS estimate. As κ

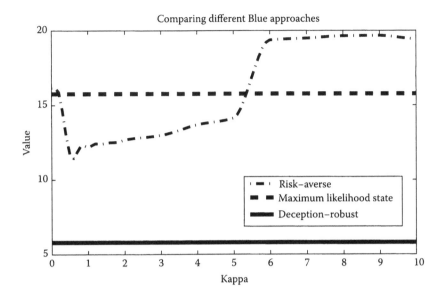

FIGURE 2.4.10
Risk-averse, deception-robust, and naive approaches.

increases, we expect the approach to achieve a lower cost for Blue because it is taking into account the expected future cost $V(X_t)$ as a risk-sensitive measure. However, in the adversarial environment, the effect of the Red player's control on the Blue player's observations has more complex consequences than that of random noise. As shown in Figure 2.4.10, the risk-averse approach gets the best cost for Blue at κ between 0.5 and 0.6 (note again that this choice will be problem-specific). As κ increases beyond this point, the expected cost begins increasing and has a horizontal asymptote and corresponds to a Blue controller that ignores all the observations and assumes the worst-case possible Red configuration.

The "bumpiness" in the results is due to the sampling error (8000 Monte Carlo runs were used for each data point in the plot.) Also note that for large κ, the risk-averse approach performs worse than the naive approach. For this specific example, the risk-averse approach does not achieve the same low cost achieved by using the deception-robust approach.

2.4.9 Implementation

In this chapter, we have discussed two approaches to handling deception in some classes of dynamic stochastic games, the deception-robust approach (which we concentrated on) and the risk-averse approach. We now discuss the main steps one goes through in the implementation of this technology.

First, one must clearly define the (finite) state space. That is, one must develop a model of all possible (physical) states of the system, and this must consist of a finite number of states. In the problems we have studied, this state space is the set of all possible entity positions and healths (where "health" is broadly defined but where we typically index this by a few numbers). For example, consider a game with six Blue entities and eight Red entities, and in which each of these entities can occupy a position on the "board" where there are 1000 positions, and we indicate the set of these positions as L. Let the Blue and Red entity positions be $L_1^B, L_2^B \ldots L_6^B$ and $L_1^R, L_2^R \ldots L_8^R$, respectively. Suppose each of these entities has one of four health states in $\mathcal{H} = \{$destroyed, damaged, needs maintenance, Okay$\}$. These health states can be denoted as $H_1^B, H_2^B \ldots H_6^B$ and $H_1^R, H_2^R \ldots H_8^R$. A state $i \in \chi$ then corresponds to a vector

$$i = \{L_1^B, \ldots L_6^B, L_1^R, \ldots L_8^R, H_1^B, \ldots H_6^B, H_1^R \ldots H_8^R\} \in L^{14} \times \mathcal{H}^{14}$$

where the superscripts on the right-hand side indicate the outer product. In this case, χ is comprised of 4000^{14} states.

In a military game such as this with a state space such as that indicated above, the possible controls for any entity might be to move from $l_{31} \in L$ to adjacent location $l_{171} \in L$ or fire at position l_{22}. They might also be more general, such as "lay low" or return fire if fired upon. We suppose that the controls for each entity take values in finite sets U_0 and W_0 (containing controls such as those above). Then the control sets for all of Blue and all of Red would be $U = U_0^6$ and $W = W_0^8$, respectively. The allowable controls can be state-dependent but we will not add that additional complication to this discussion.

Next, one must determine the transition probabilities for moving from state i to state j given controls $u \in U$ and $w \in W$, $P_{i,j}(u, w)$. For nontrivial games, these will not be enumerated for each possibility but instead will be built up from probabilities of outcomes of individual entity actions. In our example, a probability would exist for Blue Entity 2 to go from health state Okay to health state damaged, given that its control is to move from location l_1 to l_{80} while being fired upon by Red Entity 3 at position l_7, and while this Red entity is itself under fire from another Blue entity. This defines the dynamics. One must also define the Blue observation process. For our problem class, one needs to set the probability of each possible observation y given state i and controls u and w.

Let us consider the risk-averse approach first. In this case, one must also create some initial probability distribution q_0 describing Blue's lack of information about the initial Red state. For example, this could be the uniform distribution over χ if one knew absolutely nothing. Note that if χ is very large, this can be an unwieldily object. In such a case, one needs to use clever methods to represent this information. Note that to propagate this forward, one again does not want to enumerate the probabilities for every state, i.e., $[q_t]_i$ for every $i \in \chi$. For instance, one might simply carry forward the probabilities where they are above some nominal value, and set the rest to a fixed ε that guarantees we have a probability measure. One might also only allow a finite number of values of the probabilities at each step (where the particular set of values can be time-dependent). In the above military example, one can carry forward distributions for the position and health of each Red entity independently.

Note that in the risk-averse approach, one must additionally model the Red control as a state-dependent, stochastic process. For instance, in the military example, one can model a Red entity's movement as a stochastic process approximately moving toward the nearest Blue entitiy or toward the target, depending on the ranges of these objects. This motion might have some randomness in it. The certainty equivalent component of this computation will tend to put emphasis on those movement paths corresponding to intelligent Red decisions as it uses the (minimax) value function to determine its estimate.

This last statement brings up the remaining component needed for application of the risk-averse approach: Computation of the state-feedback value. Ideally, this is obtained through backward dynamic programming. More specifically, each step of the backward dynamic programming algorithm for our problem class is given by

$$V_t(i) = \min_{u \in U} \max_{w \in W} \sum_{j \in \chi} P_{i,j}(u,w)V_{t+1}(j).$$

Note that this component must be computed for each $i \in \chi$ at each time step t. Also, for each i and t, one must search for the minimum over all $u \in U$, and for each triplet i, t, and u, one must search for the maximum over all $w \in W$. (Note that this can be done off line.) For large problems, this is not feasible. Instead, one can use hierarchical techniques to decompose the problem. Further, even this might not be sufficient to make the problem computationally tractable. In that case, one can allow Blue and Red to search only over move strings of several steps where these move strings can be partially random. One then applies some heuristic value approximation at the end of the short time-horizon look-ahead. Lastly, instead of computing $V_t(i)$ for all $i \in \chi$, one can restrict the computation to only those i for which $[\hat{q}_t]_i$ is not too far below the argmax over all $[\hat{q}_t]_i$. Of course, this shortcut is only possible if the computation is done in real-time.

Now we turn to issues in the application of the deception-robust approach. This approach is more computationally demanding than the risk-averse approach. As described just above, the first steps are the specification of the state space, χ, the control spaces, U and W, the dynamics, and the observation process probabilities. One must initialize the system, i.e., specify I_0, which maps probability distributions into generalized costs. We consider only the case where I_0 is a max-plus delta function or a finite sum of such. This is the case where I_0 is $-\infty$ everywhere except at one or a finite number of points where I_0 is zero. As indicated earlier, in this case, I_0 can equivalently be represented as one probability distribution where I_0 is zero, or as a finite number of such in the case where I_0 is a finite sum of max-plus delta functions. Then to propagate I_0 forward, one merely propagates the q distributions where I_t is zero forward in time. In the deception-robust case, the Red control is not a state-dependent stochastic process but is allowed to be any $w \in W$ at each time. For a given q_t and any $\bar{w} \in W^n$, this q_t maps to #(W^n) of these q_{t+1} distributions; that is, one can have an image distribution corresponding to each possible state-feedback Red control. This branching quickly leads to an unwieldy number of distributions. In fact, one might encounter exponential growth in the number of these distributions as one moves forward in time. Various techniques are used to reduce this computational growth; for example, see the section regarding pruning earlier in this chapter.

Finally, one must discuss computation of the generalized value function, $V_t(i, q)$. Of course, this is much more computationally intensive than computation of the state-feedback value of the risk-averse approach. We have found that the following approximation works well in the example problems considered so far. In computing the value at time t, we let the first Blue control (i.e., at current time t) or the first Blue string of controls (as indicated in the risk-averse approach discussion) depend on q, and thereafter assume only state-feedback Blue controls. Again, one can choose to only compute this at values of i that correspond to relatively high values of the q.

References

1. Basar T., and Bernhard P., *H∞-Optimal Control and Related Minimax Design Problems*, Birkhäuser, Boston, 1991.
2. Basar T. and Olsder G.J. *Dynamic Noncooperative Game Theory*, Classics in Applied Mathematics Series, SIAM, 1999, Originally pub. Academic Press, San Diego, 1982.
3. Bernhard P., Colomb A.-L., Papavassilopoulos G.P., Rabbit and hunter game: two discrete stochastic formulations, *Comp. Math. App.*, 13, 1987, 205--225.
4. Elliott R.J. and Kalton N.J., The existence of value in differential games, *Memoirs of the Am. Math. Soc.*, 126, 1972.
5. Fleming W.H., Deterministic nonlinear filtering, *Annali Scuola Normale Superiore Pisa, Cl. Scienze Fisiche e Matematiche*, Ser. IV 25, 1997, 435–454.
6. Fleming W.H., The convergence problem for differential games II, *Contributions to the Theory of Games*, 5, Princeton Univ. Press, Princeton, NJ, 1964.
7. Fleming W.H. and McEneaney W.M., Robust limits of risk sensitive nonlinear filters, *Math. Control, Signals Sys.*, 14, 2001, 109–142.
8. Fleming W.H. and McEneaney W.M., Risk sensitive control on an infinite time horizon, *SIAM J. Control Optim.*, 33, 6, 1995, 1881–1915.
9. Fleming W.H. and McEneaney W.M., Risk–sensitive control with ergodic cost criteria, *Proc. 31st IEEE Conf. on Dec. and Control*, 1992.
10. Fleming W.H. and McEneaney W.M., Risk–sensitive optimal control and differential games, *Proc. of the Stochastic Theory and Adaptive Controls Workshop, Springer Lecture Notes in Control and Information Sciences*, 184, Berlin, Springer–Verlag, 1992.
11. Fleming W.H. and Soner H.M., *Controlled Markov Processes and Viscosity Solutions*, New York: Springer-Verlag, 1992.

12. Fleming W.H. and Souganidis P.E., On the existence of value functions of two–player, zero--sum stochastic differential games, *Indiana Univ. Math. J.*, 38, 1989, 293–314.
13. Friedman A., *Differential Games*, New York: John Wiley & Sons 1971.
14. Heise S.A. and Morse H.S., The DARPA JFACC program: modeling and control of military operations, *Proc. 39th IEEE CDC*, Sydney, 2000, 2551–2555.
15. Helton J.W. and James M.R., *Extending H_∞ Control to Nonlinear Systems: Control of Nonlinear Systems to Achieve Performance Objectives*, SIAM, Philadelphia, 1999.
16. Jacobson D.H., Optimal stochastic linear systems with exponential criteria and their relation to deterministic differential games, *IEEE Trans. Automat. Control*, 18, 1973, 124–131.
17. James M.R., Asymptotic analysis of non–linear stochastic risk–sensitive control and differential games, *Math. Control Signals Sys.*, 5, 1992, 401–417.
18. James M.R. and Baras J.S., Partially observed differential games, infinite dimensional HJI equations, and nonlinear H_∞ control, *SIAM J. Control and Optim.*, 34, 1996, 1342–1364.
19. James M.R. and Yuliar S., A nonlinear partially observed differential game with a finite-dimensional information state, *Sys. Control Lett.*, 26, 1995, 137–145.
20. McEneaney W.M. and Singh R., Deception in autonomous vehicle decision making in an adversarial environment, *Proc. AIAA Conf. on Guidance Navigation and Control*, San Francisco, 2005.
21. McEneaney W.M. and Singh R., Unmanned vehicle operations under imperfect information in an adversarial environment, *Proc. AIAA Conf. on Guidance Navigation and Control*, 2004.
22. McEneaney W.M., "Some classes of imperfect information finite state-space stochastic games with finite-dimensional solutions, *Applied Math. Optim.*, 50, 2004, 87–118.
23. McEneaney W.M., A class of reasonably tractable partially observed discrete stochastic games, *Proc. 41st IEEE CDC*, Las Vegas, 2002.
24. McEneaney W.M., Fitzpatrick B.G., and Lauko I.G., Stochastic game approach to air operations, *IEEE Trans. Aerospace Elec. Sys.*, 40, 2004, 1191–1216.
25. McEneaney W.M., Robust/game–theoretic methods in filtering and estimation, *First Symp. on Advances in Enterprise Control*, San Diego, 1999, 1–9.
26. McEneaney W.M., Robust H_∞ filtering for nonlinear systems, *Sys. Control Lett.*, 33, 1998, 315–325.
27. Olsder, G.J., and Papavassilopoulos G.P., About when to use a searchlight, *J. Math. Anal. Appl.*, 136, 1988, 466–478.
28. Runolfsson T., Risk–sensitive control of Markov chains and differential games, *Proc. of the 32nd IEEE Conf. on Decision and Control*, San Antonio, TX, 1993.
29. Whittle P., Risk–sensitive linear/quadratic/Gaussian control, *Adv. Appl. Prob.*, 13, 1981, 764–777.

3.1

The Role of Imperfect Information

Austin Parker, Dana Nau, and V.S. Subrahmanian

CONTENTS

An obvious source of approaches to strategy formulation is the field of classical strategic games. Classical game-tree search techniques have been highly successful in classical games of strategy such as chess, checkers, Othello, backgammon, and the like. However, all of these games are *perfect-information* games: Each player has perfect information about the current state of the game at all points during the game. Unlike classical strategic games, practical adversarial reasoning problems force the decision maker to solve the problem in the environment of highly imperfect information. Some of the game-tree search techniques used for perfect-information games can also be used in imperfect-information games, but only with substantial modifications.

In this chapter,* we classify and describe techniques for game-tree search in imperfect information games. In addition, we offer case studies of how these techniques have been applied to two imperfect-information games: Texas hold em, which is a well-known poker variant, and Kriegspiel chess, an imperfect-information variant of chess that is the progenitor of modern military wargaming [15].

3.1.1   Classical Game-Tree Search

To understand how to use a game-tree search in imperfect-information games, it is first necessary to understand how it works in perfect-information games. Most game-tree search algorithms have been designed for use on games that satisfy the following assumptions:

- *The game is a sequential-move game.* It consists of a sequence of actions called *moves*. Examples include moving a piece in a game such as chess, checkers, Othello, or backgammon, or playing a card in a game such as poker or bridge.

- *It is a two-player game.* The moves are made by two independent agents (or, in games such as bridge, two *teams* of agents) called *players*.

- *The game has real-valued payoffs.* Whenever the game ends, each player (or team of players) receives a *payoff* that can be expressed as a real number. For example, a player's payoff in poker is the amount of money that they win or lose. In chess or checkers, the payoffs can be represented numerically as 1 for a win, −1 for a loss, and 0 for a draw.

- *The game is a zero-sum game.* The two players (whom we will call Max and Min) are adversaries. Technically, a zero-sum game is one in which the sum of the payoffs is always zero, e.g., chess, checkers, and poker. But the term "zero sum" is often used to include many games in which the sum of the payoffs is nonzero, provided that these games can be translated into equivalent games in which the sum is zero (e.g., by subtracting some constant c from the payoffs of both players). Bridge is an example of such a game. Probably the best-known example of a nonzero-sum game is the prisoner's dilemma [3].

---

* This work was supported by the following grants, contracts, and awards: ARO grant DAAD190310202, ARL grants DAAD190320026 and DAAL0197K0135, the ARL CTAs on Telecommunications and Advanced Decision Architectures, NSF grants IIS0329851, 0205489, and IIS0412812, and UC Berkeley contract number SA451832441 (subcontract from DARPA's REAL program). The opinions expressed in this chapter are those of the authors and do not necessarily reflect the opinions of the funders. The figures and tables in this chapter are © 2005 Dr. Nau and are used with permission.

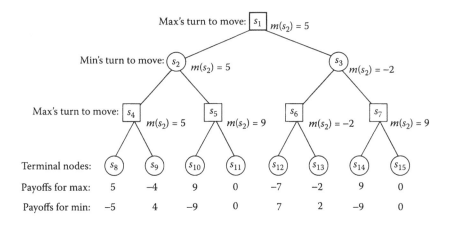

FIGURE 3.1.1
A simple example of a game tree.

- *The game is a perfect-information game.* The players always have complete information about the game's current state. This includes games such as chess, checkers, Othello, and backgammon, but it excludes most card games and some board games (e.g., Battleship and Kriegspiel chess).

Games satisfying the above requirements can be represented by *game trees* such as the simple one shown in Figure 3.1.1. In this figure, the square nodes represent states where it is Max's move, the round nodes represent states where it is Min's move, and the edges represent moves. The terminal nodes represent states in which the game has ended, and the numbers below the terminal nodes are the payoffs. The figure shows the payoffs for both Max and Min, but we will usually show only the payoffs for Max (as Min's payoff is always the negative of Max's payoff).

Suppose that two players are playing a game, the current state is s, and the player to move is p. It has become conventional to say that "perfect" play for p at s consists of choosing the move that produces the highest possible payoff if both players play perfectly from that point onwards. From this, it follows that at s, the effective payoff for Max, is

$$m(s) = \begin{cases} \text{Max's payoff at } s & \text{if } s \text{ is a terminal node} \\ \max\{m(t) : t \text{ is a child of } s\} & \text{if it is Max's move at } s \\ \min\{m(t) : t \text{ is a child of } s\} & \text{if it is Min's move at } s \end{cases}$$

where *child* means any immediate successor of s.

For example, in Figure 3.1.1,

$$m(s_2) = \min(\max(5, -4), \max(9, 0)) = \min(5, 9) = 5$$

$$m(s_3) = \min(\max(s_{12}), \max(s_{13}), \max(s_{14}), \max(s_{15}) = \min(7, 0) = 0$$

Hence, the perfect play for Max at s_1 is to move to s_2. The formula for $m(s)$ is a special case of von Neuman and Morgenstern's famous Minimax Theorem; hence, $m(s)$ is called Max's *minimax value* at s. The minimax value for Min is, of course, $-m(s)$.

If one chooses a move by applying this equation directly, this requires searching every state in the game tree, but most nontrivial games have so many states that exploring all of them is completely infeasible. Hence, a number of techniques have been developed to speed up the computation. The best known ones include:

- *Alpha-beta pruning*, which is a technique for deducing that the minimax values of certain states cannot have any effect on the minimax value of s, thus those states and their successors do not need to be searched to compute s's minimax value.
- *Limited-depth search*, which uses the following modified version of the above equation, where d is an arbitrary number called the *cutoff depth* and $e(s)$ is a *static evaluation function* that uses *ad hoc* techniques to produce an estimate of $m(s)$:

$$m(s,d) = \begin{cases} p\text{'s payoff at } s & \text{if } s \text{ is a terminal state} \\ e(s) & \text{if } d = 0 \\ \max\{m(t, d-1) : t \text{ is a child of } s\} & \text{if it is Max's move at } s \\ \max\{m(t) : t \text{ is a child of } s\} & \text{if it is Max's move at } s \end{cases}$$

- *Transposition tables*, which are hash tables where one can store the minimax values of some of the states. This way, if those states occur more than once in the game tree, computing their values more than once will not be necessary.
- *Quiescence search*, which is a modified version of $m(s.d)$ in which if $d = 0$, we will still continue to search below $e(s)$ if s is not *quiescent*, and if something is happening at s (e.g., a pending capture in chess) that is likely to make $e(s)$ inaccurate.

Most good game-tree search programs use a combination of these and several other techniques.

3.1.2 Game-Tree Search in Imperfect-Information Games

In an imperfect-information game, a player p's *belief state* is the set $b = \{s_1, s_2 \dots s_n\}$ of all states that are consistent with the information currently available to p. If the players move in alternation, then, in principle, modeling the game as an *imperfect-information game tree G* in which each node u represents a belief state b_u is possible, and the set of edges emanating from u represents the *moves(u)* of all moves that a player might be able to make at u (i.e., a move is in *moves(u)* if it is applicable to at least one state in b_u). In such a game tree, the utility value of u would depend on the probability distribution over b_u, i.e., it depends on the probability for each state $s \in b_u$, that the current state is actually s. However, in practice, this approach presents some immense difficulties.

One difficulty is that the game tree can have a very large branching factor. Generally the set *moves(b_u)* of all moves that a player might be able to make is much larger than the set of moves applicable to each state $s \in b_u$, hence the branching factor of the imperfect-information game tree is much larger than what it would be if we had perfect information. Because the size of a game tree is generally exponential in the tree's branching factor, this means that the game tree for an imperfect-information game can dwarf the game tree that we would get if we had perfect information.

As an example, consider a two-player card game in which an ordinary deck of playing cards is divided into its four suits, and each player is dealt one card of each suit. Suppose the players play cards in alternation until neither player has any cards left. If Max can see what cards are in both player's hands, then the branching factor (the number of nodes that are immediate successors) is $5 - n$ at Max's nth move and $5 - n$ at Min's nth move, for $n = 1,2,3,4$. Thus, the number of leaf nodes in the game tree is

$$4 \times 4 \times 3 \times 3 \times 2 \times 2 \times 1 \times 1 = 576$$

But suppose that Max can see the cards in its hand but not the cards in Min's hand, just the cards that Min has already played. This changes the branching factor at Min's nth move to $12 \times (5 - n)$, so the number of leaf nodes in the game tree is

$$(12 \times 4) \times 4 \times (12 \times 3) \times 3 \times (12 \times 2) \times 2 \times (12 \times 1) \times 1 = 11{,}943{,}936$$

Another difficulty is how to determine, for each possible move that an adversary might be able to make, the probability that the adversary actually can make that move. In card games where the cards are dealt to the players, this probability (or a reasonable estimate) can be computed from the probabilities of the possible card distributions. But in a game like Kriegspiel chess, in which the uncertainty arises from not knowing what moves the adversary has already made, no clear way exists to compute such a probability.

A third difficulty is that even if the above probabilities were known, still not clear is how to compute an estimate of a node's utility value. In perfect-information games, the minimax formula has been successful because it provides a pretty good (although not perfect) model of how a strong adversary might behave. But if the adversary's information about the game is imperfect, then that the adversary will make the move predicted by the minimax formula is unlikely. Some other model of the adversary is needed instead, and what this model should be is often unclear.

Several methods have been developed to try to circumvent the above difficulties. They can be classified into three main types (which are often used in combination with each other): Aggregation techniques, Monte Carlo sampling, and opponent modeling. Each are discussed below.

3.1.2.1 Aggregation Techniques

Similarity-based aggregation.   Cases are found in which two different states in a game are similar enough to be treated as equivalent. For example, in bridge, cards that have similar rank can often be viewed as equivalent: Playing one of them will usually have the same effect as playing any of the others. This effectively decreases the branching factor of the search space by reducing the number of plays that need to be evaluated. This idea was initially developed for use in the game of sprouts [1], and it has been used successfully in bridge in combination with Monte Carlo sampling [14]. More recently, in the game of poker, it has been used in the development of a computer program that plays at the level of an good human player [4].

Strategy-based aggregation.   The normal approach to game-tree generation is action-based: Each branch corresponds to an action that one might take. In strategy-based game-tree generation, each branch instead corresponds to some strategy that a player might try. For example, bridge play is composed strategies such as ruffing, cross-ruffing, finessing, cashing out, and so on. For each strategy, one can define applicability conditions telling whether the strategy is a reasonable thing to try, and partially instantiated game-tree fragments give the possible ways that the strategy might be carried out. This reduces the branching factor of the game tree because the number of applicable strategies at each point is usually smaller than the number of possible actions. The primary drawback of this approach is that a substantial amount of human effort is needed to make sure that the set of strategies is complete and correct — and for this reason, it has not been widely used. However, it has been used successfully in computer bridge [30].

3.1.2.2 Monte Carlo Sampling

In an imperfect-information game G, suppose we can generate a hypothesis h for what the missing information is. If the hypothesis h is correct, then this will reduce the game to a perfect-information game $G(h)$ that can be searched using ordinary game-tree search techniques. In general, we will not know whether h is correct, but if we have a probability distribution over the set H of all possible hypotheses, then we can use Monte Carlo techniques as follows. First, use the probability distribution to randomly generate n hypotheses $h_1 \ldots h_n$ for what the missing information might be. Next, do an ordinary minimax game-tree search on each of the games $G(h_1)$, $G(h_2)$ ... $G(h_n)$, and average the results to produce approximate utility values for the nodes of G. The larger the value of n, the better the approximations will be, and even for a large value of n, we can search $G(h_1)$, $G(h_2)$ ... $G(h_n)$ much more quickly than we could search G itself.

Statistical sampling has an important theoretical limitation [13]: It does not produce correct evaluations of information-gathering moves or moves intended to deceive the opponent (see Chapter 2.3 and Chapter 2.4) because neither type of move is even possible in the perfect-information game trees $G(h_1)$, $G(h_2)$ ... $G(h_n)$. Despite this limitation, statistical sampling has worked well in practice in several games. Examples of such games include bridge [14], Scrabble [26], and poker [4].

3.1.2.3 Opponent Modeling

Opponent modeling is an essential part of expert human game-playing. At the professional level, baseball players know which batters are susceptible to fastballs, basketball players know their opponents' better shooting hands, chess players will study the past openings of their opponents before meeting them in tournament play, and poker players are proceeded by their reputations.

In classical game-tree search on perfect-information games, the minimax formula is a simple model for the opponent: It assumes a computationally unbounded opponent capable of making the move that is worst for us at any point in the game. In perfect-information games, very little opponent modeling other than this has been done in any explicit sense* but a certain amount of opponent modeling often appears implicitly. For example, one source of static evaluation functions for chess is automated analysis of databases of the games played by chess grandmasters [16]. A chess program using such a static evaluation function implicitly attempts to push its opponent toward a board position that would be unfavorable to one of the grandmasters whose games appear in the database.

In partial-information games, opponent modeling has a much more important role to play. Most of the work on opponent modeling in partial-information games has been done in the game of poker, where the need to model an opponent's betting style is quite obvious.

---

* A notable exception is [9], an interesting theoretical model for opponent modeling in total information games that provides a syntax and algorithm for dealing with concepts such as "he thinks that I think that he thinks. ..."

For the game of Texas hold 'em (see the case study later in this chapter), one approach [7] is to keep a record of a player's past moves and assume that his future behavior will be similar to how he behaved under similar conditions in the past. A more recent approach [11] uses a neural net to aggregate the available information into a prediction of the opponent's next move. In both of these works, the programs that do opponent modeling far outperform those that do no modeling.

For some additional work on opponent modeling (specifically, a reinforcement algorithm for constructing opponent models in extensive games), see Chapter 3.5.*

3.1.2.4   Combining the Techniques

In most practical applications, two or more of the above techniques are used in combination with each other. For example, statistical sampling and aggregation can be combined by using an aggregation technique to construct a simplified version of the game tree, doing the statistical sampling on this simplified game tree and using the results of the sampling to choose a move in the original (unsimplified) game. This has been used in several bridge programs [14,30] and at least one poker program [4].

3.1.3   Case Study: Texas hold 'em

Texas hold 'em is a variant of poker that originated sometime during the 1920s. It falls into a class of poker games called "community card" or "shared card" games, which are so called because some of the cards are dealt face-up in the center of the table and are shared by all of the players. The rest of each player's hand consists of "hole cards" that are dealt specifically to that player and are not seen by the other players. Each player's hand is comprised of his hole cards together with the community cards.

Texas hold 'em is currently the most popular of the community card poker games, and a number of books have been published on how to play it [10,17,22,23,27]. It has been called the "Cadillac of Poker"** and is well-respected as one of the most strategically complex poker variants. In principle, it can be played by up to 22 players, but in practice, it is generally played by groups of 2 to 10 people.

---

* In addition, we have developed some very successful techniques for building and maintaining opponent models in the Iterated Prisoner's Dilemma with Noise [2], which is a version of the Iterated Prisoner's Dilemma in which accidents and miscommunications can occur. However, the work is beyond the scope of this book.

** This description was used, for example, in the 1998 movie *Rounders*.

Game play in Texas hold 'em works as follows: Each player is dealt two cards face down. The cards are the player's *hole cards* and represent his hidden information. There is then a round of betting referred to as *preflop*. Preflop betting is begun with a forced bet by the two players left of the dealer. This bet is called the *blind*. After this betting round, three cards are exposed face up in the center of the table. These are community cards that all players can use in their hands. These three cards are called the *flop* and following their exposure, there is another round of betting, this time with no forced bets or blinds. After this round, if players are still left, another community card called the *turn* is exposed. Following another betting round, the final community card called the *river* is shown. There is then a final betting round and if players are left in the game, there is a showdown in which the players show their highest five-card hand (created using the two hole cards and the five community cards). The player with the highest of these hands wins.

In Limit Texas hold 'em, the betting rounds have a specified structure. Players play in clockwise order. On their turn, each player has one of three options: Bet, call, or fold. The *bet* action raises the amount of money that all players must call by a fixed amount. A *fold* causes a player to leave the hands. A folded player need not put any more money into the pot but also has no ability to win the hand. When a player *calls*, they match the current bet and stay in the current hand. The initial bet is 0 (except in preflop, where the blind is generally worth one bet). There is generally a cap of four on the number of bet actions that can be made by all players in any betting round. Thus, in a two-player poker game, 17 possible ways exist for a round of betting to proceed, only 9 of which end in a call.

3.1.3.1 Play

Poker has been a subject of artificial intelligence (AI) research for yearly 30 years [12], but most work has either consisted primarily of theoretical analysis [18,34,35] or has concentrated on specific aspects of poker rather than the entire game [19,29,31].

The best-known and most successful work on building complete poker players has been done by a group of researchers at the University of Alberta [4,6,7]. Their ambition is to build a poker player for the game of Texas hold 'em that is better than the best human players. They are well on their way to doing so [32].

Their best-known approach — reported in [14] — is to use linear programming techniques to compute game-theoretic optimal strategies on a simplified version of two-player Texas hold 'em and use those strategies in the real (i.e., unsimplified) game. They have since supplanted this algorithm with one that uses game-tree search techniques along the lines of what we described in the *"Game-Tree Search"* section earlier in this chapter [5]. But, because that work is not yet published, we cannot provide the details here.

3.1.3.2 Opponent Modeling

In this section, we discuss two different opponent-modeling techniques for the game of Texas hold 'em. Both of these techniques were developed by researchers at the University of Alberta [7,11].

In [7], opponent modeling is accomplished using the probability that the opponent is holding each of the various possible hole cards. These hole cards are initially assigned weights based on the *a priori* random distribution caused by the deal. As the opponent makes actions through the game, the opponent-modeling program recomputes these weights to be consistent with the opponent's actions. For instance, if an opponent calls one bet preflop and then raises on the flop, the opponent likely has a hand that was acceptable preflop, but likely to win the hand after the flop. That is, the hand may have been expected to win with probability 0.55 before the flop and with probability 0.75 after the flop.* The player's chances of winning changed, therefore, so did his action. The key to player modeling in [7] is the idea that each player is comfortable with each possible action only when the win probability meets certain criteria, and that the criteria is particular to each individual player. That is, a player will call when his hand is likely to win with a probability above 0.5, likely to raise with hands with winning probability more than 0.75, and likely to fold otherwise. On reweighting, weights of hands consistent with opponent action increase at the expense of those hands that are not consistent.

As an example of this, consider the following situation of $9\heartsuit9\diamondsuit$. This is a good opening hand, so we raise when we get the chance. Our model of the opponent at this point gives equal weight to each of the 1225 other starting hands. The opponent then, on his action, reraises us. This affects our opinion of the opponent's hand — our opponent model tells us that the opponent is likely to reraise with a hand that will win at least 60% of the time. So, we now adjust the weights to take this into account, making only a very few hands possible. In fact, in two-player play, only pocket pairs, hands containing an ace, or very few hands containing a king are that likely to win. At this point, we call** and move to the flop. To our misfortune, $A\clubsuit J\spadesuit 2\clubsuit$ falls on the flop. The opponent bets at this point and we must reweight the opponent's hand again. Using the same heuristic model, we now increase the weight of all hands that win more than 60% of the time. At this point, an extremely high probability exists that the opponent has a pair of aces, which, in poker lingo, dominates our pair of nines. Therefore, we fold. Had we not been using any opponent modeling, we might have called, a play that has an expected payoff of about 0.05 on our bet of 1***, an undesirable situation. Thus, we see both that opponent modeling is necessary and how this particular method of opponent modeling fills that need.

---

* "Win probability" would be more accurately stated as "expected value." For purposes of presentation, this has been left out, but a full explication can be found in [7].
** This is likely not the best action at this point, but we assume it for purposes of exposition.
*** If the opponent actually does have an ace.

In Davidson et al. [11], opponent modeling is accomplished via an artificial neural network. The network takes as input all of the various aspects of the game and returns if it thinks the opponent will bet, check, or fold. How this information can be used in deciding our next move is obvious: If we know the opponent wants to fold, we should always bet, forcing the fold. The disadvantage to this technique is that it requires much data and training and it is susceptible to subtle, high-level sorts of play such as the slowplay. Davidson et al. show this technique to work significantly better than the previous weight-based approach in practice against reasonable human players.

3.1.4 Case Study: Kriegspiel Chess

We now describe our own work on the game of Kriegspiel chess.* Kriegspiel chess [20, 21] is an imperfect-information variant of chess that was developed by a Prussian military officer in 1824 and became popular as a military training exercise. It is the progenitor of modern military wargaming [15].

Kriegspiel chess is like ordinary chess except that neither player can see the other's pieces. However, a player can get information about the opponent through interactions such as captures (see Figure 3.1.2), checks, and moves that are blocked because an opponent's piece is in the way. When player x captures one of player y's pieces, a referee announces that they have made a capture, but not what piece was captured, and the referee removes the captured piece from y's board, but does not say what piece captured it. When x tries to make a move that is illegal (an attempted pawn take or moving into check or attempting to jump an opponent's piece), the referee announces that the move is illegal but not why. When x puts y's king in check, the referee tells both players that y's king is in check and gives them partial information about how the check occurred (namely by rank, file, long diagonal, short diagonal, knight, or some combination of the above). Both players hear all referee announcements.

The published literature on Kriegspiel chess is rather small. Two books have been written on how to play Kriegspiel chess [20,21]. Wetherell et al. [33] describe a program to act as the referee that advises the Kriegspiel players of illegal moves, captures, and the like. Sakuta et al. [25] describe a search strategy for some imperfect-information games that are simpler to Kriegspiel. Bolognesi and Ciancarini [8] describe some search strategies for Kriegspiel-chess endgames. Russell and Wolfe [24] describe a program that uses logical reasoning techniques to predict forced wins in Kriegspiel chess, but this technique is feasible only at points where the belief states are relatively small, such as the endgame.

How to build a really good program to play Kriegspiel chess is largely an unsolved problem. Even among human players, Kriegspiel chess is a notoriously difficult game to win [20, 21]; most games end in draws. Kriegspiel chess

---

* Most of this section is excerpted from [23], which contains some additional technical details.

FIGURE 3.1.2
A Kriegspiel chess board from the viewpoint of White. Black has just taken White's bishop in
the space marked "?." Hence, White knows Black has a piece there but not what the piece is.

presents some difficulties that do not occur in other imperfect-information
games (e.g., bridge, Scrabble, and poker):

1. Twenty moves into a Kriegspiel chess game, a conservative estimate is that at each node of the game tree, the belief-state size (i.e.,
   the number of states consistent with the current sequence of
   observations) can be more than 10^{13}. In comparison, the belief-state
   size in bridge is only about 10^7, and in two-player Texas hold 'em
   it is only about 1000.

2. In bridge and poker, usually the statistical sampling is not done on
   the game itself but on a simplified approximation in which the state
   space and belief states are much smaller. In bridge, the approximation is done by treating various sets of states as if they were equivalent, a technique that was first used in the game of sprouts [1]. In
   poker, a linear-programming approximation has been used [4]. But
   in Kriegspiel chess, how or whether such an approximation could
   be constructed is unclear. For our case study, we did not attempt
   to construct one.

3. In bridge, poker, and Scrabble, the opponent's actions are observable. The uncertainty about the current state arises from external events that can be modeled stochastically: The random deal of the cards in bridge or poker and the random choice of a tile in Scrabble. This makes telling whether or not a state *s* is consistent with a belief state *b* relatively easy, and to assign a probability to *s* given *b*.

In Kriegspiel chess, the opponent's actions are not observable, and this uncertainty has no simple stochastic model. Telling whether a state *s* is consistent with the current belief state *b* means checking whether a *history* (i.e., a sequence of moves) exists that is consistent with *b* and leads to *s*, and in the average case, this takes exponential time. No clear way exists to put a probability distribution on the states in the belief state.

For our case study, we constructed several algorithms for generating the random sample of game boards used in the tree search: AOSP, LOS, and HS. All Observation Sampling with Pool (AOSP) generates game boards that are consistent with the entire sequence *O* of observations that a player has made during the game. Last Observation Sampling (LOS) only requires consistency with the last observation o_i. Hybrid Sampling (HS) behaves like AOSP at the beginning of the game, but as the game progresses, it gradually switches over to behaving like LOS. The next section describes the algorithms in more detail.

At first glance, one might expect LOS to be the worst of the the algorithms, AOSP to be the best, and HS to be somewhere in between. But our theoretical analysis on some simplified game-tree models suggests that, in some cases, HS may outperform AOSP, and our experiments show HS outperforming AOSP in Kriegspiel chess.

3.1.4.1 Algorithms

We first introduce some notation. As the game progresses, the players' moves will generate a sequence of states $S_i = \langle s_0, s_1 \ldots \rangle$, called the *game history*. At each state s_i, each player p_j will be able to make an observation o_{ij} of s_i; usually o_{ij} will include complete information about p_j's position and partial information about the other player's position. At s_i, player p_j's *observation history* is $O_{ij} = \langle o_{1j}, o_{2j}, \ldots, o_{ij} \rangle$, and p_j's *belief state* is $b_{ij} = \{$all states that satisfy $O_{ij}\}$.

Our sampling algorithms will be based on the following properties of a state *s*: *s* is *last-observation consistent* if it is consistent with o_{ij}, and *all-observation consistent* if it is consistent with O_{ij}.

Table 3.1.1 shows an abstract version of statistical game-tree search. *S* is the sample set of states, $\gamma(s, m)$ is the state produced by performing move *m* in state *s*, Game-tree-search is a perfect-information game-tree-search algorithm such as alpha-beta, and *P* is a probability distribution over the states in *S*. Some additional code must be added to handle the case where a move *m* is applicable to some states but not others; this code is game-specific and we do not discuss it here.

TABLE 3.1.1

Abstract Statistical-Sampling Algorithm for Move Evaluation

---

procedure Choose-move(S)

$M \leftarrow$ {moves applicable to states in S}

for every $s \in S$ and every $m \in M$ do

$v_{s,m} \leftarrow$ Game-tree-search($\gamma(s, m)$)

return argmax$_{m \in M} \Sigma_{s \in S} v_{s,m} P(s)$

We now can define three different sampling algorithms that provide input for Choose-move. In each case, k is the desired number of states in the statistical sample and i is how many moves the players have played so far.

- *LOS:* If fewer than k last-observation consistent states, exist then let S contain all of them; otherwise, let S contain k such states chosen at random. Return Choose-move(S).

- *AOSP:* AOSP returns a move and stores a set of states (a *pool*) to use as input to use the next time AOSP is called. Every state in the pool is to be consistent with O_{ij}, though we do not assume that all such states are in the pool. Let S_0 be the pool AOSP returned last time and $M =$ {all of the other player's possible responses to p_j's last move}. Let $S_1 = \{\gamma(s, m) \mid s \in S_0, m \in M, m$ is applicable to s, and $\gamma(s, m)$ satisfies $O_{ij}\}$. If $|S_1| < k$, then let $S_2 = S_1$; otherwise let S_2 contain k states chosen at random from S_1. Let $m =$ Choose-move(S_2). Return $(m, \{\gamma(s, m) \mid s \in S_1\})$.

- *HS:* Like AOSP, HS returns a move and a set of states. Compute S_1 and S_2 same as in AOSP. If $|S_2| < k$ then let S_3 be a set of $k - |S_2|$ random last-observation consistent states; otherwise $S_3 = \phi$. Let $m =$ Choose-move $(S_2 \cup S_3)$. Return $(m, \{\gamma(s, m) \mid s \in S_1\})$.

3.1.4.2 Theoretical Analysis

Analyzing the performance of these algorithms is impossible without making simplifying assumptions, but more than one set of assumptions exists. Below we do two analyses based on two different sets of assumptions. The differing assumptions lead to differing conclusions about which algorithm will perform better.

Game-tree analysis. Suppose each state has exactly b children, for some constant b. Suppose that we know all of p_j's moves but not the other player's moves. If the number of states is very large (e.g., 10^{13} as described earlier), then during the early stages of the game, the number of states grows exponentially, with roughly $b^{i/2}$ possible states at the ith move. Suppose that for each state s where it is the other player's move, the observation history O_{ij} eliminates, on the average, some fraction $1/c$ of that player's possible moves, where $c > 1$. Then the number of possible states at the ith move given O_{ij} is $(b/c)^{i/2}$. Thus, the probability of any individual state at depth i being consistent with O_{ij} is $(1/c)^{i/2}$, which approaches 0 at an exponential rate as i increases.

Thus, if the game continues to grow as a tree with a branching factor of b, then our analysis suggests the following:

- AOSP's sample set S_2 will decrease in size as the game progresses. The probability of a state s's successors being consistent with b_i is $1/c$ because s is already known to be consistent with b_{i-1}. Hence, as the game progresses, S_2 will soon become too small for the results to have much statistical significance and AOSP's play will begin to resemble random play.

- Each board generated by LOS is unlikely to be consistent with the current belief state; thus the values computed by LOS are likely to be close to random.

- At the beginning of the game, HS will behave identically to AOSP. As the game proceeds and the size of S_2 decreases, HS will put more and more randomly generated boards into S_3, thus making the results more noisy. Therefore, HS's quality of play is likely to be worse than AOSP's.

Game-graph analysis.   If n possible states exist in the game, then the number of moves at each level cannot continue to grow exponentially but will eventually flatten out. The game "tree" will be a graph rather than a tree, with n nodes (at most) at each depth, one for each possible state. There will be b edges from each node at depth i to nodes at depth $i + 1$, $1/c$ of which are consistent with any given observation. Suppose these edges go to a random set of nodes. Then for each state s, the probability (under certain independence assumptions) that it is reachable in i moves is about.

$$min(1, (n-1)^{i-3}((b/c)/(n-1))^{i-1})$$

In other words, the probability that a randomly chosen state s has a history consistent with O_{ij} approaches 1 exponentially. This suggests the following:

- Rather than degrading to random play as in the game-tree analysis of the previous section, AOSP's quality of play will eventually level off at some point above that, depending on the number of states available in the pool.

- As the game proceeds, the probability of a randomly generated board being consistent with the current belief state will increase toward 1; thus, LOS will produce increasingly good quality of play. However, its play will be limited by the fact that it has no good way to assign relative probabilities to its randomly generated boards.

- At the beginning of the game, HS will behave identically to AOSP. As the game proceeds and AOSP's sample size decreases, HS will fill up the rest of the sample with randomly generated boards, but as the game proceeds, it will become increasingly likely that these randomly chosen boards are consistent with the current belief state. Thus, HS's quality of play is likely to be better than AOSP's.

Discussion. With the first set of assumptions, AOSP is likely to perform much better than LOS and somewhat better than HS. With the second set of assumptions, it is unclear which of LOS and AOSP will be better, but HS is likely to perform better than AOSP and LOS.

As both sets of assumptions represent extremal cases, our analyses suggest that the actual performance is likely to be somewhere in between. In particular, it seems plausible that HS will perform better than AOSP, i.e., that if last-observation consistent boards are included in the statistical sample later in the game, this will help rather than hurt the evaluations. A later section describes our experimental test of this hypothesis.

3.1.4.3 Timed Algorithms

To make fair comparisons among LOS, AOSP, and HS, they cannot be implemented in the exact way described in section 3.1.4.1. They must be modified to take, as an additional input variable, the amount of time t available to decide on a move. This is necessary so that the algorithm can do as well as it can within that amount of time. We call the modified algorithms *Timed LOS*, *Timed AOSP*, and *Timed HS*.

Timed LOS. Rather than taking the set S as input as shown in Table 3.1.1, Timed LOS generates the members of S one at a time and evaluates them as they are generated so it can generate and evaluate as many boards as it can during the time available. Once the time is up, it returns the move whose average value is highest, as shown in Table 3.1.1.

Timed AOSP. Timed AOSP maintains a pool of states $P = \{s_1 ..., s_p\}$ that are known to be consistent with the current belief state b. Using an estimate of how long Game-tree-search will take on each board, it calculates some number of boards k_t that it can evaluate during the available time t. The estimate k_t is deliberately a little low to try to keep Timed AOSP from running over time and to ensure that time will be left to attempt to generate more consistent boards. Three cases are found:

- If $p \geq k_t$, then Timed AOSP calls Choose-move ($\{s_1 ... s_{k_t}\}$) and returns the recommended move.
- If $0 < p < k_t$, then Timed AOSP calls Choose-move(P) and returns the recommended move.
- If $p = 0$, then Timed AOSP returns a random move.

During whatever remains of the available time, AOSP tries to generate more histories that are consistent with b; and for every such history, it adds the resultant board to the pool.

Each time the referee makes an announcement, Timed AOSP must update the pool to be consistent with the announcement. This can cause the pool to either shrink (when Timed AOSP is told a move is illegal) or to grow (when Timed AOSP is told that the opponent has moved). This computation occurs at the beginning of AOSP's turn.

If the pool is allowed to grow unchecked, it could potentially get quite large; hence, we limit its size to 20,000 boards. If the number of boards in the pool goes higher than this, we remove enough boards to get to the number of boards down to 10,000. Because the 30-second time limit allows only enough time to call Choose-move on a set about 350 boards from the pool, this is believed adequate.

Timed HS. Timed HS works the same as Timed AOSP, with one exception. If $0 \leq p < k_t$, then Timed HS generates a set R that contains $p - k_t$ random boards that are consistent with o_{ij} (we call these *last-observation* consistent boards). It then calls Choose-move $(P \cup R)$. This rules out the possibility of ever having to make a random move. It also restricts the amount of time that Timed HS can spend generating additional boards to put into the pool.

We have implemented all three of these algorithms using a combination of C and C++. For Choose-move's Game-tree-search subroutine, we used the GPL'ed chess program provided by GNU and modified it to return a minimax value for a particular board.

By the time this chapter appears in print, we intend to have made our implementations publicly available as a Kriegspiel chess game server accessible from the web.

3.1.4.4 Experiments

Our experimental hypotheses (based on the analyses in section 3.1.4.2) were that (1) Timed LOS would perform better than random play, (2) Timed AOSP would perform better than Timed LOS, and (3) Timed HS would perform somewhat better than Timed AOSP. The authors disagreed with each other about the third hypothesis because it was based on a notion that not all of us believed, that the computation time spent introducing and evaluating last-observation consistent boards would not be better spent trying to find and evaluate more all-observation consistent boards.

To test our hypotheses, we played all three algorithms against each other and against a player who moved at random. Each player plays approximately half of the games as white and half of the games as black. All experiments were run on Xeon 2.6 GHz chips with 500 MB RAM, running Linux. Each player was allowed to spend 30 seconds deciding each move, including moves that are decided after an attempted illegal move.

TABLE 3.1.2

Win/Loss/Draw Percentages with a ±95% Confidence Interval

Algorithms	Win (%)	Loss (%)	Draw (%)	Runs
LOS v. rand	39 ± 2	0 ± 0.3	61 ± 2	559
AOSP v. rand	63 ± 2	0 ± 0.3	37 ± 2	560
HS v. rand	65 ± 2	0.5 ± 0.3	35 ± 2	558

Table 3.1.2 shows the percentage of wins, losses, and draws when each of the three algorithms is played against a player who makes moves at random. Both Timed AOSP and Timed HS do much better against the random player than Timed LOS does. Timed HS does slightly better than Timed AOSP, but the difference is not statistically significant. The large number of draws is unsurprising because Kriegspiel chess is a notoriously difficult game to win.

Table 3.1.3 shows the percentage of wins, losses, and draws when the three players are played head-to-head against each other. Again, both Timed AOSP and Timed HS do much better than Timed LOS. Timed HS does somewhat better than Timed AOSP, and this time the results are statistically significant.

Figure 3.1.3 shows the number of last-observation boards used by Timed HS at each move in the games against Timed AOSP. Recall that these are the boards that Timed HS generates using the LOS algorithm when it runs out of time using the AOSP algorithm. Near the start of the game, Timed HS acts like Timed AOSP. In the middle of the game, it acts like a combination of Timed AOSP and Timed LOS. Near the end of the game, whether it acts like Timed AOSP or Timed LOS varies greatly, depending on the particular game.

This behavior is very interesting because it suggests that our hypothesis about last-observation consistent boards is correct: They become more useful as the game progresses because they are more likely to be consistent with the current belief state. Even though we do not know what probabilities to assign to them in the last line of Choose-move, they still provide useful information.

3.1.4.5 Significance of Our Results

One result demonstrated by our work is that statistical sampling approaches can be useful for game-tree search in Kriegspiel chess. This attribute was not obvious before because of the immense size of the belief states in this game.

TABLE 3.1.3

Win/Loss/Draw Percentages with a ±95% Confidence Interval at Each Move

Algorithms	Win (%)	Loss (%)	Draw (%)	Runs
AOSP v. LOS	31 ± 4.8	0 ± 1	69 ± 4.8	190
HS v. LOS	38 ± 5	0.5 ± 1	61 ± 5	190
HS v. AOSP	13.3 ± 0.4	10.7 ± 0.4	76 ± 0.5	1669

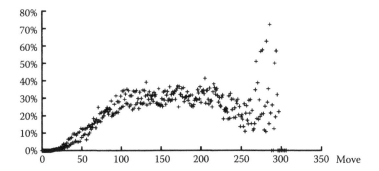

FIGURE 3.1.3
The average percentage of last-observation consistent boards that Timed HS used at each move in its games against Timed AOSP.

A second and more surprising result is that it is not necessary for the random sample to consist only of game boards that satisfy all of a player's observations. In fact, we were able to win more often by starting out with such boards but gradually switching over (as the game progressed) to boards that merely were consistent with the latest observation. The reason is that as the game progresses, a board that is consistent with the last move becomes more and more likely to be consistent with the entire set of observations, even if we have no idea what sequence of moves might have actually generated this board. To the best of our knowledge, ours is the first serious attempt to construct a good player for the entire game of Kriegspiel chess.

3.1.5 Summary

Game-tree search on imperfect-information games is much more difficult than on perfect-information games. The primary problems include exponentially larger game trees than for perfect-information games, difficulties in calculating the probability that a player can make a given move, and difficulties in calculating the probability that a player will make a given move.

We have discussed the following techniques for addressing those problems: Similarity-based aggregation, strategy-based aggregation, Monte Carlo sampling, and opponent modeling. The University of Alberta's work on Texas hold 'em shows that such techniques can provide a basis for computer programs that perform as well as very good human players. Our work on Kriegspiel chess shows that such techniques can also be useful in a game that has many orders of magnitude more uncertainty than poker.

References

1. Applegate, D., Jacobson, G., and Sleaton, D. Computer analysis of sprouts, Technical report, Carnegie Mellon University, Pittsburgh, 1991.
2. Au, T.-C. and Nau, D. Accident or intention: that is the question (in the iterated prisoner's dilemma), *Int. Joint Conf. on Autonomous Agents and Multiagent Systems (AAMAS)*, 2006. To appear.
3. Axelrod, R. *The Evolution of Cooperation*, Basic Books, Cambridge, MA. 1985.
4. Billings, D., Burch, N., Davison, A., Holte, R., Schaeffer, J., Schauenberg, T., and Szafron, D. Approximating game-theoretic optimal strategies for full-scale poker, *Proc. of the Int. Joint Conf. on Artif. Intelligence (IJCAI)*, 661–668, 2003.
5. Billings, D. October 2004. Personal communication.
6. Billings, D., Davidson, A., Schaeffer, J., and Szafron, D. The challenge of poker. *Artif. Intelligence,* 134, 201–240, 2002.
7. Billings, D., Papp, D., Schaeffer, J., and Szafron, D. Opponent modeling in poker *Proc. of the National Conf. on Artif. Intelligence (AAAI)*, 493–498, 1998.
8. Bolognesi, A. and Ciancarini, P. Searching over metapositions in kriegspiel. *Computer Games*, 2004.
9. Carmel, D. and Markovitch, S. Incorporating opponent models into adversary search. *Proc. of the National Conf. on Artif. Intelligence (AAAI)*, 1996.
10. Ciaffone, B. and Brien, J. *Middle Limit Holdem*, Bob Ciaffone, 2002.
11. Davidson, A., Billings, D., Schaeffer, J., and Szafron, D. Improved opponent modeling in poker, *Proc. of the Int. Joint Conf. on Art. Intelligence (IJCAI)*, 1467–1473, 2000.
12. Findler, N. Studies in machine cognition using the game of poker, *Comm. of the ACM*, 20(4), 230–245, 1977.
13. Frank, I. and Basin, D.A. Search in games with incomplete information: a case study using bridge card play, *Artif. Intelligence*, 100(1–2), 87–123, 1998.
14. Ginsberg, M.L. GIB: steps toward an expert-level bridge-playing program, *IJCAI-99*, 584–589, 1999.
15. Gray, B. History of wargaming, 2003 http://www.hmgs.org/history.htm.
16. Hsu, F., Anantharaman, T., Campbell, M., and Nowatzyk, A. A grandmaster chess machine, *Scientific American*, 263(4), 44–50, October 1990.
17. Jones, L. *Winning Low-Limit Hold-em*. Conjelco, Pittsburgh, 1994.
18. Koller, D. and Pfeffer, A. Representations and solutions for game-theoretic problems, *Artif. Intelligence*, 167–215, 1997.
19. Korb, K., Nicholson, A., and Jitnah, N. Bayesian poker, *Proc. of the Conf. on Uncertainty in Artif. Intelligence (UAI)*, 343–350, 1999.
20. Li, D. *Kriegspiel: Chess Under Uncertainty*, Premier, 1994.
21. Li, D. *Chess Detective: Kriegspiel Strategies, Endgames and Problems*, Premier, 1995.
22. Miller, E., Sklansky, D. and Malmuth, M. *Small Stakes Hold'em*. Two Plus Two Publications, Pittsburgh, 2004.
23. Parker, A., Nau, D., and Subrahmanian, V.S. Game-tree search with combinatorially large belief states. *Proc. of the Int. Joint Conf. on Artif. Intelligence (IJCAI)*, August 2005.
24. Russell, S. and Wolfe, J. Efficient belief-state AND-OR search, with application to Kriegspiel. *Proc. of the Int. Joint Conf. on Artif. Intelligence (IJCAI)*, 2005.
25. Sakuta, M., Yoshimura, J., and Iider, H. A deterministic approach for solving Kriegspiel-like problems, *MSO Computer Olympias Workshop*, 2001.

26. Sheppard, B., World-championship-caliber scrabble, *Artif. Intelligence*, 134(1–2), 241–275, 2002.
27. Sklansky, D. *Hold 'em Poker*, Two Plus Two Publications, Pittsburgh 1996.
28. Sklansky, D. and Malmuth, M. *Hold 'em Poker for Advanced Players*, Two Plus Two Publications, Pittsburgh 1999.
29. Smith, S., Flexible learning of problem solving heuristics through adaptive search, *Proc. of the Int. Joint Conf. on Artif. Intelligence (IJCAI)*, 422–425, 1983.
30. Smith, S.J.J., Nau, D.S., and Throon, T. Computer bridge: a big win for AI planning, *AI Magazine*, 19(2):93–105, 1998.
31. Waterman, D. A generalization learning technique for automating the learning of heuristics. *Artif. Intelligence*, 1, 121–170, 1970.
32. Wayner, P. The new card shark, *The New York Times*, p G1, G7, July 9, 2003.
33. Wetherell, C.S., Buckholtz, T.J., and Booth, K.S. A director for kriegspiel, a variant of chess, *Comp. J.*, 151(1), 66–70, 1972.
34. Zadeh, N. *Winning Poker Systems*, Prentice-Hall, Upper Saddle River, NJ, 1974.
35. Zadeh, N. Computation of optimal poker strategies, *Oper. Res.*, 25(4), 541–562, 1977.

3.2

Handling Partial and Corrupted Information

Ashitosh Swarup and Jason L. Speyer

CONTENTS

As we started to discuss in the previous chapter, the information available to the opponents in a conflict or players in a game can be full (the player knows everything and can make accurate, noiseless measurements of the game state) or partial (the player does not know everything, with the limited-measurements possibly being corrupted by noise, deception, or other factors). The nature of the information available to each player plays an important role in the analytical results of the class of problems we consider here. In the previous chapter, we explored approaches to a class of problems where the information available to players was partial. Now we are adding another complication: The available information is both partial and corrupted.

The class of games we consider in this chapter is stochastic in nature. In particular, we consider random disturbances that have a Gaussian probability distribution function. The cost function has a quadratic form (zero-sum game) and is subject to a linear stochastic dynamic equation. We limit the number of players in this game to two. In addition, the players have their own independent information sets that are not shared. This class of problems constitutes an important one; a number of physical problems can be modeled using this formulation. Examples that readily come to mind are the pursuit-evasion game problem and the problem of fault detection (where the fault in a system is modeled as an adversarial game player). In addition, the results obtained by analyzing this class of problems gives insight into the role of partial/corrupted information for not only this class of problems but also suggests the existence of similar results for a larger class of problems as well.

Problems related to stochastic dynamic games are discussed in Chapter 2.3 and Chapter 2.4, the main difference being that in these formulations, the probability space is assumed to be discrete. In this chapter, the probability space is assumed to be continuous and this fact changes the problem formulation and solution.

First, we will give an overall introduction to the game problem with perfect, shared information, with a brief explanation of the solution. To make things more clear, we will base the formulation around a pursuit-evasion game. We will then present the stochastic version of the problem along with references to past attempts at approaching the problem. We then outline our approach, which is very different from the previous approaches: An indirect approach is used to arrive at the problem solution. The solutions obtained by this approach will be examined. In particular, the effect of unshared and partial/corrupted information will be presented. In addition, the information uncertainty will be used to explain the inability of previous attempts to arrive at a solution.

While presenting the material, we assume that the reader is familiar with linear discrete-time state-space theory, linear quadratic Gaussian cost functions, probability, and Kalman filtering theory; these concepts form the basic building-blocks of this chapter.

3.2.1 The Deterministic Discrete-Time Linear-Quadratic Game Formulation

We choose to present the discrete-time linear-quadratic (LQ) game by building on an example. Consider a deterministic pursuit-evasion formulation in two dimensions. In the next section, this deterministic discrete-time LQ game is generalized to include uncertainty.

As shown in Figure 3.2.1, two players are used, u_p and u_e, and for clarity, we can assume that they are moving vehicles. The coordinates of the players at any given time are given by (x_e, y_e) and (x_p, y_p), respectively, and as shown,

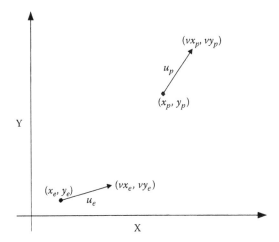

FIGURE 3.2.1
Pursuit-evasion game in two dimensions.

their respective velocities are (v_{x_e}, v_{y_e}) and (v_{x_p}, v_{y_p}). The distance at any time between the players is given by:

$$d = \sqrt{(x_p - x_e)^2 + (y_p - y_e)^2}$$

Game Objective: u_e, wants to pursue and catch u_p, whereas u_p wants to evade and escape. In other words, u_e wants to minimize d, whereas u_p wants to maximize it. Clearly, the distance between the two players is a measure of performance and, hence, is a natural choice for constructing our cost function. First, let us define the following discrete-time state variable at any time index i as:

$$x_i \triangleq \begin{bmatrix} v_{p_{x_i}} \\ v_{p_{y_i}} \\ v_{e_{x_i}} \\ v_{p_{y_i}} \\ x_{p_i} \\ y_{p_i} \\ x_{e_i} \\ y_{e_i} \end{bmatrix}$$

From state-space theory, we can model the motion of the players as a discrete-time, linear dynamic state-space model:

$$x_{i+1} = A_i x_i + \Gamma_{pi} u_{pi} + \Gamma_{ei} u_{ei}$$

For details about the state-space modeling, the reader is referred to [1]. We assume that i goes from 0 to some terminal index N.

Information Structure: We assume that at every time index i, each player knows the state x_i perfectly.

Cost Function: The cost function for the problem is defined as:

$$J(u_p, u_e) \triangleq \frac{1}{2}\left[\| x_N \|_{Q_N}^2 + \sum_{i=0}^{N-1} \left(\| u_{p_i} \|_{R_{p_i}}^2 + \| u_{e_i} \|_{R_{e_i}}^2 \right) \right]$$

where

$$\| x_N \|_{Q_N}^2 = d_N^2$$

and

$$\| x \|_A^2 \triangleq x^T A x$$

with d_N being the terminal miss distance. R_{p_i} and R_{e_i} are negative-definite and positive-definite weighting matrices, respectively, that preserve the convexity of the problem.

Definition: Saddle Point. Given a cost function $J(u_p, u_e)$, a saddle point strategy pair (u_p^*, u_e^*), if it exists, is defined as having the following two properties:

1. The order of minimization and maximization of the function with respect to u_p and u_e is interchangable:

$$\max_{u_p} \min_{u_e} J(u_p, u_e) = \min_{u_e} \max_{u_p} J(u_p, u_e) = J(u_p^*, u_e^*)$$

2. If either player deviates from his saddle point strategy, his performance in the game suffers:

$$J(u_p, u_e^*) \le J(u_p^*, u_e^*) \le J(u_p^*, u_e)$$

Thus, a saddle point can be interpreted as some sort of equilibrium where neither player has an advantage; each player is guaranteed a minimum level of performance if he plays his saddle-point strategy.

The continuous-time version of the deterministic LQ game has been solved in [2]. The discrete-time saddle-point solution is presented below.

Theorem: The saddle-point solution to the deterministic linear-quadratic pursuit-evasion cost function in above subject to the discrete-time linear dynamic system is given by the strategy pair (u_p^*, u_e^*), where at any time index i:

$$u_{p_i}^* = k_{pi} x_i$$

$$u_{e_i}^* = k_{ei} x_i$$

where

$$k_{pi} = -R_{p_i}^{-1} \Gamma_{p_i}^T \Pi_{i+1} \left[I + \Gamma_{p_i} R_{p_i}^{-1} \Gamma_{p_i}^T \Pi_{i+1} + \Gamma_{e_i} R_{e_i}^{-1} \Gamma_{e_i}^T \Pi_{i+1} \right]^{-1} A_i$$

$$k_{ei} = -R_{e_i}^{-1} \Gamma_{e_i}^T \Pi_{i+1} \left[I + \Gamma_{p_i} R_{p_i}^{-1} \Gamma_{p_i}^T \Pi_{i+1} + \Gamma_{e_i} R_{e_i}^{-1} \Gamma_{e_i}^T \Pi_{i+1} \right]^{-1} A_i$$

The matrix Π_i is generated from the following backward propagating Riccati equation:

$$\Pi_i = A_i^T \Pi_{i+1} \left[I + \Gamma_{p_i} R_{p_i}^{-1} \Gamma_{p_i}^T \Pi_{i+1} + \Gamma_{e_i} R_{e_i}^{-1} \Gamma_{e_i}^T \Pi_{i+1} \right]^{-1} A_i$$

where $\Pi_N = Q_N \geq 0$.

The saddle-point value of the cost is given by

$$J\left(u_p^*, u_e^*\right) = \| x_0 \|_{\Pi_0}^2$$

Proof: The continuous-time linear-quadratic pursuit-evasion game has been solved in [2]. The discrete-time game solution can be derived using a straightforward extension of the continuous-time results to discrete-time.

Convexity Conditions: For the problem to have a finite, bounded solution, the following convexity conditions must be satisfied simultaneously for both players at every time i:

$$\Gamma_{p_i}^T \Pi_{i+1} \Gamma_{pi} + R_{pi} < 0$$

$$\Gamma_{e_i}^T \Pi_{i+1} \Gamma_{ei} + R_{pi} > 0$$

If either of these conditions is not satisfied, the corresponding player can shift the cost in their favor by an arbitrarily large value. Ususally, the convexity conditions represent physical energy or power constraints on the input strategies.

Remark 1: Note that each player's strategy at any time i is a linear function of the state at that time index. Assuming that the system matrices and cost function weightings are known *a priori* to both players, each player can compute their opponent's saddle-point strategy at every time i. Thus, this problem falls into the class of problems with *perfect information*. Also note that only the current value of the state is required to implement the saddle-point strategy at any time, i.e., the saddle-point strategies are finite-dimensional, as opposed to being a function of the entire state history.

The fact that the information structure is perfect is key to the existence of a saddle-point structure; at any time instant, each player knows for certain the best strategy his opponent can use against him. As we shall see, partial/ uncertain information can break down the saddle-point structure in certain cases due to the fact that each player cannot be sure of his opponent's moves. We will introduce the linear-quadratic-Gaussian (LQG) game in the next section along with previous approaches to obtaining a saddle-point solution.

3.2.2 The Discrete-Time LQG Game: Formulation and Previous Work

Three possible ways exist in which random uncertainties can enter into the system (other than the players' controls):

1. Through the initial state $x_0 \sim N(\bar{x}_0, \bar{P}_0)$.
2. As Gaussian white process noise, $w_0 \sim N(0, W_1)$, which is added linearly to the right-hand side of the state equation.
3. As Gaussian white observation noise, $v_i \sim N(0, V_1)$, coupled with imperfect measurements of the state as

$$z_i = H_i x_i + v_i$$

To account for the random processes, the cost function is now modified to include the expectation operator, E. We also include the state at every time index i in the cost rather than just a terminal weighting on the state. This makes the problem more general,

$$J(u_p, u_e) \triangleq E[S(u_p, u_e)]$$

where

$$S(u_p, u_e) \triangleq \frac{1}{2}\left[\| x_N \|_{Q_N}^2 + \sum_{i=0}^{N-1}\left(\| x_i \|_{Q_i}^2 + \| u_{p_i} \|_{R_{p_i}}^2 + \| u_{e_i} \|_{R_{e_i}}^2 \right) \right]$$

Due to the significance of the saddle-point structure, all subsequent game-theoretic analysis will be centered around this structure. We would like to examine the existence of a saddle-point solution for this class of problems in the presence of uncertainties. Let us now present the different problem categories depending on the information structure of the system, which in turn is decided by how the uncertainties enter the system.

1. *Both players measure the state perfectly, and process noise enters the system linearly.* This case still falls under the class of problems with perfect information because both players measure the state perfectly. The only quantity that changes is the cost function, which is modified by the variance of the process noise. The saddle-point structure is preserved due to the perfect information structure. Relating to our practical two-vehicle example, this scenario would be the pair of vehicles riding over rough or rocky terrain. The variation in the surface could be modeled as process noise, and this would only affect the final value of the cost function but not the saddle-point structure. We get a similar result for a linear quadratil regulator (LQR) control problem with perfect measurements and linear dynamics with process noise: The optimal controller remains unchanged from the noiseless case and only the final value of the cost function changes.

2. *No process noise, initial state uncertainty exists with both players making a common (or shared), noise-corrupted measurement of the state.* In this case, we assume that the common, noisy measurement is of the form of z_i. In this case, a saddle point structure was shown to exist if all the conditions discussed in the previous section apply, with an additional condition that a Riccati equation with a dimension equal to twice that of the state has no conjugate points. This problem was solved by [3] under the restriction that only observation histories, not control histories, were shared. Therefore, this problem falls into the class of problems with *partially shared information.*

   An equivalent condition for the existence of saddle points was derived in [1], where a necessary and sufficient condition shown for the existence of saddle points is that two Riccati equations, each of the dimension of the state, have no conjugate points. The first Riccati equation is the control Riccati equation, hence, the first condition is equivalent to the existence of a solution to the Riccati equation Π_i. The second condition takes into account the uncertainties in the information structure. If conjugate points do indeed exist for the second Riccati equation, deception becomes a possibility in the game and the player who can successfully deceive the opponent wins the game. For our two-vehicle problem, this translates into the deceiving vehicle making an unexpected maneuver that the other vehicle cannot catch, in which case the deceiving player wins the game.

   Note that in this problem, the use of a Kalman filter involves certain pitfalls. To estimate the state, each player constructs a Kalman filter. The filter is constructed by guessing the opponent's strategy in the linear filter structure. While the Kalman filter is a good estimator when solving a control problem with random uncertainties, it is prone to failure when used against an intelligent adversary. This is because the Kalman filter is constructed by trying to guess the opponent's strategy. Random variables are predictable, on the average, but an intelligent adversary is not. Hence, it may be possible for a player to take advantage of the opponent's estimation error and play a strategy other than what is being "guesstimated" by the opponent. Doing this can violate the convexity conditions outlined in the previous section, in which case the deceiver can shift the cost in their favor by an arbitrarily large value. For this particular problem, the existence of a solution to the second Riccati equation guarantees immunity from deception. However, as we increase the complexity of the partial information structure, we will see that no such condition exists to prevent deception. Hence, another task we face is to develop an estimation algorithm that yields a state estimation error independent of the opponent's controls.

3. *No process noise or initial state uncertainty exists, one player makes perfect measurements of the state, and the other makes partial, noisy measurements of the state.* This problem increases the complexity of the information pattern and has never been solved. The only approach that yielded a saddle-point solution for this problem was [4], but only when the partial information structure was greatly relaxed. While solving the problem, the player with perfect state information was assumed to have access to their opponent's Kalman filter error via some "mystical third party." While valid from the point of view of deriving a solution to the problem, this assumption is physically not realizable. Also, it goes against the notion of solving adversarial problems in the presence of uncertainty; one player is given information that they should not have.

   Conjectured by [5] was that the saddle point strategies would be infinite-dimensional, i.e., each player, at any time instant, would play a linear strategy that would be a linear kernel operating on their own *entire measurement history*. Clearly this presents an impediment in realizing a practical implementation of such a strategy (if it exists). Each player would have to store their own entire measurement history, which in turn would lead to memory constraints and limitations. Thus, after a certain time, when a player's memory capacity has been reached, their controller would be suboptimal. A variation of this problem is the one in which the state-space is finite, and such a problem has been investigated in [6] and also in the Chapter 2.4.

4. *Process noise is added to the state, and both players make independent, unshared, imperfect, noisy measurements.* This is the most general

problem in the class. A numerical algorithm to compute supposed saddle-point strategies was proposed by Willman [7]. The algorithm involved each player constructing a Kalman filter to estimate the state. The Kalman filters were of growing dimension at every time step. Furthermore, each player constructed the Kalman filter by putting in an estimate of the opponent's optimal controller. By fixing the opponent's (linear) optimal strategy, the problem was converted into a one-sided, linear-quadratic-Gaussian, optimal control problem that was solved to find the optimal control gains. These gains were then fixed and used to construct a one-sided LQG optimal control problem for the opponent, and so on. Thus, a series of numerical iterations were set up and the problem was run until it converged. However, no formal proof of optimality was given, and the algorithm was found to converge for a very limited number of cases. Also, the convergence of the algorithm assumed that no deception occurred by either opponent. Furthermore, a counterexample to this algorithm was found in [1], where a player could cheat and shift the cost in his favor. This is done by using the *cross-correlations* that exist between the Kalman filter state estimation error and the state itself.

Consider the significance of the class of problems with unshared, partial/corrupted information. The very fact that no known saddle-point solution exists to the more complex formulations in a continuous probability space is very intriguing. The past approaches trying to solve the problem in a continuous probability space did not have the analytical tools available today and, hence, struggled to find a saddle-point structure. In the next section, we will consider the LQG problem in which one player makes perfect measurements and the other player makes noisy measurements, with the measurements themselves being unshared. We will discuss an indirect approach used to arrive at a very elegant solution to this problem. We will also see that for this class of problems, saddle points do not exist in pure strategies. For our two-vehicle problem, we conclude that no one pure strategy will guarantee a certain minimum performance level. However, we will propose an alternative filtering and control scheme that guarantees that the cost function stays within a certain bound.

3.2.3 LQG Game with Partial Information: An Indirect Approach

All previous approaches to this problem tried to merge the approaches to the LQG control problem and the deterministic game problem. All approaches assumed that the Kalman filter would be the state estimator of choice because it is the natural choice for LQG problems. The approach taken here is the one used in [8], where the linear exponential Gaussian (LEG) control problem (first solved in [9] and then modified in [10]) is used as the starting point. In this section, we will modify the LEG control problem into the LEG game problem. Then, just as the LEG control problem converges to the LQG control problem in the limit as the LEG parameter $\theta \to 0$ (as discussed in [9]), the LEG game problem will converge to the LQG game problem as $\theta \to 0$. Thus, instead of computing $E[S]$, we consider the following cost function

$$\Psi = E[e^{-\theta S}]$$

where θ is a scalar parameter, taken here to be negative. This is the linear exponential Gaussian game cost function, where the negative value of θ ensures that the random uncertainties play alongside the player with perfect information adversarial to the player with partial, noisy information. We now want to find:

$$\Psi^* = \max_{u_p} \min_{u_c} \Psi$$

The LQG game problem solution is obtained from the LEG game problem solution by computing the following limit as in [8]:

$$J^* = \lim_{\theta \to 0} \frac{\Psi^* - 1}{\theta}$$

Note that the computation of an expected value is really the integration of the argument of the expectation operator multiplied by the probability density function of the random variable, the latter also being an exponent of a quadratic form. The key to solving the LEG problem is the fact that the expectation operator can be replaced by an extremization operator, with the extremization operator acting on the argument of the exponent. This is explained explicitly in [9]. After casting the problem in this form, we are left with the following problem:

$$\min_{u_e} \max_{u_p} \max_{x_0} \max_{v} \max_{w} \left\{ S + \frac{1}{2} \left[\| x_0 - \bar{x}_0 \|^2_{(\theta \bar{P}_0)^{-1}} + \| v_N \|^2_{(\theta V_N)^{-1}} \right.\right.$$

$$\left.\left. + \sum_{i=0}^{N-1} \left(\| w_i \|^2_{(\theta W_i)^{-1}} + \| v_i \|^2_{(\theta V_i)^{-1}} \right) \right] \right\}$$

Remark 2: Note how the random variables now appear as game players, as opposed to random variables, on the side of u_p. u_e must design a filtering/control scheme accordingly.

Because the actual optimization process is out of the scope of this text, we will present the results directly in the form of a theorem. The interested reader is referred to [8] for the complete derivation.

Theorem 2: Consider the following quadratic cost function

$$J(u_p, u_e) = \frac{1}{2} E \left[\|x_N\|_{Q_N}^2 + \sum_{i=0}^{N-1} \left(\|x_i\|_{Q_i}^2 + \|u_{p_i}\|_{R_{P_i}}^2 + \|u_{p_i}\|_{R_{e_i}}^2 \right) \right]$$

subject to the state equation

$$x_i + 1 = A_i x_i + \Gamma_{p_i} u_{p_i} + \Gamma_{e_i} u_{e_i} + w_i$$

u_p makes perfect measurements of the state x, while u_e makes imperfect measurements z of the state, given by:

$$z_i = H_i x_i + v_i$$

The process noise w_i and the observation noise v_i are both Gaussian white noise processes with statistics $(0, W_i)$ and $(0, V_i)$, respectively. The initial state x_0 is Gaussian with statistics $(\bar{x}_0, \bar{P}_0)$. The solution to the game problem

$$J^* = \max_{u_p} \min_{u_e} J(u_p, u_e)$$

then has equilibrium controllers of the form:

$$u_{p_i}^* = k_{p_i} x_i$$

$$u_{e_i}^* = k_{e_i} \hat{x}_i$$

where

$$k_{e_i} = -R_{e_i}^{-1} \Gamma_{e_i}^T \Pi_{i+1} (I + \Gamma_{e_i} R_{e_i}^{-1} \Gamma_{e_i}^T \Pi_{i+1} + \Gamma_{p_i} R_{p_i}^{-1} \Gamma_{p_i}^T \Pi_{i+1})^{-1} A_i$$

$$k_{p_i} = -R_{p_i}^{-1} \Gamma_{p_i}^T \Pi_{i+1} (I + \Gamma_{e_i} R_{e_i}^{-1} \Gamma_{e_i}^T \Pi_{i+1} + \Gamma_{p_i} R_{p_i}^{-1} \Gamma_{p_i}^T \Pi_{i+1})^{-1} A_i$$

Π_i is found by the following backward equation:

$$\Pi_i = Q_i + A_i^T \Pi_{i+1} (I + \Gamma_{e_i} R_{e_i}^{-1} \Gamma_{e_i}^T \Pi_{i+1} + \Gamma_{p_i} R_{p_i}^{-1} \Gamma_{p_i}^T \Pi_{i+1})^{-1} A_i$$

$$\Pi_N = Q_N$$

Also, $\hat{x}_i$ is the estimate generated by the filter equation:

$$\hat{x}_i = P_i \bar{P}_i^{-1} [A_{i-1} \hat{x}_{i-1} + \Gamma_{e_{i-1}} u_{e_{i-1}}] + P_i H_i^T V_i^{-1} z_i$$

$$\hat{x}_0 = P_0 \bar{P}_0^{-1} \bar{x}_0 + P_0 H_0^T V_0^{-1} z_0$$

where the matrix P_i satisfies the following recursions:

$$\bar{P}_{i+1}^{-1} = M_i^{-1} - M_i^{-1} A_i \left(A_i^T M_i^{-1} A_i + P_i^{-1} \right)^{-1} A_i^T M_i^{-1}$$

$$P_i = \left(\bar{P}_i^{-1} + H_i^T V_i^{-1} H_i \right)^{-1}, \quad i = 0, 1, \ldots, N-1$$

where

$$M_i^{-1} = W_i^{-1} \left[I - \Gamma_{pi} \left(\Gamma_{pi}^T W_i^{-1} \Gamma_{pi} \right)^{-1} \Gamma_{pi}^T W_i^{-1} \right]$$

For the filter matrix P_i to exist, the following condition must be satisfied:

$$H_i \Gamma_{pi-1} \neq 0$$

The equilibrium cost function for this problem is

$$J\left(u_p^*, u_e^*\right) = \lim_{\theta \to 0} \Upsilon^* = \frac{1}{2} \left[\| \bar{x}_0 \|_{\Pi_0}^2 + \mathrm{tr}(\Pi_0 \bar{P}_0) + \sum_{i=0}^{N-1} \left[\mathrm{tr}(\Pi_{i+1} W_i) + \mathrm{tr}\left(\Gamma_i^0 P_i \right) \right] \right]$$

with

$$\Gamma_i^0 = k_{ei}^T \left[\Gamma_{ei}^T \Pi_{i+1} \Gamma_{ei} + R_{ei} \right] k_{ei}$$

Remark 3: Note that $J(u_p^*, u_e^*)$ is *not* a saddle point; a saddle point structure does not exist for this class of problems. This property will be discussed in detail in a subsequent section.

Remark 4: A very interesting filter structure results as we take the LEG to LQG limit $\theta \to 0$. We shall, henceforth, refer to it as the "blocking filter," a name given because it blocks out the opponent's inputs and has an error independent of the opponent's inputs. Consider the term M_i^{-1} we presented in the theorem. Clearly, $M_i^{-1} \Gamma_{pi} = 0$. The matrix M_i^{-1} is used to construct the matrix $\bar{P}_{i+1}^{-1}$, and from the equation for $\bar{P}_{i+1}^{-1}$, we see that $\bar{P}_{i+1}^{-1} \Gamma_{pi} = 0$. This property is what we refer to as the "blocking property" of the filter; the control matrix of the opponent u_p falls into the null space of the filter matrix $\bar{P}^{-1}$. As shown in [8], this property ensures that the filter error of u_e's filter is independent of all of u_p's inputs. In fact, the filter error is a zero-mean Gaussian random variable, with variance equal to P_i presented in the above theorem.

Remark 5: In the limit as $\theta \to 0$, for the matrix P_i to exist, and for the problem to have a bounded cost, we require that $H_i\Gamma_{p_{i-1}} \neq 0$. This is evident from the remark above, and from the equation for P_i: because $P_i^{-1} = \bar{P}_i^{-1} + H_i^T V_i^{-1} H_i$ and $P_i \Gamma_{p_{i-1}} = 0$, for the matrix P_i to exist, it is necessary that $\Gamma_{p_{i-1}} \varepsilon R(H_i)$. From a game-theoretic point of view, this translates to an observability condition; the control actions of u_p — even though they are noise-corrupted or deceptive — must be observable by u_e.

Remark 6: Note that θ approaches zero from the left, i.e., $\theta < 0$. The cost function itself is continuous and finite for $\theta > 0$, but this translates to the case where the noise uncertainties play with the player with noisy measurements. This does not translate to a meaningful interpretation in the game-theoretic sense.

Remark 7: Note that the we use the term "equilibrium" instead of saddle point. This is because for pure strategies, a saddle point does not exist for this class of problems. We shall discuss this property in detail as we go along.

Remark 8: The equilibrium controllers are linear controllers, operating on the state and state estimate, respectively, and the gains are the same as those from the corresponding deterministic game problem.

Remark 9: The controllers are finite-dimensional; no kernels are operating on state/measurement histories.

Remark 10: For a numerical example given in [1, 8], with both players playing their equilibrium strategies, the theoretically computed equilibrium value of the cost is essentially the same as the numerically simulated value, thus validating our results.

The structure we have outlined above has some very interesting properties. In particular, we can directly implement our two-vehicle problem using the above formulation and get very predictable and consistent results. The blocking filter properties are outlined in the next section. These properties make this filter immune to deception, and are to be contrasted with the Kalman filter, which is constructed by guessing the opponent's strategy in the linear dynamic filter equation at every time step. The guesswork is done in the *a priori* state equation:

$$\bar{x}_i^k = A_{i-1}\hat{x}_{i-1}^k + \Gamma_{e_{i-1}}u_{e_{i-1}} + \Gamma_{p_{i-1}}u_{p_{i-1}}^k$$

where the superscript k on the state estimates indicate that these estimates are generated by the Kalman filter, and the superscript k on the value of u_p indicates that this is a guessed value. Note that the accuracy of the state estimates, i.e., the state estimation error is highly dependent on the accuracy of the guessed value of u_p. In the next section, we will discuss how the Kalman filter is vulnerable to deceptive moves by the opponent; a wrong guess can ruin the game for the player using the Kalman filter.

3.2.4 Properties of the Blocking Filter

The respective equations for the blocking filter and estimation error are

$$\hat{x}_i = P_i \bar{P}_i^{-1} \left[A_{i-1}\hat{x}_{i-1} + \Gamma_{e_{i-1}} u_{e_{i-1}} \right] + P_i H_i^T V_i^{-1} z_i$$

$$e_i = P_i \bar{P}_i^{-1} \left[A_{i-1}e_{i-1} + w_{i-1} \right] - P_i H_i^T V_i^{-1} v_i$$

Shown in [1,8] is that the state estimation error is a Gaussian random variable with statistics $(0, P_i)$. Note that no attempt is made in the state estimator to estimate u_p's control. The matrix $\bar{P}_i$ has the property $\bar{P}_i \, \Gamma_{p_{i-1}} = 0$, i.e, the control direction of u_p is "blocked out" at every time index. This means that the dynamics associated with the control direction of u_p are blocked out at every time index and the associated state is estimated with a zero-memory estimator (the measurements are used directly because $\Gamma_{p_{i-1}}$ is in the range space of H_i). In addition, we see that the estimation error, and, hence, the statistics of the error, are independent of u_p's inputs. Thus, in no way can u_p take advantage of u_e's imperfect measurements and play deceptive strategies. This is the main difference between the blocking filter and the Kalman filter.

Another difference between the two filtering schemes is that if the estimated strategy for u_p in u_e's Kalman filter is correct, then the state estimate $\hat{x}_i^k$ is orthogonal to the state estimation error, e_i^k. For the blocking filter, this is not true; a component of the state estimate is correlated with the estimation error. A component of the estimation error is actually uncorrelated with the entire state history. If all of u_e's guesses are correct when implementing the Kalman filter, the estimation error variance P_i^k will be less than that of the blocking filter P_i. Thus with perfect guesswork, the equilibrium cost obtained with the Kalman filter will be less than that obtained with the blocking filter. However, one cannot guarantee the accuracy of guesswork, and, hence, the added security provided by the blocking filter from deception is worth the tradeoff in performance.

In [1], the performance of the Kalman filter and blocking filter are compared for a simplified scalar pursuit-evasion problem formulation. If u_e's guesses about u_p's strategy are correct, then the values of the cost for the blocking filter and the Kalman filter are 5.90206 and 5.46695, respectively. Observe how the Kalman filter does slightly better in reducing the cost for u_e due to the smaller error variance. For this particular problem, u_p is demonstrated to inject a large-variance white noise process at the initial time-step, which changes the cost to $-57{,}920.7$ and $63{,}141$, respectively, for the blocking filter and the Kalman filter. Observe how u_p can increase the cost arbitrarily if the Kalman filter is used, whereas if this trick is tried against the blocking filter, the performance in the game is ruined.

Going back to our two-vehicle problem, we see that if u_e uses a Kalman filter to estimate the state, guessing u_p's strategy all along the way, then correct guesswork would give better performance than if the blocking filter were used; however, u_p could also take advantage of the fact that u_e is trying to guess and then actually escape by playing a deceptive strategy that ruins u_e's state estimation error. If u_e uses a blocking filter to estimate the state, there is no way u_p can deceive u_e and escape.

3.2.5   Effects of Partial Information

Recall that we used the term "information" to denote everything each player "knows" at any time instant. In this case, the *information set* of each player is defined as the union of their control history and observation history sets. At first glance, u_p, being the player with perfect state information, may appear to have a major advantage in the game. However, in the presence of process noise, u_p has no way of knowing what his opponent has played at any point in time, aside from the fact that u_p has no access to u_e's observation set. Hence, u_p, just like u_e, has *partial information*. Therefore, whereas u_p does have the advantage of not having to estimate the state from a noisy measurement, with the right estimation scheme employed by u_e, the advantage that u_p has is not as large as one would think it to be.

The breakdown of the saddle-point structure for this class of problems occurs because information is *unshared* and because random uncertainties exist. Therefore, for each value of the cost function, either player can improve on his part of the cost by taking advantage of the unshared information structure. This is done by guessing; a player could try to guess/estimate his opponent's information set and then use the assumed statistics to attempt to improve the cost. Alternately, the player could be conservative and use a filtering scheme like the blocking filter that does not require "guesstimation." Of course, a player could choose to play a mixture of the above two approaches. As we no longer have the saddle point as a measure of performance, we measure performance by evaluating strategies at a nominal *equilibrium point* and then examine how much either player can improve his performance about that equilibrium point. This concept is covered in the next section. Before going ahead, note that while a correct guess on the opponent's strategy will, in general, improve performance, if the guess is wrong or the guess is somehow caught by the opponent, the player trying to guess can do much worse. The point the authors are trying to make is that in the presence of unshared and partial information, reasonably good performance can be obtained by playing a conservative strategy that does not attempt to guess what the opponent is doing. Guesswork can be used to attempt an improvement in performance at the expense of a possible performance degradation.

For our two-vehicle problem, this is equivalent to implementing a variety of strategies and then seeing how much either vehicle can improve performance about the equilibrium point.

3.2.6 Properties of the Equilibrium Cost: The Saddle Interval

We can mathematically formulate our discussion in the previous section as follows:

For every equilibrium strategy pair (u_p^*, u_e^*), we can separately find a u_p^δ and a u_e^δ such that $J(u_p^\delta, u_e^*) \leq J(u_p^*, u_e^*)$ and $J(u_p^*, u_e^\delta) \leq J(u_p^*, u_e^*)$, respectively. The values of u_p^δ and u_e^δ are not unique. Let us denote the strategy values that maximize the deviations from the equilibrium points by $u_p^{\delta*}$ and $u_e^{\delta*}$ respectively. Then the interval $(J(u_p^*, u_e^\delta), J(u_p^{\delta*}, u_e^*))$, is called a *saddle interval*. The endpoints of the interval depend on what control/filtering strategies are used.

Let us now examine the saddle intervals for different control/filtering schemes.

3.2.6.1 Saddle Interval for the Blocking Filter

For the blocking filter, we can find a u_p^δ such that $J(u_p^\delta, u_e^*) \geq J(u_p^*, u_e^*)$, provided all of u_p's guesses about u_e's control are correct. A bound exists on the improvement that u_p can get if u_e plays u_e^*; u_p cannot make the cost infinitely large, i.e., we can find a $u_p^{\delta*}$ such that $J(u_p^{\delta*}, u_e^*) \geq J(u_p^*, u_e^*) \geq J(u_p^*, u_e^*)$, with $J(u_p^{\delta*}, u_e^*) < \infty$. Note that $u_p^{\delta*}$ is a function of u_e's filter error, e_i, and therefore, the upper bound on the cost is never achieved; the maximum cost perturbation possible by u_p is always bounded and less than the theoretical maximum. Hence, the equilibrium strategies we derived are immune to the noise-injection problem that exists for the Kalman filter and Willman strategies discussed earlier. Similarly, we can find a $u_e^{\delta*}$ such that $J(u_p^*, u_e^*) \geq J(u_p^*, u_e^{\delta*}) \geq J(u_p^*, u_e^{\delta*})$, with $J(u_p^*, u_e^{\delta*}) > -\infty$. For u_e, achieving this bound would imply that a player knows his own estimation error, which is equivalent to making perfect state measurements. Clearly, even though $u_p^{\delta*}$ and $u_e^{\delta*}$ exist and are finite in general, they are functions of quantities that are unknown to them and, therefore, the bounds $J(u_p^{\delta*}, u_e^*)$ and $J(u_p^*, u_e^{\delta*})$ are never reached in practice. To conclude, we have:

- If the blocking filter is used by u_e, the strategy pair (u_p^*, u_e^*) forms an equilibrium point about which exists a range over which either player can improve on their cost, given that the other player plays their equilibrium strategy,

$$\infty > J(u_p^{\delta*}, u_e^*) \geq J(u_p^\delta, u_e^*) \geq J(u_p^*, u_e^*) \geq J(u_p^*, u_e^\delta) \geq J(u_p^*, u_e^{\delta*}) > -\infty$$

- We define the *saddle interval* as $(J(u_p^{\delta*}, u_e^*), J(u_p^*, u_e^{\delta*}))$. This interval is an open interval for the blocking filter as the upper and lower bounds are never achieved.

- This concept is an extension of the notion of a saddle point in deterministic games to games with uncertainty. Note that if u_p plays $u_p^{\delta*}$ and u_e guesses this correctly, u_e can change his strategy to make the cost even less than $J(u_p^*, u_e^{\delta*})$, i.e. u_p's guess goes against him. The reverse is true as well: If u_e attempts to improve on his strategy by guessing what u_p played and this is wrong or is caught by u_p, u_e can do much worse instead of doing better.

3.2.6.2 Saddle Intervals for Kalman Filter and Willman Strategies

If the Kalman filter is used in place of the blocking filter, under certain circumstances, $J(u_p^{\delta*}, u_e^*) = \infty$. At the same time, u_e cannot make the cost $-\infty$ because u_p does not construct a filter of any sort. Clearly, the player u_e is at a disadvantage here. For the Willman algorithm, both players are at a disadvantage because they both construct Kalman filters. This demonstrates the superiority of the blocking filter; u_e can play their equilibrium strategy using the blocking filter to estimate the state because they know that no matter what u_p does, the cost will always be within a definite known bound. Also, if a Kalman filter is used by u_e, even if the convexity conditions on u_p are not violated, u_p can still improve on the cost by using cross-correlations. For example, u_p could use the cross-correlations between the current state x_i and u_e's state estimation error e_i^k. For the Kalman filter, the error and state are correlated to a much larger degree than in the blocking filter because the entire state is correlated with the Kalman filter error. In addition, the Kalman filter error is dependent on u_p's control history, which gives u_p an additional parameter with which to improve the cost. Clearly, the amount by which u_p can improve his cost is far greater with the Kalman filter than with the blocking filter. Similar logic can be applied to the Willman algorithm or any other strategy that attempts to smooth over u_p's control history [4]. This new concept in filtering theory as applied to games with intelligent adversaries as opposed to stochastic processes is significant: Filtering theory applied to a stochastic process can be optimized because the behavior of any stochastic process is predictable on the average. However, no way exists to predict the average behavior of an intelligent adversary and, hence, it is futile, or even dangerous, to attempt to estimate such behavior.

3.2.7   Application of Results to an Adversarial Environment

Not having to estimate one's opponent's moves in a game while making a reasonable good estimate of the state that is immune to deception is a very desirable place to be. However, estimating one's opponent's maneuvers with some degree of certainty might be possible. Based on this, we can outline two extreme approaches towards game play in an adversarial environment with partial information.

3.2.7.1 Conservative Approach

A conservative approach by a player would be to play the equilibrium strategy at each point, knowing that the worst can happen to them. If the blocking filter is used, the worst-case scenario is actually bounded.

3.2.7.2 Aggressive Approach

If a player is absolutely sure of their opponent's moves, he can at each point attempt to improve his performance by intelligently deviating from his equilibrium strategy. As we mentioned earlier, this occurs at the risk of doing much worse than the equilibrium point.

The above two cases are the two ends of a spectrum of possible approaches. Each player can — with educated guesswork — choose to play a combination of conservative and aggressive strategies at different times in the game. A tradeoff exists between estimating the adversaries motion and the lag associated with it (Kalman filter) and blocking out that motion, but not the state with faster response (blocking filter). The performance of the player would, of course, depend on what the opponent actually plays. If we look to do actual simulations and compute an average, a player could play the same type of strategy during each run of the averaging process or choose to vary it. This brings us to the notion of *mixed strategies*. Each player could also assign a probability statistic to a strategy and implement it over the simulation runs. At this point, the role of mixed point strategies with reference to the saddle point structure for this class of problems remains an open question.

In this chapter, we saw the importance of the information structure in an adversarial environment. In particular, we considered the scenario where information is unshared and imperfect and looked at how this affects each player's decision-making capability. We outlined an algorithm that eliminates the requirement to try to guess an opponent's maneuvers, which gives a reasonably good state estimate that is immune to deception. We discussed the breakdown of the saddle-point structure in such games where information is imperfect, noisy, and unshared. A conservative approach guarantees a minimum level of performance, whereas an aggressive approach could improve performance, but also renders the aggressive player vulnerable to deception.

References

1. Swarup, A., Linear Quadratic Gaussian Differential Games with Different Information Patterns, Ph.D. Dissertation, University of California, Los Angeles, 2004.
2. Bryson, A.E. and Ho, Y.C., *Applied Optimal Control*, Hemisphere Publishing Corp., Bristol, PA, October 1979.

3. Başar, T. On the saddle-point solution of a class of stochastic differential games, *J. Optimization Theory Appl.*, 33(4), 539–556, April 1981.
4. Behn, R.D. and Ho, Y.C., On a class of linear stochastic differential games, *IEEE Trans. Auto. Cont.*, AC-13, 3, June 1968.
5. Rhodes, I.B. and Luenberger, D.G., Differential games with imperfect state information, *IEEE Trans. Auto. Cont.*, AC-14, 1, February 1969.
6. McEneaney, W.M. Some classes of imperfect information finite state-space stochastic games with finite-dimensional solutions, *Appl. Math. Optimiz.*, 50, 87–118, August 2004.
7. Willman, W., Formal solutions for a class of stochastic pursuit-evasion games, *IEEE Trans. Autom. Cont.*, October 1969, AC-14.
8. Swarup, A. and Speyer, J.L., Characterization of LQG differential games with different information patterns, *Proc. of the 43rd IEEE Conf. on Decision and Control*, The Bahamas, 3459–3466, December 2004.
9. Whittle, P. Risk-sensitive linear/quadratic/Gaussian control, *Adv. Applied Prob.*, 13, 764–777, 1981.
10. Fan, C-H., Speyer, J.L. and Jaensch, C.R. Centralized and decentralized solutions of the linear-exponential-Gaussian problem, *IEEE Trans. Autom. Cont.*, 39, 10, 1986–2003, October 1994.

3.3

Strategies in Large-Scale Problems*

Boris Stilman, Vladimir Yakhnis, and Oleg Umanskiy

CONTENTS

From the practical perspective, most of the existing computational techniques for adversarial reasoning are yet to reach the point where they can, in near real-time, formulate strategies required by realistic problems such as military Command and Control (C2). Here we describe an approach, linguistic geometry (LG), that has demonstrated such capability in several problems characterized by practical scale and complexity.

* This research is supported in part by the DARPA contract NBCHC040152. Approved for public release, distribution unlimited.

We begin by exploring the nature of a key challenge facing a military strategist: The friendly side (Blue) is trying to anticipate and predict the enemy action; the enemy (Red) is actively trying to do the same with respect to Blue while simultaneously trying to deny Blue sufficient information with which Blue could predict Red's actions. Many existing automated tools, particularly military modeling and simulation tools, attempt to model the intelligent enemy by using a fixed battle plan for the enemy while using flexible decisions of human players for the friendly side [9,22]. Such approaches tend to create artificially biased strategies for Blue that might not be able to withstand actions of a thinking, dynamic enemy. Clearly, to form a basis for automated adversarial reasoning and decision making, one would need an ability to automatically generate unbiased advantageous strategies for Blue.

Game-theoretical approaches are natural for problems involving contenders with various levels of adversity, from partial cooperation to full hostility. It is also popular, and several chapters in this book, including Chapter 2.3 and Chapter 3.1 through Chapter 3.5, are game theoretical in nature. Whereas other game-theoretical chapters provide interesting solutions to important classes of problems, the distinction of this chapter's approach is in the significantly larger size of the problems considered here. We will briefly discuss the relation of the present chapter to other chapters' approaches in the next section, but we would like to notice the importance and historical significance of the approaches rooted in classical game formalization and game tree searches. (The reader is encouraged to review Chapter 3.1 prior to reading this chapter.)

Game-theoretical approaches greatly benefited from formalization and understanding of numerous game-related problem domains. However, the main obstacle to employing such techniques to large-scale problems, such as the military strategist challenge, is the size of the game tree. For instance, consider the game theoretical domain that the authors are facing in the RAID program [11,12]. Let us evaluate a lower bound of the size of the game tree associated with the RAID problem. In a simplified form, the game involves 23 Blue entities fighting against 20 Red entities in an urban environment. Ignoring the issues related to the use of weapons, each entity can make at least 20 physical moves. The actual number of moves is higher (21 to 23 in a flat area, with the ability to move up and down the floors in buildings); it would be significantly larger if actions such as application of weapons were taken into account. However, to illustrate the large size of the game tree, the lower bound is sufficient and, thus, we will not analyze application of weapons at this point. Because all the entities move concurrently, at each game move we are facing at least 20^{43} possibilities. The requirements for a solution [11,12] include prediction for at least the next 30 minutes and the entities are making on the order of 5 moves per minute, so we must predict 150 moves. This gives a lower bound of the size of the game tree as $10^{\log(20) \times 43 \times 150} \cong 10^{8392}$. No present-day computer or a reasonable combination thereof could search such game trees in a lifetime, even using time-saving techniques such as alpha-beta pruning ([10], see also Chapter 3.1 and the next section).

To find a solution, we focus here on *linguistic geometry* (LG), a game-theoretic technique that has demonstrated a significant increase in size of problems solvable in near-real time. It appears to be a viable approach for solving such practical problems as mission planning and battle management. LG can be structured into two layers — game construction and game solving. Construction involves a hypergame approach based on a hierarchy of abstract board games (ABG). Game solving includes both resource allocation for constructing an advantageous initial game state and dynamic strategy generation for reaching a desirable final game state in the course of the game.

3.3.1 Game-Solving Approaches in Practical Problems

Let us first consider the classical game-theoretic approaches. The games used by most game-based approaches are usually classified [13] as *continuous vs. discrete*, as *strategic versus extensive*, and as *games with perfect information vs. games with imperfect information*. Commonly, continuous games are considered to be within the realm of strategic games, whereas discrete games are divided between the strategic and extensive ones.

Continuous games are often described mathematically in the form of *differential games*. The classical foundations of theory of differential games can be found in [8], whereas more modern dynamic, multiagent models of differential games are presented in [4,18]. An interesting approach to continuous strategic games with imperfect information can be found in Chapter 3.2. Problems for several autonomous aerial vehicles planning a route through territory guarded by aggressive counterparts are usually described mathematically in the form of pursuit-evasion differential games. Problems of generating and real-time regenerating adversarial courses of actions for ground and naval operations can also be formulated employing pursuit-evasion differential games. A promising combination of discrete-event simulation with pursuit-evasion differential games can be found in [25,26]. Unfortunately, according to [5,15,25,26], for the large-scale games, the differential games approach is insufficient due to combinatorial explosion (see also the section 3.3.6 in this chapter).

Discrete strategic games were introduced and investigated by Von Neumann and Morgenstern [43] half a century ago and were successfully employed in various domains including economics. This tradition is exposed in many textbooks [24,44]. This approach allows analyzing full-game strategies, representing entire games. It does not allow breaking a game into separate moves and comparing them. Chapter 3.1 provides a short exposition of strategic games, where their main limitation is noted as follows: "The primary drawback of this approach is that a substantial amount of human effort needed to make sure that the set of strategies is complete and correct — and for this reason it has not been widely used." This significant limitation makes this approach inconvenient for large-scale problems where a complete set of strategies is too large for a reasonable completeness analysis.

Discrete extensive games specify the possible orders of events; each player can consider their plan of action not only at the beginning of the game but also whenever they have to make a decision [13,24]. Extensive games are usually represented as trees, which include every alternative move of every strategy of every player. Application of this class of games to real-world problems requires discretization of the problem domain, which can be done with various levels of granularity. The extensive (unlike strategic) games can represent concurrent moves. This condition is similar to the real world, where all the pieces (ships, tanks, aircraft, UAVs, ballistic/cruse missiles, satellites) and players (Red and Blue) move and act concurrently. Thus, the extensive games would allow us to adequately represent numerous real-world problem domains including modern wargaming.

Sources ([13,24] and Chapter 3.1) describe successful applications of extensive games to various problems employing searches through the game tree combined with various search reduction techniques, from those based on heuristics to alpha-beta pruning. However, such approaches have not been adequate for large-scale problems due to the large size of the respective game trees (see the above evaluation of the game tree size for RAID). Several search reduction techniques are discussed in [13,24] and Chapter 3.1, e.g., alpha-beta pruning, limited-depth search, similarity-based aggregation, and others. Although useful in various applications, these techniques are insufficient for the game trees of the magnitude considered here. According to [10], in the best case, the number of moves to be searched employing alpha-beta algorithms grows as the square root of the original exponentially growing game tree. Using this estimate, in the case of the RAID game tree discussed above, the alpha-beta search would have to go through 10^{4196} cases, which is clearly impossible with modern-day computers. While useful for some problems, limited depth search is not feasible for certain classes of problems that require predictions of very high precision, e.g., RAID [11,12] with a required depth of at least 150 moves. The similarity-based aggregation might be beneficial for large-scale problems in combination with other techniques.

To move further, we need the notion of the game state. Although Chapter 3.1 does not explicitly define the internals of the game state, the state is implicitly defined as a node of the game tree considered there. In contrast, we look at the internals of the game state that could be constructed by placing game pieces on the game board.

In solving games, different types of states might need to be considered. For example, one of the approaches to solving games with imperfect information is to include the *belief states* significantly enlarging the size of the game tree with respect to the games with perfect information (Chapter 3.1). The belief states are defined in Chapter 3.1 as sets of "all [game] states that are consistent with the information currently available" to the player. However, our need to look into the internal structure of the game state leads to an alternative (but still compatible) definition of the states of belief and the notion of information and, therefore, to an alternative treatment of solutions for imperfect information (see section 3.3.4.3 in this chapter). Finally, Chapter 2.3, Chapter 2.4, Chapter 3.2, and others deal with imperfect information in a more complex manner than through the "belief states" and the reader is encouraged to review these interesting approaches.

Another approach to discrete extensive games stems from the decidability theory in mathematical logic and employs strategies based on finite state machines (FSM), so that the memory size needed for the strategy to operate is limited by the amount of the states in the respective FSM (Figure 3.3.14) [3,6,19,49,50,51]. Such strategies are called state-strategies [3], or strategies with restricted memory [6] because the required memory should be restricted as the games within that approach include infinitely long plays. Figure 3.3.14 describes the application of a state-strategy for Player A for alternating (the players make moves one after another) or concurrent (the players move simultaneously) two-player games with perfect information. Sequence $a_0, b_0, a_1, b_1 \ldots$ represents the game play, where $a_0, a_1 \ldots$ are moves of Player A and $b_0, b_1 \ldots$ are moves of Player B, and for each n, a_n and b_n are moves at game turn "n." Sequence $S_0, S_1, S_2 \ldots$ represents the states of the strategy. In the case of alternating games, the scheme in Figure 3.3.14 corresponds to Player A making first moves in each turn; if Player B plays first, the pairs a_n, b_n must be transposed for each n. For other games, the interpretation of the input sequence $b_0, b_1 \ldots$ must be correspondingly adjusted. For instance, for games with more than two players, each b_n represents the combined moves of the other players. For games with imperfect information, each b_n represents either the information that becomes available after the move a_n was completed or an assumption about possibilities (for "what if" analysis), or combination thereof. A strategy is called winning (optimal) if a player using it would reach a desired outcome no matter what the opponents actions [13].

In contrast to [3,6,19], in [49] and subsequently in [50,51], the game rules for generating permissible plays for infinite games with perfect information were defined as recursively constructed FSMs generating such plays and permitting considerations of either finite or infinite plays. Even if the game trees were potentially infinite, the games could be redefined as games on a finite graph (essentially, the state transition graph for the FSM) and, thus, were called graph-games. A type of games on graphs is also considered in Chapter 3.1, although not in the tradition of [49,50,51] where such graphs were constructed from specific winning conditions (such conditions define which set of finite or infinite plays is a "win" for each player). In addition, FSMs are utilized in Chapter 3.4, although the purpose pursued in Chapter 3.4 differs from that pursued in this chapter as follows. In Chapter 3.4, FSMs are utilized as a simulation engine for the entire game to validate a plan or strategy that is not formulated via FSM. The simulation FSM then models the enemy response via random moves and is run multiple times to gather evidence that the plan or strategy is beneficial. In contrast, we are investigating FSM-based strategies that are advantageous for a given player in the following sense. If the player would utilize the strategy (i.e., would run the strategy FSM in parallel with the run of the game and would perform each of his moves as prescribed by the strategy FSM), he would have an advantage over the other players. To demonstrate this advantage, either the FSM strategy is played against human opponents (as was done in RAID [11,12]) or against opposing FSM strategies (see section 3.3.5 of this chapter).

Although at least four new constructive mathematical algorithms finding winning state-strategies have been described in [3,6,19,49] ([50,51] are enlargements of [49]), they were still subject to combinatorial explosion. However, the formal definition of various notions related to graph-games in [50,51] had a significant impact upon the approach described in this chapter.

Yet another approach to discrete extensive games is dispensing with tree search altogether by defining explicit game states, the so-called game boards. Such game boards must have sufficiently rich structure so that a "projection" of the game tree on the board could be defined. If considered in its entirety, this projection essentially forms the graph of the game [50,51] such that each node in the graph represents multiple nodes of the game tree. However, even if the resultant graph is much smaller than the game tree, it could still be too large for a meaningful search. In addition, each game state might be sufficiently large, so that maintaining multiple states necessary for such a search could be a problem by itself. For example, in the RAID problem, the board included about 100,000 cells. Within this approach, only portions of the projected game tree are constructed and only those portions that represent meaningful flow of events, the so-called *trajectories*. Moreover, such "flows" are not constructed in isolation, but are intertwined together as action-reaction-counteraction constructs.

Both game trees — especially those for games with imperfect information — and graphs of games include myriad paths representing meaningless event flows. In this approach, they are not even considered and, thus, they do not influence the algorithm run time. This result is illustrated on several small examples in [29] where the game trees of 10^{20} to 10^{40} nodes are reduced down to 10^2 nodes. This approach is called linguistic geometry (LG) [27–42]. Originally, LG arrived at the "construction" paradigm by formalizing heuristics of champion game players (e.g., [1]) into a mathematical theory for finding advantageous strategies for state transition systems (see Appendix), referred to as *complex systems* [27–29]. The present form of LG utilizing the game board was first described in [46,47] where the complex systems and graph-games of [50,51] were fused and transformed into the notion of *abstract board games* (ABG). Later, the notion of ABG was generalized into the notion of an LG hypergame, a structured collection of ABG. LG hypergames were described in several publications [33,35,37,38,40]. We use the notation "LG hypergames" because after 2002, the term "hypergame" appeared elsewhere with a different meaning, apparently not related to this research.

3.3.2   Overview of LG

The strategic gaming ideology of Botvinnik [1] was encapsulated by Stilman within the formal theory of LG [29]. The LG approach can be structured into two layers — game construction and game solving.

- *Game construction* includes modeling a set of related real-world campaigns, missions, or nonmilitary conflicts by constructing an LG hypergame — a hierarchy of ABGs. The result of any specific game construction is twofold — a formal definition of an LG hypergame and a link between the formal hypergame entities and real-world entities within the set of conflicts being modeled.
- *Game solving* includes decision making and automated reasoning about the hypergame by:
  - Generating an advantageous start state for a selected side.
  - Generating and dynamically regenerating advantageous strategies, tactics, and COA for all the sides at each game turn.
  - Reasoning about imperfect information, including deception.

Due to the link between the formal and the real-world entities, the game solving permits translating the formal solution (e.g., strategies or deceptions) into the courses of action for the real-world entities, providing solutions to the real-world conflicts. Conversely, the real events could be mapped into the hypergame in real-time. For example, the immediate battle damage assessment or new intelligence might result in the removal or addition of game pieces or in changes to their current status in the course of the game. For brevity, we will not be making a distinction between the formal and corresponding real-world entities wherever it is clear from the context.

3.3.3   Game Construction

3.3.3.1   Abstract Board Games

An ABG is essentially a FSM coupled with a string automaton (SA) evaluating the current value of the states as they are transitioning from each other during a game play (also called a run due to the FSM nomenclature). With respect to a player, the aforementioned SA is usually referred to as a cost function if minimizing its value is desired, or a pay-off function if maximizing its value is desired. The definition below is an extended form of the notion of *complex system* defined in [27–31,46,47].

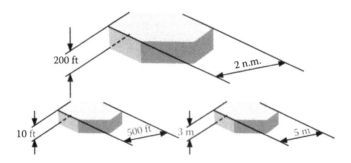

FIGURE 3.3.1
3D hex cells for various ABGs (not to scale).

Definition 1. ABG (also known as a complex system [29]) is the following nine-tuple:

$$\langle \mathbf{B, P, R, SPACE,} \ \textit{Val,} \ \mathbf{S}_i, \ \mathbf{S}_t, \ \mathbf{TR, W} \rangle$$

where the components are described below.

The game board (B). The game board is a complex structure including sets, functions, and relations. The basis of this structure is a finite set of locations (or cells), X. Other important relations include the adjacency relation that describes which cells are adjacent to a given cell. Although this relation could be entirely abstract (i.e., not related to any conceivable 2D or 3D space), we often employ a 3D hexagonal cell pattern (Figure 3.3.1). In this case, eight adjacent cells would be present — on the sides, bottom, and top. Each cell could represent an FSM in its own right. For instance, its states could capture the notion of being filled with abstract "substance" that can be interpreted as air, water, earth, and so on. The state transitions could be understood as follows: Assume that a cell represents the surface of a concrete highway. In this case, the current state of the cell represents the notion of "being filled with concrete capable of supporting vehicles." The notion that the cell is on the surface is represented by setting the state of the cell adjacent to it on the top as "filled with air." If the highway was bombarded, the cell's state could be transitioned to a state representing the notion of "being filled with damaged concrete incapable of supporting a vehicle."

Another aspect of state transitions of a cell is changing its permeability. For instance, an adjacent pair of cells could represent a wall between the cells, e.g., a part of a building's wall. It can be assigned several permeability states with respect to various types of pieces. For instance, it could be permeable by people (indicating that a door exists) but not by vehicles, or it might not be permeable by any piece. In the latter case, if pieces representing combatants act upon the cell by creating a breach, the state of permeability of the cell could be changed, permitting permeability by people.

The structure of the game pieces (P). The other major component of ABG is the set of game pieces, such as pawns, knights, and kings in chess or tanks,

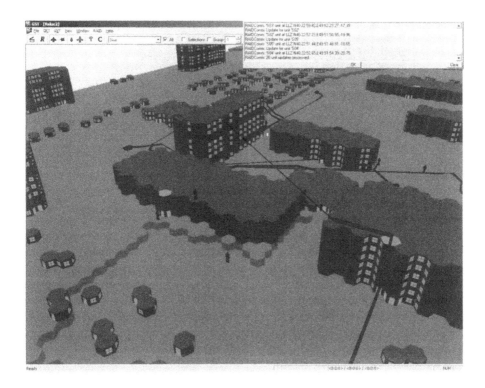

FIGURE 3.3.2
A part of the game board from a RAID experiment (in grayscale).

aircraft, and infantry units in wargames. Let us designate the set of all pieces in the game as P. This set is broken into a disjoint collection of subsets, each associated with a unique player (side). The sides could have various levels of adversity toward each other as defined by their winning conditions.

The game pieces or entities in ABG can act in various ways: Move in space, "take" other pieces as in chess, or apply weapons, apply sensors, refuel other entities in the air, or repair other entities as in military games. Actions that are not simply changing the piece placement function are related to changing the states of the cells or changing the states of the pieces. A game piece is also an FSM; its state could include ammunition, fuel, and so on. The actions presently represented in LG software are the actions of motion, application of weapons, and application of sensors. This list will be extended as our research progresses.

The structure of reachabilities (R). The aforementioned actions of pieces are defined via reachability relations (motion reachability, weapon reachability, sensor reachability, and so on). Relations of motion reachability represent moving abilities of various pieces for various problem domains: Piece p can move from location x to location y in one step if and only if relation $R_p(x, y)$ holds. Some of the pieces can crawl; others can jump or ride, sail and fly, or

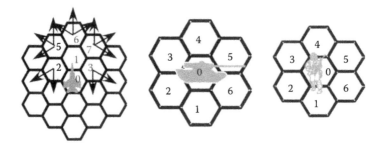

FIGURE 3.3.3
Aircraft, tank, and soldier reachabilities for a various ABG (not to scale).

even move from one orbit to another. Some of them move fast and can reach location y in one move, i.e., $R_p(x, y)$ holds; others can do that in k steps only, and many of them cannot reach certain locations at all. For example, a tank cannot reach a location completely surrounded by antitank obstacles such as thick concrete walls or deep wide trenches. During one move, certain vehicles can move only to the adjacent cell. However, pieces with more advanced moving abilities can jump over adjacent cells and reach remote cells during one move. Moreover, during the operation, a piece can change its speed, be replicated, or be transformed into a piece q with a new reachability $R_q(x, y)$. In this way, we can represent a launch of a missile from the aircraft or a change of the spacecraft mobility after refueling or docking.

When the cells cover the game board via repeatable patterns, reachability relations can also be represented as reachability patterns. For example, the left-hand figure in Figure 3.3.3 represents a motion reachability pattern for a striker aircraft modeling its cruising speed during an approach to target. The hex cells used for this reachability are 2 nautical miles (nm) across (Figure 3.3.1, top). The game turn interval is 30 sec. Thus, the speed is 8 nm/min (480 nm/hr). The arrows represent possible directions the aircraft can face at the end of the 30-sec. interval, assuming the initial direction in cell 0 as depicted. This figure is only a 2D projection of a 3D pattern. The 3D pattern permits the piece representing the aircraft to either stay in the same layer or to go one layer up or down in the same pattern as the 2D projection.

The middle figure in Figure 3.3.3 represents the cross-country reachability for a tank. The hex cell dimensions for this ABG are 500 ft across (Figure 3.3.1, bottom left). The game turn interval is 15 sec. Thus, the engagement cross-country speed modeled is 2000 ft/min (20 mi/h). No arrows are in this picture because the tank is more agile and can face any direction within this constraint. Similarly, the right figure in Figure 3.3.3 represents a slow infantry advance in an urban area. The cells are 5 m across and 3 m tall, and the game turn interval is 12 sec. This corresponds to 1.5 km/h in real-world speed. This speed was combined with two other speeds, 3 km/h and 4.5 km/h in DARPA RAID experiments. Also, similar to the aircraft reachability, the reachability pattern for infantry permits it to go to the floor above or to the floor below in one game move.

Another type of reachability, called weapon reachability (or *strikability*), reflects the application of weapons. For example, the reachability used for long-range air-to-air missiles in several ABGs is shown in Figure 3.3.5. This figure is a 2D projection of a 3D region. It represents an air-to-air missile with the range of up to 20 miles (10 hex cells away). The checkered cells are those within the range of the aircraft's missiles, provided that the aircraft is in the center cell as represented via a gray aircraft icon. Various guns, conventional artillery, strategic and tactical ground and submarine-based missiles, laser weapons — all could be represented by the weapon reachability relations. Additional requirements reflecting weapons' specifics could be imposed upon the weapon reachabilities. For example, this could be a requirement of an obstacle-free line of sight (LOS) to the object to be destroyed. This would model the fact that the object must be first acquired by the missile radar, which means that it should be visible from the aircraft (i.e., at the moment of shooting, a straight line connecting the aircraft and the target in 3D physical space should not cross any obstacles). In terms of the ABG abstract board, this line should not cross hex cells "filled" as part of terrain. For example, the gray areas on Figure 3.3.5 "behind" the obstacles (black hex cells) are unreachable for the long-range missile.

Relations of sensor reachability represent the application of various sensors, such as the eyes of soldiers, infrared sensors for heat detection, sonar, radar (fire control, detection, airborne or ground based), and so on. For example, the pattern in Figure 3.3.5 also represents the sensor reachability for the onboard target acquisition radar. Other actions could be modeled via reachability relations or patterns as well.

Finally, generation of trajectories based on the reachability relations for the large-size game boards might be time-consuming. For the LG systems developed so far, this run time was reduced by computing reachabilities for all the board locations in advance and storing them in large hash tables for future use.

The space of states (SPACE). The state space has three aspects — the states of cells, the states of pieces, and the placement function of the pieces. The component of the game state corresponding to the placement of pieces on the board is a multivalued function from X to P of the form $f: X \to Power(P)$, where *Power* is the power set operator, called the piece placement function. For a given state f and a location x, the meaning of $f(x)$ is the (possibly empty) set of all pieces placed in the cell x. The space of all possible game states is the following Cartesian product:

$$\prod_{i \in X} CellStateSpace_i \times \left\{ \left(f, \prod_{p \in \bigcup_{x \in X} f(x)} PieceStateSpace_p \right) \middle| f: X \to Power(P) \right\},$$

where $CellStateSpace_i$ is the set of all states of the cell i, $PieceStateSpace_p$ is the set of all states of the piece p, and $\bigcup_{x \in X} f(x)$ is the set of all pieces currently on the board with respect to the piece placement function f. The above Cartesian

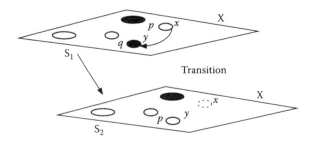

FIGURE 3.3.4
A state transition of ABG caused by moving a single piece.

product is not necessarily identical to *SPACE*, but is a superset of *SPACE*. This relation is because the specific game rules might not permit certain combinations of the cell and piece states to emerge.

The worth function (Val). The worth function *Val* is a function on P with positive integer values describing the initial values of pieces.

The initial and target sets of states, respectively, S_i and S_t. These states formally describe the beginning and the end of the game. S_t is not desirable or undesirable but merely an indicator of the end of the game.

The set of permissible state transitions (TR). Various means are used to describe the state transitions (Figure 3.3.4), usually via a collection of game rules. For example, a rule can be described by the *guard* describing the applicability of the rule to the source state, the *remove list* consisting of the pieces to be removed from the specific cells of board, the *add list* consisting of pieces to be added to the specific cells of the board, and the *change list* consisting of the description of state transitions for cells and pieces. The guard can be described via an *applicability list* consisting of items pertaining to the presence or absence of pieces in specific cells, their states, or the states of cells, e.g., of the form $ON(p) = x \land R_p(x, y)$, where the syntax $ON(p) = x$ means that for the current placement function f, $p \in f(x)$.

The winning condition (W). The winning condition W is a structure indicating the desired outcome of the game for each side. For instance, the goal of a side could be reaching a state within a subset of target states, or it might be to achieve the highest possible value of certain game parameters in the course of the game, e.g., maximum damage for the opponent, in which case it might not be possible to express it merely via a final state.

Definition 2. ABG can be divided into three classes:

- An *alternating serial* (AS) system is an ABG where only one element at a time can be moved. A move could be a combination of a physical move within the board and an action, as defined via the game rules. The opposing sides alternate turns.

- An alternating concurrent (AC) system is an ABG where all, some, or none of the elements of one side can move simultaneously (plus some the opposing elements located at the destinations of the concurrent moves can be destroyed). The opposing sides alternate moves.

- A *totally concurrent* (TC) system is the ABG where all, some, or none of the elements of both sides can move simultaneously or be destroyed.

3.3.3.2 LG Hypergames

Hypergame representation is a decomposition of complex problems into smaller and more uniformly described problems. In this manner, many problems can be conveniently represented as multiple games. Within a single hypergame, we can link together a number of military and nonmilitary ABGs with different space-time resolutions representing various spatial domains (battlespaces or theaters, in military nomenclature).

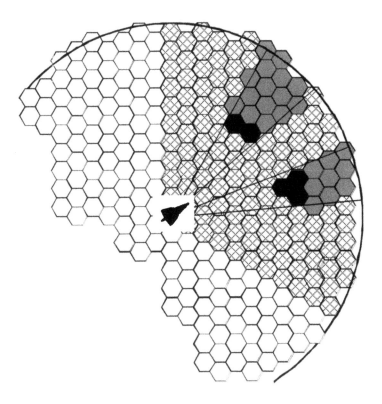

FIGURE 3.3.5
Long-range missile reachability relation, 2D projection.

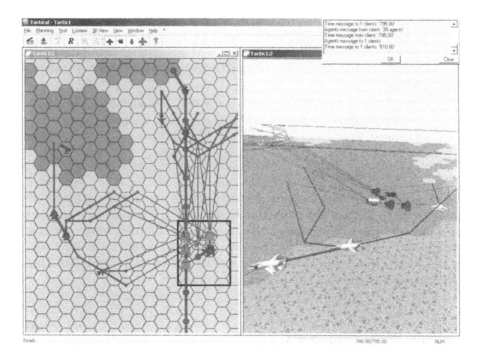

FIGURE 3.3.6
The Air ABG of a Joint hypergame. The small rectangle on the left represents the Land ABG
(see Figure 3.3.7) within the Air ABG.

Formally, a hypergame is a hierarchical confederation of several interlinked
concurrent ABGs [33,40]. To define and implement such a system, we do the
following: We define each component ABG, then for every pair of the interacting hypergame components, we define *interlinking mappings* that provide
information links (hyperlinks) between the game elements (i.e., pieces and cell
locations) in one game and their counterparts in the other game. Intuitively,
due to the hyperlinks, a game piece could be thought as being spread out
among the component ABG. A specific list of permitted activities is assigned
to each game piece. For every such piece, each activity of the piece is dedicated
to a unique component game. That is, only within this game the players are
free to engage the piece in this activity, whereas the hyperlinks reflect this
activity into the other connected games. For instance, the tank movements
(with respect to the hypergame depicted in Figure 3.3.6 and Figure 3.3.7) are
determined in the Land Game, but only reflected in the Air Game, whereas
the actions of tanks shooting aircraft or aircraft shooting tanks are determined
in the Air Game and are only reflected in the Land Game.

The hyperlinks together with the dedication of activities to specific game
components permit us to utilize concurrent activities of various pieces while
avoiding encoding the system of the component ABGs as their Cartesian

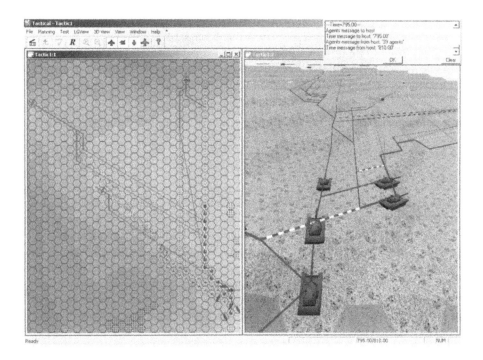

FIGURE 3.3.7
The Land ABG of a Joint hypergame (see Figure 3.3.6).

product. Instead, concurrent moves are considered only within the individual component ABG while maintaining their interdependence via the hyperlinks.

The current implementation of LG hypergames allows executing hypergames on multiple computers located in geographically remote locations (linked over TCP/IP protocol) with insignificant time spent on execution of the interlinking mappings. Therefore, the LG hypergame run time is on the order of the run time of the largest component game. Even a linear growth of computation time (with respect to the number of the component ABGs) has been avoided.

The hypergame capability has been implemented for various military operations including Joint Space/Air/Ground operations [17,20,33–40,45]. For instance, one of the implemented hypergames permits experiments with a scenario combining two ABGs for ground and air operations (Figure 3.3.6 and Figure 3.3.7). The Blue (depicted in gray in the foreground of Figure 3.3.7) and Red tanks (seen as dark gray dots in the background of Figure 3.3.7) operate in a separate ABG within a 5×5 mile area with the game turn period of 15 seconds, whereas the aircraft are performing the air-to-ground offensive operations in a $100 \times 100 \times 4$ nautical mile area with the game turn period of 30 seconds. The goal of the Blue Air Force is to destroy ground-based targets and to provide close air support for the Blue ground forces when requested. They are opposed by the Red integrated air defenses including fighter interceptors and surface-to-air missiles. The goal of the Blue ground forces (consisting of a group of tanks) is to destroy certain ground targets, and they are opposed by the Red tanks. When the Blue tanks are beset by the Red force, they call on the Blue Air Force for fire support and win the engagement with few losses. When the Air ABG is not executing, or when the communication between two ABGs is terminated, the Blue tank losses are much higher.

3.3.4   Game Solving

3.3.4.1   Strategy

Generation of LG Trajectories. At the lower level of the hierarchy of LG constructs is a trajectory — a planning path — with a piece moving along it. When it moves forward, part of a trajectory that is left behind should disappear, and re-appear when an entity backtracks during the search to explore another path.

Within LG, trajectories are represented as strings of symbols: $a(x_0)a(x_1) \dots a(x_l)$ over the alphabet $\{a\} \times X$, where a is a symbol and X is the abstract board of the ABG. Each successive point x_{i+1} is reachable from the previous point x_i, i.e., $R_p(x_i, x_{i+1})$ holds. Formal tools, i.e., grammars of trajectories [28,29], generate specific types of trajectories encountered in a number of problem domains, e.g., a shortest path, a roundabout path, and so on. Various types of trajectories generated in a given state form the Language of Trajectories for this state [29]. Strings of the Language of Trajectories serve as symbols for the Language of Zones.

Examples of the bundles of trajectories (2D and 3D) generated for aircraft and tanks in the Joint hypergame are shown in Figure 3.3.6 and Figure 3.3.7 as a part of an LG zone. Such bundles include the best shortest trajectories of the aircraft or tanks enabling them to attack or protect a target. The algorithms for LG trajectory generation [28,32] are fast due to prior generation of the tables of distances induced by reachability relations and pruning of low-quality trajectories before they are fully formed.

Several pruning criteria are present including the "smoothness" criterion, by which only the trajectories with the least deviation from the direction to the target are retained in the bundle. The direction is given by the straight line (in 3D space) connecting the start and the end of the bundle of trajectories. Another criterion for pruning allows us to select (i.e., keep) the trajectories that have the greatest parts common to other trajectories. A trajectory is always generated and analyzed within the context of an LG zone. One of the major criteria within a zone is the projected survivability of the piece. Trajectories for a piece with survivability less than a preselected threshold are pruned. Several other pruning criteria are domain specific.

Generation of LG Zones. The basic building block for the LG strategies is the LG zone. Zones contribute to the solution of team composition, tasking and subtasking, team dynamics and tactics, cooperative path planning, and uncertainty management. Intuitively, a zone is a network of trajectories drawn

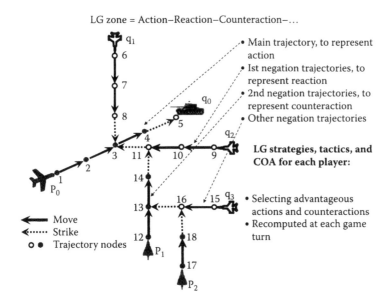

LG zone = Action–Reaction–Counteraction–...

• Main trajectory, to represent action
• 1st negation trajectories, to represent reaction
• 2nd negation trajectories, to represent counteraction
• Other negation trajectories

LG strategies, tactics, and COA for each player:

• Selecting advantageous actions and counteractions
• Recomputed at each game turn

Move
Strike
Trajectory nodes

FIGURE 3.3.8
An LG zone.

in the game board representing action-reaction-counteraction-counter coun-teraction, and so on. For every domain, several types of LG zones are specific to that domain, representing "building blocks" for the LG strategies in the sense that every LG strategy for this domain could be constructed from the LG zones of these types. For example, for the game of chess, the essential zone types are *attack, retreat, unblock,* and so on [29]; for a subdomain of military operations in urban terrain, they are *attack, protect, relocate, rout, block, evade,* and so on. Essentially, this is a "genetic code" of the abstract board games.

Consider bundles of the attack zones that include bundles of trajectories. In Figure 3.3.8, the white aircraft and the tank represent the Blue side, whereas the gray aircraft represent the Red side. Roughly speaking, an attack zone has a main (friendly or adversarial) piece — p_0 in Figure 3.3.8, where $a(5)$ is a target location. The main trajectory represents a path that the main piece needs to pursue to attain a local goal. A zone includes one or more pieces opposing to the main one, e.g., $q_1, q_2,$ and their first *negation* trajecto-ries, e.g., $a(6)a(7)a(8)a(3)$ attempting to prevent the main piece from achieving the goal. It also includes second negation trajectories of the pieces friendly to the main one, e.g., $a(12)a(13)a(14)a(11)$ for p_1 counteracting some of the above actions of the enemy, counter-counteractions of the opponent, and so on. Trajectories in a zone are linked together employing *relation of connectivity.* For example, in Figure 3.3.8, trajectory $a(6)a(7)a(8)a(3)$ is connected to trajec-tory $a(1)a(2)a(3)a(4)a(5)$ via location $a(3)$.

A *concurrent* zone [29] is constructed in a way that the length of any negation trajectory t is equal to the number of moves that the acting piece on the negated-by-*t* trajectory must make to reach the location targeted by *t*. In Figure 3.3.8, black solid arrows indicate the directions of physical moves, whereas the dotted arrows indicate the actions such as weapon release. Assuming that the Blue pieces are UAVs, the Red Bomber is manned, and the Red Fighters are either manned or unmanned, the intuitive meaning of the strategy represented by a single zone in Figure 3.3.8 is the following: Pieces q_2 and q_3 distract the Red fighters while q_1 finishes off the Red Bomber and prevents the destruction of q_0, which is the goal of the Red forces.

In LG, a zone is represented as a string of symbols, $t(p_0, t_{0,-0}) \, t(p_1, t_{1,-1}) \, \cdots$ $t(p_k, t_{k,-k})$, where $t(p_i, t_i, i)$ represents a trajectory *ti* for piece *pi* with time *i* allocated for moving along this trajectory. From the point of view of formal grammars, zones generated in a certain game state form the *Language of Zones* for this state [29]. From the point of the FSM representation of strategies, the Language of Zones in a current game state represents the current state of the LG state-strategy.

As was mentioned before, a zone is a projection of a part of the game tree onto the game board. Mathematically, a strategy is a sub-tree of the game tree [3,6,13,49], and a zone represents a portion of a game strategy as assigned to the pieces included in the zone. Furthermore, because a zone can be executed in isolation, its game-theoretical value to a player can be evaluated in terms of friendly pieces lost (or affected through their states), enemy pieces destroyed or damaged, grounds gained, or other cost functions. The zone evaluation permits the player to compare possible strategies based on the selection of zones where the piece is permitted to participate. In fact, the cost or value functions are evaluated not with respect to the game state but with respect to a set of zones generated for the state. This action, in addition to the aforementioned aspect of constructing strategies rather than searching through the game tree, constitutes another difference between LG and other gaming approaches.

Finally, the zone generating algorithm is fast, just as the trajectory generating algorithm it incorporates. This speed is achieved by pruning the majority of low-quality zones before they are fully generated. Only high-quality zones remain. A number of quality functions for the pruning purposes, such as projected probability of success, projected survivability, following rules of engagement, avoiding collisions with friends, and avoiding selected threats, are defined [14,31,32]. The algorithms for trajectory and zone generation are published in [27,28,29,32].

3.3.4.2 Example

The game defined below is totally concurrent (per Definition 2). Although we describe the elements of the game informally, all the steps below correspond to formal constructions or to elements of a mathematical proof in accordance with the definitions above. In our example, the two players are Blue and Red. The original disposition of forces is given in Figure 3.3.9. Blue pieces are depicted as white icons with a black border; Red pieces are depicted as borderless gray icons. Each player has a fighter (more streamlined

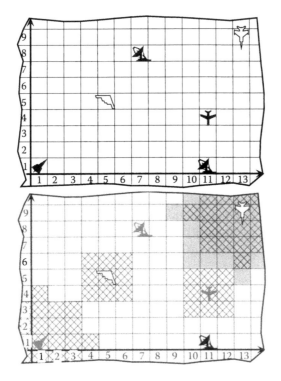

FIGURE 3.3.9
The abstract board, with reachabilities and weapons ranges of pieces.

arrow-like icon), a UAV bomber, and a ground installation (radar icon). The board is 2D, of unlimited size, and composed of square cells.

We can describe the mission objective for Blue as a list of prioritized goals:

- Priority 1: Protect the Blue Radar (G1)
- Priority 2: Destroy the Red Radar (G2)
- Priority 3: Protect the Blue Bomber or destroy the Red Fighter (G3)

This list yields the following evaluation function (also known as a pay-off function) *Eval*:

- 0 if not G1.
- 1 if G1 and not (G2 or G3).
- 2 if G1 and exactly one of (G2 or G3).
- 3 if G1 and G2 and G3.

In general, we do not limit ourselves to zero-sum games and, thus, Red might have a list of goals not necessarily symmetric to the one for Blue. However, for simplicity, we will assume that all Red wants is to hinder Blue as much as they can. Thus, in terms of the abstract board games, the adversaries have the following opposing goals:

- Blue: maximize *Eval*
- Red: minimize *Eval*

We need to describe how the pieces move and act (Figure 3.3.9):

- All pieces may move and act concurrently.
- Bombers (the motion and weapon reachability patterns are identical for both bombers):
  - The motion reachability pattern is composed of checkered cells around the bomber icon, one cell in any direction from the central cell (nine cells total).
  - The weapon reachability pattern is its current location (one cell).
- Fighters:
  - The motion reachability patterns are identical for both fighters. This pattern is composed of checkered cells around the fighter icon. To understand the entire pattern, one must examine Figure 3.3.9 and Figure 3.3.10 (29 cells total).
  - The weapon reachability patterns are different for the Red and Blue fighters:
    - Lighter gray squares describe the weapon reachability pattern for the Blue fighter (53 cells total).
    - The weapon reachability pattern for the Red fighter is identical to its motion reachability pattern (29 cells total).

In this simplified scenario, if a piece is within the weapons range of an adversarial piece, its destruction is immediate, i.e., without wasting a move. In general, other interpretations of the weapons range could be utilized, e.g., the adversarial piece might launch a missile that would be represented as a separate piece. In such a case, the destruction of the piece under attack would not be immediate but might happen only during the move occurring when the missile piece would reach the piece under attack.

Size of the game tree. The evaluation below illustrates that even for small problems, the size of the game tree can be considerable, in this case on the order of 10^{14}. We can compute this as follows:

- Assume the depth of 3 game turns.
- Amount of legal moves at any given position:
  - $29 \times 29 \times 9 \times 9 = 68,121$
- Search tree size:
  - $68,121^3 \cong 3 \times 10^{14}$

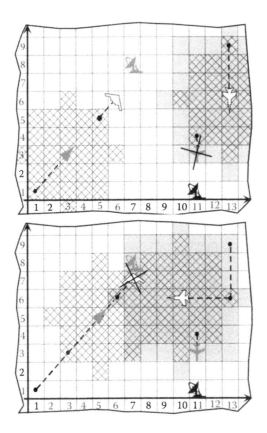

FIGURE 3.3.10
Intuitive solution: Move 1 (top) and move 2 (bottom).

Intuitive solution. An intuitive attempt to maximize *Eval* is described in Figure 3.3.10. This solution results in *Eval* = 1. However, a strategy exists with *Eval* = 2, and we will apply the LG approach to find it.

LG Solution. We start with construction of zones. Two shortest main trajectories of the Blue Bomber leading from (5,5) to (7,8) are shown in Figure 3.3.11 (top). Two first negation trajectories are also present of the Red Fighter from (1, 1):

$$a(1,1)a(3,3)a(4,5)a(6,7) \quad \text{and} \quad a(1,1)a(3,3)a(5,5)$$

Existence of at least one such a trajectory means that the Red Fighter has enough time to intercept the Blue Bomber at (6,7) or (7,7), respectively. Also, an interception of the Blue Bomber is possible at the destination (7,8), where the Blue Bomber will be destroyed after it already hits the Radar. However, any first negation trajectory having the first three nodes as $a(1,1)a(3,3)a(5,5)$

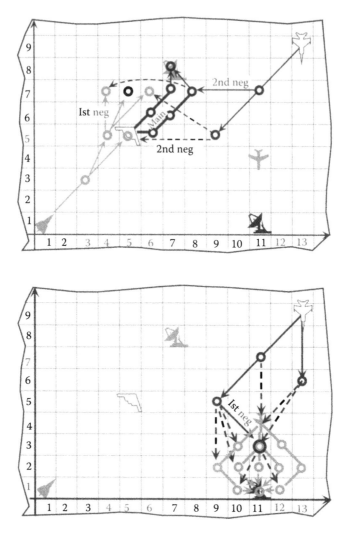

FIGURE 3.3.11
The zones for Blue Bomber, Zone 1 (top) and Red Bomber, Zone 2 (bottom).

is not safe for the Red Fighter. Indeed, the existence of second negation trajectories of the Blue Fighter from (13,9) designated as

$$a(13, 9)a(11, 7)a(9, 5) \quad \text{and} \quad a(13, 9)a(11, 7)a(8, 7)$$

and shown in Figure 3.3.11 (top) makes the Red Fighter at $a(5,5)$ vulnerable to destruction by the Blue Fighter. The safe second move position closest to both $a(5,5)$ and $a(7,8)$ is $a(4,5)$, thus any shortest first negation trajectories for the Red Fighter permitting it to potentially prevent destruction of the Red Radar, or at least destroy the Blue Bomber, will start from $a(1,1)a(3,3)a(4,5)$ (Figure 3.3.11, top). This reasoning explains the zone of Blue Bomber (Zone 1) depicted in Figure 3.3.11 (top). This zone guarantees either G2 or G3 because the only way for the Red Fighter to intercept the Blue Bomber in time is to select $a(1,1)a(3,3)a(5,5)$, which would result in its destruction by the Blue Fighter.

All the main trajectories of the Red Bomber are shown on Figure 3.3.11 (bottom). The Red Bomber will be intercepted by the Blue Fighter moving along one of the first negation trajectories that include either path $a(13,9)$ $a(11,7)a(9,5)$ or $a(13,9)a(13,6)$. The weapons range of the Blue Fighter applied from location $(9,5)$ shows that none of the shortest main trajectories of the Red Bomber are safe because the Blue Fighter "dominates" all the locations (Figure 3.3.11). The only way for the Red Bomber to approach the Radar at $(11,1)$ is to try to use a longer trajectory. Let us generate all the main trajectories of the length 4, shown on Figure 3.3.11 (bottom). Again, taking into account the weapons range of the Blue Fighter applied from $(9,5)$, we conclude that the only main trajectory of the Red Bomber that might be safe from the Blue Fighter after the first move is $a(11,4)a(12,3)a(13,2)a(12,1)a(11,1)$. This route is the highest-quality main trajectory. Notice that the sub-trajectory $a(12,3)a(13,2)a(12,1)a(11,1)$ is safe because no intercepting trajectories of the Blue Fighter from $(13, 9)$ lead to this location; it does not have enough time (one time interval). This explains the zone for the Red Bomber (Zone 2) depicted in Figure 3.3.11 (bottom). No second negation trajectory is found for this zone because Red does not have a capability to harm the Blue Fighter. Execution of this zone guarantees G1.

The crucial point in constructing the strategy for the Blue Fighter achieving *Eval* = 2 is the fact that it has a choice of participating either in Zone 1 or Zone 2. We may apply a well-known problem-solving principle called deferred selection: Whenever a choice exists between two options that are both desirable, try to delay such selection and keep both options open as long as possible. The only trajectory permitting such a course of action for the Blue Fighter is $a(13, 9)a(11, 7)a(9, 5)$. This corresponds to the zones in Figure 3.3.12 (top). Checking that the execution of this strategy gives *Eval* = 2 is easy (Figure 3.3.12, bottom, and Figure 3.3.13). The zones also permit us to analyze the low score of the intuitive solution. The reason for that score is the precipitous selection of Zone 2 without an attempt to explore Zone 1.

This example demonstrates the application of the LG approach to construct a winning strategy for Blue with respect to a winning condition *Eval* ≥ 2. A slight reformulation of every step of the above construction would result in the proof of the following theorem that we leave to the reader.

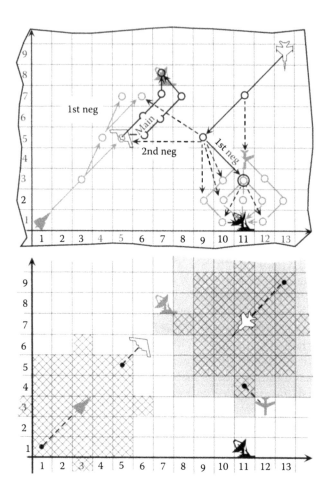

FIGURE 3.3.12
Highest quality zones (top) and Step 1 of the corresponding strategy execution (bottom).

Theorem. There exists a winning strategy for Blue with respect to a winning condition *Eval* ≥ 2.

3.3.4.3   Imperfect Information

In [13,24] and Chapter 3.1, the imperfect information is treated via belief states. Within LG, a belief is defined in a different way, via the notion of worldviews. A *worldview* is an FSM with a board reflecting the player's beliefs or knowledge regarding the current disposition of enemy pieces, noncommunicating friendly pieces, or the states of the cells. Such beliefs are formalized via constraints on the piece placement function, states of

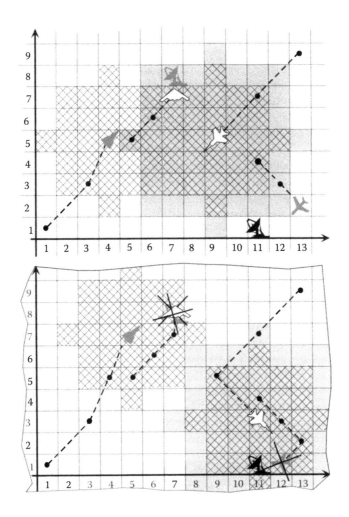

FIGURE 3.3.13
Step 2 (top) and Step 3 (bottom) of an LG Strategy execution.

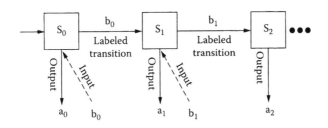

FIGURE 3.3.14
Application of a state-strategy.

the pieces, or states of the cells. To reflect multiplicity of beliefs, LG employs multiple worldviews permitting modeling of various types of knowledge, e.g., full knowledge currently available to a side, "true" knowledge representing the objective reality, various assumptions of a side regarding the other sides or even its own pieces' communication with whom is temporary broken. Essentially, a worldview could be treated as an ABG (or an LG hypergame) in its own right, and thus LG is capable of generating advantageous strategies and COA for each side with respect to a worldview. The LG approach employs the following approaches to uncertainty management of gradually increasing sophistication.

Reactive Approach (with Red, Blue, and True Worldviews). Each worldview can contain information about the Red and Blue forces and the environment. The Blue and Red Worldviews differ in such a way that each of these worldviews contains only the information known to the respective side *a priori*, or via its sensors, automatic feed from databases, or direct input from the operator. The True Worldview is needed when a third party is defining the objective reality, e.g., umpires or a simulator where the game is being conducted. For example, in the RAID program, such a simulator is OTB (U.S. Army's OneSAF Testbed Baseline, see http://www.onesaf.org). The LG tools generate strategies, tactics, and COA within each worldview. Consider a contesting side (Red or Blue). Its sensors operate in the True Worldview, not in the side's Worldview. If these sensors uncover discrepancies between the side's worldview and the True Worldview, the side would react by updating the faulty knowledge in its worldview. The LG algorithms then recompute the side's strategy. However, if the discrepancy were the result of a deception deliberately engineered by the opposition, the side might be unable to discern the deception without the following proactive approach.

Proactive Approach (with Multiple Virtual Worldviews). Because the state of beliefs changes dynamically, we need an ability to create ("spawn") or eliminate worldviews as the game progresses. For example, within the Blue Worldview, the LG algorithms will be able to spawn a number of Virtual Worldviews, e.g., a Virtual Red Worldview (VRW) that can represent "what Red thinks the world ought to be" as far as Blue knows. Thus, when computing the strategies, Red in VRW would not see (as a consequence of formal constraints on the game states) what Blue intends to conceal or, contrary, would see the decoys created by Blue. Thus, Blue within the Blue Worldview would be able to evaluate Red strategies and COA should the Blue deception be successful. This would allow Blue to shift forces to where Blue otherwise would not dare move them. Another Virtual Worldview could assist Blue in uncovering Red deception by modeling possible ambushes, feints, and so on, undertaken by Red. The capabilities for other sides are similar to what was discussed above for Blue. Creation and elimination of various virtual worldviews is explained via two different comprehensive examples in [34,41].

3.3.4.4 Resource Allocation

The LG approach permits the development of algorithms allocating resources for various problem domains [39,42]. The resource allocation capability can be used in several ways, for example:

- To determine the best minimal cost defense force to counter an expected enemy assault, while insuring that
  - A threshold probability of successful defense is met and the threshold for the losses is not exceeded.
- To determine the least amount of attack force to carry out an assault while insuring that
  - A threshold probability of successful offense is met.
  - To assure that the threshold for the losses is not exceeded.

As an example, we discuss such an algorithm for the case of Blue conducting defensive operations against Red, e.g., as in [39].

We assume the case of a single ABG and assume that the board is already defined. We are given several types of attacking Red entities (Cruise Missile, Bomber Aircraft, Infantry Unit, and so on), so that the various reachabilities, probability tables (the so-called probabilities of kill), and ranges of weapons and sensors are defined. We also assume that all the Red attacking assets are placed on the board. The mission for the Red attacking assets is to destroy the Blue pieces designated as defensive assets.

With respect to Blue, we assume that we are given several types of defensive Blue entities (e.g., Missile Ship, Fire Unit, Airborne Interceptor), so that the various reachabilities, probability tables, and ranges of permitted weapon and sensor loads are defined. Pieces instantiating these types of Blue entities are called the defensive assets. We assume that several Blue entities designated as defensive assets are already placed on the board. Finally, we are given a threshold probability of success (PS) and several stockpiles of defensive assets. Each stockpile includes an entity instantiating one of the defensive asset types, a number of such entities available for the mission, and an opportunity cost. The opportunity cost is a relative cost (in artificial units) representing the difficulty of delivering any of the pieces assigned to the stockpile to the theater of operation combined with perceived importance of the piece type, i.e., the more the demand for usage of the piece type for other theaters, the more important the piece type is. The opportunity cost could be determined by subject matter experts. That several Blue defensive assets are prepositioned on the board is entirely possible. These pieces will participate in the defense of the defensive assets, but they are not considered to belong to any of the stockpiles. The opportunity cost of the prepositioned defensive assets is defined as zero.

Algorithm outline. The Blue defensive assets are separated into two dynamically changing groups, on-the-board pieces (OnBoard) and off-the-board pieces (OffBoard). Initially, OnBoard consists of the prepositioned defensive assets, whereas OffBoard consists of all the pieces in the stockpiles. During the execution of the algorithm, the Blue pieces from the stockpiles would be switched between OnBoard and OffBoard in either direction.

The purpose of the algorithm is to determine the least costly placement of the defensive assets on the board so that the probability of destruction (PD), also called destructibility, of each attacking asset would be greater or equal to the PS. The cost of placement is defined as the cumulative opportunity cost of the Blue defensive assets OnBoard. The destructibility of each Red attacking entity is to be determined from the construction of the LG zones.

The computation is to be conducted in several stages, each consisting in a number of steps. At each step, a group of Blue defensive assets from OffBoard is placed on the board and thereby becomes a member of OnBoard. That such a placement would cause a rearrangement of the pieces already on the Board to maintain various constraints imposed on the Blue pieces is possible.

After the placement of the defensive assets at this step, the LG attack zones for the Red attackers are generated. Each zone has the main trajectory from a group of Red attackers toward one of the Blue defended assets as well as first negation trajectories from the Blue defensive assets, so that the protected assets are defended in an effective way. Within this zone structure, the cost of percentage of average destructibility increase is computed. In several steps, by varying the Blue defensive assets as well as respective first negation trajectories, LG selects such a setup of zones that maximizes the minimal destructibility of the attackers (within the threshold of the PS) while minimizing the cost of percentage of average destructibility increase achievable in this setting. This setup corresponds to an advantageous resource allocation of minimal cost, i.e., the advantageous start state of the game.

■■■■■■

3.3.5   Accuracy of the Solution

The LG approach has been validated theoretically and via experiments with software applications in industrial and research projects. Below we describe several of those projects.

3.3.5.1   Mathematical Proof for Reti-Like Problems

The Reti endgame is a well-known chess problem involving two kings and two pawns. In [29], a comprehensive mathematical proof that the LG algorithm generates an optimal draw strategy for the Reti problem is presented. Furthermore, the problem is generalized to a larger class of the so-called Reti-like problems including n-dimensional boards of arbitrary size as well as concurrent moves by the players. The proof in [32] can be readily extended to this larger class.

3.3.5.2 Specific Chess Examples Investigated by Experts

LG has solved various chess problems including such difficult ones as the Nadareishvili Endgame and the Botvinnik–Capablanca problem [1,29]. Chess experts, including several World Chess Champions, analyzed the zone-based reasoning behind the solutions and concluded that at every move, the zones provided such action-counteraction reasoning that they were unable to counter or to produce a better motivation for the moves. These issues are discussed in [1,29] and in private communications with grandmasters Smyslov, Eive, and others.

3.3.5.3 Industrial Projects

The Ministry of Energy of the former U.S.S.R. utilized the LG approach (then called the PIONEER approach) for year-long scheduling of the centralized power equipment maintenance for its 1121 power stations. LG was selected because other scheduling algorithms could not overcome the combinatorial explosion due to the large scale of this problem, especially if multiple resources were taken into account [1,2,21,23,29,48]. For instance, according to [21], various enhancements of the dynamic programming approach generated schedules that satisfied only 10% of scheduling requests on average. In contrast, the PIONEER-based schedules satisfied from 83 to 89% of requests [2]. The quality of the PIONEER-based schedules exceeded the ones produced by traditional means. Indeed, a smaller-scale monthly scheduling a comparison with schedules produced manually by experts following the then-existing standard procedures demonstrated that PIONEER-based system generated schedules that improved the manual ones by 18% on average with respect to the total power of the plants included on the schedule [23].

3.3.5.4 LG-PROTECTOR for Boeing

LG was utilized in a research project for Boeing related to resource allocation for the defense against cruise missiles [36,39]. A total of 109 experiments were conducted [36]. Subject matter experts determined that using the traditional resource allocation techniques, they could not allocate resources better than the LG algorithm [36,39]. Moreover, each resource allocation experimented upon was computed by LG-PROTECTOR in under 1 minute, whereas the experts acknowledged that manually, under a standard procedure, such work would have required several experts days to complete [36,39].

3.3.5.5 The RAID Program

The LG approach was utilized in the RAID project (Real-time Adversarial Intelligence and Decision-making) [11,12] along with an approach

TABLE 3.3.1

RAID Experiment Scoring Criteria

Red casualties
Collateral Damage
Blue Casualties
Advance To Objective
Time to Complete the Mission
Facility Protection

described in Chapter 1.3. LG served as a key "brain" behind the software that predicted the future for human adversarial teams, Blue and Red, in an urban environment. As a part of such prediction, this system suggested the best courses of action for the Blue team against the actions of the Red team (also predicted by LG) in real-time. Following these recommendations, the Blue team fought Red in a simulated battle employing OTB, a U.S. Army battle simulation package (U.S. Army's OneSAF Testbed Baseline). Both teams were staffed with retired military professionals. Multiple comparative experiments with assisted and unassisted Blue teams were conducted (Figure 3.3.2). The scoring criteria are presented in Table 3.3.1; the experiments results, in Table 3.3.2 and Table 3.3.3.

TABLE 3.3.2

Results of One of the RAID Experiments

	Pair ID	RAID Score	Non-RAID Score	Difference
• Experiments show that the RAID-supported commander noticeably outperforms the staff-supported commander.	1	71.91	69.76	2.15
• Statistics:	2	78.34	75.07	3.27
– Number of Valid Run Pairs = 9	3	84.66	86.81	2.15
– Mean Difference = 2.78				
– StDev of Difference = 5.21	4	74.22	78.11	3.89
• RAID advantage is significant:	5	83.04	73.35	9.69
– 6 times out of 9 Outperformed the Human team	6	80.25	81.41	1.16
– In 2 runs, the difference was higher than StDev (86% and 128% higher)	7	94.83	82.93	11.90
	8	89.31	85.92	3.39
• RAID disadvantage is negligible	9	81.09	79.30	1.79
– Out of 3 runs where the Human Blue team outperformed RAID, the difference never exceeded StDev	Mean	81.96	79.18	2.78
	StDev	7.12	5.74	5.21

TABLE 3.3.3

Results of One of the RAID Experiments

	Pair ID	RAID Score	Pair ID RAID Score	Difference
• Experiments show that RAID-supported commander noticeably outperforms the staff-supported commander	3	74.300	72.500	1.80
• Statistics:	2	76.890	75.240	1.65
– Number of Valid Run Pairs = 9	6	57.840	67.440	−9.60
– Mean Difference = 3.14				
– StDev of Difference = 10.10	4	88.650	71.750	16.90
• RAID advantage is significant:	8	70.390	76.350	5.96
– Outperformed the Human team 5 times out of 9	10	77.810	79.710	1.90
– In 2 runs, the difference was higher than StDev (67% and 99% higher)	9	86.390	78.170	8.22
	1	77.500	57.380	20.12
• RAID disadvantage is negligible				
– Out of 4 runs where the Human Blue team outperformed RAID,	7	69.530	72.520	2.99
the difference never exceeded StDev	Mean	75.48	72.34	3.14
	StDev	9.20	6.72	10.10

3.3.6   Scale of the Problems

The major difficulty of developing tools for adversarial reasoning is related to the issue of scalability. This means that even modest increases in problem complexity, such as adding several tanks, aircraft, or platoons, could cause an exponential increase in computation time to generate plans or make decisions, a problem called combinatorial explosion. The difficulties of overcoming the combinatorial explosion for problems of practical scale and complexity were discussed in the beginning of this chapter.

As was mentioned before, the LG approach overcomes the combinatorial explosion by dispensing with the game tree altogether via constructing only meaningful flows of events. However, one would need evidence that the techniques we utilize actually work. We provide such evidence on two levels:

- The first level is theoretical. A mathematical proof exists that the LG approach has a low-degree polynomial run time [29].
- The second level is experimental. Software implementations could be inefficient, leading to exponential run times despite the theoretical results. Thus, the claim of scalability for the LG-based software systems must be confirmed experimentally.

- The LG-PROTECTOR studies for Boeing concluded that the LG-based software tools of mission planning and execution, resource allocation, and COA generation and assessment have a low-degree polynomial run time, whereas several of those tools demonstrated even better, linear run-time growth [36,39].

- In the aforementioned RAID program, one of the requirements was the ability to compute a 30 minute prediction within 300 seconds. This requirement was met, indicating that the LG-based reasoning and decision-making tools do not suffer from the combinatorial explosion.

In the period of 1999 to 2005, more than 15 LG-based software systems and prototypes were developed. They include decision aids, decision making, C2, and training prototypes. Two of them, LG-PROTECTOR for Boeing and RAID, are discussed in this chapter. The rest are described in [16].

3.3.7 Appendix: State Transition Systems

We will formally describe three notions, a state transition system (STS), a finite state machine (FSM), and string automaton (SA). STS is a four-tuple $\langle S, S_{in}, S_t, TR \rangle$ where S is a set of states, S_{in} S is a nonempty set of initial states, S_t S is a set of (possibly empty) terminal states, and TR is a set of state transition rules. A state transition is just an arbitrary pair of states. A transition rule is a triple $\langle StateTrig, TranTrig, AdmTrans \rangle$ where $StateTrig$ is a set of states called trigger states, $TransTrig$ is a set of state transitions called transition triggers such that either $StateTrig$ or $TransTrig$ is nonempty, and $AdmTrans$ is a nonempty set of state transitions called admissible transitions. A run of the STS is a possibly infinite sequence of states $s_0, s_1 \ldots$, where $s_0 \in S_{in}$; if the sequence is finite, then the last state is terminal and no state may follow a terminal state; and lastly, each successive pair s_i, s_{i+1} in the run satisfies the following transition condition:

"For each s_i, s_{i+1}, a transition rule $\langle StateTrig, TranTrig, AdmTrans \rangle$ exists from TR such that: $(s_i, s_{i+1}) \in AdmTrans$ and either $s_i \in StateTrig$ or $(s_{i1}, s_i) \in TranTrig$."

An FSM is an STS with a finite set of states. An SA is an FSM with the following caveats: SA "accepts" a string of symbols $a_0, a_1 \ldots$ in an alphabet A, and for each transition rule in SA is associated with a function $f: A \times S \to Power(S)$, where $Power$ is the power set operator, such that $AdmTrans$ consists of transitions of the form of (s, σ) with $\sigma \in f(a, s)$. Furthermore, the transition condition is augmented as follows:

"$s_0, s_1 \ldots$ corresponds to a sequence $a_0, a_1 \ldots$, and $s_{i+1} \in f(a_i, s_i)$"

Various types of FSM and SA are explained in [7].

References

1. Botvinnik, M.M., *Computers in Chess: Solving Inexact Search Problems*, Springer-Verlag, New York, 1984.
2. Botvinnik, M.M., Petryaev, E.I., Reznitskiy, A.I., et al., Application of new method for solving combinatorial problems to scheduling repairs of equipment of power plants, *Economics and Mathematical Methods*, Moscow, 1983 [in Russian].
3. Büchi, J.R. and Landweber, L.H., Solving sequential conditions by finite state strategies, *Trans. of the Am. Math. Soc.*, 138, 295–311, 1969.
4. Dunnigan, J., *The Complete Wargames Handbook*, William Morrow & Co., New York, 1992.
5. Garcia-Ortiz, A. et al., Application of semantic control to a class of pursue-evader problems, *Comp. Math. with Appl.*, 1993, 26(5), 97–124.
6. Gurevich, Y. and Harrington, L., Trees, automata and games, *Proc. of the 14th Annual ACM Symp. on Theory of Computing*, 60–65, San Francisco, 1982.
7. Hopcroft, J. and Ullman, J., *Introduction to Automata Theory, Languages, and Computation*, Addison-Wesley, Reading, MA, 1979.
8. Isaacs, R., *Differential Games*, John Wiley & Sons, New York, 1965.
9. Keefer, D.L., Corner, J.L., and Kirkwood, C.W., Decisions analysis applications in the operations research literature, 1990–1999, 2004, http://www.public.asu.edu/~kirkwood/Papers/DAAppsSummaryTechReport.pdf.
10. Knuth, D., and Moore, R., An analysis of alpha-beta pruning, *Artif. Intelligence*, 6(4), 293–326, 1975.
11. Kott, A. and Ownby, M., Tools for real-time anticipation of enemy actions in tactical ground operations, *10th Intl. Command and Control Res. and Tech. Symp.*, McLean, VA, 2005
12. Kott, A. and Ownby, M., Adversarial reasoning: challenges and approaches, in Trevisani, D.A. and Sisti, A.F. (Eds.), *Proc. of SPIE, Enabling Technologies for Simulation Science IX*, 5805, May 2005, 145–152.
13. Kuhn, H.W., and Tucker, A.W. (Eds.), *Contributions to the Theory of Games*, Volume II (Annals of Mathematics Studies), 28, Princeton University Press, Princeton, NJ, 1953.
14. Lee, J., Chen, Y-L., Yakhnis, V., Stilman, B., and Lin, F., Discrete event control and hostile counteraction strategies, *DARPA JFACC Final Report*, Rockwell Science Center, Thousand Oaks, CA, February 2001.
15. Lirov Y., Rodin, E.Y., McElhaney, B.G., and Wilbur, L.W., Artificial intelligence modeling of control systems, *Simulation*, 50(1), 12–24, 1988.
16. *Linguistic Geometry Tools: LG-PACKAGE*, with Demo DVD, 46 pp., STILMAN, 2005. This brochure and recorded demonstrations are also available at http://www.stilman-strategies.com.
17. *Linguistic Geometry Workshop, with STILMAN's Comments*, 17 pp., REPORT, Dstl, Ministry of Defence, Farnborough, U.K., February 25–26, 2003.
18. Lirov, Y., Rodin, E.Y., McElhaney, B.G., and Wilbur, L.W., Artificial intelligence modeling of control systems, *Simulation*, 1, 12–24, 1988.
19. McNaughton, R., Infinite games played on finite graphs, *Ann. Pure Applied Logic*, 65, 149–184, 1993.
20. McQuay, W., Stilman, B., and Yakhnis, V., Distributed collaborative decision support environments for predictive awareness, *Proc. of the SPIE Conference "Enabling Technology for Simulation Science IX,"* Orlando, FL, 2005.

21. Method and Algorithm of Optimization of Capital and Medium Repair Schedules of Main Generation Equipment for Energy Systems, Report of VNIIE - National Research Institute for Electrical Engineering, Moscow, 1977 [in Russian].

22. Naval Studies Board, *Technology for the United States Navy and Marine Corps, 2000–2035: Becoming a 21st-Century Force*, Washington, D.C., 1997.

23. Reznitskiy, A. and Stilman, B., The PIONEER method in computer-aided scheduling of power facility maintenance, *Auto. and Telemechanics*, USSR Academy of Sciences, Moscow, 1983 [in Russian].

24. Osborn, M. and Rubinstein, A., *A Course in Game Theory*, Cambridge, MA: MIT Press, 1994.

25. Rodin, E., Semantic control theory, *Appl. Math. Lett.*, 1(1), 73–78, 1988.

26. Shinar, J., Analysis of dynamic conflicts by techniques of artificial intelligence, INRIA Report, Antipolis, France 1990.

27. Stilman, B., A formal language for hierarchical systems control, *Intl. J. Languages Design*, 1, 4, 333–356, 1993.

28. Stilman, B., A linguistic approach to geometric reasoning, *Int. J. Comp. Math. Appl.*, 26, 7, 29–58, 1993.

29. Stilman, B., *Linguistic Geometry: From Search to Construction*, Kluwer Academic Publishers, Boston, MA, 2000.

30. Stilman, B., From games to intelligent systems, *Proc. of the 2nd ICSC Intl. Symp. on Eng. of Intelligent Systems — EIS'2000*, June 27–30, 2000, University of Paisley, U.K., 779–786.

31. Stilman, B. and Yakhnis, V., Solving adversarial control problems with abstract board games and linguistic geometry (LG) strategies, *Proc. of the 1st Symp.: Adv. in Enterprise Control*, JFACC Program, DARPA, ISO, November 15–16, 1999, San Diego, CA, 11–23.

32. Stilman, B. and Yakhnis, V., Adapting the linguistic geometry — Abstract board games approach to air operations, *Proc. of the 2nd Symp.: Adv. in Enterprise Control*, JFACC Program, DARPA, Information Systems Office, July 10–11, 2000, Minneapolis, MN, 219–234.

33. Stilman, B. and Yakhnis, V., *LG War Gaming for Effects Based Operations*, STILMAN Advanced Strategies, Technical Report to Rockwell and Boeing, 47 pp, July 2001.

34. Stilman, B. and Yakhnis, V., Linguistic geometry: new technology for decision support, *Proc. of the SPIE Conference "Enabling Technology for Simulation Science VII,"* April 22–25, 2003, Orlando, FL.

35. Stilman, B. and Yakhnis, V., *LG War Gaming for Effects Based Operations*, STILMAN Advanced Strategies, Technical Report to Rockwell and Boeing, 47 pp, July 2001.

36. Stilman, B. and Yakhnis, V., LG Anti-CM Defense Project in September–December 2001, STILMAN Advanced Strategies, Final Report to Boeing with raw data and charts, 35 pp, January 2002.

37. Stilman, B., Yakhnis, V., and Umanskiy, O., Winning strategies for robotic wars: defense applications of linguistic geometry, *Artif. Life Robotics*, 4, 3, 2000.

38. Stilman, B., Yakhnis, V., and Umanskiy, O., Knowledge acquisition and strategy generation with LG wargaming tools, *Intl. J. Comp. Intell. Appl.*, 2, 4, December 2002, 385–409.

39. Stilman, B., Yakhnis, V. Umanskiy, O., and Hearing, J., Operational level decision aids with LG-based tools, *Proc. of the SPIE Conference "Enabling Technology for Simulation Sci. VI,"* April 1–5, 2002, Orlando, FL.

40. Stilman, B., Yakhnis, V., and McCrabb, M., LG wargaming tool for effect based operations, *Proc. of the SPIE Conference "Enabling Technology for Simulation Science VI,"* April 1–5, 2002, Orlando, FL.

41. Stilman, B., Yakhnis, V., Curry, P., and Umanskiy, O., Deception discovery and employment with linguistic geometry, *Proc. of the SPIE Conference "Enabling Technology for Simulation Science IX,"* Orlando, FL, 2005.

42. Stilman, B., Yakhnis, V., Umanskiy, O., and Boyd, R., LG-based decision aid for naval tactical action officer's (TAO) workstation, *Proc. of the SPIE Conference "Enabling Technology for Simulation Science IX,"* Orlando, FL, 2005.

43. Von Neumann, J. and Morgenstern, O., *Theory of Games and Economic Behavior*, Princeton University Press, Princeton, NJ., 1944.

44. Walker, P.A., Chronology of game theory, 2001, http://www.econ.canterbery.ac.nz/hist.htm.

45. Weber, R., Stilman, B., and Yakhnis, V., Extension of the LG hypergame to "inner games" played over the topology of competing "mind nets," *Proc. of the SPIE Conference "Enabling Technology for Simulation Science IX,"* Orlando, FL, 2005.

46. Yakhnis, V. and Stilman, B., Foundations of linguistic geometry: complex systems and winning conditions, Symposium "Linguistic Geometry and Semantic Control," *Proc. of the First World Congress on Intelligent Manuf. Processes and Systems (IMP&S)*, Mayaguez-San Juan, Puerto Rico, February 1995.

47. Yakhnis, V. and Stilman, B., A multi-agent graph-game approach to theoretical foundations of linguistic geometry, *Proc. of the Second World Conf. on the Fund. of Artif. Intelligence (WOCFAI 95)*, Paris, July 1995.

48. Yakhnis, A., Yakhnis, V., and Stilman, B., Linguistic geometry and board games approach to automated generation of schedules, *Proc. 15th IMACS World Congress on Sci. Comp., Modeling and Appl. Math.*, Berlin, 1997.

49. Yakhnis, A. and Yakhnis, V., Extension of Gurevich-Harrington's restricted memory determinacy theorem: a criterion for the winning player and an explicit class of winning strategies, *Ann. Pure Applied Logic*, 48, 277–297, 1990.

50. Yakhnis, A. and Yakhnis, V., Gurevich-Harrington's games defined by finite automata, *Ann. Pure Applied Logic*, 62, 265–294, 1993.

51. Zeitman, S., Unforgettable forgetful determinacy, *Logic Comp.*, 4, 273–283, 1994.

3.4

Learning to Strategize

Gregory Calbert

CONTENTS

Strategy development in warfare is difficult partly because of the inherent problem of scale. The interaction of large numbers of agents, both human and machine, means that planning for even small operations will involve reasoning both at small and large spatial and temporal scales. Traditionally, military planners have dealt with the problem of scale by demarking the planning process into strategic, operational, and tactical levels. The time-scales involved in military operations range from years or even decades at the strategic level down to minutes and seconds for the tactical. Even the language used to describe strategic, operational, and tactical plans is different. Planning at the tactical level might involve terms akin to the kinetic reach of forces, such as precision or firepower. At the operational level, the language used is derived from logistics, placement, or the maintenance and sustaining of forces. Strategic-level plans involve forays into the influence and shaping both of physical and political arenas.

We saw earlier that imperfect information increases the scale or number of strategic actions that must be considered because the opponent will be in one of a large number of probable states. In Chapter 3.1, the authors limited the strategy space by pruning states that were not consistent either with the current observations or the history of past observations. Progress was made for strategy development in an abstract game of utmost difficulty, Kriegspiel.

Yet even if the opposing sides have perfect information of the battlefield, the large scale of strategic actions can also arise simply from the number of elements within the game. Unlike classical abstract games such as chess or Go, warfare has no rule to simplify the dynamics of the individual elements. Indeed, concurrent or synchronized actions are seen as crucial factors in modern maneuver-based warfare.

In developing strategies, planners and modelers must develop systematic approaches to dealing with the scale of combat. In the current practice of military planning, an exhaustive structured process, sometimes termed the "military appreciation process" [2], has been developed through which distributed teams of planners analyze the commander's overall intent or objective, consider various strategic options, conduct wargaming of these options, and finally choose which course of action is most appropriate. At each stage of the military appreciation process, exhaustive checks are made, ensuring all important military intelligence is understood and major risks or opportunities are not ignored.

In the modeling and analysis domain, a collection of approaches exists to deal with the scale of warfare. One such approach is to construct a high-resolution wargame in which the elements, such as tanks or jet fighters, have carefully scripted behaviors. Strategic or course-of-action options are then simulated using the best available information regarding the strategies of the adversarial force. For the probabilistic analysis of strategy, structural aspects of the variables involved, such as conditional independence and hierarchical measures of effectiveness, can be exploited using Bayesian networks [19] or Bayesian knowledge bases, as shown in Chapter 1.1.

In this chapter and the chapter following, we explore machine-learning approaches to the development of strategy. Machine-learning methods in the context of games can be defined as algorithms used in the selection of strategies that improve some performance measure, such as the number of wins, as experience with the game or simulation dynamics increases. The term *experience* is taken here as the number of moves or games the agent plays against an opponent (which may or may not be learning). Advances in machine learning, particularly reinforcement learning (RL) and coevolutionary algorithms, have demonstrated that constructing an agent and applying algorithms such as the method of temporal differences — which we describe below [30] — is feasible to learn games such as backgammon and chess to the level of a master player.

Games with three or more players, such as the Settlers of Catan, are now the subject of machine-learning research [23]. In this game, the effectiveness of reinforcement learning becomes evident when combined with various structural observations of well-known game features, such as force mobility, and the hierarchical decomposition of the strategies from higher-level goals down to lower-level actions. Using spatial and temporal structure to develop hierarchical decompositions of complex problems into a series of simpler nested abstract subproblems is also present partly in the linguistic geometry strategy development approach, as shown in Chapter 3.3. We begin this chapter by constructing a simulation-based wargame, broadly based on an operational-level military scenario. The wargame, termed TD-Island (Temporal Difference Island) has two sides, Blue and Red, pitted against one another with the objective expressed in the end or terminal states of securing a strategically important island. Blue and Red agents have a number of elements, including jet fighters, transporters, and land forces, under their control. One agent is used for each side and, therefore control, is centralized. We define the state-dynamics of the wargame. Interactions between opposing elements (for example, a Blue brigade in the same location as a Red) are governed by a set of probabilistic tree-based rules. Importantly, each side can make concurrent moves, generating an extremely high action-space or possible number of moves per turn. The dynamics of the wargame are couched in the language of a Markov decision process or dynamic game.

Once we review the rules governing wargame dynamics and the terminal states, we then discuss exploiting symmetries to reduce the action-space dimension. By exploiting such symmetries, we generate what is termed a *model homomorphism* [12]. In the homomorphic model, the dynamics remain the same as that of the original wargame. However, choosing only one of a number of symmetric actions results in a reduced action-space. We also exploit heuristics to further reduce the action-space, these being derived from observations of human-vs.-human play of the wargame.

Having described wargame dynamics and the use of symmetries and heuristics to reduce complexity, we review reinforcement learning methods, both in the single-agent and adversarial contexts. We then describe the results from the application of one such algorithm in combination with techniques to approximate the action-value or Q-function using important game features. Finally, we discuss our results and draw some insights into promising avenues for feature research.

3.4.1 Our Wargame

Given our task of implementing a computational approach to operational-level military operations planning, a fair amount of effort is required to design an abstracted model representing environmental factors, such as geography or ports, element dynamics, such as the movement rules of jet fighters or brigades, and the terminal states of the game. At all stages of wargame construction, we face the tradeoff between the expressiveness or detail of the model and its computational tractability. At the operational level, modeling the actions of brigades, as opposed to individual soldiers, is better. At a strategic level, modeling whole-of-force states such as the number of offensive and defensive weapons systems [17] might be better. Here we describe the processes of this abstraction in the simulation-based wargame we call TD-Island [7].

Before proceeding, we must introduce some standard definitions and notation for describing our wargame. Assuming that we have two agents playing, our game is formally described as the collection of sets $\langle S, A_1, A_2, \Psi, P, R, P_0, S_T \rangle$, where S is the set of possible states, the set of actions for agent i is denoted by A_i, Ψ is the set of admissible state-action pairs, the transitions and rewards are denoted by P and R, respectively, with P_0 and $S_T \subset S$ denoting the initial distribution of states and the set of terminal states. We have, thus, defined a stochastic dynamic game [5].

Our abstraction is inspired by the classical abstract games of chess and checkers (draughts) in the sense that the game uses pieces or elements of varying diversity, a discrete space, a set of rules determining element dynamics, and rules that define the end-states of the game. Chess and checkers capture some of the fundamental aspects of warfare such as attrition of forces, maneuver, and static or dynamic centers of gravity [26]. However, these factors are not sufficient. Warfare also involves synchronization of maneuver and probabilistic interactions — for example, one can attempt to strike a target with a jet fighter only to be destroyed by some land-based missile defense system. To this effect, we allow concurrent actions for each side and probabilistic interactions when two opposing pieces occupy the same spatial state. Furthermore, when a strike occurs in a spatial state occupied by opposing pieces, those pieces may defend or retaliate.

3.4.1.1 Space and Geography

Games that represent tactical-level conflict usually assume that space is continuous or fine-grained [14,15,20]. Because we are modeling an operational-level representation of a wargame, we use an abstraction often used by military planners and termed *tile-coding* in the artificial intelligence community [28]. Here continuous space is grouped into a number of strategically important regions or tiles. Planners often partition space into three regions labeled near, in-transit, or far to represent regions of space near the home-base, transit

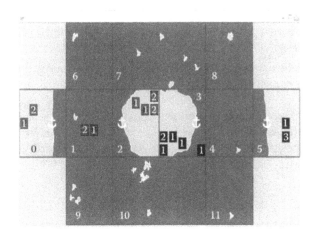

FIGURE 3.4.1
Diagram showing the partition of space in the operational level game.

regions, or areas within the direct zone of conflict. Our game is divided into twelve regions. Each region is either classified as a land or sea region, which broadly describes its geography. This classification then partly determines the dynamics of the elements within the wargame.

Our wargame is intended to represent what might be termed an island scenario, in that the aim is to take or secure some strategically important island. In this regard, we label the land tiles as numbers 0, 2, 3, and 5 as shown in Figure 3.4.1. The remaining tiles are classified as sea.

3.4.1.2 Elements, Actions, and Concurrent Moves

The game has numerous element types, that of jet fighters, brigades, destroyers, air transport, sea transport, land-air defense, command and control (C2), bases, mobile bases, and logistics. As shown in Figure 3.4.1, the sea-based elements, destroyers and sea transports, make the transition from a land region to a sea region at what might be loosely termed points of embarkation, denoted by the anchor symbol. Each element has rules that govern its dynamics and interactions with other elements. We classify the dynamics of each element into one of four actions:

- *General Actions*: These are moves from a land or sea tile to a land or sea tile. If the element is a jet fighter or an air transport, these move from base to base, or base to mobile base, or mobile base to mobile base.
- *Strike Actions*: A jet fighter can move from a base to any tile and strike an opposing side's piece, returning to the same base.

- *Transport Actions*: Brigades, manpads, logistics, and mobile bases cannot move across sea tiles. They are transported via sea or air transports.
- *Null Actions*: If you don't move an element, it stays there. Bases and C2 are assumed not to move.

A move by some agent or controller on a particular side is then defined as the set of concurrent actions of the individual elements of that side. Suppose n elements are on a side. Let A_i denote the possible set of actions for element $i \in \{1 \dots n\}$ and let

$$C : A_i \rightarrow \{G, S, T, N\}$$

be a classification mapping of the action, as General, Strike, Transport, or Null. Furthermore, let us specify the element number of the cargo transported by element j as $T(j)$. For a particular game state denoted $s \in S$, we define the admissible moves as a function of the state s to be

$$\Psi_s = \left\{ (a_1, \dots, a_n) \in \otimes_{i=1}^n A_i \middle| \forall (i, j) \in \{1, \dots, n\}, \text{ if } C(A_i) = G \Leftrightarrow i \neq T(j) \right\}$$

This definition restricts the set of moves, or concurrent actions, to forbid the simultaneous general action of an object while it is also being transported or carrying cargo.

Having defined the set of concurrent actions or moves, we can describe the state-dynamics of each element type.

- Jet fighters can fly independently from their own base to their own base (or mobile base), if the base or mobile base is on land. Jet fighters can fly from base to a target, strike the target, and return to the same base in a single concurrent move.
- Destroyers can move from a port to an adjacent sea tile, one tile per concurrent move; for example, from 5 to 4 in one turn, then from 4 to 8 to 11 in the next turn, or from 11 to 10 to 9 in three turns.
- Air transports can move from their own base to their own base (mobile base) in one concurrent move, with or without cargo. The cargo elements of manpads, brigades, logistics, or mobile base can be transported in this way. Pick-up and put-down of cargo can only occur at a base or a mobile base with the transported piece at that location. Sea transports move the same way as the dynamics of a destroyer, with the option of transporting brigades, manpads, mobile bases, or logistics pieces. These pieces must be at the same port of embarkation. Only one piece per time may be transported.
- Brigades can be transported across sea or air, as previously described, or move from land tile 2 to 3 or from 3 to 2 in one concurrent turn.

- Bases are assumed not to move.
- C2 elements cannot move.
- Land-Air-Defense have identical rules as for a brigade.
- Logistics elements move as per brigades; however, this element cannot move from 2 to 3 or vice versa and must be air-transported.
- Mobile bases have identical rules as for logistics elements.

3.4.1.3 Internal States

Each element is assumed to have its own internal state specifying what might be termed its health. Jet fighters, destroyers, air transports, sea transports, logistics, and land-air-defenses are assumed to be in one of two states, alive or dead, whereas the remaining elements can be in one of four states: Alive, damaged, heavily damaged, or dead.

3.4.1.4 Interactions

When two or more opposing pieces occupy the same spatial region, interactions may occur depending on the element types and a set of probabilities specified in the simulation model. For example, if a jet fighter attempts to strike a target in the same region as that of opposing jet fighters, destroyers, or land-air-defense systems, a chance exists it will be shot down before it is able to prosecute its target.* Therefore, the dynamics of the internal health states of elements are determined by a set of interaction rules. Our interaction rules are defined by a set of probabilistic decision trees. The overall form of the decision tree is as follows:

```
1    if(in the same tile as opponent pieces)
2       {//is there an interaction?
3       Generate p~U [0,1]
4    if (p<p (interaction))
5       {Count (opposing pieces you can interact with).
6       Choose one of the opposing pieces at random.
7       Generate p~U [0,1]
8    if (p<p (attack|interaction))
9       {decrement your internal health}
10   else
11      {decrement opposing pieces health}}}
```

---

* This situation never occurs in the classical games of chess and checkers. If you are in a position to take an opponent's piece and you choose to do so, this move occurs with certainty (probability equals 1).

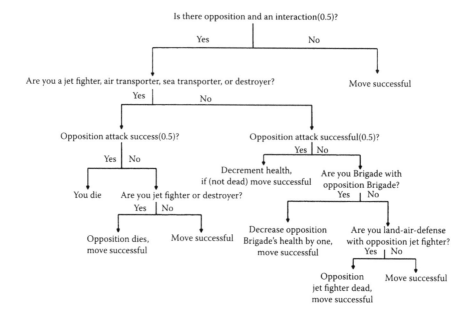

FIGURE 3.4.2
Decision tree for a general action of some element. The probabilities for interaction and a successful opposition attack are specified in parentheses.

Thus, one must specify probabilities determining the chance of interacting with opposition forces, and the chance — given an interaction occurs — that the opposition is successful in decrementing your health state by 1. For each action, a decision tree specific to the action type — either General, Strike, Transport, or Null — determines the transition to a new state. Figure 3.4.2 shows the decision tree for a general action.

3.4.1.5 Ordering of Moves

Though we define our moves as concurrent actions, strictly speaking, we implement or simulate them serially. Furthermore, we assume that for a particular side, the actions occur in the following order: Strike, then General, then Transport. For example, suppose we have two concurrent moves, one for each side. To execute these moves, one side first runs its Strike, followed by General, followed by Transport moves. The opposition move is then executed in the same way. Thus, for a particular side, a series of state-transitions take place as each action is executed before the opposition is allowed to make its concurrent move. Once a particular concurrent move is chosen and executed, no intervention is allowed by the agent who chose that move. This means that each agent is only able to exhibit control in batched concurrent actions and is unable to readjust its concurrent move in light of an unfavorable outcome of a particular action. One can think of this restriction as loosely mimicking the inherent command and control delays from tactical to operational levels.

Each element is only allowed to execute one action per move. In terms of state-transitions, suppose one side's concurrent move is denoted by $a = (a_1, a_2 \ldots a_n)$ and the opposition's by $b = (b_1, b_2 \ldots b_n)$. Both moves are assumed to be ordered following the "Strike, then General, then Transport" assumption. Under our approach of simulating concurrent moves serially, transitions from state s_t are made in the following fashion:

$$s_t \xrightarrow{a_1} s_t^1 \xrightarrow{a_2} s_t^2 \xrightarrow{a_3} \cdots \xrightarrow{a_n} s_t^n \xrightarrow{b_1} s_t^{n+1} \xrightarrow{b_2} \cdots \xrightarrow{b_m} s_t^{n+m} = s_{t+1}.$$

Truly concurrent moves would make the transition

$$s_t \xrightarrow{a,b} s_{t+1}.$$

Note that this approach to simulating truly concurrent moves, termed *sequential execution* [12], induces a perfect information game. The set of states that the opponent could occupy as a move is made, that is, the information set of each player, is therefore unique [13]. We chose this approach to generating the state-transitions in the game for a number of reasons. First, it is the simplest to implement computationally. Second, though it can be argued that real-time, tactical-level games are of simultaneous extensive form, it is difficult to argue that simultaneous moves occur at operational levels. If this were the case, both sides would move all their elements at precisely the same time, an unlikely situation. Here an equally good assumption is that strategic moves are made in reaction to opponent's strategies, given that defense will automatically be instigated in response to these moves, as is the case in our game. However, we could have chosen to inter-leave execution of Strike, General, and Transport moves across sides in the following fashion:

$$s_t \xrightarrow{a_1} s_t^1 \xrightarrow{b_1} s_t^2 \xrightarrow{a_2} \cdots \xrightarrow{b_m} s_t^{n+m} = s_{t+1}.$$

3.4.1.6 End-States

Games like chess and checkers have clearly defined end-states. The end-states for our game denoted by S_T should, in some way, reflect those seen in operational level warfare. We use the notations J, B, D, AT, ST, $C2$, Ba, Mba, and L to denote the number of jet fighters, brigades, destroyers, air transports, sea transports, command and control, bases, mobile bases, and logistics, respectively. Furthermore, we use the subscript b or r to denote the Blue and Red sides, respectively. Our end-states are defined by a number of indicator functions of each state, $I_e(s)$. If the indicator function has value 1, then this state is a subset of the terminal states, that is, $s \subset S_T$.

One possible end-state is that of materiel dominance of the opposition force. Let e be a subset of the state-space specified by*

$$e = ((J_b = 0) \wedge (B_b = 0) \wedge (D_b = 0) \wedge (J_r > 0) \wedge (B_r > 0) \wedge (D_r > 0)).$$

If this condition is true, then the Red side is said to win through materiel dominance. If the first three conditions are met, then the Blue side has a minimal means of defending itself because its jet fighters, brigades, and destroyers are eliminated, whereas the last three conditions specify that the Red side can still strike with its jet fighters, occupy the island with its brigades, and attack the Blue sea lines of communication with destroyers.

Now suppose $|A_{s,b}|$ and $|A_{s,r}|$ denote the number of concurrent moves (excluding the purely Null moves where all elements execute a Null move) for the Blue and Red sides, respectively. Then if the Boolean variable

$$e = ((|A_{s,b}| = 0) \wedge (|A_{s,r}| > 0))$$

is true, the Red side wins. This condition occurs when no possible concurrent moves are left for the Blue side and is termed the *trapped end-state*. As a simple example, suppose the Blue side possesses jet fighters only but all bases are destroyed. Here no feasible moves exist for the jet fighters, as they cannot exit or return to a base, and the Blue side is, therefore, trapped.

Next, let the Occupy function $Occ(x, element)$ be true if the element is at tile x and define the Boolean variable

$$e = \left(\begin{array}{c} \left(Occ(2, red\ Brigade) \right) \wedge \left(Occ(3, red\ Brigade) \right) \\ \wedge (J_b < J_r) \wedge (B_b < B_r) \wedge (AT_b = 0) \wedge (AT_r > 0) \wedge (ST_b = 0) \wedge (ST_r > 0) \end{array} \right).$$

If this variable is true, the Red side wins through island occupation and defense. Essentially, this subset of states has the Red force occupy both sides of the island with brigades and a greater strike and transportation capability. Note that though Blue brigades might be on the island, no possibility exists that they might be resupplied, as no Blue side transporters remain.

We also modeled what might be termed "social will" in the following way. After a set number of moves, each side calculates the probability that it will cease playing. Here we took

$$\Pr(stop) = \begin{cases} 1 - \exp(\xi(\Delta J + \Delta B + \Delta D)), & \text{if } \Delta J + \Delta B + \Delta D < 0, \\ 0 \text{ otherwise.} \end{cases}$$

---

* Here, we refer to "and" as the symbol $\wedge$.

where ΔJ, ΔB, and ΔD represent the balance between your and your opponent's jet fighters, brigades, and destroyers, respectively. The parameter $\xi \geq 0$ measures the level of pessimism, in the sense that as $\xi \to \infty$, if the balance terms are negative, the probability that a side will stop approaches unity with greater sensitivity to the value of the materiel balance.

Our final end-state occurs when the number of moves exceeds a maximum number of turns.

3.4.1.7 Initial Conditions

We assume that three jet fighters, three destroyers, two brigades, "three air transporters, three sea transporters," two land-air-defense units, one base, and one mobile base are placed at tile 0 for the Blue force, and the same elements placed at tile 5 for the Red force. Furthermore, we assume each side has a base on the center island (tile 2 and 3 for the respective Blue and Red force).

3.4.2 Reducing the State-Action Space Dimension Through Symmetries and Heuristics

Our simulation-based wargame is complex due to the large state-action space dimension of the game. One can estimate the approximate state-space dimension by assuming that each element can occupy any one of the 12 tiles and be in two states, either alive or dead. For n elements, this condition generates a state-space dimension of

$$|S| = 24^n \approx 10^{1.4n}.$$

The action-space dimension is only slightly more complicated to estimate. One can obtain an approximate lower bound by assuming that an element can execute two possible actions, so the dimension of the action-space for concurrent moves is approximately

$$|A| \approx 2^m = 10^{0.3m}$$

where m is the number of elements that move. Assuming 19 elements move, this generates an action-space dimension on the order of 1 million moves. However, this estimate is only a lower bound because jet fighters can strike any opposition target and many permutations of cargo (such as brigades) are carried by air and sea transports. Indeed, by executing the simulation model using only valid concurrent moves, we found that $\log(|A|) \approx 7.6 \pm 1.2$ over 1000 games averaged across each game. In essence, because we are able to execute concurrent moves, we generate an explosion in the action-space dimension.

A number of ways exist to reduce the action-space dimension. First, one might look to multiagent control of individual elements. Second, one might use a number of heuristics to prune the space of concurrent actions. We could also reduce the action-space by observing symmetries in the game. Though adopting a multiagent approach is inevitable when each side has a large number of elements, we looked at reducing our action-space dimension through the observation of symmetries and the application of a number of heuristics, as described here. Multiagent approaches are discussed later.

3.4.2.1 Symmetries

Intuitively, a number of symmetries might be exploited to reduce the action-space dimension. Before we look at these symmetries in an applied context, let us review some of the definitions related to model reduction in Markov decision processes (MDP).

Symmetries and model reduction in MDPs are discussed extensively in the work of Ravindran and Barto [24]. Given an MDP of $M = \langle S, A, \Psi, P, R, P_o, S_T \rangle$, one can define an MDP homomorphism onto MDP $M' = \langle S', A', \Psi', P', R', P'_o, S'_T \rangle$ denoted by the surjective map

$$h : \Psi \to \Psi', \quad h(s,a) = (f(s), g_s(a)), \quad f : S \to S', \quad g_s : A_s \to A'_{f(s)}.$$

Intuitively, a homomorphism is a map that preserves the transition dynamics and rewards of the original MDP. As a simplified example, suppose the actions of the MDP are deterministic. For this MDP M, let $T(s,a)$ denote the new state s_1 found from choosing action a in state s, that is $P(s,a,s_1) = 1$. Under MDP M', $T'(s',a')$ is similarly defined as the new state found by applying action a' in state s'. Then, under a homomorphism, the map f must satisfy

$$T'\big(f(s), a\big) = f(T(s,a)) \quad \text{and} \quad R(s,a) = R'(f(s), a).$$

The MDP M' is said to commute with the original MDP M under the homomorphism h if such a map exists [11]. An isomorphic mapping from M to M' under h occurs if the functions f and g_s are bijective. Under an isomorphic mapping, we have the probability of making a transition from s to s_1 under action a is

$$P(s,a,s_1) = P'(f(s), g_s(a), f(s_1)).$$

One can define mappings from an MDP M onto itself, termed an *automorphism* of M if it is an isomorphism. Automorphisms describe symmetries in the MDP M in the sense that one can transfer policies from one subset of the state-dependent admissible actions Ψ to another through simple transformations [24].

As an applied example, consider an ordered set of jet fighters in our game, denoted by $J = \{1, 2, \ldots j\}$ and an ordered set of targets $L = \{1, 2 \ldots l\}$. We can define the simplest automorphism if we make the restriction that a jet fighter can strike only a unique target during a move; that is, no two jet fighters can strike the same target. For l targets, the number of ordered permutations P_j^l generates the number of ways the jet fighters can strike targets. We can then define automorphisms that map one collection of permutations of jet fighters onto the same set. For example, suppose there are three jet fighters and three targets. Six such permutations describe jet fighters to targets, denoted by (i, j, k), assigning jet fighters i, j, k to targets 1, 2, and 3, respectively. The bijective mapping g_s might be described as the operation that induces a cyclic permutation in each assignment of jet fighters to targets, for example,

$$\{(1,2,3), (1,3,2), (2,1,3), (2,3,1), (3,2,1), (3,1,2)\}$$

$$\downarrow \ g_s$$

$$\{(3,2,1), (2,1,3), (3,2,1), (1,2,3), (1,3,2), (2,3,1)\}.$$

Under the composition operator, the set of automorphisms forms a group that is simply the group of permutations under j objects, which we denote S_j. This is true because for any two automorphisms p and q,

$$p, q \in S_j \Leftrightarrow p \circ q \in S_j.$$

To exploit this symmetry, one need only choose one such permutation of jet fighters onto targets because all permutations are equivalent, as identified through the group of automorphisms [6]. By choosing one such permutation, we generate a smaller homomorphic MDP M'. For example, one could simply choose the trivial permutation of assigning jet fighters to targets if both jet fighter and target have the same index in their respective sets. By allowing jet fighters to strike targets only with the same indices, and further restricting the transportation of cargo assigned to transporters in a similar way, one induces a homomorphic map g_s such that the state-action dimension of the homomorphic MDP $|\Psi'| < |\Psi|$. This is conceptually illustrated in Figure 3.4.3.

Such a homomorphic map only exists when the internal states of the jet fighters are identical. If we include an internal fuel supply, for example, this symmetry is broken or only approximately met if the fuel supplies of the jet fighters are not identical. When targets are destroyed or cargo transported, new assignments of jet fighters to targets and transporters to cargo must be calculated. Thus, the map g_s must be recalculated as new states are encountered, and a number of algorithms for achieving this are listed in [6].

3.4.2.2 Heuristics

Introducing state-action symmetries ameliorates the problem of a high state-action space dimension. One can go farther by playing the game and

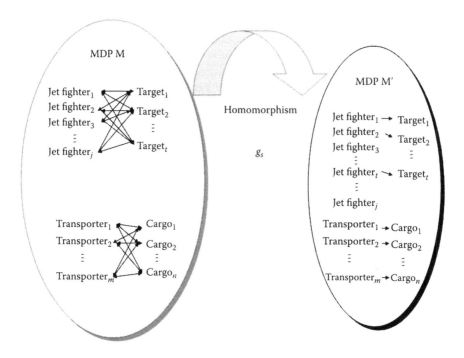

FIGURE 3.4.3
Diagram illustrating state-action reduction through the symmetry braking, which induces a homomorphic map from MDP M to reduced MDP $M_\_$.

observing a number of heuristics that reduce the number of possible state-action pairs that must be sampled. In our current version of the game, we include two such heuristics. The first heuristic is derived from the observation that cargo is particularly vulnerable when being transported. Though a brigade has four health states — alive, damaged, heavily damaged, or dead — it may be destroyed in one strike while in transit on a sea transport. Thus, we restricted ourselves to actions that satisfy the following rule:

- Any sea transport action to some tile must be accompanied with a destroyer escort in that same tile, unless no destroyer is available. For example, if a sea transport moves from tile zero to tile one, that move is considered safe or valid if either a destroyer takes the same action or the destroyer already occupies tile one.

A similar observation exists for air transportation:

- Only air transport to bases protected by jet fighters or land-air-defenses. For example, an air transport can only move from a base on tile 0 to a base on tile 2 if tile 2 already has either a jet fighters, land-air-defense, or both.

The last heuristic assures that the air transport is protected from an adversary strike move, given the presence of a jet fighter or a land-air-defense element.

3.4.3 Review of Reinforcement Learning Methods

Now that we have defined the stochastic dynamic game, we are in a position to review our machine-learning approach to the development of wargame strategies. Pioneered by Arthur Samuels in his experiments in checkers and refined by Richard Sutton, *reinforcement learning* (RL) is an approach to developing an optimal or good policy (set of state-dependent actions) in a controlled Markov chain. As opposed to supervised machine-learning approaches, RL exploits the temporal structure of a problem to find such a policy. In his seminal paper, Sutton [27] formulated an algorithm termed the *method of temporal differences* to learn the time-dependent expectation of achieving a terminal reward, r_T, as $E(r_T | \theta, s_t)$, a function of statistical parameters θ and the current state $s_t \in \{1, 2 \dots T\}$. By making parameter adjustments as states are encountered, one could make better predictions compared to supervised learning, where such adjustments are only made once the absorbing or terminal state is encountered. By calculating the temporal difference $E(r_T | \theta, s_{t+1}) - E(r_T | \theta, s_t)$, one can adjust the parameters toward what is a better prediction by taking the gradient. In the temporal difference algorithm, an increment in the parameters is calculated as

$$\Delta\theta = \alpha(E(r_T | \theta, s_{t+1}) - E(r_T | \theta, s_t))\nabla_\theta E(r_T | \theta, s_t),$$

where $\alpha \in (0, 1)$ is the learning rate, which usually must satisfy a number of standard stochastic convergence conditions found in [28]. Let $V(s_t) = E(r_T | \theta, s_t)$ denote the value function. Sutton introduced the $TD(\lambda)$ family of parameter updates, defined by

$$\Delta\theta_t = \alpha\left(V(s_{t+1}) - V(s_t)\right) \sum_{k=0}^{t} \lambda^k \nabla_\theta V(s_{t-k})$$

and showed that for $\lambda = 1$, the parameter updates are equivalent to the supervised Widrow–Hoff algorithm used in neural network machine-learning [27]. Some neurophysiologic evidence exists that humans use temporal-difference learning as shown in a functional magnetic resonance imaging experiment described in [25].

The theory of Markov decision processes — or more generally, stochastic dynamic games — are a natural way to frame the process of control through reinforcement learning [28]. Given a Markov chain and corresponding series of rewards $r(s_t) = r_t$, $t \in \{1, 2 \dots T\}$, we define the Q-function and value function given the state s_t and the action a_t, respectively as

$$Q(s_t, a_t) = \mathrm{E}\left(\sum_{i=t}^{T} r_i \middle| s_t, a_t\right), \quad V(s_t) = \mathrm{E}\left(\sum_{i=t}^{T} r_i \middle| s_t\right).$$

Here we have assumed that the Markov process is finite or regenerative and undiscounted. One can define the Bellman equation, relating the Q-function of the current state to the value function of the next state, as

$$Q(s, a) = r(s, a) + \sum_{s'} P(s, a, s') V(s')$$

where $P(s, a, s')$ determines the transition probability from state s to s' under action a. The optimal Q-function satisfies

$$Q^*(s, a) = r(s, a) + \sum_{s'} P(s, a, s') \max_{a'} Q(s', a').$$

When the number of state-action pairs is sufficiently low and the transition matrix is defined explicitly, one can solve for the optimal policy, which is the probability of choosing an action $a \in \Psi$ for state $s \in S$, $\pi(s, a) = \Pr(a \mid s)$, using methods such as backward induction for finite-horizon problems or value-iteration for infinite horizon problems [28].

For RL, one updates the estimates of the Q-function and, hence, the policy, as states are encountered, so a transition matrix need not be explicitly defined, only sampled through a simulation model. The Q-learning algorithm describes such an update as is described here and in Chapter 3.5 as

$$Q(s_t, a_t) \leftarrow Q(s_t, a_t) + \alpha_t(r_t + \max_{a'} Q(s_{t+1}, a_{t+1}) - Q(s_t, a_t)).$$

Provided all state-action pairs are visited infinitely often, application of the Q-learning algorithm results in convergence to the optimal Q-function with a probability of 1.0 [34]. If one chooses actions in an ε-greedy fashion, a similar update rule describes what is known as the $SARSA(0)$ algorithm [28].

3.4.3.1 Function Approximation

When the number of state-action pairs is too large, one must turn to an abstraction of the domain to learn policy improvements. A number of ways of achieving this abstraction are used. One way is to generalize over state-actions pairs through a function approximation technique [30]. As with the $TD(\lambda)$ algorithm, we approximate the Q-function with a set of relevant statistical parameters, through a function approximator

$$Q(s, a, \boldsymbol{\theta}) \approx Q(s, a).$$

This is our approach in this chapter, though one would potentially use the structural abstraction approach of decomposing our original MDP into a hierarchy of sub-MDPs and learning a hierarchically optimal policy, as is done in feudal RL or through the MAXQ decomposition approach [10,11]. When defining each sub-MDP, under some circumstances, one is able to abstract away or ignore states that are irrelevant to solving the optimal policy. We discuss the potential application of hierarchical problem decomposition at the end of this chapter.

With function approximation, the Q-function equivalent of the $TD(\lambda)$ algorithm, $SARSA(\lambda)$, is described through the introduction of an eligibility trace $\mathbf{e}_t \in \mathbb{R}^{|\theta|}$. If we set

$$\mathbf{e}_t \leftarrow \lambda \mathbf{e}_{t-1} + \nabla_\theta Q(s_t, a_t, \boldsymbol{\theta}_t)$$

and the temporal difference as

$$\delta_t = r_t + Q(s_{t+1}, a_{t+1}, \boldsymbol{\theta}_t) - Q(s_t, a_t, \boldsymbol{\theta}_t)$$

then the $SARSA(\alpha)$ parameter update has the form

$$\boldsymbol{\theta}_{t+1} \leftarrow \boldsymbol{\theta}_t + \alpha_t \delta_t \mathbf{e}_t.$$

A thorough description of the convergence properties of the $TD(\lambda)$ algorithm with function approximation can be found in [31].

3.4.3.2 Adversarial Reinforcement Learning

RL has been extended to account for adversarial responses in stochastic dynamic games. Chapter 3.5 describes the extension of RL to learning strategies in extensive play games. With an adversary, the environment is nonstationary. For alternating move games, as is the case for our TD-Island game, rather than observing the value of the Q-function after executing an action, we can use the value returned by following the principal variation [4] of a minimax tree search — to some depth — as our Q-function value [3]. Here we are adopting a pessimistic approach, assuming that the opponent will choose actions that minimize our Q-function (which we are trying to maximize). This algorithm, formalized by [4] in the game of chess and backgammon, is termed the $TDleaf(\lambda)$ method. An agent termed KNIGHTCAP adopting the $TDleaf(\lambda)$ method in combination with a detailed evaluation function was able to achieve play at the level of a chess Grandmaster, as reported in [3]. However, this paper noted when the game dynamics possessed inherent stochasticity, such as backgammon, the value of the tree-based minimax search to a high depth was eroded. In backgammon, authors that experimented with a minimax search tree of depth three (three-ply) could not see an improvement over using a simple one-ply search [4].

When agent moves are made simultaneously, researchers have combined techniques for finding the minimax policy, as in the case of zero-sum games or Nash equilibria with general sum games by combining mixed strategy game-theoretic methods with reinforcement learning algorithms. For simultaneous move games, the policies are generally stochastic or mixed [13]. In a method termed minimax Q-learning [21], instead of using the maximum of the Q-function for updates, as would be done in Q-learning, the minimax Q-value $\min_{a_1} \max_{a_2} Q(s, a_1, a_2)$ is used for the update. For general sum games, this value is replaced by the value at a Nash equilibrium in the method called Nash-Q [16]. Though these algorithms are of considerable interest, their application is strictly limited to small numbers of state-action pairs where values can be calculated either through linear programming approaches for zero-sum games or other approaches, such as the Lemke–Howson algorithm for general sum games [33]. The minimax approach again is pessimistic because it assumes the opponent chooses policies that minimize your payoff. An agent using the minimax-Q learning algorithm will not be able to exploit weaker opponents or opponents using set policies.

Another class of algorithms use the methods of fictitious play to model the opponent [32]. As the game or process changes, an agent using fictitious play stores the empirical frequency of the opponent's actions and uses this as a predictor the opponent's next action. The agent can then apply standard RL approaches, such as a modified Q-learning algorithm, to update Q-function estimates. Again, using this fictitious play approach, the agent must store empirical frequencies for all state-action pairs, so the possibility to scale to larger domains is limited.

Of greatest interest is an algorithm that does not seek to find an equilibrium solution, but rather the agent will adjust its learning rate according to a comparison with the current Q-function algorithm and some averaged Q-value. The algorithm "win or learn fast," or *Wolf* [5], stores the average Q-function for a particular state-action. If the current Q-function value for this state-action is greater than this average, the agent is said to be winning and the learning rate is adjusted to α_w; otherwise, the agent is losing, so the learning rate is adjusted to α_l, where $\alpha_w < \alpha_l$. No assumptions are made regarding the way the opposing agent learns, as is the case for the minimax-Q and Nash-Q algorithms. Furthermore, the algorithm scales to domains where applying function approximation is necessary.

3.4.3.3   Application of Reinforcement Learning Algorithms to the TD-Island Game

The TD-Island game has a number of factors limiting the applicability of the *TDleaf(λ)* algorithm to search depths greater than one-ply. First, though we have used symmetries and heuristics to prune our action-space at each move, the action-space is still large. In practice, only a subset of all the possible concurrent actions can be sampled. This fact makes search in depth difficult, selectively sampling opponent responses to form some sort of minimax tree might be possible. The TD-Island game also has inherent stochasticity. For example, in the parameters we used for our simulations, a probability 0.6 existed that a strike action is conducted successfully. Q-learning and *SARSA*(λ) have also been shown to perform well when implemented in agents using other reinforcement learning algorithms such as minimax-*Q* and Wolf. For these reasons, we took the pragmatic approach of implementing *SARSA*(λ) only with a one-ply search.

3.4.3.4 Choice of Function Approximator

One of the real challenges of applying reinforcement learning with function approximation is the choice of state-action features deemed important to winning the game. Agents controlling multiple-elevator scheduling and backgammon used multiple layer feed-forward neural networks [30] as the basis of the *Q*-function approximator. Our approach is to use a single layer, smoothed function approximator, as this has the advantage that all values of the parameters have clear interpretations, whereas the parameter meanings in the hidden layers of a multilayer neural network defy clear interpretations. The TD-Island game can end in either a win, draw, or loss, and we assumed that the terminal reward, r_T, was defined as follows:

$$
r_T = \begin{cases} -1 & \text{for a loss,} \\ 0 & \text{for a draw,} \\ 1 & \text{for a win.} \end{cases}
$$

We chose to use a linear function approximator, mapped onto the interval $(-1, 1)$ through the hyperbolic tangent function. Thus,

$$
Q(s, a, \boldsymbol{\theta}) = \tanh\left(\beta \sum_i \phi_i(s, a)\theta_i\right),
$$

where $\phi_i(s, a)$ is the *i*th state-action feature with parameter θ_i and β is a tuning or bias parameter. The *i*th component of the eligibility trace update will then be

$$
e_{t+1,i} \leftarrow \lambda e_{t,i} + \beta \phi_i(s, a)\text{sech}^2\left(\sum_i \phi_i(s, a)\theta_i\right)
$$

though, in practice, calculating the gradient numerically is easier.

3.4.3.5 Choice of Features, Tuning Parameter, and Learning Rate

Without a good choice of appropriate features, any machine learning algo-rithm fails. To choose our features, we experimented with the TD-Island game and spoke to a number of military operations planning staff to ascer-tain what was seen as important in terms of intermediate states or objectives to achieve. Features can generally be divided into three classes. First were feature sets relating to the materiel or mass balance in the game. The second set of features corresponded to the number of possible courses of action one could take. Finally, we generated a list of features corresponding to important intermediate points.

For purposes of explanation, this chapter details results obtained from a limited feature set, that of materiel balance and concurrent action bal-ance. Thus, we looked to the balance of each element type and the balance of the number of possible concurrent moves each side could take. For example, if the Blue side possessed ten jet fighters and the Red two, our resulting jet fighter balance was eight. In total, our number of features amounts to nine. Because concurrent action-space dimension was large compared to the materiel balance terms, we chose to calculate the loga-rithm ratio of the action-space dimension over the opponent action-space dimension,

$$\phi_{Action}(s) = \log\left(|A_{s,agent}| \Big/ |A_{s,opponent}| \right).$$

Some experimentation was required for the choice of the tuning param-eter, β. One simple way of obtaining a baseline value is to remember that if the agent possesses all 19 pieces and the opponent 0, as is the initial condi-tion, the agent by default wins, receiving a score of 1.0. We could have, thus, set the value of β to solve

$$\tanh(19\beta) = 0.999,$$

which is $\beta = 0.2$. Instead, we chose the value of $\beta = 0.1$ to avoid over-sensitivity of the function approximator to changes in the parameters.

We chose our learning rate α_n, where n is the total number of moves, to be

$$\alpha_n = a/(a+n)$$

where $a = 500$ determines the rate of learning decay.

3.4.3.6 Overall Structure of TD-Island Game

We have described in detail the TD-Island simulator, the use of symmetries, and heuristics to reduce and prune the action-space, end-states, and learning

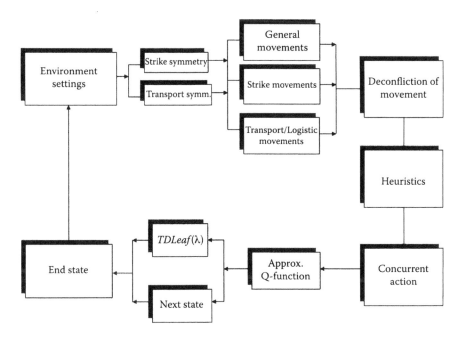

FIGURE 3.4.4
Schematic diagram showing the general flow of computation as learning proceeds in the TD-Island game.

algorithms. Schematically combining all the methods into one diagram (Figure 3.4.4) showing the general flow of computation is useful.

3.4.4 Results

We applied the $SARSA(\lambda)$ algorithm over 3000 games to observe the learned parameter values and the resultant game play. Because the concurrent action-space was large, we could not sample every possible action. Instead, we sampled 1000 possible concurrent moves per turn. In turn, each of the moves was simulated and the resulting Q-function evaluated. We used the greedy strategy of choosing the concurrent move that returned the maximum of the sampled values. As we sampled only a subset of all possible concurrent actions, no assurance existed that the optimal concurrent action was chosen, hence a large component of exploration is inherent in our policy. The ability to sample only a finite set of available actions is certainly the reality in any military planning process, thus, the finite sampling ability of our agent is congruent to what we see in real-world military practice.

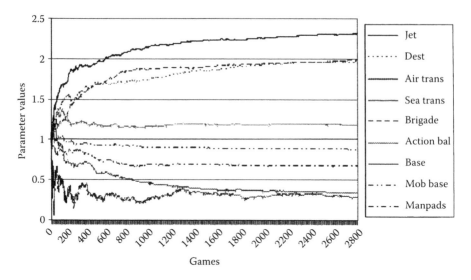

FIGURE 3.4.5
Graph of the parameter values θ as a function of the number of games played.

The opposing side also adopted a greedy strategy, with parameter values all set to 1. Hence, for our opponent, none of the features stood out as being particularly important. Figure 3.4.5 shows us the materiel and action balance parameter values as a function of the number of games played, with the parameter value of the base normalized to 1.

Of interest is the interpretation of the learned values for the element balance. Having an advantage in the number of jet fighters figures highest in the learned evaluation function. This attribute is not unreasonable as the jet fighter has the dual advantage of mobility and strike. Furthermore, the jet fighter is able to strike transporters in-transit, destroying cargo such as brigades, when this element is most vulnerable. The importance of destroyers and brigades reflects their prominent role in winning the TD-Island game. Destroyers are the only defense to sea-transported items, with brigades necessary for island occupation and defense. The success of the $SARSA(\lambda)$ algorithm is shown by the cumulative score (Figure 3.4.6) of the learning agent over the series of games played.

Of note here is the observation that the $SARSA(\lambda)$ agent's cumulative score rises quickly toward its equilibrium value after approximately 1000 games. With computation time restrictions, this rapid learning can be seen as advantageous when applying learning to the TD-Island game with differing scenarios based on different initial conditions. End-state conditions are reached with differing frequencies. Figure 3.4.7 shows how the number of end–state conditions reached for the learning agent (Blue) compared to the equal parameter agent (Red).

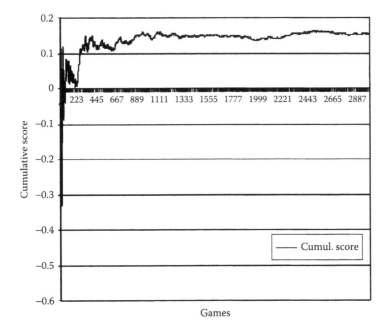

FIGURE 3.4.6
Graph of the cumulative score of the $SARSA(\lambda)$ agent against the opponent choosing equal parameter values, of value 1.

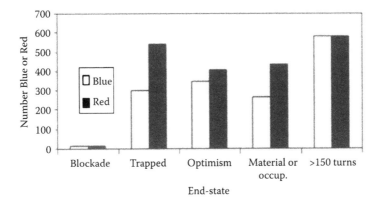

FIGURE 3.4.7
Number of times a side succumbed to a particular end-state over 3000 games. The agent with the learned parameter values is Blue, that of equal parameter values, Red.

3.4.5 Future Possibilities for Abstraction and Approximation in Complex Domains

Function approximation is a viable way to learn an approximate Q-function when computing the exact Q-function over all state-action pairs is not feasible. To improve the agent behavior, one can extend the function approximation parameter set to include temporal dependence. Alternatively, learning can be done through a multiagent or hierarchical approach. In the RL agent KNIGHTCAP, parameters were extended to include the temporal phases of the chess game [4]. In chess, a well-defined classification of states exists into the opening, middle, and end games. For the KNIGHTCAP agent, a different set of parameters is used for the three stages of the game. Observing the play of the TD-Island game, two distinct phases are seen, prior- and post-jet fighter dominance. Thus, extending the function approximation approach to include temporally dependent parameters is possible.

Because of the high action-space dimension, a multiagent approach could be successfully applied to the TD-Island game. Indeed, if the TD-Island game is scaled up to a large number of elements, a multiagent approach would be vital. An important paper detailing the successful application of multiagent RL methods to complex domains comes in the area of multiple elevator control [9].

A number of ways exist to assign agency in the TD-Island game. One could assign each element an RL agent. Though this is possible, agents would have to coordinate extensively in the transportation moves. Agency could also be assigned in similar ways to the command and control arrangements found at an operational level military campaign. Separate agents might be assigned to control strikes (jet fighters), the sea movements of destroyers, land movements on the island tiles, and transportation movements. Again, any approximation of the Q-function would have to address the coordination between agents. For example, a land agent might decide to move a brigade within the island tiles while the transportation agent decides to transport this element back to the home base. This coordination conflict must be resolved. The agents might learn to coordinate themselves, as do agents in cooperative games, such as [8].

Though hierarchical control [1] has been used to develop complex agents, a great potential exists for the combination of hierarchy with machine-learning [29] to coordinate agents, for example, the feudal reinforcement learning approach of [10]. The top level of the hierarchy would resolve the conflicts mentioned previously between transportation and general movements of elements. One can also exploit hierarchy for structural abstraction. In a seminal paper on hierarchical reinforcement learning [11], the author broke the task of taxi passenger pickup and delivery into a hierarchy of subtasks. At the top level of the hierarchy was the overall task, which was decomposed into pick-up passenger and put-down passenger subroutines. These were further decomposed into a navigation subroutine controlling the primitive actions of movement to north, south, east, or west. Though this hierarchical decomposition — termed MAXQ — was more costly in terms of memory storage than flat Q-learning (storing $Q(s, a) \; \forall \; (s, a) \in \Omega$), the structural characteristics of the problem implied that some state components could be ignored in certain subroutines without changing the nature of what is defined as a recursively optimal policy. For example, in the navigate subtask of the taxi problem, one could ignore the state variable describing whether the passenger was in the taxi or not as this has no influence on the navigation task per se. After employing structural abstraction across each of the sub-routines, the memory storage required to solve the problem was significantly less than that of the flat Q-learning. Thus, structural abstraction is a viable alternative to flat function approximation under some circumstances, though how well the recursively optimal strategies generated through hierarchical decomposition will perform in adversarial settings is unclear at this stage of research. An interesting area of research is the utility of structural abstraction in adversarial settings [18].

One could employ structural abstraction in the TD-Island game. For example, if a subroutine was allocated to strike, only the states of the jet fighters, bases (a base is required for ingress and egress from a strike-move), and opposing pieces are required to execute the strike or a series of strike moves. The states of the other elements may be ignored. If we exclude logistics and fuel consumption, assuming all of the supplies are adequate to execute a strike move, then the positions of the opposition's elements may be further abstracted away without any loss in the quality of the policy.

We have discussed the roles of dynamic abstraction, multiagency, and hier-archical problem decomposition as ways of potentially improving both the policy and the storage requirements of the TD-Island game. The notions of hierarchy and multiagency have been combined in reasonably simple domains such as the two-taxi, two-cargo problems, and in more complex domains such as autonomous guided vehicle routing [22]. Research is also being conducted into combining game-theoretic approaches to strategy development, such as the Wolf algorithm, with hierarchical problem decomposition.

References

1. Atkin, M.S., King, G.W., and Westbrook, D.L., SPT: Hierarchical agent control: A framework for defining agent behaviour, 2001, http://eksl-www.cs.umass.edu/papers/atkin-aa01.pdf.
2. Australian Department of Defense, *The Joint Military Appreciation Process Handbook*, 2003.
3. Baxter, J., Tridgell, A., and Weaver, L., Learning to play chess through temporal differences, *Machine Learning*, 40(3), 243–263, 2000.
4. Baxter, J., Tridgell, A., and Weaver, L., Reinforcement learning and chess, in Furnkranz, J. and Kubat, M. (Eds.), *Machines that Learn to Play Games, Advances in Computation: Theory and Practice*, Vol. 8, Nova Science Publishers, Huntington, New York, 2001.

5. Bowling, M. and Veloso, M., Multi-agent learning using a variable learning rate, *Artif. Intelligence*, 136, 215–250, 2002.

6. Calbert, G., Exploiting action-space symmetry for reinforcement learning in a concurrent dynamic game, *Proc. of the Intl. Conf. on Optimisation Techniques and Appl.*, 2004.

7. Calbert, G., Operational wargaming through machine-learned temporal differences, submitted to *J. Battlefield Tech.*

8. Claus, C. and Boutilier, C., The dynamics of reinforcement learning in cooperative multiagent systems, *Proc. of the Fifteenth Intl. Conf. on Artif. Intelligence*, Madison, Wl, 746–752, 1998.

9. Crites, R.H. and Barto, A.G., Elevator control using multiple reinforcement learning agents, *Machine Learning*, 33(2), 235–262, 1998.

10. Dayan, P. and Hinton, G.E., Feudal reinforcement learning, *Proc. of Neural Info. Processing Systems 5*, Denver, CO, 271–278, 1993.

11. Dietterich, T.G., Hierarchical reinforcement learning with the MAXQ value function decomposition, *J. Artif. Intelligence*, 13, 227–303, 2000.

12. Fitch, R., Hengst, B., Suc, D., Calbert, G., and Scholz, J., Structural abstraction experiments in reinforcement learning, submitted to the Australian Joint Conference on Artificial Intelligence, Sydney, New South Wales, Australia, 2005.

13. Fudenberg, D. and Tirole J., *Game Theory*, Cambridge, MA: MIT Press, 1991.

14. Galligan, D.P., Anderson, M.A., and Lauren, M.K. *Map Aware Non-Uniform Automata* ver. 3.0 Handbook, Defence Technology Agency, New Zealand Defence Force, 2004.

15. Hoffman, F.G. and Horne, G., *Maneuver Warfare Science*, United States Marine Corp Combat Development Command, Washington, D.C., 1998.

16. Hu, J. and Wellman, M.P., Multiagent reinforcement learning: theoretical framework and an algorithm. *Proc. of the Fifteenth Intl. Conf. on Machine Learning*, Morgan Kaufman, San Francisco, 242–250, 1998.

17. Johnson, R.W., Melich, M.E., Michalewicz, Z., and Schimidt, M., Coevolutionary optimisation of fuzzy logic intelligence for strategic decision support, submitted to *IEEE Trans. on Evolutionary Optimisation*, 2005.

18. Kwok, H-W, Uther, W., and Calbert, G., Hierarchy and structural abstraction experiments in an adversarial game, in preparation, 2005.

19. Kuter, U., Nau, D., Gossink, D., and Lemmer, J.F., Interactive course-of-action planning using casual models, *Proc. of the Third Intl. Conf. on Knowledge Systems for Coalition Operations*, 2004.

20. Lauren, M. and Stephen, R., Map aware non-uniform automata (MANA)-A New Zealand approach to scenario modelling, *J. Battlefield Tech.*, 5(1), 27–31, 2002.

21. Littman, M.L., Markov games as a framework for multi-agent reinforcement learning, *Proc. of the Eleventh Intl. Conf. on Machine Learning*, Morgan-Kaufman, San Francisco, 157–163, 1994.

22. Makar, R., Mahadevan, S., and Ghavamzadeh, M., Hierarchical multi-agent reinforcement learning, *Proc. of the Fifth Intl. Conf. on Autonomous Agents*, 246–253, Montreal, Quebec, Canada, 2001.

23. Pfeiffer, M., *Reinforcement Learning of Strategies for Settlers of Catan*, Institute of Theoretical Computer Science Preprint, Graz University of Technology, Austria, 2004.

24. Ravindran, B. and Barto, A.G., Symmetries and model minimization in Markov decision processes, Computer Science Technical Report 01-43, University of Massachusetts, Amherst, MA, 2001.

25. Seymour, B., O'Doherty, J.P., Dayan, P., Koltzenberg, M., Jones, A.K., Raymond, J.D., Friston, K.J., and Frackowiak, R.S., Temporal-difference models describe higher order learning in humans, *Nature*, 429, 664–667, 2004.

26. Smet, P., Calbert, G., Scholz, J., Gossink, D., Kwok, H-W., and Webb, M., The effects of materiel, tempo and search depth on win-loss ratios in chess, *Proc. of the Australian Joint Conf. on Artif. Intelligence*, Perth, Western Australia, Australia, 2003.

27. Sutton, R.S., Learning to predict by the method of temporal differences, *Machine Learning*, 3, 9–44, 1998.

28. Sutton, R.S. and Barto, A., *Reinforcement Learning: An Introduction*, Cambridge, MA: MIT Press, 2002.

29. Sutton, R.S., Precup, D., Singh, S., Between MDPs and semi-MDPs: A framework for temporal abstraction in reinforcement learning, *Artif. Intelligence*, 112, 181–211, 1999.

30. Tesauro, G.J., TD-Gammon, a self-teaching backgammon program, *Neural Computation*, 6(2), 215–219, 1994.

31. Tsitsiklis, J.N. and Van Roy, B., An analysis of temporal difference learning with function approximation, *IEEE Trans. on Automatic Control*, 42(5), 674–690, 1997.

32. Uther, W. and Veloso, M., Adversarial Reinforcement Learning, Carnegie-Mellon University Department of Computer Science Technical Report-03-107, 2003.

33. Von Stengel, B., Computing equilibria for two-person games, in Aumann, R.J. and Hart, S. (Eds.), *Handbook of Game Theory*, Vol. 3. Amsterdam: North-Holland, 2001.

34. Watkins, C.J.C.H. and Dayan, G., Q-Learning, *Machine Learning*, 8, 279–292, 1992.

3.5

Learning from and about the Opponent

Pu Huang and Katia Sycara

CONTENTS

In the preceding chapter, we have seen how a battlefield can be modeled as a stochastic game, and how an agent can learn from its opponent's actions to form its own strategy accordingly. The learning approach taken there, reinforcement learning, has been shown to be very effective in a single-agent, stochastic environment (see [1,8,14] and references therein). To apply the same approach to a multiagent game, the basic algorithm of reinforcement learning must be modified because as every agent in a multiagent game is learning, their interaction creates a *time-variant* environment, whereas the original formulation of the reinforcement learning algorithm assumes a time-invariant environment. To see why multiagent learning can create a time-variant environment, consider an individual agent X in a multiagent game. Because every agent is learning, the other agents' reactions to the strategy improvement of agent X will depend on how agent X improves its strategy. Alternately, as all the other agents learn to react to agent X, the learning environment of agent X shifts. (To any individual agent, all the other agents constitute its learning environment.) Therefore, the learning approach taken by a single agent will affect how its own learning environment will shift over time.

To learn from and about the opponent, we need to address the environment shifting problem. Many multiagent learning algorithms have already been proposed, including minimax-Q [9,10], Nash-Q [6], "win or learn fast" algorithm [2], and so on. Though of considerable interest, all these algorithms have limited application to simple games like 2×2 matrix games, zero-sum games, games with dominant strategies, and others. In fact, all these algorithms have only been proved to converge for such simple games. In this chapter, we will provide two multiagent learning algorithms and show that they are both convergent for a fairly large set of games, namely, the extensive games. Convergence of a multiagent learning algorithm is not only of theoretical but also of practical interest. Without a convergence guarantee, an algorithm might actually chase an ever-shifting learning target. This is because, as explained in the previous paragraph, any multiagent learning algorithm will inevitably change its own learning environment. Practically speaking, this means that an agent may never learn to act properly if it applies an algorithm without a convergence guarantee, i.e., even after learning for an infinite time, the agent may still not be able to find the "proper" action to respond to its opponent.

An extensive game (introduced earlier in Chapter 3.1 and Chapter 3.3) is a natural model for negotiation, bargaining, and wargames. A major characteristic of these games is that agents take actions alternately to interact with each other, for example, submit offers and counteroffers alternately in a bargaining game, which can be easily captured using the extensive game model. Many board games like chess and Go have this characteristic also and, thus, can be modeled as extensive games as well. A well-known extensive game is Rubinstein's bargaining game in which two agents alternately propose how to split a certain amount of profit [5]. With the rapid development of e-business, we expect more and more autonomous agents will be deployed on the Internet to negotiate/bargain with each other on behalf of their human masters. The extensive game model can serve as an analytical foundation to develop such agents. Learning is obviously a very important feature of these bargaining agents, as we cannot foresee every possible scenario and program the agent accordingly. The algorithms we developed have their root in the two basic learning approaches for games, namely, fictitious play and reinforcement learning, which we review in the following two sections.

3.5.1   Fictitious Play

A common criticism of the game theory is that agents must have unbounded rationality to find an equilibrium. Essentially, to find the equilibrium, an agent A must assume that its opponent agent B is rational, that agent B knows that agent A is rational, and that agent B knows that agent A assumes agent B is rational, and so on. Sometimes an agent also needs infinite computational resources to find the equilibrium, as finding the equilibrium of many real-world games involves searching over prohibitively large spaces. In response to this criticism, game theorists have developed a learning process called *fictitious play*, and have showed that equilibrium can arise as the result of this process. In fictitious play, an agent tries to learn its opponent's strategy by observing and recording the history of actions it took. More specifically, the agent maintains a belief about its opponent's strategy, continuously adjusts its belief through repeated plays, and then forms its own strategy accordingly based on the belief. An agent's belief is usually represented by a probability distribution over its opponent's strategy space.

Formally, fictitious play can be represented as the following process: Let B_i^t denote the belief of play i about its opponent's strategy at time t, and π_i^t denote player i's own strategy at this time. Then in every time period t, a player i

1. Updates its belief from B_i^{t-1} to B_i^t
2. Selects its own strategy π_i^t based on B_i^t

Usually, the Bayesian rule is applied in Step 1 to update the belief. In Step 2, a variety of methods can be used to select π_i^t. An obvious choice is to select a π_i^t that maximizes the immediate payoff. Other approaches, like randomly selecting a π_i^t, are also possible. Depending on the exact form of the prior distribution and the likelihood function used in Step 1, the selection method used in Step 2 has many variants.

If the empirical belief B_i^t of every agent does converge as t goes to infinity, then all agents' strategies collectively converge to a Nash equilibrium [4]. However, B_i^t might not converge. In this case, fictitious play does not converge either. Here we give such an example for the simple bargaining game shown in Table 3.5.1. In this game, if agents A (the row player) and B (the column player) agree on a deal, they both get reward 1; otherwise, they get 0. The unique Nash equilibrium of this game is that every agent plays a mixed strategy $\frac{1}{2}, \frac{1}{2}$. Suppose that agents A and B's initial believes are $(0, 1)$ and $(1, 0)$, respectively, i.e., agent A believes that agent B will play strategy BH with probability 1, and agent B believes that agent A will play strategy AL with probability 1. We also assume that (1) in fictitious play Step 1, each agent adds weight 1 to the strategy its opponent played, and (2) in Step 2, each agent selects the strategy that generates the maximum immediate reward. If all these assumptions are satisfied, it is easy to see that agent A will always play AL and agent B will always play BH, which does not match the

TABLE 3.5.1

A Two-Player Bargaining Game Where
Fictitious Play Does Not Converge

	BL	BH
AL	0, 0	1, 1
AH	1, 1	0, 0

Nash equilibrium. One can argue that by simply changing the belief updating rule and the strategy selection method, this problem can be easily fixed. However, even for more sophisticated fictitious play rules, counterexamples where the learning process does not converge have been found. For a more detailed discussion about those counterexamples, the reader should refer to Fudenberg and Levine [4], who studied fictitious play extensively.

3.5.2   Reinforcement Learning

In its original form, reinforcement learning addresses the problem of single-agent learning in an uncertain environment. The uncertain environment is modeled as a Markov chain, as shown in Figure 3.5.1. In each environment state s, the agent must decide which action to take. Its decision will stochastically determine the successive state to which it will transit. For example, suppose that the agent takes an action a in state s, then with probability 0.3 (0.7), it will transit to state s' (s''). In every state, the agent will get some reward. The agent's goal is to find an optimal policy (i.e., decide which action to take in every environment state) that maximizes its infinite-horizon discounted or average reward through learning. This process is called a *Markov decision process* (MDP). In such a Markov environment, an agent tries to learn which action to take at each state to maximize its reward. With the assumption that the environment is time-invariant, i.e., the probabilities that characterize the Markov chain do not change over time, the reinforcement learning algorithm converges to the optimal policy, i.e., the agent is guaranteed to collect the maximum reward it can possibly get by following the reinforcement learning procedure (see [14] and references therein).

One major feature of the reinforcement learning model is that it introduces a structural framework — namely, the Markov state-transition framework — to model the uncertain environment with which the agent

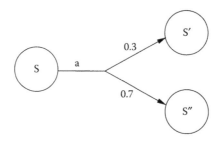

FIGURE 3.5.1
In an uncertain environment, an agent can transit from state s to either s' or s'' even after the agent executes a definite action a.

interacts. This framework has such a general structure that it can be used to model other types of uncertainty also, say, uncertainty about the opponent's strategy in a game. This leads to Littman's multiagent learning model for stochastic games [9]. In Littman's model, instead of directly collecting an immediate reward in each state, an agent must play a matrix game with another agent and the outcome of the game determines the reward in that state. For each individual agent, even if it fixes its strategy for the matrix game in every state, the agent is still not sure about what the next state would be because the next state will depend on its opponent's strategy, too. It has been shown that if each agent treats the uncertainty about its opponent's strategy as the same as the environment uncertainty in an MDP and the matrix game in each state is simple enough, say, 2×2 games, zero-sum games, games with dominant strategies, and so on, a variety of multiagent reinforcement learning algorithms converge to the equilibrium [2,6,10,13].

3.5.3 Extensive Game

Both learning approaches we discussed so far converge only for simple matrix games. In the rest of the chapter, we discuss another learning model — learning in extensive games. We present two algorithms (one originates from fictitious play and another one from reinforcement learning) and show that both are provably convergent.

An extensive game played by I players can be represented by a tree G. Every nonleaf node s of G is owned by a player $i \in I$. A player owning a nonleaf node s can take any action $a \in A(s)$ when it is its turn to play, where $A(s)$ is the set of all available actions in node s. After this player takes an action a, the game moves to a successive node $s' = <s, a>$. Depending on whether s' is a nonleaf node or a leaf node, the game continues or stops: If s' is a nonleaf node, the game progresses and the player who owns node s' takes its turn to move; otherwise, if s' is a leaf node, the game ends and every player i gets a reward (payoff) $r_i(s')$. Rewards in a leaf node s' are represented by a vector $r(s')$, and the ith component $r_i(s')$ represents player i's reward.

In every nonleaf node s, player i follows a strategy (policy) $\pi_i(s)$ to play the game. Player i's strategy $\pi_i(s)$ in node s is a probability distribution over $A(s)$. In other words, when the game progresses to a node s owned by player i, it selects an action $a \in A(s)$ to play according to the probability distribution $\pi_i(s)$. All the π_i in all the nodes owned by player i constitute player i's strategy π_i for the whole game. All the π_i's of all the players constitute a strategy profile $\pi = \{\pi_1, \pi_2,..., \pi_I\}$. A player i's strategy π_i is a contingency plan that specifies which action to take in every node it owns. All these contingency plans of all the players form a strategy profile of the game. Let π_{-i} denote the strategy profile of all the other players excluding i, $\pi = \{\pi_i, \pi_{-i}\}$. Once the structure of the game tree G and the strategy profile π are given, any

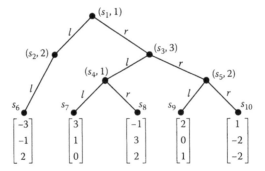

FIGURE 3.5.2
An extensive game played by three players. Nonleaf nodes are labeled with a pair representing the name and the owner; leaf nodes are labeled with the name only. The payoffs of the players are shown as vectors below the leaf nodes.

individual player i's expected reward, $R_i\,(\pi_i|\pi_{-i},\,G)$, is determined as well. We can calculate $R_i\,(\pi_i|\pi_{-i},\,G)$ as

$$R_i(\pi_i|\pi_{-i}, G) = \sum_{s \in LF(G)} P^\pi(s)r_i(s)$$

where $LF(G)$ is the set of all leaf nodes in the game tree G, and $P^\pi\,(s)$ is the probability that the game ends at a leaf node s, given that the strategy profile of all the players is π.

Figure 3.5.2 is an extensive game played by three players. In this game, nonleaf nodes are labeled with a pair representing the name and the owner; leaf nodes are labeled with the name only. For example, label $(s_1, 1)$ of the root node represents that this node is named s_1 and owned by player 1; label s_6 is the name of a leaf node that is the direct successor of node $(s_2, 2)$. Two actions — we call them l and r — are available in each nonleaf node except s_2, where only action l is available. The payoffs are shown in the figure as vectors below the leaf nodes. The first entry in every vector is the payoff of player 1, the second entry is the payoff of player 2, and so on.

An important solution concept of extensive games is *subgame perfect equilibrium* (SPE). A subgame of an extensive game is the game represented by a subtree G_s, rooted at a node s, of the original game tree G. A strategy profile $\pi^* = \{\pi_i^*, \pi_{-i}^*\}$ is an SPE if for every subgame $G_s \subseteq G$ and every player i, strategy π_i^* of player i maximizes its expected reward, i.e.,

$$R_i(\pi_i^*|\pi_{-i}^*, G_s) \geq R_i(\pi_i|\pi_{-i}^*, G_s)$$

for any strategy π_i other than π_i^*. An equilibrium strategy profile is a stable profile in the sense that any individual player i will not deviate from its strategy π_i^* if all the other players stick to their equilibrium strategy π_{-i}^*, which in turn holds because no player deviates.

If the reward vector in every leaf node is known to every player, backward induction can be used to find the SPE [5]. This is done by propagating the reward vectors in the leaf nodes to the nonleaf nodes, starting from the leaf nodes and ending at the root. The reward vector $\overrightarrow{r(s)}$ of a nonleaf node s represents the rewards all the players would obtain by playing the SPE strategies in the subgame G_s rooted at node s. The procedure of backward induction is described as follows.

Let $<s, a>$ denote the successor node if action a is taken in node s, and $B(1)$ denote the set of nodes whose successors are leaf nodes only, i.e.,

$$B(1) = \{s | < s, a > \in LF(G), \quad \forall a \in A(s)\}.$$

Then in every node $s \in B(1)$, the owner of s (suppose it to be player i) would choose an action a that leads to a leaf node $<s, a>$ where it can get the maximum reward, i.e., player i would choose an action a in every note $s \in B(1)$ such that

$$a = \arg \max_{b \in A(s)} \{r_i(<s, b>)\}.$$

The reward player i gets in node s by choosing action a is

$$r_i(s) = r_i(<s, a>)$$

and every other player $i' \neq i$ gets reward

$$r_{i'}(s) = r_{i'}(<s, a>).$$

Putting these equations together, the reward vector $\overrightarrow{r(s)}$ in node s can be represented by

$$\overrightarrow{r(s)} = \overrightarrow{r(<s, a>)}, \forall s \in B(1).$$

We call $B(1)$ the level-1 set. Similarly, we can define the level-2 set $B(2)$ as the set of nodes whose successors are leaf nodes *or* nodes in $B(1)$, i.e.,

$$B(2) = \{s | <s, a> \in LF(G) \cup B(1), \quad \forall a \in A(s) \quad \text{and} \quad s \notin B(1)\}.$$

For every node $s \in B(2)$, the owner of s (say, player j) would choose an action a such that

$$a = \arg \max_{b \in A(s)} \{r_i(<s, b>)\}$$

and, therefore, the reward vector in node s is determined by

$$\overrightarrow{r(s)} = \overrightarrow{r(<s, a>)}, \quad \forall s \in B(2).$$

In general, the level k set $B(k)$ is defined as

$$B(k) = \{s \mid < s, a > \in LF(G) \cup B(1) \cup ... \cup B(k-1),$$

$$\forall a \in A(s) \quad \text{and} \quad s \notin B(1) \cup ... \cup B(k-1)\}.$$

For every node $s \in B(k)$, the owner of s would choose an action a that maximizes its own reward and the reward vector in node s is, thus, determined by

$$\overline{r(s)} = \overline{r(<s,a>)}, \quad \forall s \in B(k).$$

Continue this procedure until reaching the root of the game tree. The reward vector in the root then is the SPE reward, and every player's strategy in every node constitutes the SPE strategy profile.

In this chapter, we assume for every play i and every pair of distinct terminal nodes s and s', $r_i(s) \neq r_i(s')$, i.e., there is no tie for every player. This type of extensive games is called *generic* and has a unique SPE. In the game shown in Figure 3.5.2, the unique SPE reward is the reward vector in the leaf node s_9.

3.5.4 Learning in Extensive Games

If only one player in an extensive game is learning, then the environment this single learning player faces is an MDP. To give a concrete example, refer to Figure 3.5.2. Suppose both players 2 and 3 have a fixed strategy (they are not learning). Player 2's strategy is $\pi_2 (s_2) = \{1\}$ and $\pi_2 (s_5) = \{0.9, 0.1\}$, i.e., player 2 always chooses action l in state s_2 and selects action l and r in state s_5 with probability 0.9 and 0.1, respectively. Player 3's strategy is $\pi_3 (s_3) = \{0.4, 0.6\}$. Then the MDP the single learner, player 1, faces is shown in Figure 3.5.3.

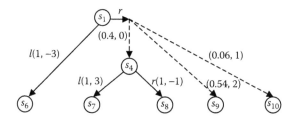

FIGURE 3.5.3
The tree-like MDP player 1 faces if it is the only learner and all other players move according to some fixed strategies.

The states of the MDP consist of all the nonleaf nodes owned by player 1 and all the leaf nodes. The actions available in every state are l and r, represented in the figure by solid-line arrows. Taking certain actions in some states leads to another state with probability 1. We mark these actions with two numbers — the first is the probability, and the second is the payoff. For instance, if player 1 chooses action r in node s_4, it will move to s_8 with probability 1 and get payoff −1. Taking other actions probabilistically leads to several other states. For instance, if player 1 takes action r in state s_1, then it will move to state s_4, s_9, and s_{10} with probabilities $p_1 = 0.4$, $p_2 = 0.54$, and $p_3 = 0.06$, respectively, getting payoffs 0, 2, and 1, respectively. We use dashed-line arrows to represent the transition from one state to several other states. Each dashed-line arrow is marked with the probability of this transition and the payoff obtained by player 1. Note that all the probabilities in Figure 3.5.3 is deterministic because we assume only player 1 is learning and players 2 and 3 have a fixed strategy. If all players are learning simultaneously, these probabilities change over time.

If the single learner in an extensive game does not own the root of the game, such as player 2 in Figure 3.5.2, then the learning problem of this learner consists of several tree-like MDPs. For example, if players 1 and 3 have fixed strategies and player 2 is learning, then player 2 learns on two separate tree-like MDPs — one consists of states s_2 and s_6, the other consists of states s_5, s_9, and s_{10}. Learning on two or more MDPs poses no extra difficulty here. The learner updates its strategy in an MDP only when some states in this MDP are visited in a round of game play; otherwise, if no state is visited in a play, the learner just keeps its previous strategy.

Players in an extensive game learn through repeatedly playing the same game. Every player has its own goal of maximizing its own long-run average reward. We call a round of game play an episode and index episodes by t. Given an extensive game G, if player i is the only learner (thus, only its strategy π_i^t changes over time) and all the other players move according to a fixed strategy π_{-i}, then player i's average reward in N episodes is defined as

$$AR_i^N(\pi_i^t) = \frac{\sum_{t=1}^{N} R_i\left(\pi_i^t | \pi_{-i}, G\right)}{N}$$

where $R_i\left(\pi_i^t | \pi_{-i}, G\right)$ is the expected payoff player i obtains in episode t. The long-run average reward of player i is defined as the limit of $AR_i^N(\pi_i^t)$ as N goes to infinity, i.e.,

$$AR_i\left(\pi_i^t\right) = \lim_{N \to \infty} AR_i^N\left(\pi_i^t\right).$$

For any fixed strategy π_{-i} of player i, a strategy exists π_i^* for this player such that π_i^* maximizes its expected reward $R_i\left(\pi_i^t | \pi_{-i}, G\right)$ in one round of game play.

If, through learning, player i's long-run average reward $AR_i(\pi_i^t)$ converges to $R_i(\pi_i^* | \pi_{-i}, G)$, we say the learning algorithm adopted by player i is individually convergent.

If all players are learning, then everyone's strategy changes over time. Let $\pi^t = \{\pi_i^t, \pi_{-i}^t\}$ denote the strategy profile of all the players in episode t, and again define player i's average reward in N episodes and long-run average reward as

$$AR_i^N\left(\pi_i^t | \pi_{-i}^t\right) = \frac{\sum\limits_{t=1}^{N} R_i\left(\pi_i^t | \pi_{-i}^t, G\right)}{N}$$

$$AR_i\left(\pi_i^t | \pi_{-i}^t\right) = \lim_{N \to \infty} AR_i^N\left(\pi_i^t | \pi_{-i}^t\right)$$

Let $\pi^* = \{\pi_i^*, \pi_{-i}^*\}$ denote the SPE strategy profile as in the inequality above. Then if every player i's long-run average reward converges to its SPE reward $R_i(\pi_i^* | \pi_{-i}^*, G)$, we say the learning algorithm adopted by the players is *collectively convergent*. The distinction between individual convergence and collective convergence is that the former assumes a time-invariant environment, whereas the latter does not.

Note that rewards are averaged over episodes and every round of game play increases the episode index by one. This is different from the definition of average-reward in MDPs, in which the time index increases every time a state transition happens.

During the learning process, every player chooses an action randomly according to its strategy π_i^t, which is a probability distribution. One commonly asked question is why a player would do so instead of picking up the best, pure action in every node? To give an example, say, why would player 1 not choose action l in node s_4 no matter what strategies the other players might have? There are two reasons: First, in the learning process, playing greedily is not necessarily in a player's best interest. For example, if player 1 always takes action l in node s_4 (this will lead it to get the best immediate reward of 3), then player 3 will eventually learn this fact and may never take action l in node s_3 because it will always get reward 0 in node s_7. Consequently, player 1 would have no chance to get the best immediate reward it might be able to get in leaf node s_7. Therefore, players randomize their strategies to explore the best rewards they can get. Secondly, we assume a player only knows its own final payoff in the leaf nodes but not its opponents' payoffs. Neither of our algorithms (MLA or MQ-Learning, see the two sections below) requires a player to know its opponents' payoff. Without knowing other players' payoff, a player cannot decide which pure action is in its best interest and, therefore, needs to randomize its strategy to explore its options. This latter feature of our algorithms makes them very useful for negotiation and bargaining games. In such games, it is usually true that an agent can only observe it's opponent's move, but does not know its final rewards or payoffs.

3.5.5 Multiagent Learning Automaton (MLA)

Learning automaton is a fictitious-play type of algorithm in which an agent maintain a belief about its opponent's strategy. The single-agent version of this algorithm has been shown convergent for average-reward learning in *ergodic** MDPs [11,12]. Because of the special tree-like structure of the MDPs derived from extensive games, we can slightly change the single-agent learning automaton algorithm and prove that the modified version is actually both individually and collectively convergent. We call the modified version multiagent learning automata (MLA). We state MLA for multiagent learning in extensive games, and the single-agent version for learning in tree-like MDPs is the same. The algorithm is as follows:

In every nonleaf node s of the game, the owner of this node (assume to be player i) keeps a probability distribution $\pi_i^t(s)$ over all actions available in this node, i.e., $\pi_i^t(s) = \{p_i^t(a)\}$, where $a \in A(s)$ and $\sum_{a \in A(s)} p_i^t(a) = 1$. Every time it is player i's turn to move, it takes an action according to this probability distribution. Assume player i takes an action a in episode t, then at the end of this episode, the probability distribution $\pi_i^t(s)$ is updated according to

$$p_i^{t+1}(a) = p_i^t(a) + \alpha\beta(1 - p_i^t(a)),$$

$$p_i^{t+1}(b) = p_i^t(b) - \alpha\beta p_i^t(b), \qquad \forall b \neq a,$$

where $0 < \alpha < 1$ is a learning rate and β is the *scaled* reward received in episode t. To ensure that $\pi_i^t(s)$ is a probability distribution at any time, β is scaled to fit into interval $[0,1]$, with 0 representing the lowest reward and 1 representing the highest reward.

Theorem 1: For any $\varepsilon > 0$, a learning rate $0 < \alpha < 1$ exists such that if the learning rate of every player is less than α, then the long-run average reward every player gets by following the MLA algorithm shown above will converge to the ε-range of its SPE reward.

Proof: We prove this theorem by induction on the depth of the game tree. Define the level-1 set $B(1)$ as previously given, then in every node $s \in B(1)$, taking an action will lead to an immediate reward. By the convergence of the single-automaton algorithm [12], given any $\varepsilon > 0$, there exists $0 < \alpha(s) < 1$ such that if the owner of the node s (suppose it to be player i) chooses a learning rate less than $\alpha(s)$, then its strategy $\pi_i^t(s)$ will converge close enough to the optimal strategy $\pi_i^*(s)$ (under Euclidean metric) such that $AR_i(\pi_i^t(s))$, the long-run average reward player i gets by following strategy $\pi_i^t(s)$, satisfies

$$|AR_i(\pi_i^t(s)) - r_i(s)| < \varepsilon$$

---

* An MDP is ergodic if every policy results in a single recurrent class, though different policies can result in different recurrent sets. See [11] for details.

where $r_i(s)$ is the maximum reward player i can obtain in node s, as defined previously. For any other player $i' \neq i$ who does not own node s, $\pi_i^t(s)$ converges to $\pi_i^*(s)$, meaning that the long-run average reward player i' gets in node s will also converge to the reward it would get if player i follows the optimal strategy $\pi_i^*(s)$, i.e.,

$$|AR_i\left(\pi_i^t(s)\right) - r_i(s)| < \varepsilon,$$

where $r_i(s)$ is defined above. Note that $\varepsilon_{i'}$ may not equal ε in the prior equation. However, by decreasing $\alpha(s)$, the upper-bound of learning rate in node s, we can always control how closely $\pi_i^t(s)$ will converge to $\pi_i^*(s)$ and thus control $\varepsilon_{i'}$; therefore, without loss of generality, the following statement holds.

For any node $s \in B(1)$, given any $\varepsilon > 0$, there exists $0 < \alpha(s) < 1$ such that if the owner of the node s (suppose it to be player i) chooses a learning rate less than $a(s)$, then

$$|\overline{AR\left(\pi_i^t(s)\right)} - \overline{r(s)}| < \varepsilon\overline{1}, \quad \forall s \in B(1),$$

where $\overline{1}$ is a vector with all entries equal to one; $\overline{AR(\pi_i^t(s))}$ is a vector representing the average rewards all players will get in node s if player i, the owner of node s, follows strategy $\pi_i^t(s)$; and $\overline{r(s)}$ is the SPE reward vector every player gets if it plays SPE strategy in the subgame rooted in node s.

Now we move onto the level-2 set $B(2)$. In any node $w \in B(2)$, taking an action leads to either a leaf node or a node in $B(1)$. Without loss of generality, assume all actions lead to a node in $B(1)$. After the average reward vector in every node of $B(1)$ has converged to the ε-range of the SPE reward of this node, the learning problem in the nodes of $B(2)$ is the same as that in the nodes of $B(1)$, except that we cannot pinpoint the rewards to exact numbers, but instead constrain them into intervals. More specifically, suppose player j owns a node $w \in B(2)$ and takes an action $b \in A(w)$ that leads to a successive node $s = <w, b> \in B(1)$. Then because of the convergence of the learning process in node $s \in B(1)$, the reward player j gets by taking action b in node w would fall into the interval $[r_j(s) - \varepsilon, r_j(s) + \varepsilon]$, where $r_j(s)$ is the jth entry of $\overline{r(s)}$. Therefore, by the convergence of the single-automaton algorithm, an upper bound $0 < \alpha(w) < 1$ exists such that if player j chooses a learning rate less than $\alpha(w)$, its average reward in node w converges to the SPE reward of the subgame rooted in node w, i.e.,

$$|AR_j\left(\pi_j^t(w)\right) - r_j(w)| < 2\varepsilon$$

where $r_j(w)$ is SPE reward player j gets in the subgame rooted in node w. Again, because we can always control the convergence range by controlling $\alpha(w)$, we have

$$|\overline{AR\left(\pi_j^t(w)\right)} - \overline{r(w)}| < 2\varepsilon\overline{1}, \quad \forall w \in B(2).$$

By induction, we conclude that Theorem 1 holds. Also clear is that the upper bound α of the whole game is the minimum of the upper bounds in all nodes.

Theorem 1 says that the MLA algorithm is collectively convergent for multiagent learning in extensive games. If only one player is learning and all others follow fixed strategies, then as shown in the preceding section, the extensive game degenerates to a tree-like MDP. By using the same induction technique as shown above, we can show that the MLA algorithm is also individually convergent.

Corollary 1: Given any $\varepsilon > 0$, a single learning player in an extensive game can use the learning automaton algorithm and choose a small enough learning rate to guarantee that its long-run average reward converges to the ε-range of the maximum reward it can get.

3.5.6 MQ-Learning

The MLA algorithm uses the reward obtained in every episode to reinforce the strategy in every node of an extensive game. If we keep a value for each node-action pair and use the reward obtained in every episode to reinforce these values, we get another provably convergent algorithm, *MQ-learning*. The name stands for multiagent Q-learning because the idea of reinforcing values is derived from the Q-learning algorithm. Here is the algorithm:

In every nonleaf node s of the game, the owner of this node (let it be player i) keeps a vector $Q_i^t(s)$ storing the q-values of all actions available in this node, i.e., $Q_i^t(s) = \{q_i^t(s,a)\}$, for every $a \in A(s)$. Every time it is player i's turn to move, it favors the action with the maximum q-value and at the same time uniformly explores other actions. More specifically, player i's strategy in node s is

$$
\pi_i^t(s) = \begin{cases} \arg\max\limits_{b \in A(s)}\left\{q_i^t(s,b)\right\} & \text{prob. } 1-\sigma \\[2ex] \text{uniform}\left\{d \mid d \neq \arg\max\limits_{b \in A(s)}\left\{q_i^t(s,b)\right\}\right\} & \text{prob. } \sigma, \end{cases}
$$

i.e., with probability $1 - \sigma$, player i chooses the action with the maximum q-value, and with probability σ, player i chooses other actions uniformly.

Assume player i takes an action a in episode t, and then at the end of this episode, the q-vector in node s is updated according to

$$
q_i^{t+1}(s, a) = (1 - \gamma)q_i^t(s, a) + \gamma\beta,
$$

$$
q_i^{t+1}(s, b) = q_i^t(s, b), \qquad \forall b \neq a,
$$

where $0 < \gamma < 1$ is a learning rate and β is the reward received at the end of episode t. Here we do not need to re-scale the reward β.

Theorem 2: For any $\varepsilon > 0$, an exploration threshold $0 < \sigma < 1$ exists such that if the exploration threshold of every player is less than σ, then for any node s and any $a \in A(s)$, the expected q-value of this pair $E[q_i^{\tau} (s, a)]$ converges to the ε-range of the SPE reward of the subgame rooted in node $<s, a>$.

Proof: Again, we prove this theorem by induction on the depth of the game tree. Take an arbitrary node $s \in B(1)$ and assume the owner of this node is player i; our first observation is that for any $a \in A(s)$, $q_i^{\tau} (s, a)$ converges to the reward player i would get if the game ends at the leaf node $<s, a>$. Actually, updating this procedure defines a difference equation and the solution of this difference equation is

$$ q_i^{\tau}(s, a) = \beta + \left(q_i^0(s, a) - \beta \right)(1 - \gamma)^{\tau}, $$

where $q_i^0 (s, a)$ is the initial q-value of action a and τ indexes the number of times action a has been taken*. Given that $0 < \gamma < 1$, the above solution is globally stable, i.e., $q_i^{\tau} (s, a)$ converges to β from any initial point $q_i^0 (s, a)$. Note that taking an action in $s \in B(1)$ leads to a leaf node $<s, a>$, and, thus, the reward β is a deterministic number equal to $r_i (<s, a>)$. Therefore, given $0 < \gamma < 1$, $q_i^{\tau} (s, a)$ converges to $r_i (<s, a>)$ exponentially with any given initial value.

Now we move on to level-2 set $B(2)$. In any node $w \in B(2)$, taking an action b leads to either a leaf node or a node in $B(1)$. If it is a leaf node, for the same reason stated above, the q-value converges. Otherwise, if $s = <w, a>$ is a non-leaf node belonging to $B(1)$, then the reward player j gets by taking action b in node w is a random variable: If the owner of node s chooses the SPE strategy (with probability $1 - \sigma$), the reward is $r_j(s)$, where $r_j(s)$ is the SPE reward player j gets in node s; if the owner of node s does not choose the SPE strategy (with probability σ), then the reward is a random variable u depending on which suboptimal action has been taken. Put together, player j's reward is $\beta = (1 - \sigma)r_j (s) + \sigma u$. Because the above solution is globally stable, the expected q-value $E[q_j^{\tau} (w, b)]$ converges to $E[\beta] = (1 - \sigma)r_j (s) + \sigma E[u]$. With a small enough exploration threshold σ, $E[q_j^{\tau} (w, b)]$ can be bounded as

$$ \left| E\left[q_j^{\tau}(w, a) \right] - r_j(s) \right| < \varepsilon, \quad \forall w \in B(2) \quad \text{and} \quad \forall b \in A(w) $$

where $s = <w, a>$ is a node in $B(1)$. By induction, we conclude that Theorem 2 holds. The exploration threshold for the whole game is the minimum of the exploration threshold in all nodes.

Two methods are available for a player j to estimate the expected q-value $E[q_j^{\tau} (w, b)]$: The first is to average $q_j^{\tau} (w, b)$ over *local time* τ (long-run average reward) to approximate $E[q_j^{\tau} (w, b)]$. Due to the Theorem of Large Numbers,

---

* We call this the *local time* in node s and do not use episode index t here because any specific action a is not activated in every episode.

this average converges to the expectation. The second method is to decrease the learning rate γ to suppress the variance of $q_j^\tau(w, b)$. Theoretically, as in Q-learning, if player j's learning rate γ^τ at local time τ satisfies

$$\sum_{\tau=0}^{\infty} \frac{1}{\gamma^\tau} = \infty, \quad \text{and} \quad \sum_{\tau=0}^{\infty} \frac{1}{(\gamma^\tau)^2} < \infty,$$

$q_j^\tau(w, b)$ itself converges to its expectations and player j can directly use q_j^τ (w, b) to estimate $E[q_j^\tau(w, b)]$.

Again, if only one player is learning and all others follow fixed strategies, then by using the same induction technique, we can show that the MQ-learning algorithm is also individually convergent.

Corollary 2: Given any $\varepsilon > 0$, a single learner in an extensive game can use MQ-learning and chose a small enough exploration rate to guarantee that its long-run average reward converges to the ε-range of the maximum reward it can get.

3.5.7 MLA Experiment

In the first experiment, we show the convergence of the MLA algorithm by applying it to the game illustrated in Figure 3.5.2. We set the learning rates as $\alpha_1 = 0.005$, $\alpha_2 = 0.003$, and $\alpha_3 = 0.01$. Figure 3.5.4 shows the evolution

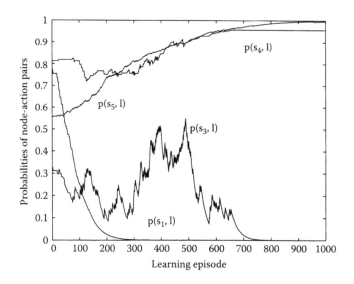

FIGURE 3.5.4
The evolution of three players' strategies when using the automaton learning algorithm. The learning rates are set to be $\alpha_1 = 0.005$, $\alpha_2 = 0.003$, and $\alpha_3 = 0.01$.

of probability vectors in four nodes of the game. We only show the probability of taking action l in every node. Because only two actions are available in every node, the probability of taking action r in every node equals 1 minus the probability of taking action l. Node s_2 is not included in this figure because only one action is available in s_2 and thus $p(s_2, l) = 1$. As we can see, after about 1000 learning episodes, all players' strategies converge very closely to the SPE profile. In the SPE profile, $p(s_4, l)$, the probability of player 1 taking action l in node s_4, equals 1. Figure 3.5.5 shows that $p(s_4, l)$ actually converges to 0.957. The reason is that after $p(s_3, l)$ converges very close to 0, player 1 — who owns node s_4 — has little chance to visit this node any more.

If we decrease the maximum learning rate, the error between the SPE profile and actual strategy profile can decrease as well. In Figure 3.5.5, we change the learning rate of player 3 from $\alpha_3 = 0.01$ to 0.002 and keep everything else the same as in Figure 3.5.4. Compared with the previous experiment, two observations about Figure 3.5.5 are clear: First, because of the small learning rate of player 3, the convergence speed of $p(s_3, l)$ is slower. (For the convenience of direct comparison, we put Figure 3.5.5 in the same time scale as Figure 3.5.4. Even though we cannot see the convergence of $p(s_3, l)$ in Figure 3.5.5, it actually converges very close to 0.) Second, $p(s_4, l)$ in Figure 3.5.5 converges closer to one compared with the convergence in Figure 3.5.5. In Figure 3.5.5, $p(s_4, l)$ converges to 0.998, in contrast with 0.957 in Figure 3.5.4.

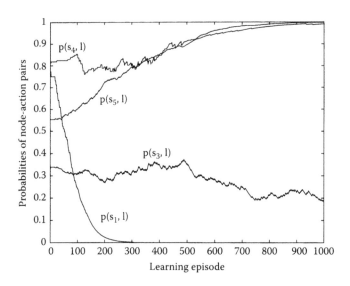

FIGURE 3.5.5

The evolution of three players' strategies when using the automaton learning algorithm. Compared with Figure 3.5.4, only player 3's learning rate is changed to $\alpha_3 = 0.002$; all other parameters are the same.

3.5.8 MQ-Learning Experiment

We showed the convergence of MQ-learning on the same game used in the MLA experiment. The learning rates of the three players are set to be $\gamma_1 = 0.01$, $\gamma_2 = 0.02$, and $\gamma_3 = 0.01$, and the exploration thresholds are set to be $\sigma_1 = 0.1$, $\sigma_2 = 0.05$, and $\sigma_3 = 0.2$. All the initial q-values are 0. Figure 3.5.6 shows the result.

As we can see, the q-value of every node-action pair eventually converges to a neighborhood of the SPE reward of the successive node of this pair. Note that $q(s_4, r)$ converges extremely slowly; the reason is that this specific node-action pair has little chance to be activated. We can accelerate the convergence speed by two methods: First, choose larger exploration thresholds to ensure every node-action pair is sufficiently activated in the learning process. Second, choose larger learning rates to speed up the learning process. However, both acceleration methods have undesired side effects — large exploration thresholds enlarge the ε-range that constraints the expected q-values, and large learning rates amplify the variance of q-values.

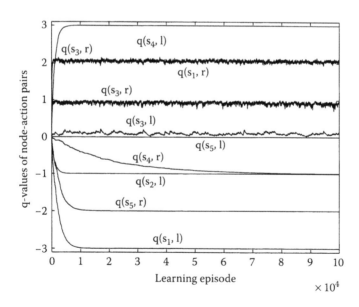

FIGURE 3.5.6
The evolution of q-values when using the MQ-learning algorithm. The exploration thresholds of three players are set to be $\sigma_1 = 0.1$, $\sigma_2 = 0.05$, and $\sigma_3 = 0.2$.

3.5.9   Toward Practical Applications

Games of practical interest, like the TD-Island game discussed in the previous chapter, and board games like chess and Go, often have a prohibitively large number of states, which prevents direct application of our algorithms. Two general approaches are used to address this problem: Use heuristics to limit the state space being searched, or approximate the state-action function (q-function). Though effective heuristics are often problem-specific, as they exploit a specific problem structure (like the symmetric structure of the TD-Island game), one heuristics called hierarchical state decomposition [3] is usually applicable to many practical games. The basic idea of this approach is to organize game states into groups, view a state group as a virtual state, and iteratively apply the learning algorithm on the virtual and real states. Many practical problems can be hierarchically decomposed, as decomposition seems to be the natural way we humans organize and reason on complicated information. Approximation is another way to deal with the state explosion problem. In this approach, the state-action function, which has its domain on the state and action spaces, is approximated.

Potentially any function approximation method can be applied for this purpose. In practice, one has to carefully investigate the problem and choose an approximation function that fits. Generally speaking, a good approximation function should have at least the following two properties: Flexible enough to fit the target (i.e., has enough parameters adjustable to fit the shape of the target function) and easy to converge in the learning process (i.e., not over parameterized). If possible, the final approximation function learned should contain information useful for behavior interpretation, i.e., answer the question why an agent takes an action a in a state s. One successful application of approximation method is Tesauro's backgammon program [15]. Tesauro used a neural network to approximate the state-action function for the backgammon game and let his program play against itself to learn the right move. His program is so successful that it can rival human experts.

One requirement of both our algorithms is that every player must be able to observe the actions its opponents take in each move. If this is not true, a player might not know exactly at which tree node it is located during the learning process. Instead, it only has uncertain information about the nodes at which it might be located, and this information is represented by a probability distribution over all possible nodes. This type of extensive game is games with incomplete information, such as discussed in Chapter 3.1 and Chapter 3.2. Again, if we assume only one player is learning, the problem of learning in extensive games with incomplete information degenerates to the problem of learning in *partially observable Markov decision processes* (POMDPs), with the hidden states corresponding to nodes in the game. It would be interesting to see whether single-agent learning algorithms for POMDPs [7] can also be extended for learning in extensive games with incomplete information.

References

1. Bertsekas, D.P. and Tsitsiklis, J., *Neuro-Dynamic Programming*. Belmont, MA: Athena Scientific, 1996.
2. Bowling, M.H. and Veloso, M.M., Multiagent learning using a variable learning rate, *Artifi. Intelligence*, 136(2), 215–250, 2002.
3. Dietterich, T., Hierarchical reinforcement learning with the MAXQ value function decomposition, *J. Artif. Intelligence Res.*, 13, 227–303, 2000.
4. Fudenberg, D. and Levine, D.K., *The Theory of Learning in Games*. Cambridge, MA: MIT Press, 1998.
5. Fudenberg, D. and Tirole, J., *Game Theory*, Cambridge, MA: MIT Press, 1991.
6. Hu, J. and Wellman, M.P., Multiagent reinforcement learning: theoretical framework and an algorithm in *Proc. 15th Int. Conf. on Machine Learning*, Madison, WI, 242–250, 1998.
7. Kaelbling, L.P., Littman, M.L., and Cassandra, A.R., Planning and acting in partially observable stochastic domains, *Artif. Intelligence*, 101, 99–134, 1998.
8. Kaelbling, L.P., Littman, M.L., and Moore, A.P., Reinforcement learning: a survey, *J. Artif. Intelligence Res.*, 4, 237–285, 1996.
9. Littman, M.L., Markov games as a framework for multi-agent reinforcement learning, in *Proc. of the 11th Int. Conf. on Machine Learning (ML-94)*, San Francisco, 157–163, 1994.
10. Littman, M.L., Friend-or-foe q-learning in general-sum games in *Proc. of the 18th Int. Conf. on Machine Learning*, 322–328, Williams College, Williamstown, MA, 2001.
11. Mahadevan, S. Average reward reinforcement learning: foundations, algorithms, and empirical results, *Machine Learning*, 22(1–3),159–195, 1996.
12. Richard, J., Wheeler, M., and Narendra, K.S., Decentralized learning in finite markov chains, *IEEE Trans. Automatic Control*, AC-31(6), 519–526, 1986.
13. Singh, S., Kearns, M., and Mansour, Y., Nash convergence of gradient dynamics in general-sum games; in *Proc. of the 16th Conf. on Uncertainty in Artif. Intelligence*, 541–548, Stanford, CA, 2000.
14. Sutton, R.S. and Barto, A.G., *Reinforcement Learning: An Introduction*. Cambridge, MA, MIT Press, 1998.
15. Tesauro, G., Programming backgammon using self-teaching neural nets, *Artif. Intelligence*, 134(1–2), 181–199, 2002.

Index

A

Abstract board games, 256
Abstraction in complex domains, 310–311
AdmTrans, 282
Adversarial models, opponent intent
    inferencing, 1–22
  adversary intent inferencing model, 7–19
    adversarial intent inferencing, 12–19
    architecture of adversarial intent
      inferencing model, 8–9
    model construction, 9–11
    reasoning over model, 11–12
    wargaming, 12–19
  intent inferencing, 2–5
  representing, reasoning under uncertainty,
    5–7
Adversarial reinforcement learning, 303–304
Adversary intent inferencing, 7–19
  architecture of adversarial intent
    inferencing model, 8–9
  construction, 9–11
  reasoning over model, 11–12
Aggregation techniques, game-tree search,
    imperfect information, 214
AII. *See* Adversary intent inferencing
Algorithmic complexity, scalability, 87–91
Alpha-beta pruning, 212
Alternating concurrent, 263
Alternating serial, 262
Analysis of competing hypotheses, 105–112,
    125
Ant-like agents, humanistic behavior, 54–58
Applied Optimal Control, 248
Approximation in complex domains, future
    possibilities, 310–311
Attrition, 182
AvoidCombat, 56
AvoidDetection, 56

B

Battle of Midway, application, 115–121
Bayesian knowledge bases, 6

Bayesian networks, 5
BEE. *See* Behavioral evolution and
    extrapolation
Behavior of humans, changes, 127–129
Behavioral evolution and extrapolation, 51
  hybrid approach, 54
Belief networks, converting plans to, 107–110
Belief revision function, 26
Belief state, 2, 26
Blackhawk Down, 31
Blocking filter
  properties of, 244–245
  saddle interval, 246–247
BlueAlive, 55, 57–58
BlueCasualty, 55, 57–58
BlueThreat, 55
BNS. *See* Bayesian networks
BRB. *See* Bayesian knowledge bases

C

CDPR. *See* Cross-domain security plan
    recognition
CellStateSpace$_i$, 261
Chess, 332
Cognitive approach to modeling opponents,
    26–28
Cognitive attacks, 126
Cognitive hacking, 126
Community card game, 216
Conditional probability rule, 6
Conditional probability tables, 7
Convexity conditions, 235
Corrupted/partial information, 231–250
  adversarial environment applications,
    247–248
    aggressive approach, 248
    conservative approach, 248
  blocking filter, properties of, 244–245
  deterministic discrete-time linear-quadratic
    game, formulation, 232–236
  discrete-time linear-quadratic game game
    formulation, 236–239
    previous work, 236–239

Milton Keynes UK
Ingram Content Group UK Ltd.
UKHW031127141024
449569UK00006B/397